UNKNOWN KNOWNS

On Economics, Investing, Progress, and Folly

Laurence B. Siegel

Edited by Wayne H. Wagner

Foreword by Theodore R. Aronson

Montesquieu
Press

Copyright © 2020 by Laurence B. Siegel
Published by Montesquieu Press
Del Mar, California

MontesquieuPress.com

First Edition: June 2021
Hardcover ISBN 978-1-7361484-0-2
Intl. Paperback ISBN 978-1-7361484-1-9
ebook ISBN 978-1-7361484-2-6

Library of Congress Cataloging-in-Publication Data
Names: Siegel, Laurence B., 1954-, author. Wagner, Wayne H., 1938-, editor
Title: Unknown Knowns: on economics, investing, progress, and folly / Laurence Siegel.
Description: First edition. | Del Mar, CA: Montesquieu Press [2021]
Includes foreword by Theodore R. Aronson and index.
Library of Congress Control Number: 2021907440

Cover image: Public domain
Cover design by Klazina Stanwick
Print book interior design by Dave Stanwick

If you would like permission to use material from the book (other than for review
purposes), please contact lbsiegel@uchicago.edu. Thank you.

Interested in bulk copies? Visit MontesquieuPress.com or email lbsiegel@uchicago.edu

The author is available for speaking events. Please contact him at **lbsiegel@uchicago.edu**. He is
also a CFA Institute recommended speaker. See https://speakerhub.com/agency/society-speaker-
directory

10 9 8 7 6 5 4 3 2 1

Cover painting:
Work, by Ford Madox Brown

The cover painting, *Work* by Ford Madox Brown (British, 1821-1893), celebrates the importance of work to human existence. The workers vary in skill, dress, and the difficulty of their labor, but all are shown with dignity. On the margins of the original painting are idlers (to the right — one rich, one poor) and supervisors (above, receiving the benefits but not participating). The beautiful buildings at the top and the parkland to the right emphasize the wealth of the city to which the workers are contributing. The city is modeled after Hampstead in London. Artistically, Brown is associated with the Pre-Raphaelite Brotherhood, a group of British artists in the mid-nineteenth century who rejected the formalism of some of the Old Masters and brought drama, energy, and social themes into their paintings. This version, one of two originals, is exhibited in the Birmingham (U.K.) Museum and Art Gallery and was painted in 1863.[1]

Unknown Knowns explores the relationships between work, human capital, financial capital, the broad sweep of economic history, and the progress we can expect in the future. It is composed of essays written between 2010 and 2020 for investors and the general public. Deep thanks are due to Ted Aronson (AJO Partners) and Bob Huebscher (Advisor Perspectives) for the sponsorship and publication of most of these articles, and to Steve Sexauer for co-authorship of a few of them and helpful suggestions on many others. Happy reading.

---

[1] Source: https://upload.wikimedia.org/wikipedia/commons/2/2e/Ford_Madox_Brown_-_Work_-_Google_Art_Project.jpg, public domain.

Also by Laurence B. Siegel

As author

Fewer, Richer, Greener: Prospects for Humanity in an Age of Abundance (Wiley, 2019)

Puzzles of Money, Inflation, and Debt, with Thomas S. Coleman and Bryan Oliver (CFA Institute Research Foundation, forthcoming 2021)

Benchmarks and Investment Management (CFA Institute Research Foundation, 2003)

As editor

Robert C. Merton and the Science of Finance: A Collection, with Luis Garcia-Feijóo and Timothy R. Kohn (CFA Institute Research Foundation, 2020)

The Productivity Puzzle: Restoring Economic Dynamism, with David E. Adler (CFA Institute Research Foundation, 2019)

Rethinking the Equity Risk Premium, with P. Brett Hammond and Martin L. Leibowitz (CFA Institute Research Foundation, 2011).

Insights into the Global Financial Crisis (CFA Institute Research Foundation, 2009).

The Future of Life-Cycle Saving and Investing (in three volumes), with Zvi Bodie, Dennis McLeavey, Rodney N. Sullivan, and Lisa Stanton (CFA Institute Research Foundation, 2007, 2009, and 2012)

Stocks, Bonds, Bills, and Inflation Yearbook (annual), Ibbotson Associates, Inc., Chicago, 1984-1994

Also by Wayne H. Wagner

Investment Management: Meeting the Noble Challenges of Funding Pensions, Deficits and Growth, with Ralph A. Rieves (Wiley, 2009)

Millionaire: How an Index Fund Can Turn Your Lunch Money into a Fortune, with Al Winnikoff (Renaissance, 2001)

The Complete Guide to Securities Transactions: Enhancing Investment Performance and Controlling Costs (Wiley, 1989).

Table of Contents

Part VI: Policy and Governance

Part VII: Provocative

List of Figures

UNKNOWN KNOWNS:
Things that you know, but don't know you know

There are known knowns;
there are things we know we know.
We also know there are known unknowns;
that is to say we know there are some things we do not know.
But there are also unknown unknowns —
the ones we don't know we don't know.
…[Those] tend to be the difficult ones.
–*Donald Rumsfeld*

Penetrating so many secrets, we cease to believe in the unknowable.
But there it sits nevertheless, calmly licking its chops. –*H. L. Mencken*

The trouble with people is not that they don't know,
but that they know so much that ain't so.
– *"Josh Billings" (Henry Wheeler Shaw)*

You know more than you think you know,
just as you know less than you want to know. –*Oscar Wilde*

TO CONNIE

And to friends of progress, freedom, and enterprise everywhere.

Foreword

Spend enough time in our business, and you will meet everyone. At least everyone worth meeting. And so it was, my meeting Larry.

Over the course of many years, a friend, Liz Hilpman, shared snippets of a dude she knew who shuttled between New York City (job) and Chicago (home). She always described him as really intelligent... and "different." Of course, lots of Wall Streeters are really intelligent, but I assumed she also meant he was not your typical Wall Street guy. Fortunately for me, I would come to know "different" meant so much more than not typical.

My curiosity eventually got the best of me, and I wrangled a meeting with Larry at his perch at the Ford Foundation. My first impression of Larry was that of a gentleman — literally, a *gentle man*. He was so interested in what I had to say, I immediately felt important in his presence and almost forgot *I* arranged the meeting with *him*. Over the next quarter century, I learned what lies beneath his gentle exterior — a powerful wit, a hilarious sense of humor, and a muscular intelligence that feeds on a curiosity and interest for everything he encounters.

In fact, the diversity of Larry's interests is only superseded by the copiousness of his output — the reviews, articles, books, and monographs he produces far exceed the material he consumes, if not in quantity, certainly in caliber. Eventually, I volunteered my firm, AJO, to serve as a distributor of Larry's materials. That may sound generous, but I must admit, my motives were a bit more selfish...

AJO's mailing list was established from 35 years of industry relationships. It includes clients, prospects, reporters, and FOAJOs (friends of AJO). In fact, 35 years in the world of investing is actually enough time to both meet everyone and have them included on your mailing list — even the thought-leaders in the investment world. The selfish part of using our publishing partnership? Not only did AJO receive his work hot-off-the-press, but the reaction of our recipients from the anticipation and excitement he created only redounded to our benefit.

AJO will eagerly continue to be one of the vessels delivering anything Larry produces. Of course, Larry doesn't lack venues to publish — key among them are his own website (https://larrysiegel.org/) and his perch as Research Director of the CFA Institute's Research Foundation. This book is yet another!

In the able hands of Wayne Wagner, many pieces from the AJO/Siegel collaboration (Larry's work, AJO's delivery) grace the following pages.

I'm sure you'll find Larry's writing as I've often described it — insightful, erudite, articulate, and opinionated — with the added advantage of being right! And when he isn't, he's interesting anyway.

Theodore R. Aronson
Philadelphia, Pennsylvania
February 2021

Ted Aronson is the founder of AJO, a trustee of Spelman College, and past chair of the CFA Institute. When this was written he was chair of the CFA Institute Research Foundation.

About Larry Siegel

Wayne H. Wagner

I first met Larry Siegel at a Q Group meeting in Florida.

In the late 1960s, a young man named Dale Berman had the idea for a seminar series which he entitled The Institute for Quantitative Research in Finance, universally known as the Q Group. The goal was to create a forum where the young academics could interact with practitioners who were attempting to find real world applications for the new field of quantitative investment management. I spoke at one of the early sessions at the Hanover Inn at Dartmouth College. The audience at the time was fourteen, although by now the number of attendees is approaching two hundred.

The seminars, lasting two and a half days, are held twice a year in very pleasant resort-style locations. The format provides each speaker 45 minutes to make a presentation, followed up by a half hour of question-answer interchange with the audience. The question and answer session was often as insightful as the formal presentation. All in all, the Q Group was quite a success, with academics striving to be on the program and practitioners eager to be in the audience.

The speakers are leading academics and well-known practitioners such as Marty Leibowitz, Mark Kritzman, and Jack Treynor. Many Nobel Laureates in economics have spoken there, including Harry Markowitz, Bill Sharpe, Bob Merton, Myron Scholes, Dick Thaler, Gene Fama, and others. The presentations stretched the knowledge and awareness of the participants, who often challenged the assumptions of the academics.

I recall giving a presentation and awaiting the questions from the audience. Most started out with a compliment or thank you, and then got into the meat. The questions were polite and knowledgeable and could be devastatingly incisive. Often the speaker learned more than the audience. *Definitely* true in my case.

Somewhere along the way, I became aware of the deep thinking coming from the Ford Foundation representative, a curmudgeonly, slightly rumpled man whose Q Group questions were always penetrating and insightful. This was my first exposure to Larry Siegel. The Q Group cherished Larry's insights, featuring him many times as a speaker and panel member.

I got to know Larry much better when I was invited to be a Trustee of the CFA Institute's Research Foundation. The CFA Institute is a professional group promoting the knowledge and integrity of the financial advice profession. The related Research Foundation funds several monographs a year written by leading academics and practitioners.

The Research Foundation, run by a big ball of energy named Bud Haslett, retains Larry as its Director of Research. My job was Chairman of the Research Committee, a job made simple by the dynamic drive of Bud and Larry.

My chief responsibility was to aid Larry Siegel, then (and now) the indispensable Gary P. Brinson Director of Research. As Chairman of the Research Committee, I helped guide the direction of the research topics and development efforts. My position required frequently interaction with Larry Siegel, and I learned to respect his unique powers of analysis, sardonic wit, and exacting editing standards.

Going back a step, as I progressed though my career I became good friends, very good friends, with investment manager Ted Aronson, whose company is now known as AJO. I was unaware that Ted has published thought pieces on a regular schedule, and that many of the original pieces were authored by Larry Siegel.

Ted commissioned Larry to produce these pieces, which were circulated to clients. prospects, and friends. Several a year were produced, and I found them both wide-ranging and profound.

Unfortunately, these little gems were privately published and not widely distributed.

I knew they deserved wider exposure, and I encouraged Larry to let me edit a volume of these short, stimulating, and highly readable pieces. Larry has done intensive work re-editing and refining the selected pieces.

Most of the articles are readily available from AJO or from the CFA Institute. Some of the best were published in journals that retained the re-publication rights, so they are not included in this book, but can be read in the *Journal of Portfolio Management*, the *Journal of Investing*, the *Journal of Retirement*, and the *Journal of Wealth Management*. They are well worth your interest.

It was my suggestion to put selected items together in a book. Together we sorted out the not-so-relevant. I learned a lot by carefully reading the entries in this book. And I developed a deep respect for Larry's drive and talent.

Larry's boundless curiosity leads him to seek knowledge in many ways:

Reading a book, then summarizing the key thoughts in a review. Many of the authors, such as Michael Lewis and Nassim Taleb, will be familiar to you. Others, all deep thinkers but more focused on specific areas, are distilled to present important ideas to a more general audience (you, dear reader).

> Example: "Michael Lewis on the Hidden Benefits of Competent Government," in the POLICY AND GOVERNANCE section of this book.

Interviewing. Larry is constantly seeking out interesting thinkers and getting them to share their wisdom.

> Example: "'Uneasy lies the head that wears a crown': A Conversation with Jack Bogle," in the INVESTING section of this book

Co-authoring. Larry can't do it all alone, and he engages deep thinkers in cooperative writing.

> Example: "Floods and Deserts: Why the Dream of a Secure Pension for Everyone Is Still Unattained," with Stephen C. Sexauer, in the SAVINGS AND RETIREMENT section.

Synthesizing. Drawing parallels and consequences from multiple sources. The best example of this is Larry's 2019 book, *Fewer, Richer, Greener*.

> Example: "Why Fewer, Richer, Greener," an interview published in Welling on Wall Street, in the PROGRESS, GROWTH, AND PRODUCTIVITY section.

Fewer, Richer, Greener, published in 2019 by John Wiley & Sons, is Larry's first book outside the fields of finance and investing. Enjoy the salient but brief essays, then delve deeply into *Fewer, Richer, Greener*. You'll enjoy the trip.

It has been an honor for me to work closely with Larry on this book. I wish I could think and write like him.

Wayne H. Wagner

Progress, Growth, and Productivity

While Larry's primary focus in his career has been on investment management and finance, many of his more recent insights revolve around the history of successful economies, and how that portends the future.

In this area, Larry's ability to draw from varied sources is on full display. The first article gives you an overview of his book, *Fewer, Richer, Green*er, which was published by Wiley in late 2019.

Wayne's personal favorite: To Hell in a Handbasket?

—WHW

Chapter 1. Why "Fewer, Richer, Greener"

Investment Thinker Larry Siegel Dares to Be Contrarily Optimistic

An interview by Kathryn M. Welling in *Welling on Wall Street*, January 11, 2013

What does a "retired gentleman of leisure" do if his golf game, well, isn't up to par? If you're investment maven and author Laurence B. Siegel, who until July 2009 was director of research in the investment division of the Ford Foundation and before that did nothing more notable on the investment scene than help found Ibbotson Associates, you take on all sorts of official and unofficial roles so that you can keep having "fun." You see, fun, to Larry, is stirring the biggest pots of intellectual ferment he can find in the sometimes all-too-arid landscape of investment thought.

1-1 Kate Welling

No surprise, then, that Larry has taken on the responsibilities of working as the Gary P. Brinson Director of Research at the CFA Institute Research Foundation in the nonprofit sector, and has set up a consulting practice to serve the investment industry. Or that he keeps up with a wide-ranging torrent of postings, here, there and everywhere in the blogosphere, all the while penning emails and pieces of his own at a pace that would have challenged Voltaire.

Lately, Larry has been having lots of his special brand of fun upending stereotypes of retired investment types as economic pessimists and, well, grumpy old men, by coming out in print with lengthy, provocative, and thoroughly researched rebuttals to the headline-grabbing, "Woe Is Us" economic predictions of a couple of the economic and investment world's most prominent forecasters. Indeed, Larry dares to optimistically characterize the world we're leaving to our children and grandchildren as "fewer, richer, greener." I was lucky enough to catch up with Larry the other day and got him to explain.

Listen in. –**KMW**

Kate Welling: Let's talk about "Fewer, Richer, Greener." Your paper is making waves.[2] Stirring up opposition to the dirge-like "the world is going to hell in a handbasket" commentaries we've seen recently from the likes of GMO's Jeremy Grantham and Northwestern's Robert Gordon. Is Chicago big enough these days for both you and Prof. Gordon?

Larry Siegel: Absolutely. He's an engaging guy. He makes a lot of valid points. If you only make the points that support your side, which is what he and I both did, it looks like you want to fight — that you're only trying to persuade, rather than to understand. But that's really not me. There are headwinds and tailwinds to growth. There always have been and there always will be. They offset each other in various ways and produce varying degrees of growth and prosperity.

Gordon made a very effective argument for what he believes, but I thought it was one-sided, so I had fun trying to take it apart. But I did so from a position of respect for his knowledge and erudition — which is why we can have a reasonable discussion.

Kate: Does that likewise apply to how you're getting along with Jeremy Grantham these days?

Larry: Jeremy is a friend with whom I often disagree. I also respect his erudition, but I think he's strongly inclined to overstatement.

Kate: Well, his views could scarcely be more diametrically opposite — a future "too crowded, too poor, too polluted."

Larry: Jeremy's position is self-inconsistent. The problems Jeremy anticipates – soaring food and other resource prices, worsening environmental pollution — are, if they occur, the result of massive income and consumption growth in countries that haven't had much of a break until recently. Jeremy Grantham's big concern is that the demand for high-protein food, industrial materials, and

---

[2] My article, "Fewer, Richer, Greener," published in the *Financial Analysts Journal* in November/December 2012, was the basis for my book of the same name, published by John Wiley & Sons in 2019 and available at https://www.amazon.com/Fewer-Richer-Greener-Prospects-Abundance/dp/1119526892

other goods is going to push up the prices of natural resources to the point where they become the limiting factor for growth —

Kate: And push the environment into a tailspin, just to ice his argument.

Larry: Yes. But growth is good for the environment. I'll get to that later.

Kate: I can't wait. But first, tell me what you're concerned about if we get too little growth?

Larry: If you have too much growth, that is an easy problem to solve. When there is a lot of growth, inputs get expensive, acting as a natural governor on the growth rate.

But if there's too little growth, there isn't a lot you can do. You can cut taxes, but taxes are already inadequate to pay for the amount of government that people seem to want. You can improve education. There are only so many levers to push at the public policy level. The classical idea is that, if you have too little growth, people will work harder for less money, causing growth to reappear after a recession or depression — but that outcome is not all that attractive. We *did* get growth that way in 1933, '34, '35 — but who wants that?

Kate: It's not an outcome that you'll find very many people rooting for, that's for sure.

Larry: Nope. That was actually one of the best growth periods in our history — but it was from very low levels.

Kate: So you are concerned about growth being too slow, yet you're making something of an industry out of writing optimistic futurist essays?

Larry: I'm concerned that growth will be slow in the short run, as aging, developed economies work their way out of government debt and entitlement difficulties. I'm very optimistic in the long run — and I'm optimistic right now for emerging markets. In fact, long-term growth has turned into kind of a hobby for me. When you hit on a theme and people start to identify you with it, you keep working it. I wrote a piece on moral hazard for the CFA Institute Research Foundation after the crash of 2008. I only got a little positive feedback, and frankly the essay was a little unfocused, so I didn't write about moral hazard again. But growth is more fun – following the literature and analyzing the arguments.

Kate: And finding yourself at the center of some. You've been pretty shrewd to position your articles as the reasoned antidote to the "sky is falling" warnings from Grantham and Gordon that grabbed the headlines.

Larry: Well, "man bites dog" sells. "Man doesn't bite dog" or "dog doesn't bite man" doesn't sell because no news, or moderately good news, is what people are used to. So it's hard to get people to listen to a forecast that says, "The world has been going to hell in a handbasket for as long as anyone can remember, but it never quite seems to get there. Instead, we're going in the opposite direction."

Kate: The world isn't really going to hell in a handbasket?

Larry: Measured by just about any objective measure you choose, the health and wealth of the human race have been improving rapidly and almost continuously for at least the last 200 years. And there is every reason to expect this trend to continue, most dramatically in the developing world but also, more slowly, in the developed world.

Kate: Because?

Larry: The biggest contributor to this favorable outlook is the astonishing and too-little-appreciated fact that the population explosion is almost over. Sometime in our children's or grandchildren's lifetimes, global population will peak somewhere between 10 and 11 billion and then either level off or begin to decline. And this world of fewer and richer people will also be greener —

Kate: Hold it right there. There are only, what, 7 billion people on this planet now, and our economic growth of the last 200 years is being blamed for all sorts of pollution, melting ice caps, and floods engulfing parts of New York City and environs.

Larry: My analysis is based on the idea that environmental quality is an economic good like any other. Subsistence or primitive living is about the most environmentally destructive lifestyle imaginable, but it's hard to see the destruction because the population is small under those conditions and the destruction is just beginning; the environment looks pretty. As an economy begins to develop, it gets dirtier.

Heavy industry is the way out of abject poverty. And it's dirty. But, as a society gets richer, it can afford to pay for large helpings of environmental quality. The whole point of getting rich is to buy things one wants. Of course, nearly everyone wants a beautiful, clean, and safe natural environment, but people also have other priorities — eating, for example. The human body makes implacable calorie demands.

Kate: Tell me about it!

Larry: Seriously, when calories are scarce, future benefits are discounted at very high rates — all people care about is the present. When there's abundance, people can invest in the future, including in environmental quality. This is all well-documented and represents what economists call the "environmental Kuznets curve" — the tendency of societies to become environmentally dirtier as they begin to develop, then cleaner as they pass a certain threshold of affluence. But I'm acutely aware that my fewer, richer, greener thesis is at odds with what mostly passes as received wisdom these days — that natural resources constraints will result in a future that's crowded, poor and dirty.

Kate: As you basically said, dystopia sells.

Larry: The tradition of pessimism among intellectuals of all sorts runs very deep. Maybe, as Joseph Schumpeter once said, "pessimistic visions about almost anything usually strike the public as more erudite than optimistic ones." And, essentially, what I'm saying is that the long-term prospects are fine — not that everybody is doing fine right now, of course. But the kind of economic slowdown that we have had in the last five or six years [2007-2012] is a normal fluctuation, in line with other slowdowns throughout history. You might have forecast it —

Kate: As not a few did —

Larry: That's right. The financial crisis was entirely predictable — if you saw the fiscal policies in developed countries, where basically the governments were going crazy with debt —

Kate: As were quite a few in the private sector; don't forget the banks, insurers, and derivatives that the governments went deeper into debt to bail out.

Larry: Yes. The financial crisis was a kind of perfect storm of stupidity, fueled by poorly designed incentives. In the U.S., Congress required lenders to give mortgages to people who couldn't pay them. The private sector responded by saying, "Sure. Let's give them two or three mortgages!" Similar problems arose in other countries. The problem that I didn't foresee was the contagion to other institutions caused by massive derivatives bets.

Kate: It was plain scary. And we really haven't accomplished much in terms of fundamental reform or deleveraging —

Larry: I concede that the twin mountains of household and government debt that Gordon cites as his sixth and final headwind to growth are probably a legitimate concern over the intermediate run. (Government debt is a greater concern because households can be presumed to keep their self- interest in mind at least a little, while governments are spending other people's money.)

But the concern won't last forever; the nice thing about debt is that it matures. In the long run, the last of the baby boom generation will die and the problem of a large population of entitlement collectors supported by a smaller population of producers will die with it. The so-called age pyramid will turn into an age pagoda everywhere and hopefully by then society will have created the institutional arrangements needed to have a smaller population of workers supporting a larger population of children and retirees. It's inevitable that people will work longer and save more for their old age, either through pension systems or private savings — it's just going to be bumpy reaching that equilibrium.

In other words, "structural" deficits won't last forever. Eventually they'll get repudiated or paid back.[3]

Kate: "Bumpy" may be putting it mildly —

Larry: Well, in the meantime, equity markets discount long-term earnings growth, not what's going to happen in the next year and a half. Fixed-income markets are different, so if you have a one-year Greek bond, maybe you should worry. Somebody told me — I don't know if it's true — that Russia, which is one of the investment darlings of the last 10 or 15 years, has never issued a long-term bond that was paid off in full.

Kate: That certainly has the ring of truth —

Larry: But I don't know if it is. To be sure, I'd have to hire an economic history Ph.D. student to go back and look at the bond prices in Russian newspapers. Otherwise, that comment might circulate as urban legend, so take it with a large grain of salt.

Kate: I like the way, by the way, that your essays footnote and document your claims, instead of falling into the internet trap of endlessly repeating urban legends. Your stated skepticism, for instance, about the frequently repeated claim that only about half the people in the world have ever made a phone call.

Larry: I *was* careful to say that it was a quote that had been repeated by a number of prominent people in various noteworthy settings: Newt Gingrich, Al Gore, and Kofi Annan. That doesn't make it true, but it has the ring of truth to it.

Kate: Just consider the sources!

Larry: None of them is stupid, but many smart people are gullible. Plus, I do think cell phones have changed that situation because, even in some of the poorest countries of Africa, many people now have a cell phone. Yet, for the first 120 or 130 years after the invention of the telephone, that claim was probably roughly true. Even today, I'm wondering what percentage of the world's inhabitants have

---

[3] When a debt is repudiated, that simply means it is paid back by someone else – the lender, a credit guarantor, the taxpayers, and so forth.

never ridden in a car.

Kate: It can only be people in the poorest and most remote places on the globe.

Larry: I bet there are 10% or 15% of people in the whole world who have *never* made use of a motor vehicle in any way. If that's true, there is an 1880s technology the benefits of which still have not seeped through to everybody.

Kate: I don't know, private cars are one thing, but motor scooters and such can be found in pretty remote places. Anyway, how did you happen to start writing about "Fewer, Richer, Greener"? Generalizations are dangerous, but most "retired gentlemen of leisure," as you call yourself, tend to be pretty pessimistic about the course of the economy — at least the ones I know.

Larry: Well, most retired gentlemen of leisure actually just play golf. (So do I, but my score for 9 holes is about what a good golfer scores in 18. I used to think that was a good thing until someone told me that it's not.) The retired gentlemen who do take pen to paper are usually the ones who feel most strongly about something. The first thing that got me thinking about "fewer, richer, greener" it was Ben Wattenberg's book, called *Fewer*, which is where I got the first part of my title.

He basically said the world's going to hell in a hand basket because we're running out of people. I liked him and I liked the book, but I thought, "That can't be right."

Kate: Why not? The world needs young people.

Larry: I agree there is a downside to low population growth or zero population growth — a small number of young workers supporting a lot of old people. If you go to certain parts of Italy or Japan, and see almost no children, you realize that a world without children would be depressing. But, in fact, a lot of the problems we've been facing come from trying to bring the benefits of technology, including food technology and that sort of thing, to rapidly increasing numbers of people.

So, when some of that pressure comes off, those problems become much less severe, and it becomes easier to save the environment. It occurred to me that, although Wattenberg's book is great in some ways, the environmentalists are right about population growth not being an unalloyed good. Some problems we're facing are easier to solve if we have slow instead of fast population growth — which is what we're seeing, not just in the developed world, but in some of the most unexpected places in the developing world.

Kate: The fertility rates that you discussed in your *Financial Analysts Journal* piece, reported in a somewhat different (and more dramatic) style as Exhibit 1.1, is a real eye-opener —

Exhibit 1.1 Total fertility rates in selected countries and regions, 1950-2015.

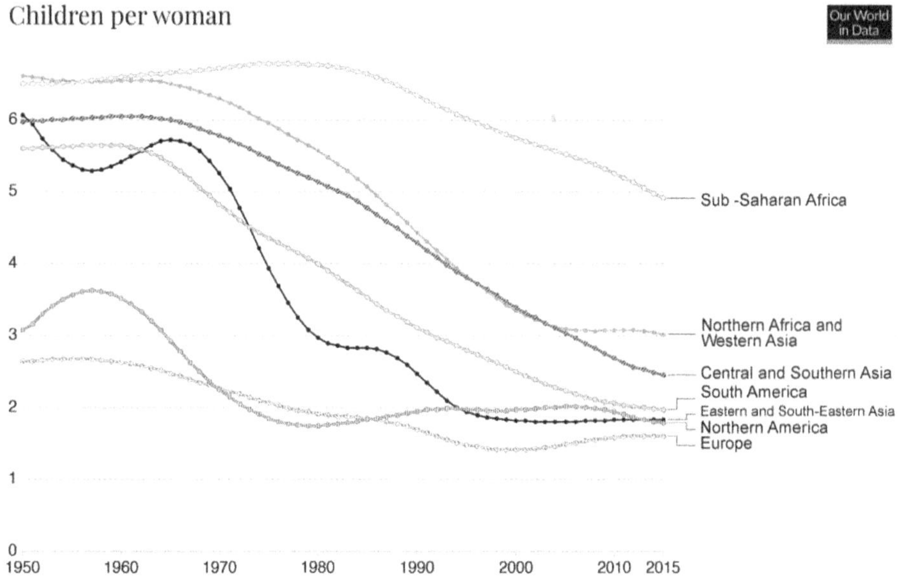

Children per woman

Source: Our World In Data http://ourworldindata.org/ United Nations Population Division (2012 revision). The interative data visualization is available at OurWorldInData.org.

Larry: Right. Many people are already aware that a number of European countries plus Japan and Russia have fertility rates below the replacement rate of 2.1, which is the rate at which a couple reproduces itself, with the extra 0.1 representing children who don't live long enough to reproduce. However, many don't appreciate how low the lowest fertility rates are — or how profound the resulting social changes they imply are. But what really surprises lots of people is how relatively low population growth rates already are in places like India, Indonesia, Thailand, Mexico, and Brazil. While these places are still pretty poor by developed world standards, they have evidently progressed enough to start offering advanced-country trade-offs to parents deciding how many children to have.

Kate: Or simply can now offer them the ability to make an economic choice — instead of being ruled by biology.

Larry: That's an interesting way to express the concept. Matt Ridley really gave me the impetus to write this up when he wrote *The Rational Optimist.* I reviewed it for *Advisor Perspectives* — and to do that, I had to do a lot more reading. There's an extensive body of literature on long- term change — and almost all of it says that the change, at least so far, has been much more positive than most people appreciate.

Kate: Really? Why? People usually tend to be optimists.

Larry: Well, in an e-mail exchange the other night, among members of this discussion group that I'm in with Rob Arnott and Cliff Asness, the question was, "Would you rather be in the top 1% in 1900 or at the 50th percentile, or median, today?" The question had actually been raised by Thomas Frank, the lefty University of Chicago history Ph.D., who used to write a magazine called *The Baffler.* I'm not sure what he does any more—

Kate: A column in *Harper's* among other things —

Larry: He's kind of a left-wing thinker and even he was saying that you're better off in the 50th percentile today. You have a car, an air conditioner, access to penicillin, all of which, in 1900, didn't exist. Frank almost nailed it in terms of a breakeven proposition — because in 1900 technology was actually pretty far along. If you were in the top 1% in 1900, or for that matter the top 15%, you could take the train. It could go about 75 miles an hour and is only a little slower now. You could hire, if you were in the top 1%, an army of servants to cater to your every whim.

Kate: Look no further than *Downton Abbey.*

Larry: Yes! You lived in sumptuous surroundings. Yet if you got sick and needed a pill, the only pills available were cod liver oil — and did absolutely nothing. So how would you like to be in the top 10% in 1900 or in the top 1% in 1600? There are lots of ways to show that the amount of progress we've made is tremendous and that, basically, economic growth means that people of ordinary means can enjoy benefits or services that only the rich could afford in earlier ages.

Kate: Or that we can actually enjoy a level of something like health care that was completely unattainable in the past.

Larry: Let's call it "medicine." One of my personal peeves is that "health care" has become jargon for "health insurance." Anyway, medicine is an area where we really are turning over new ground every year — every day. It was possible, before the record player was invented, to hire local musicians to play Mozart over dinner. It was very expensive, but it was possible. But it wasn't possible, even in 1900, to hire a team of doctors to give you the kind of medical care you can get from a nurse practitioner in the drugstore today. My wife just had a knee replaced. She walked out of the hospital the same day, got into our car, and I drove her home.

Kate: Totally replaced, as an outpatient? That *is* amazing.

Larry: Yes, and no one had ever had their knee replaced until 1968. You got in a wheelchair and stayed there.

Kate: Still, rehab is no fun, I am sure.

Larry: True. But the surgery was a minimally invasive procedure in which they somehow actually break up your busted knee, take it out, and put in a titanium one, through a five-inch incision that looks like a shark bite. The progress we've seen is astounding.

Kate: I don't think anyone denies that, even Prof. Gordon or Jeremy Grantham. Their point is that the pace of innovation witnessed since the Declaration of Independence can't continue — and in fact has slowed dramatically.

Larry: Which is where I part company with them. My follow-up article to the Financial Analysts Journal piece, which is essentially a critique of Grantham and Gordon, published by Advisor Perspectives and then reprinted by my friends at AJO Partners, discusses some of the examples that Gordon uses to buttress his argument that the revolutionary innovations of the past which have driven growth over the last couple of centuries aren't likely to be repeated anytime soon. My article points out how suspect the examples are.

Kate: Such as?

Larry: Well, first off, the six headwinds to growth that he identified mostly have to do with the U.S., which is only 5% of world population. While there's no doubt that the U.S. faces wrenching adjustments in education, entitlements, and industrial structure, I do expect them to be made, eventually. But in the meantime, the outlook for the developing world has never been better — and Gordon doesn't give sufficient weight to that. Beyond that, Gordon tries to use things like transportation speed to show that we're losing the ability to innovate. The speed at which passenger travel occurred, he writes, "increased steadily until the introduction of the Boeing 707 in 1958. Since then, there has been no change in speed at all, and, in fact, airplanes fly slower now than in 1958 because of the need to conserve fuel."

Kate: You can't deny that the airlines fly slower these days —

Larry: No, but that misses the point. We know perfectly well how to fly at three times the speed of sound, and the military does it every day. But it's fuel-intensive and very costly. So we've chosen not to spend valuable resources on faster passenger travel. There are also environmental constraints. People don't like sonic booms.

Anyway, the early adopters, people who flew in the Concorde, had to pay most of the costs and there weren't enough people willing to do that to make a go of it. But it's fatuous to think we *never* will do it — or *never could*. It's just that we choose our fights and we didn't pick that one. Eventually, that will change.

Right now we have the physical capabilities to be energy independent in the United States. We're choosing not to do it. Is that a good idea?[4]

Kate: Good question. How about answering it?

Larry: Well, it depends on whether you only care about people in the United States. If you do, energy independence makes sense, but it would be a very costly decision both for Americans and for the foreign energy suppliers that we trade with. I don't just care about the U.S., and I think that a world energy market is much more efficient than local energy "autarkies." (An autarky is a country or economy that trades only with itself.) Energy independence is not on my list of top ten things to achieve and there's only so much water I'd like to pollute in pursuit of that.

Kate: While we're discussing energy, Jeremy Grantham has said that the very rapid progress of the last 200 years is due to cheap energy, which, he says, is a thing of the past. Is it?

Larry: No. Because fossil fuels have in fact been cheap, we haven't tried to develop new sources of relatively cheap energy, so of course we don't have them. How long do you think it would take to develop a safe nuclear reactor? One that doesn't fall apart in an earthquake? Melt down in a tsunami? That's impervious to terrorism? And that has multiple back-up systems in case something goes wrong — is that within the power of human imagination?

Kate: Sure, it's only a matter of cost — and mass psychology.

Larry: Absolutely. That technology has been around for some time. For a while, we tried to develop it and then we stopped. But we could figure it out.

---

[4] After this was written, the U.S. became energy independent (in the sense that it is a net energy exporter).

Kate: Isn't part of the Gordon/Grantham argument, though, that productivity growth has slowed because the supply of further innovations has simply gotten too thin?

Larry: Well, what Gordon did was to follow convention by attributing the productivity surge of the last 250 years to three distinct industrial revolutions. The first included the cotton gin, the mechanized loom, the steam engine, the railroad, and the factory system. He dates it from 1750 to 1830, and I use 1776-1826 (choosing to break up American history into 50-year periods to reduce the temptation to monkey with the periods to get a desired result). The second revolution, from 1876 to 1926, saw the telephone, electrical transmission, audio and video recording and playback devices, electric appliances, the car, the airplane, radio, and even early TV.

Kate: And the third industrial revolution is computers and the internet?

Larry: Yes. For the sake of data analysis, I say the third epoch started in 1976, when both Microsoft and Apple were founded, but Gordon argues that much of the benefit of computers came earlier, and there is some validity to that if accurate credit card bills and military draft notices are what you think is important. Still others, like Kevin Kelly, the futurist and *Wired Magazine* founder, contend at least as passionately that it didn't start until the beginning of the commercial internet, when computers were married with telecommunications.

Kate: Now, essentially, as I understand the "sky is falling crowd," the latest technological advances don't hold a candle to those of the previous industrial revolution, in terms of their potential for improving the lot of mankind?

Larry: Well, Gordon's essay is skillfully argued and offers many illuminating facts showing how profoundly the daily lives of ordinary people changed in the developed world between, say, 1870 and 1950. Having made that transition from a relatively primitive lifestyle in which women, for example, spent much of their day carrying water, to modern life, we aren't going to again experience that magnitude of change, he argues. And there's something to his thesis — another 50-fold increase in the U.S. standard of living over the next 250 years isn't terribly likely.

So he concluded that further improvements in the standard of living will be less profound and have a smaller impact on per capita GDP. But the U.S. isn't the world — and there are plenty of places in the world where people have barely begun to experience the second industrial revolution, much less the third. Women still carry water in some places. Did you notice the chart of long-term real per capita GDP growth that I included in my critique?

Kate: The one showing it growing at a remarkably consistent rate all the way back into the 18th century?

Larry: Exactly. A 1.8% constant growth rate from 1789 to 2012, as shown in Exhibit 1.2. The thing to notice, though, is that, despite the way the growth rate looks so steady over time, when I broke it down into the three industrial revolutions and the periods in between, considerable variations in growth rates showed up — as well as pretty dramatic stagnation recently, which probably explains all of the hand-wringing. But it's the lack of any visible relationship on the chart between industrial revolutions and growth rates that demands an ex-

Exhibit 1.2 Real per capita GDP growth in the United States by subperiod, 1789-2012

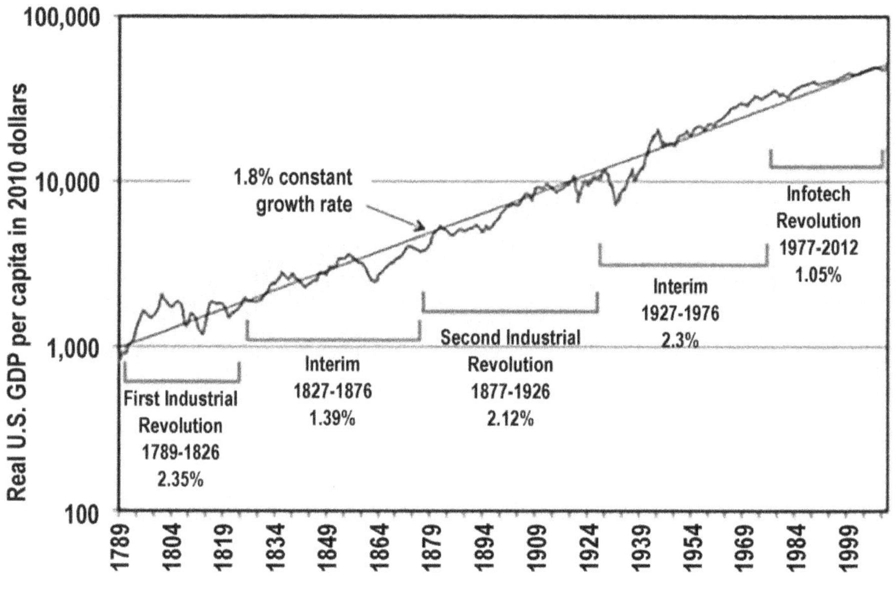

planation.

Kate: So what's yours? Surely there is some connection between industrial revolutions and GDP growth —

Larry: My conjecture is that it simply takes a long time for cutting-edge, productivity-enhancing technology to be absorbed into the general economy — and that causes the benefits of any given breakthrough to be spread out over generations or even centuries. Imagine someone in a remote African village only now able to make a phone call, thanks to a cell phone, more than 130 years after

Alexander Graham Bell. So it's small wonder that the dates of industrial revolutions don't line up neatly with periods of rapid GDP growth.[5]

Kate: Let's back up and talk about where economic growth comes from in the first place. Your chart starts in what, 1789? But if it started earlier it would have to show almost no GDP growth for centuries on end —

Larry: That's right. At the aggregate level, there wasn't much growth before 1800, as the great economic historian Angus Maddison showed. But at favored times in favored places, there was plenty of growth. Do we seriously think that Mozart's Vienna of 1790 wasn't better off than Vienna in 790, or 1290? Of course it was.

People in Ancient Greece, Ancient Rome, the high Middle Ages in Europe, the Italian Renaissance, and the English and French Age of Enlightenment were all much richer than the people who preceded them. Nobody devotes tremendous energy to philosophy or sculpture when they're starving. And all this occurred before 1800.

Kate: Why couldn't that growth be sustained, then?

Larry: Each time that the growth occurred, it kept getting squashed back down again. Growth, and for that matter technological change, comes from an organic process of people saying, "What can I do to make my life easier? How can I accomplish more?" So economic growth is, arguably, an inherent property of the human species. But wars, natural disasters, artificial barriers to trade, to enterprise, to entrepreneurship, can slow down or stop growth, even make it run in the wrong direction. What wealth was built up during the periods I just named was mostly destroyed through wars and disease.

Kate: Then it's not terribly comforting to see growth tailing off here in the U.S. When you broke up American history into four 50-year periods, plus a fifth period from 1976 to 2012 that is 36 years long, this contemporary period had the slowest growth, around 1%. What's happening?

Larry: The U.S. has become a mature economy, and there's a little bit of evidence that very rich countries grow more slowly. Something about substituting

---

[5] In later work, I pointed out that much recent technological progress reduces the effort or expenditure needed to accomplish a given goal, such as making an international video call. This shows up as a reduction in GDP (because GDP measures the dollar value of transactions, not the benefit of the good or service procured), even though it is obviously an improvement in aggregate well-being. Thus GDP growth does not fully capture economic progress. See chapters 16 and 23, "The Mismeasurement of Growth" and "Dematerialization," in my 2019 book, *Fewer, Richer, Greener*.

leisure for work, or being satisfied with the living conditions you have. In the 1950s and 1960s this was seen as a major problem, and futurists wrote about a glut of leisure time. It didn't materialize, and in the 1980s and 1990s we worked harder than we did a generation earlier; but hours worked and the percentage of people in the work force have both declined recently. So there's a possible wealth effect on growth.

Kate: Maybe, but the majority of Americans haven't been feeling particularly wealthy for the last five years or so.

Larry: Well, that slowing has taken place only in the U.S., which is the only place where we have decent historical data — and in a few other rich countries. The relevant growth rate for investors is the *world's* growth rate, since they can hold global portfolios that take direct advantage of GDP growth throughout the world — in places that are only now starting to benefit from even the second industrial revolution, with a few remnants left over from the first one, 200 years ago! Just consider that China, which had a negative rate of growth between 1500 and Chairman Mao's time, has four times the population of the U.S. and is growing faster than the U.S. ever did, except for a few scattered years in the distant past.

But most future growth will not come from China! They've already achieved what economists (although not most ordinary people in the developed world) would call middle-income status. A lot of future global growth is going to come from what a Goldman Sachs study calls "The Next 11," places like Indonesia, Nigeria, Turkey, and Vietnam. It's a very exciting time to be in those parts of the world because they've never had a chance. Now they do.

Kate: Okay, but what fundamentally sparks economic growth, especially in places that have been lacking in it, basically forever?

Larry: Places that have been lacking in growth are the victims of one force or another keeping them from getting ahead. People always have and always will try to make more money, to produce more goods, to leave their children some things that they themselves did not have. But something gets in the way — war or disease or bad monetary policy that causes a hyperinflation. Still, the natural course of things — and we have centuries of evidence to back this up — is for people to compete and cooperate with each other to do more with less. That's what growth is, and it's not a big mystery. The mystery is when it doesn't happen: Who or what is stopping it?

Kate: You don't buy Jeremy Grantham's argument that the disappearance of cheap energy is putting a lid on growth?

Larry: Oh, there's little doubt that sharply higher energy costs have contributed to the recent stagnation in the U.S. economy. But he offers no evidence that it's anything but a temporary – albeit large – reversal of the sort we've seen time and again in the commodities markets.

And the recent run-up in commodities was unusual in that a lot of seemingly unrelated commodities moved up in price together.[6]

There's no reason to believe that the prices of unrelated commodities, each of which has its price uniquely set based on the ever-shifting tension between resource discovery, resource exhaustion, new extraction and production technologies, and substitution, will move in lockstep in the future as they did in the recent past.

Kate: You mentioned Deirdre McCloskey's "great fact" in your *Financial Analysts Journal* piece —

Larry: Yes. She is a very innovative and prolific professor with whom I studied at the University of Chicago. What she called the "great fact" is the monumental economic growth that the developed world has experienced for the last 200-plus years. She argues that it had very little to do with "improved supply and demand efficiency" or any of the other conventional economic explanations. Nor did it have to do with private property rights, an explanation favored by many illustrious scholars. As she pointed out, "China had secure property for millennia before failing to have an industrial revolution," and the rule of law and property rights existed in ancient Rome and in Mesopotamia. But, by contrast, in Holland and England between 1600 and 1800, there was an "obvious and historically unique improvement in the dignity and the liberty of the bourgeoisie." In fact, she wrote, "none of the allocative, capital accumulation explanations of economic growth since Adam Smith have worked

scientifically... None of them have the quantitative force and the distinctiveness to the modern world to explain the Great Fact..."

Kate: Then what does explain it, according to McCloskey?

---

[6] In the years after this interview took place, commodity prices, including the price of energy, fell sharply.

Exhibit 1.3 The world in 1800 - Poverty and short lifespans almost
everywhere

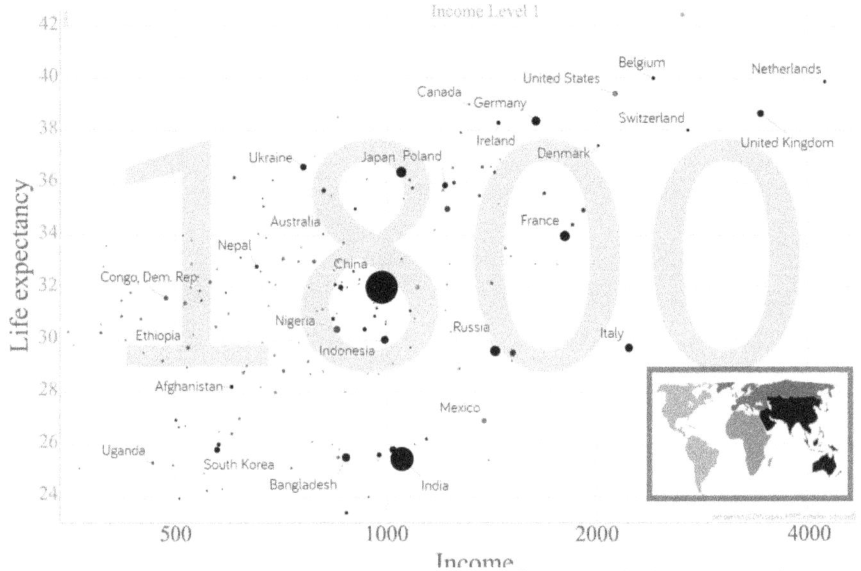

Note: GDP is measured in current (2011) U.S. dollars at purchasing-power parity.
Each bubble represents a country, with the area of the bubble proportional to the
country's population in the year shown in the exhibit title.

Larry: The explanation that works, she says, is "Creativity. Innovation. Discovery. And where did the discovery come from? It came from the releasing of the West from ancient constraints on the dignity and liberty of the bourgeoisie, producing an intellectual and engineering explosion of ideas. As... [Matt] Ridley has recently described it, ideas started breeding, and having baby ideas, who bred further." The upshot is that the decision to save some of what one produces and invest it for the future is not nearly enough to explain economic growth that has been self-sustaining now for 250-plus years. Only an explosion of creativity and invention is.

Kate: Do you agree that ideas having babies — not capital accumulation — is responsible for the greatest increase of wealth and well-being in history?

Larry: Yes. I wish I thought of that metaphor myself. How great the Great Fact is can be summed up in one data point: The per capita GDP, adjusted for purchasing power parity, for the *world* in 2010 — $11,200 — was equal to the per capita GDP (in the same units) for the U.S. in 1929, when this country had the highest living standard in the world and was, by any reasonable measure, very much a developed country. This is mindboggling growth, yet we tend to take it for granted, so I'm including some ingenious data graphs generated using the late Swedish physician and statistician Hans Rosling's data and software to drive home the point. See the income and life expectancy charts in Exhibits 1.3, 1.4, and 1.5.[7]

Kate: If the Great Fact explains economic growth in the past, is it also a forecast for the future?

Exhibit 1.4 The world in 1950 - The developed world is wealthy, the rest of the world poor

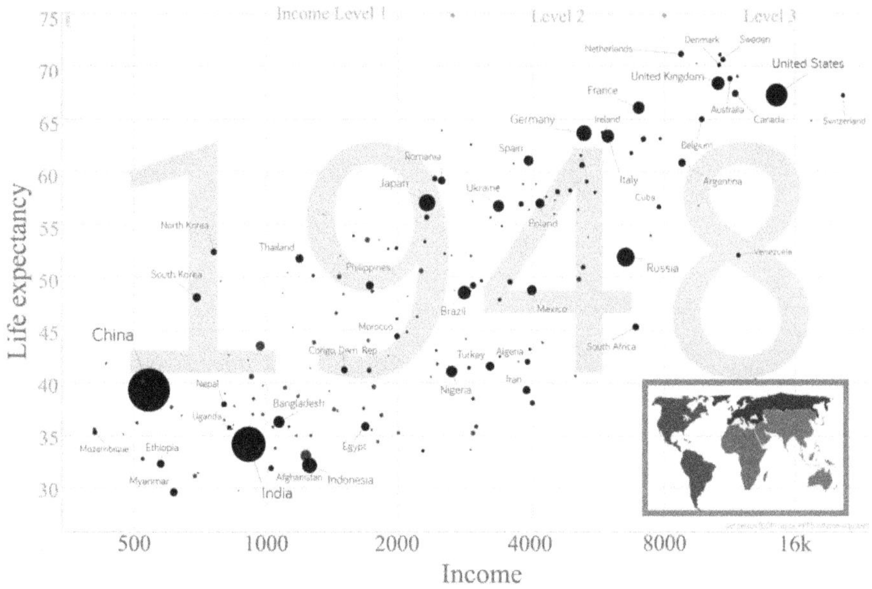

Note and source: See Exhibit 1.3.

Larry: There is no guarantee of it, but it is very likely. Developed country growth rates, as I said, have been amazingly stable for over two centuries, while developing countries' have only accelerated. The data give virtually

no hint of deceleration. Moreover, creativity and invention seem to be accelerating further.

Kate: Let's segue here into the environmental Kuznets curve, which underlies your "greener" optimism.

---

[7] Update: The 2019 per capita GDP for the world, in purchasing-power parity terms, is $18,381. The large increase since 2010 is due to the combined effects of real growth and inflation, not just real growth. This number is roughly equal to U.S. per capita GDP in 1949. Much of the increase is due to growth in China, India, and other developing countries. The charts in this reprint of the original *Welling on Wall Street* article are from my 2019 book, *Fewer, Richer, Greener*.

Exhibit 1.5 The world today - Developing countries begin to join the developed world in prosperity and longevity

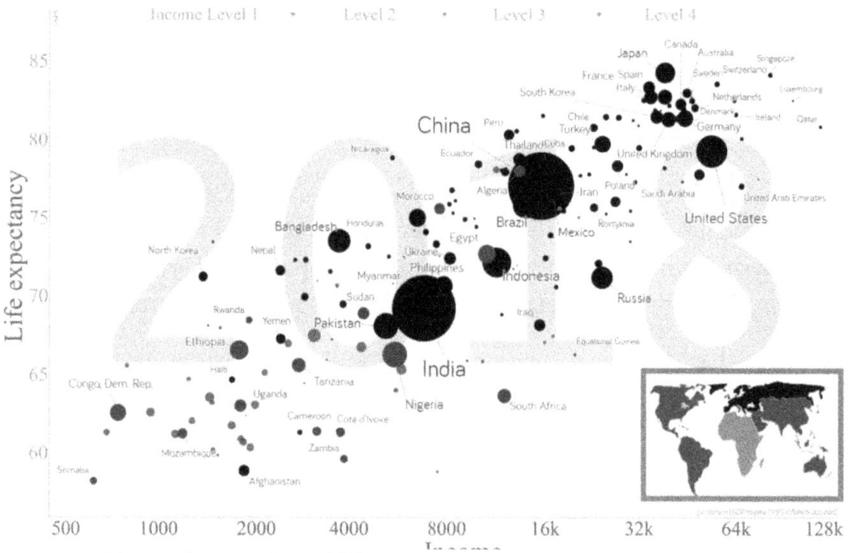

Note and source: See Exhibit 1.3.

Larry: The economist Simon Kuznets, in the 1950s, found that income inequality tends to increase as a country develops from poor to middle-income, but then decreases as (or if) the country becomes rich. This is the original Kuznets curve.

Economists in the 1990s found that the same principle applied to environmental quality, which dips considerably as a country industrializes, then rises as the country becomes rich and people are willing to make sacrifices to clean up the environment. This phenomenon shows up in the data. Sulfur dioxide emissions in the U.S., for example, first rose as the country industrialized, and then fell dramatically in recent decades as environmental legislation was passed and a post-industrial economic mix substituted for heavy industry. Today, China is beginning to achieve better air and water quality standards after decades of degradation. My conclusion is that growth in the stage where middle-income countries become rich is good for the environment, because environmental protection then becomes affordable and almost universally desired.

Kate: Yet there has to be a social or governmental decision to create and enforce environmental standards, doesn't there?

Larry: To clean up, say, the air, either the government has to regulate emissions directly, or it has to create property rights in emissions and allow trading to occur. The second solution is much fairer and more efficient.

Kate: A role for government, what? There are things that the private sector can't do?

Larry: Mm-hmm.

Kate: Really, what role do you have in mind for government...

Larry: Government has to do plenty! Just less than it's doing now.

Some people imagine that capitalists, or libertarians, whatever you want to call people who favor small government, are actually opposed to *any* role for government. That is not the case (setting aside a few ridiculous extremists).

Economics says that there is a role for government in providing public goods, which are goods that everyone benefits from whether or not they pay for them, and in managing externalities. An example of a public good is a fire department: governments should put out fires because, if that were done by private enterprise, people might not pay for fire protection because they might depend on their neighbors putting out the fire so that the fire would not spread.

Kate: And, by "externalities," you mean?

Larry: An example of an externality is air pollution, where a transaction between two private parties (say, the buyer and seller of whatever a factory produces) harms a third one (me, when I try to breathe the air). If air pollution isn't regulated or controlled in some way by the government, everyone will pollute as much as they feel like, because it's profitable to pollute – you are consuming a resource but not paying for it.

Kate: Okay, if we are headed towards a world that is fewer and richer and greener, yet still not *so few* that natural resources cease to be attractive investments, aren't commodities good things for investors to be tucking into the portfolios they manage?

Larry: In principle, sure, but commodity investing is very complex.

Kate: Spoken like a man from the University of Chicago. Why?

Larry: Commodity futures are not a pure capital asset like a stock or a bond but are derivatives that have to equilibrate three markets: (1) the spot market for the physical commodity, (2) the insurance market in which sellers lock in a price so they can be profitable, and (3) the storage market, which arises from the fact that the supply and demand for a commodity are never exactly matched up. So there's an inventory or storage market that is created by leaving the commodity in the ground until it is needed, or else storing it in a warehouse.

The end result of all these interacting forces is that some commodity futures positions have a higher return than the "spot" or physical commodity, and some have a lower one. It takes careful analysis to decide exactly how to position a commodity portfolio, taking into account your forecast for spot prices as well as for the insurance and inventory services that are implicitly priced through the commodity futures market. I told you it was complicated.

Kate: In other words, "Don't try this at home." So let's return to the topic of long-term economic growth. Do you have a specific forecast?

Larry: I'm not forecasting the much-desired 3% rate of real GDP growth in the United States because our population growth is only 0.75% per year. If you add that to 1.8% real per capita GDP growth, that's a total of 2.55%. That is my forecast unless the population growth rate changes materially.

Kate: Okay...but I thought you were an optimist.

Larry: A 2.55% real GDP growth rate in the U.S. is enough to bring about massive increases in prosperity over the long run, at the same 1.8% real per capita rate of increase that we've experienced in our long history. Isn't that enough? We Americans are not trying to build an empire. We're trying to get personally more prosperous, so we care about real *per capita* growth. Individual well-being is what's important.

Besides, investors don't need to worry about U.S. growth being a little slower than it used to be. As I said, investors are exposed to global growth. Even if they only invest in the S&P 500, those companies get about 46% of their sales and 40% of profits from outside the U.S. And investors should not hold only the S&P 500. To be fully exposed to the growth that I've been talking about, they should hold global portfolios, which include developed, emerging, and frontier markets.

Kate: Do you have other advice for investors?

Larry: Natural resource-related equities. Energy stocks, both conventional and alternative.

Water. Farmland, agriculture stocks, and food technology – fertilizer, GMO foods, whatever will enable farmers to grow more food and allow engineers to expand the amount of arable land. Minerals and metals. Real estate will recover and gradually move to new highs. Right now, while the governments of the world work out their debt travails, I'd avoid bonds except for the very shortest durations. Human capital — the returns to labor — will benefit more than financial capital from the growth I've been describing, so if you can invest in human capital, you should.[8]

Kate: And just how do you suggest doing that — given that, in a free society, workers own their own human capital, in the sense of having the right to sell it to the highest bidder or whomever they want?

Larry: It's hard, but companies that find ways to make a profit educating large numbers of people are a start. Those could include companies that educate their own workers as a sidelight to their main business.

Kate: Great, Larry. Thanks for cheering me up. Any final thoughts?

Larry: All this growth will not happen by magic. It's a lot of work.

Kate: You would add that! But thanks, again.

---

[8] I plead the perennial excuse of investment managers to their clients: I wasn't wrong, just early. (Very early.)

Chapter 2. To Hell in a Handbasket? No Way, Says Johan Norberg

March 20, 2017

Is the world going to hell in a handbasket? Are most people getting poorer while the rich get richer? Have we destroyed the planet? In a sparkling — and delightfully short — new contribution to the econo-optimist genre, Johan Norberg, author of *Progress: Ten Reasons to Look Forward to the Future*, emphatically answers "no."

Consider the following:

- In 1981, "extreme" poverty — living on an income of $1.90, or less, per person per day in today's money — characterized 52% of the world's population. Today, the comparable figure is 12% of a much larger population.

- Global life expectancy at birth has more than doubled since 1900. It is now 71 years, more than that of the United States in 1965.

- The environment is better adapted to human life. "In 1981," writes Norberg, "half of the world's population had access to safe water. Now, 91 per cent do. On average, that means that 285,000 more people have gained access to safe water every day for the past 25 years."

This is not cherry picking. Practically every economic, social, and environmental indicator is in a long-term uptrend, if not an accelerating one. Norberg does not deny that bad things still happen — and I devote some attention to them toward the end of this article — but in his narrative they recede into near-insignificance when compared to both the long-term and the recent pace of improvement.

Political freedom, while losing a few battles, is gradually winning the war: in 1950, 31% of the world's people lived in electoral democracies; today, 63% do. Violence is down, Norberg argues, and in many countries equality under the law has been extended to women, blacks, and gays.

Norberg's book chronicles the advancements of the last few centuries, with emphasis on the last half-century when progress has become globalized and the developing world played a convincing game of catch-up with the developed. While his subtitle asks us to look toward the future, his book is about the recent past and its startling and unexpected gift of prosperity, safety and good health to a majority of the world's people.

Understanding Rational Optimism

In *Progress*, Norberg, a Swedish economic historian and now a senior fellow at the Cato Institute and executive editor at Free to Choose Media, sets forth a vision of the future that I call "econo-optimism." Norberg's principal theme is that economic growth has, in the relatively recent past, brought comforts and conveniences once known only by the rich to an increasingly broad swath of humanity. He is confident that such progress will continue.

Econo-optimism is rational optimism. Optimists have long been parodied, starting with Voltaire's *Candide* ("this is the best of all possible worlds"), as people whose connection to reality is a wispy thread. They do not see the challenges, the misery, the possibility of disaster. There is something to this critique. Any particular brand of optimism can be blind to reality, or it can be based on data, history, human capability, and an acute sense of limitations and how they can or cannot be overcome. Only the latter is legitimate.

Technologically-driven abundance will never solve, or render irrelevant, the fundamental problem of economics — that of allocating scarce resources to unlimited wants. Some optimists believe, wrongly, that production will be sufficient to satisfy all true needs, and likely much more. They argue that the chief challenge will be to distribute the fruits of production fairly.

Rational optimists, whose knowledge embeds the immutable nature of the economic problem, believe something fundamentally different: the "real prices" of most of the world's important goods and services, which have been falling rapidly, will continue to fall in the future, making it easier and easier to achieve a given standard of living. By the real price of a good or service, I mean the *amount and difficulty of labor* required to buy that good or service. It not only takes far fewer hours of labor to buy most necessities and luxuries than it once did; the work is much less backbreaking. But we will not be able to sit on our haunches and live richly on the fruit that falls out of technological trees. We will always have to put forth effort, and there will be setbacks, including big ones.

It is enough, in the rationally optimistic view, for markets to provide the possibility of at least a decent standard of living for everyone in the world. And, following Norberg's argument, that lofty goal is within a few generations, perhaps less, of being achieved — for the first time in the history of humankind.

Julian Simon established the econo-optimist genre with his groundbreaking 1981 book, *The Ultimate Resource*. Simon argued that human capital is the most important natural resource. Matt Ridley, in *The Rational Optimist*, which I reviewed in *Advisor Perspectives* in 2011,[9] locates the source of these advances in the market economy and the freedom to cooperate and compete. In *The Skeptical Environmentalist*, Bjorn Lomborg applied similar thinking to environmental issues. Taking an academic perspective and enriching these arguments with detail, Deirdre McCloskey and Joel Mokyr have each strengthened the econo-optimists' case tremendously.[10]

I recommend Norberg's *Progress* as a worthy addition to this canon. Readers who want a brief introduction to economic futurism will find it sufficient; I hope that some will be tempted by it to begin a serious exploration of the topic.

Structure of the Book

Norberg follows a formula that characterizes many popular science books: state the author's pet theory, then show how it applies to each of the major spheres of human life (one per chapter) to which it could conceivably apply. The author thereby hopes to convince the reader that the pet theory is valid and universal.

Richard Dawkins is one of the most celebrated authors to use this structure, and he may have invented it. In *The Selfish Gene* (1976), he showed how his proposition — that genes (instead of individuals) seek to maximize their reproductive success — answers questions as varied as why life exists, why people exist, why parents are at odds with their children, why husbands and wives quarrel, why people cooperate and why they are altruistic. Each "why" is a chapter. An endless series of nonfiction titles followed this recipe.

Here's Norberg's pet theory, set forth in his first chapter, entitled "The Good Old Days Are Now": the world is getting better in multiple dimensions, the benefits are widespread, the extent of the improvement is very large and the pace is accelerating. Of course, human life does not always get better and better; terrible

---

[9] https://larrysiegeldotorg.files.wordpress.com/2017/07/ap-ridley-pdf.pdf

[10] See McCloskey's Bourgeois trilogy (*Bourgeois Dignity*, *The Bourgeois Virtues*, and *Bourgeois Equality*) and Mokyr's *A Culture of Growth*. All are heavy stuff, highly recommended but only accessible to readers with a generous time budget. A more recent McCloskey entry, co-authored with Art Carden, popularizes the Bourgeois trilogy in a much shorter book, *Leave Me Alone and I'll Make You Rich: How the Bourgeois Deal Enriched the World*, University of Chicago Press, 2020.

things happen. But the general trend is sharply upward.

The 10 areas in which Norberg says massive progress has occurred are food, sanitation, life expectancy, poverty, violence, the environment, literacy, freedom, equality and the living conditions that the next generation can expect. These areas correspond to Norberg's chapter titles, and it's a pretty impressive list. If some major area of human life has gotten worse in the last half-century, he doesn't seem interested in it. (But I'd be willing to bet on vehicular traffic and the quality of a U.S. high-school education.)

The Causes of Progress

The literature on long-term economic growth and its takeoff in northwestern Europe between about 1750 and 1820 offers a lot of explanations for progress: a growing population; laws that protected private property; the Republic of Letters; and the political fragmentation of Europe, allowing innovators to compete and find patronage.

In this literature, the more recent globalization and acceleration of progress have been attributed to factors as varied as cheap and fast communication, the spread of democracy, the widespread use of English and the acceptance of central banking. I am not sure any one explanation is fruitful. It will take a lot more effort to understand this long and exciting moment in history.

To his credit, Norberg does not hang either the Industrial Revolution or the recent wealth explosion on any of these nails, although he is a strong believer in free markets. But, in his final chapter, Norberg puts forth a tentative explanation: Progress depends on keeping new knowledge out of the hands of élites opposed to change. Think of the scholastics who couldn't stomach Galileo's discoveries: If one man with a telescope could overturn centuries of priestly thought, then the priests did not have a monopoly on all knowledge and had no natural right to rule.

This hypothesis is worth developing, and perhaps Norberg will do so in future work. Here, he does not put much energy into explanations, being more interested in documenting the amount of progress that has occurred and convincing us to be optimists about it continuing.

The Accelerating Rate of Change

Acceleration in the trend toward improvement is one of Norberg's most powerful points. It took from the beginning of time until 1981 for half the world to escape extreme poverty; four-fifths of the other half escaped between 1981 and today. And, surprisingly, the most rapid progress against poverty has been in this young century. For many Americans the 21st century has been a disappointment; for much of the world's population it is the only decent break they've ever gotten.

We don't want that to stop.

The Elements of Progress

Food

Of all human needs, food is the most basic. When I was a child, "There are children starving in Africa" was a common parental response to complaints about the food at my dinner table. If I had an older brother, he would have heard that there were children starving in China or India, and my father probably heard that children were starving in Belgium.

There is still hunger in the world, but most of it is related to warfare and attempts by rulers to control their population. (What an execrable practice.) If all of the food produced in the world were distributed evenly, there would be more than enough for everybody. Even fairly recently, that was not the case. It is the result of the Green Revolution, largely the product of one man:

> In one episode of the TV series *Bullshit!* the magicians Penn and Teller play a game of "The Greatest Person in History," with all the pretenders, religious leaders, presidents, and revolutionary leaders in one deck. Like poker, each player places bets based on how good their cards are – but they might be bluffing. Penn draws one card and immediately goes all in, because he knows he is going to win... He drew Norman Borlaug.

Clearly, Norberg is having fun. But a case can be made that the Iowa agronomist was the greatest person in history. Because of his invention of Green Revolution techniques and his work in bringing them to the world's poorest countries, we've gone in a little more than a generation from a condition where the Club of Rome, in 1972, could plausibly forecast worldwide famine by the end of that decade to one where it is unimaginable (obesity is a bigger problem). And all of that was accomplished while the world's population doubled!

Life Expectancy

Along with food, the length of life is a basic measure of well-being. Exhibit 2.1, from *Our World in Data* (not cited by Norberg), shows life expectancy at birth from 1770 to 2019 for the world and by region.

Exhibit 2.1 Life expectancy, 1770 to 2019

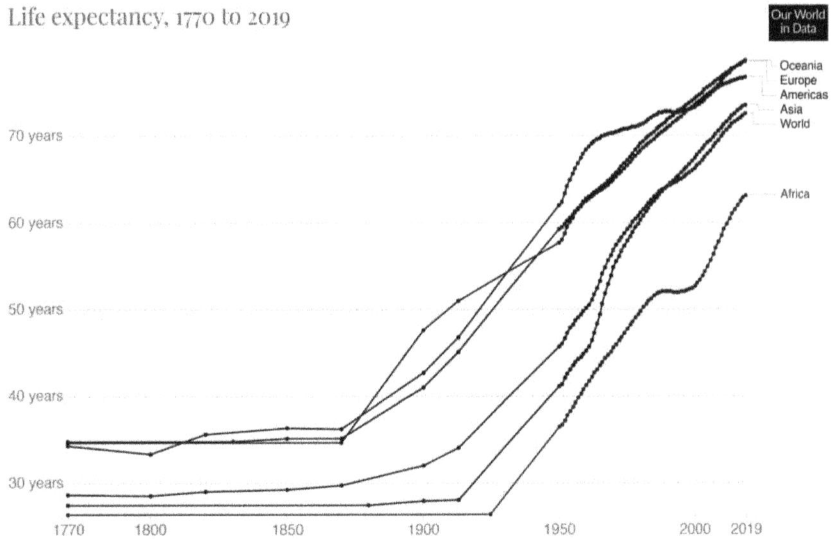

Source: OurWorldInData.org/life-expectancy
Note: Shown is period life expectancy at birth, the average number of years a newborn would live if the pattern of mortality in the given year were to stay the same throughout its life.

Note the slopes of the lines. Asia's advance from age 41 to 68 in a half-century (1950-2000) represents a life expectancy increase of 5.4 years per decade! (If the increase were 10 years per decade, we would never die.) Of course, not all of those years of life were tacked on at the end; decreases in child mortality were responsible for much of the improvement. But the whole world, including Africa, now enjoys a length of life that was unattained even in the most advanced countries in 1930.

Poverty

Exhibit 2.2, again from *Our World in Data*, illustrates the point I made in the introduction. While economic growth between 1820 and 1970 boosted more than a billion people into non-poverty, population growth caused the absolute number of people in extreme poverty to grow even more. By 1970, some two billion lived on less than $1.90 a day in today's money.

Exhibit 2.2 World population living in extreme poverty, 1820-2015

World population living in extreme poverty, 1820–2015

Extreme poverty is defined as living on less than 1.90 international-$ per day
International-$ are adjusted for price differences between countries and for price changes over time (inflation).

Our World in Data

Source: OurWorldInData.org/extreme-poverty
Note: See OurWorldInData.org/extreme-history-methods for the strengths and limitations of this data and how historians arrive at these estimates.

Then, starting around 1970, something changed. The absolute number of poor began to decline, at first slowly but, after the year 2000, so quickly that the United Nations seriously discusses ending extreme poverty completely by 2030.

What changed? Globalization, the opening of China, the reform of India and expansion of trade. (By "globalization," I mean the integration of the whole world into one economy; whatever you produce in one place is for sale anywhere in the world you can find a buyer.) It's not that complicated a formula, and the amount of misery that has been eliminated is immense.

The Environment

But isn't all this progress and prosperity achieved at the expense of nature?

No, argues Norberg. At earlier times in human history it might have been, but at today's level of affluence it is not.

Norberg relies heavily on the idea of the environmental Kuznets curve, a phenomenon in which environmental variables first decay as economies move from primitive to developing status, then improve as those economies transition from developing to developed. He writes, "Technology and affluence are not an obstacle to environmental sustainability, but its precondition."

There are two reasons this is the case. The most important reason is that "preferences change...with better living conditions." The further from bare survival your life is, the more resources you can devote to environmental protection, both personally and through the actions of government. The second reason is that technology provides the tools needed to achieve a clean environment and to bring about the substitution of abundant resources for scarce ones.

Norberg is not blind to the ongoing environmental harm done by certain human activity:

> The number of people breathing unsafe air has risen by more than 600 million since 2000, to a total of almost 1.8 billion. Many cities in India, Pakistan, and Bangladesh suffer from pollution levels that are ten times higher than what is deemed safe.

Yet even this despoilment, caused by the transition from extreme poverty to what economists call lower-middle-income status (although Americans would still call it poverty), will be reversed when lower-middle-income countries become upper-middle-income or high-income. The Kuznets curve, Norberg argues, will rescue the global natural environment in the long run. And it will only happen if economic progress continues at a robust pace.

By touching on food, the length of life, poverty, and the environment I've given a sampling of the ways in which Norberg documents recent advancements. I discuss equality below. The others are beyond the scope of this essay, but if you read Norberg's book you'll get the full picture.

The Conundrum of Moral Progress

In addition to chronicling mankind's material progress, Norberg invokes an old idea that is worth resurrecting: moral progress. How else can one describe a persistent decline in violence (carefully documented by Steven Pinker in

The Better Angels of Our Nature), a rise in the number of democracies, and an increase in the status of women and minorities?

While many economists are reluctant to address moral issues in any way, the most astute of them remember that their field was once called "moral philosophy" and that its founder, Adam Smith, wrote *The Theory of Moral Sentiments* before he wrote *The Wealth of Nations*. Economics, intended to help us live better lives, should acknowledge all of the important aspects of it. Norberg is very much with this program.

Equality of Outcomes or Equality Before the Law?

Equality of economic outcomes is a recent passion, sparked by the work of Thomas Piketty in 2013 and bolstered by thousands of stories in the media. (To be fair, early economists such as Thorsten Veblen were also concerned with equality of economic outcomes; such concern faded as economic growth boosted formerly poor workers into the middle class.) I'll return to equality of outcomes in a moment.

Norberg's conception of equality is quite different: He is concerned with equality before the law. We are unequal in a very profound sense if women cannot vote, if blacks are denied admission to public universities because of their skin color, if gays can be prosecuted and, like Alan Turing, hounded by his government to the point of suicide.

In Western societies and many others, we've made huge strides in the pursuit of equality before the law. That progress has reduced the urgency of this issue because, in these societies, almost no one is on the other side. Again, such progress is astoundingly recent. The treatment of African Americans and of gays and lesbians that I just described occurred in my lifetime, the inability of women to vote in my parents' lifetimes.

Yet Norberg overlooks the most visible social issue of our time, that of radical inequality of outcomes in the largely affluent societies of the West. Why is it visible, and why doesn't Norberg think it is important?

The Elephant Graph: Income Inequality in Perspective

In the United States, Europe, and other developed parts of the world we hear a great deal about the "hollowing out" of the working or middle class. The factory system, which provided moderately well-paid employment to the unskilled, is almost dead in the First World; in its place, we are told, is an élite population of professional, managerial, and technical workers, comprising 15% or 20% of the population and lording it over the rest, a *lumpenproletariat* that earns survival wages or lives on government benefits. (The ratio is often described, very inaccurately, as the 1% versus the 99%.)

What is overlooked is that our *lumpenproletariat* is, by global standards, upper middle income, hovering around the 80th percentile (where 1 is bad and 99 is good) of worldwide incomes. Let's look at this situation a little more closely.

Exhibit 2.3 shows the growth over 1988-2008 in global incomes, sorted by percentile of income distribution. People at the 2nd percentile, who are among the world's very poorest, saw their incomes grow by about 22% in real terms. At the 50th percentile, or median, they saw their incomes grow by about 80%; these are typically industrial workers in rapidly developing countries such as China. As we all know, the top 1% did very well (although we must remember that there is a lot of rotation in the top 1%; they are not the same people every year.

Exhibit 2.3 Growth of Real Incomes Over 1988-2008 by Percentile of Global Income Distribution

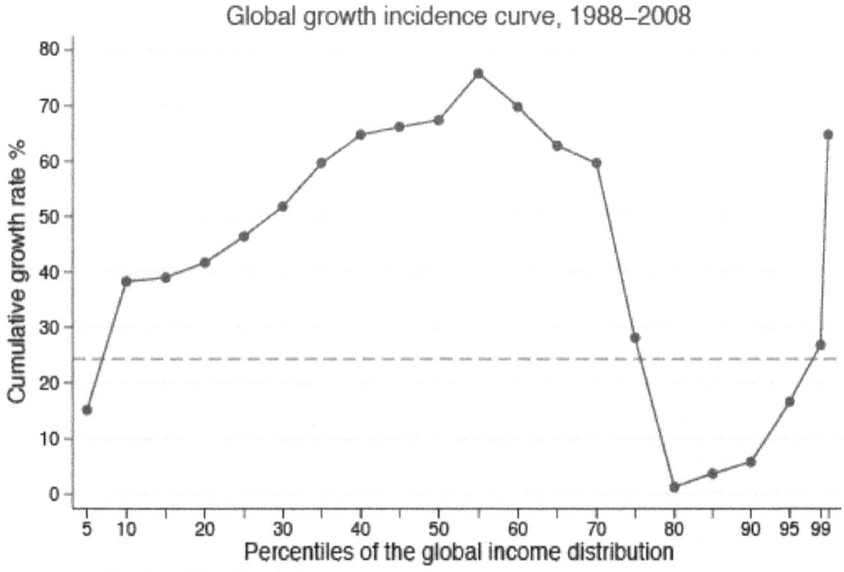

Global growth incidence curve, 1988–2008

Source: Worldbank.Org
Note: Y-axis displays the growth rate of the fractile average income (in 2005 PPP USD). Weighted by population. Growth incidence evaluated at ventile groups (e.g. bottom 5%); top ventile is split into top 1% and 4% between P95 and P99. The horizontal line shows the growth rate in the mean of 24.34% (1.1% p.a.)

At the 80th percentile of global income distribution, however, there was no gain at all. The 90th percentile did not do much better. Who are these people? They are, by and large, the present or former industrial workers of the First World, our "losers."[11]

This diagram, discussed widely in the popular media by its originator Branko Milanovic, the New York Times columnist Paul Krugman and others, is widely called the elephant graph. Since it's a little hard to see why, Caroline Freund, a World Bank economist, drew in the elephant in Exhibit 2.4.[12]

Exhibit 2.4 Elephant Graph Showing the Elephant

Global inequality has declined: Growth incidence curve, 1988-2008

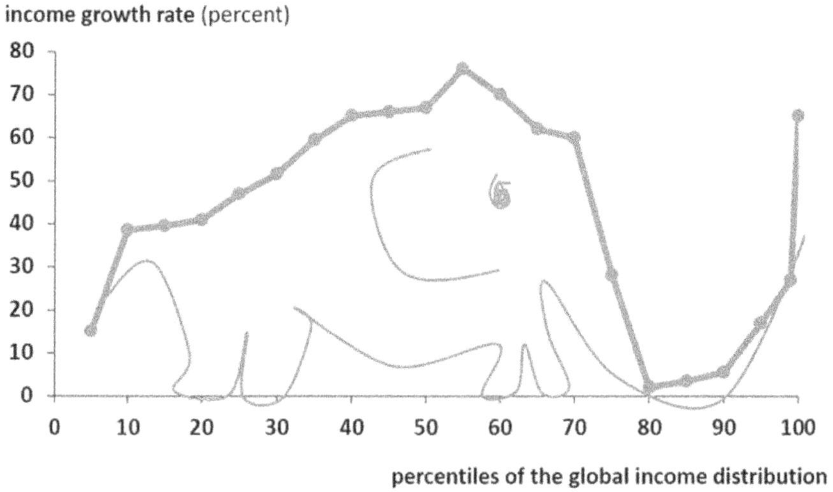

income growth rate (percent)

percentiles of the global income distribution

Source Freund, Caroline. 2016.

No wonder the rest of the world — including Norberg, who takes a global rather than a First World view — is a little puzzled when they hear American and European complaints about middle-class stagnation or decline! The developing world is doing fine relative to its own history and standards, but not as well as our

---

[11] As Adam Corlett of the Resolution Foundation points out, the low point on the elephant graph also includes a lot of people in the former Soviet Union, eastern Europe, and Japan, which had lagging economies over the period.

[12] Freund, Caroline. 2016. "Deconstructing Branko Milanovic's 'Elephant Chart': Does It Show What Everyone Thinks?" Peterson Institute for International Economics, blog post (November 30), https://www.piie.com/blogs/realtime-economic-issues-watch/deconstructing-branko-milanovics-elephant-chart-does-it-show.

"losers." They would love to have our problems.[13]

But the fact that global growth and poverty reduction have been very rapid is little consolation to those at the low point, where wages have stagnated for at least 20 years and possibly for 40. Moreover, there is variation around this average wage growth rate of zero, so that any given working-class individual may have experienced an actual decline in well-being over multiple decades. These concerns, while receding into near-insignificance when measured on a global scale, are not to be taken lightly and are partly responsible for the resurgence of nationalism and populism in recent elections.

I am concerned that, organized politically in advanced countries where they may constitute a majority, these nationalist- and populist-oriented voters will redirect resources toward themselves and close the borders to trade and immigration, possibly alleviating their distress for a while but seriously damaging the engine of global growth that made the income-growth diagram elephantine in the first place, instead of flat lining around zero as had been the case for millennia before the Industrial Revolution.

Global economic growth relies on free markets, free trade and the relatively free movement of people. (Completely free movement of people cannot be achieved.) Should we worry? Yes, in the short run — and also in the longer run if the trends toward isolation and autocracy are simply allowed to run unchecked. But, as I'm about to demonstrate, they will not be.

The End of Progress?

Some observers look at the negative side of today's way of life and detect an end to the progress that Norberg has documented. In the First World, the work ethic, the love of learning and the desire to start enterprises all seem to be flagging. There is an apparent failure of nerve and ambition. History gives us reasons for concern. While progress got off to a good start in ancient Greece and Rome, medieval China, Renaissance Italy and at various other places and times in the past, it fizzled out and extreme poverty returned. Are we repeating the mistakes of those societies?

No. This time, progress is not going end. The thrust toward modernity is too broad and powerful — it is literally worldwide. If decline begins to take root

---

[13] I am being a little facetious. People perceive changes in their socioeconomic status much more keenly than levels, so the people in a poor country that is booming may be happier than the people in a stagnating rich country.

somewhere, people will imitate their more successful neighbors or else move in with them. With cheap and instantaneous global communication, an African peasant, able to see on her village TV or her smartphone how life is lived in more prosperous lands, will not tolerate being condemned to a life of poverty. Using the same tools, an Indian villager can not only discern why it's profitable to move to a city but can buy a bus ticket and go there. Someday, even eastern Kentucky will cease to be overpopulated and impoverished.

Conclusion

Johan Norberg's *Progress* is an outstanding introduction to the science of economic growth. It will not make anyone into an expert in the field, but it's an eye-opener if you haven't been exposed to the ideas Norberg is promoting. It can be read by a high school student, so it could be used as a supplemental school text.

If you have friends who think the world is coming to an end, buy some copies and give it to them.

Chapter 3. The Age of Experts: A Review of Marc Levinson's *An Extraordinary Time*

Stephen C. Sexauer and Laurence B. Siegel

Published in *Business Economics*, October 26. 2017. Reprinted with permission.

How good were the good old days? Was the post-World War II economic boom in the United States and other developed countries a truly special period, one that we cannot expect to repeat, even over centuries-long time frames? Where did those exceptional growth rates come from, and what — if anything — can we do to bring them back?

In *An Extraordinary Time: The End of the Postwar Boom and the Return of the Ordinary Economy*, the economist and journalist Marc Levinson, author of *The Box*, poses these questions. His answer is that the quarter-century from 1948 to 1973, was truly exceptional and that the good times are not coming back. They were, he writes, "an economic golden age across the world" [inside cover] and, because of the rapid rise in oil prices in the 1970s and the economic ups and down since then, "we are not likely to see its equivalent again" [p. 270].[14]

To begin to understand those times, Levinson presents a richly detailed account of the development of macroeconomic models and their use in the postwar period by governments trying to harness the chaos of economic innovation and growth. That tale is the sterling contribution of this book. The emergence of the partnership between business and government in those times is now largely forgotten and Levinson recounts it effectively.

But Levinson's pessimism about future growth asks that we ignore essential elements of the human story and of economic history. The global economy made great progress before 1948 and after 1973; if you do not care only about people in the United States, the most recent quarter-century is the most special one of all.

---

[14] This latter quote is from the last sentence of the book.

Levinson's conclusion — that we are destined to revert to an "ordinary economy," one characterized by stagnation and unproductivity — is deeply wrong.

Although the era of *dirigisme* coincides with the years Levinson calls special, Levinson acknowledges that *dirigisme* did not work miracles: "The entire economic model that had brought the world a quarter-century of unprecedented prosperity was broken" [p. 78]. And, despite Levinson's kvetching, we had some of our best years after the love for central planning in developed economies faded and a more laissez-faire approach was adopted. Thatcherism and Reaganism were not failures; they restored economic growth to a respectable rate, but at the cost of stability.[15] In most places and times, the artificially imposed stability of inflexible union rules, strong government control, and monopolistic corporations would choke off economic growth; in 1948-1973 they did not.

The Marriage of Innovation and Stability

As a general rule, the tensions and balances between governments, the entrepreneurial and professional classes, and rank-and-file workers ebb and flow depending on which economic growth variable dominates: innovation or stability. It is difficult to have both.

But, in the U.S. in 1948-1973, we found instead an unprecedented marriage of innovation and stability. The U.S. had earlier experienced rapid innovation, or growth, in many of the years between the Civil War and World War I and then again in the 1920s. But such growth is usually chaotic and disruptive, and many people are hurt by the side effects of innovation. The 1948-1973 period was indeed special in that the fast-growing U.S. economy is remembered as relatively stable, with few people hurt. Social cohesion provided the lubricant for great change without great *angst*.

You'd be forgiven if you just scratched your head: *what* social cohesion? The civil rights battle raged over the entire period. In 1960, the sunny midsummer of our history, John Kennedy ran for president on a platform of "get[ting] this country moving again"; the 1958 recession, the third in eight years, was the deepest since

---

[15] We are tempted to say "and equality," but we strongly suspect that the rise in inequality after 1970 has more to do with technological advances that made unskilled labor less valuable, while enabling highly skilled labor to extract spectacular rents. Those advances are a good thing: Substituting BTUs for muscle power is the oldest and most important way of making the average person better off, and leveraging human capital with connected computers and almost instantaneous communication increases the overall quality of life. We are concerned that providing opportunity for the less capable will be a critical challenge for the future, but we must rise to it, not turn backwards.

the Great Depression. The chaos that reigned from the Kennedy assassination through the end of the Vietnam war more than a decade later is nobody's idea of social cohesion. And that last period took up two-fifths of the special quarter-century; it was no brief interruption.

And that was just the United States. For much of the world, 1948-1973 was a turbulent and sometimes violent period. From the Soviet Union to the Cultural Revolution in China to the coups and kleptocracies in emerging markets, life was chaotic and desperately poor: "There is no sugarcoating the brutality that, for many people...in many corners of the world...was part of everyday life" [p. 44].

Levels Matter

Then why do so many of us, at least in the industrialized world, remember 1948-1973 so fondly? Is it because, despite lower *levels* of output and productivity (thus standard of living), the *growth rates* of these variables were high, making us feel as though we were getting ahead substantially every year?

Yes. Rates of change are felt more keenly by the human mind than levels. And some of the social cohesion was real: as many as 80% of Americans saw themselves as middle class, they went to the same schools, spoke the same language, and shared the recent memory of a war that was almost lost.[16] Despite increasing urbanization, small-town living — where people from all walks of life rub shoulders and are forced to get along — was still the predominant memory, if not the present reality.

But, setting aside emotion and invoking rationality, would you rather live in a $15,000 GDP per capita country that is growing at 8% or a $52,000 GDP per capita country that is growing at 2%?[17] We'd choose the latter, simply because we don't want to struggle. We can find emotional satisfaction in ways other than anticipating prosperity that may or may not come. Levels matter.

---

[16] We should not forget that most African Americans did not go to the same schools as the majority. Even after schools became legally integrated, most remained segregated due to living patterns.

[17] U.S per capita GDP in 2017 dollars ranged between $15,000 and $16,000 in 1951-1954, and was $52,000 at the time this article was written in 2017. Source: Federal Reserve Bank of Saint Louis, https://fred.stlouisfed.org/series/A939RX0Q048SBEA.

Do You Only Care About People in the First World?

If you ignore the three-quarters of the world population that live in less developed countries, the case for 1948-1973 being "special" is stronger. First-world incomes rocketed ahead, and the middle class did especially well. But if you lived in China or India, and "in many [other] corners of the developing world, the third quarter of the twentieth century was a truly terrible time" [p. 44]. You were about as well off in 1973 in those countries as you were in the Middle Ages.

The big break for the Chinese people came after the liberalization of 1978, and for India after 1992. Because of the large populations of these countries and of some of their neighbors, more wealth has been created worldwide since 1978 than in the special quarter-century. And the recent success of the emerging economies has not been limited to those two population giants. Growth in almost all of the less developed countries has been faster in this century than ever before,[18] and has even started to accelerate in Africa.[19]

No Economic Period Is Ordinary

When thinking about Levinson's overall contention, that 1948-1973 was a unique instance of massive economic progress that never happened before and never will again, one cannot help thinking, "Really?"

In the long sweep of human achievement across all peoples before 1948 and after 1973, the competing epochs of progress are also quite extraordinary. Levinson mostly pooh-poohs them, writing:

> The effects of innovation on the economy were slight in the early twentieth century, very strong from the 1920s to 1973, quite weak between 1973 and 1995, fairly strong between 1995 and 2003, and considerably weaker in the years thereafter. ... [I]n the late 1990s...the

---

[18] For growth rates by country since 2000, see International Labour Organisation, *World of Work Report 2014: Developing with Jobs*,
http://www.ilo.org/wcmsp5/groups/public/@dgreports/@dcomm/documents/publication/wcms_243961. pdf, p. 21.

[19] Maddison Project historical data for all countries and years are at
https://www.rug.nl/ggdc/historicaldevelopment/maddison/?lang=en. The web site is periodically updated.

commercialization of the Internet [led] to a burst of productivity growth...that exhausted itself in just half a dozen years. [p. 263]

Maybe the telephone, the automobile, electrical appliances, and the factory assembly line didn't boost productivity data until 1920. Maybe the introduction of statins in 1987, which increased life spans by *three years*, didn't move the needle because they don't cost much.[20] And maybe Amazon, Uber, and the use of the Internet in the global supply chain, which seem tremendously productive to us, don't show up in the data either. But we would fault the data collection methods, not the technologies. The early 20th century and the last few years have seen changes that are both hugely disruptive and impressively productive.

This observation brings us to our most basic objection to Levinson's theme: *no economic period is ordinary*. Was any time more special than the end of the 18th and the beginning of the 19th century, when substitutes for human muscle power, stored in carbon, were harnessed to begin the release of all of mankind from a Malthusian existence? Was any time more extraordinary than the opening of China and the end of the Cold War, enabling two or three billion people to apply their skills in a world economy that had previously been the province of the Europeans, Americans, and Japanese?

What the Nobel Prize-winning economist Angus Deaton calls "the great escape," from dangerous and backbreaking work in fields, mines, and primitive factories, came largely before 1948 in the industrialized West and is still proceeding today in emerging markets.[21] The drive to bring sanitation and clean water to the masses began early in modern history but continues to be a challenge in developing countries today.

Medical innovation has produced a decrease in suffering and gains in the quality and length of life that can hardly be comprehended; in 1840 surgery had to be performed without anesthetics. (Let that sink in.) The first cure of an infectious disease using antibiotics was in 1935 — and we have barely seen the beginning of these advances, which continue today with gene sequencing. Gains in human rights and political freedom, along with occasional losses, have also proceeded without reference to any particular quarter-century.

These, not the increase in housing and automotive and appliance wealth that we associate with economic growth, are mankind's great achievements and they did not stop coming, or even slow down, in 1973. *No period is ordinary*.

---

[20] In an ironic twist, no matter how beneficial, only expensive innovations add measurably to GDP.

[21] Deaton, Angus. 2013. *The Great Escape*. Princeton, NJ: Princeton University Press.

In the Postwar World, a New Leaf: Government by Experts

In making his case, Levinson does provide us with a valuable and richly detailed view into two powerful postwar trends. The first consists of the emerging availability of government data on the economy and the rise of operations research as a discipline that could be used by government experts for macroeconomic planning. The second is that governments made the leap to being accountable for economic outcomes, combining the need to please voters with the capacities newly acquired through macroeconomic data and theory.

This trend toward management of non-centrally planned economies by government experts is apparent from the wording of the U.S. Employment Act of 1946, which "promote[s] maximum employment, production, and purchasing power."[22] It lives on in the July 2012 statement by European Central Bank president Mario Draghi that the bank would do "whatever it takes to preserve the euro."[23]

Experts and the Magic Square

Levinson recounts the effort by experts to manage four macro variables to desirable and stable levels to achieve growth and stability, a strategy called the Magic Square. The variables were unemployment, inflation, real GDP growth, and trade balances.[24]

In the U.S., the reigning expert was Walter W. Heller, a Kennedy confidant and strong Keynesian.[25] In the developing world it was Raúl Prebisch, an Argentine economist who tried to steer a middle course between capitalist orthodoxy and the radicalism then in vogue in Latin America and other emerging economies.

And in West Germany the rock-star expert was Kurt Schiller, *Stern*'s Man of the Year in 1969, described by Levinson as "work[ing] late into the night [with] his 'team of eggheads.' After crunching the numbers, they specified the most

---

[22] http://www.federalreservehistory.org/essays/employment_act_of_1946

[23] https://www.nytimes.com/2016/01/22/business/international/ecb-stimulus-mario-draghi.html

[24] In addition, they were committed to maintaining fixed exchange rates, a system that failed by 1971; it's a matter of interpretation whether the foreign exchange value of one's home currency is a fifth variable or just a manifestation of trade balances.

[25] Not Walter E. Heller, the Chicago financier and philanthropist.

desirable rate of economic growth," which turned out to be 4%, with 0.8% un-employment and 1% inflation. The cadre of experts used linear programming, input-output analysis, and other new items in the economist's toolkit to balance the unpredictable behavior of markets and capitalists against the legal obliga-tion to foster growth.

In the end, however, such incredibly rosy macro goals were unachievable. As Levinson indicates, 1973, when the first large OPEC oil price increase occurred, was the year when the macroeconomic indicators all seemed to agree that things had started to go badly. Yet, as the failure in 1971 of the Bretton Woods fixed exchange-rate system proved, the magic square had been deteriorating for some time; OPEC was merely the catalyst.

By the time of the second oil shock, in 1979, any pretense of maintaining the magic square had been abandoned. U.S. inflation was running at 9%, unemploy-ment was around 6%, and real GDP growth was a paltry 1.3%. President Carter may not have uttered the word *malaise* in a speech but he should have. In the end, Levinson states, "The idea that government planning could assure prosper-ity and rising living standard for all proved to be a cruel hoax" [p. 46].

I don't think any economist today would propose that you can hold all of the Magic Square variables constant at the same time, when each is affected by mil-lions of independent decisions and several of the variables are pushing against each other. (For example, some factors that cause high GDP growth tend to also cause high inflation.) "Only belatedly," Levinson writes, "would [Kurt Schiller] accept that the magic square was a technocrat's fantasy" [p. 34]. Governments have learned their modesty lesson, although it could also be argued that the outcomes are also modest: in what seems like the main challenge we now face, First World economies are hardly growing faster than their populations.

The problem is not that the experts don't know anything; they do. With a few exceptions, they are diligent and well-meaning students of the economy and of human behavior. The difficulty is that the rational expectations hypothesis is roughly right: people do what they want, and react poorly to policies that push them to do things they think are unprofitable. As a result, there are severe limits to what proactive economic policy can accomplish. Mostly we need to establish good laws and institutions and hope for the best, figuring that people acting in their own interest will produce the "right" amount of economic growth.

The Return of the Ordinary Economy?

Levinson's insights into the role of economic planning, in both developed and emerging economies, make *An Extraordinary Time* worth reading even if its conclusions are suspect. We'll close by noting that the last half of the book's subtitle, "The Return of the Ordinary Economy," posits that there is such a thing as an ordinary economy. What is it, and what will it look like when it returns?

Perhaps, for many people, it is a steady-state economy where one day, year, or decade is much like another, lacking in abrupt surprises and limited in the amount of change. Unfortunately, the only steady-state economy in the historical record is one that, according to Angus Maddison, produced output equal to $3 per person per day — just enough that many people could survive long enough to reproduce; a lucky few survived longer, and an even luckier few did so at some degree of affluence. This was the reality faced by most of the world's people for most of its history.

This Hobbesian way of life, "solitary, poor, nasty, brutish, and short," is, of course, not what Levinson thinks is in store for us. His ordinary economy looks more like today's economy: affluent yet sluggish, unequal, unfamiliar, and continually disruptive. Like other forecasters of our economic future, Levinson has projected the present forward indefinitely, making the familiar behavioral mistake of overemphasizing the most recent observation.

We have more faith in humanity than that. The evidence is on our side.

Chapter 4. A Nation of Slugs?

April 2017

Have we all gone lazy? Are Americans no longer the restless go-getters they once were? Has our culture changed in ways that impede economic progress instead of naturally promoting it? In his new book, *The Complacent Class,* Tyler Cowen, one of the most eclectic and inventive of today's authors on economic issues, says yes to all of these.

Not so fast, Professor. The United States is still the richest large country in the world. Three decades after Japan gave us a run for our money, and two decades after Europe unified, we're way ahead of both. The U.S. recovery from the global financial crisis of 2007-2009, while lacking in vigor, is stronger than in most other developed societies. While some small countries have higher per-capita income and China's total output is on par with that of the U.S. (depending on the measure), Chinese incomes are one-quarter those in the United States and will probably not catch up in this century. And the U.S. standard of living has increased in ways that are not captured by GDP statistics — the air Americans breathe and the tap water we drink is the envy of hundreds of millions around the world.

Tyler Cowen is one of the most prolific and original authors the economics profession has yet produced. It's hard to figure out when the blogging superstar, George Mason University professor, online educator, and author of more than a dozen books ever sleeps.

Yet *The Complacent Class* is strangely unsatisfying. Without presenting much in the way of data, Cowen portrays Americans as contented with modest achievements, dug in, working harder to protect small gains than to achieve large ones. This image collides with the America I know. There is a vocal minority that is deeply distressed, a condition common over America's turbulent economic history. But a great many people, the majority, work hard and are doing fairly well to very well.

Oy Vey...

Cowen, who I think of as an optimist,[26] has joined the chorus of commentators who say that the country is going to hell in a handbasket. He foreshadowed the current work with a 2010 book called *The Great Stagnation: How America Ate All the Low-Hanging Fruit of Modern History, Got Sick, and Will (Eventually) Feel Better,* but the emphasis in that book, on how we can and will someday feel better, is mostly missing from *The Complacent Class.*

The hell-in-a-handbasket genre is as old as the ancient Greeks and has filled American library shelves for our entire history. But it is enjoying a robust revival.

Of course, just because an idea has become faddish does not mean it isn't true. Relative to its glorious history, the U.S. has indeed suffered in this new century, with two wars and a long, shallow depression. We never fully recovered from the global financial crisis. It's not surprising that there should be a rash of pessimistic books in the stores.

But, despite making a large number of worthwhile points, *The Complacent Class* is not one of the better books in this genre. A cleaner and more persuasive case for American decline is made by Nicholas Eberstadt, writing in *Commentary.*[27] Eberstadt focuses on the newly disadvantaged category of young and middle-aged white men. He is rightly concerned about the separation of this group from the upwardly mobile mainstream, which includes many members of minority groups.

Cowen, in contrast, says that a mainstream group, the professional upper middle class, *is* the problem. That is Cowen's most serious mistake. Those who are falling behind should be emulating the professional class's success, not deploring or resenting it.

Three Complacent Populations

Cowen finds three groups in American life to be unsuitably complacent. They are: educated professionals; middle-status people who are "dug in," desperate to

---

[26] https://object.cato.org/sites/cato.org/files/serials/files/policy-report/2012/11/culture.pdf

[27] https://www.commentarymagazine.com/articles/our-miserable-21st-century/

preserve their modest successes; and the "stuck" poor.[28] But he makes it clear that the book's title refers to the first group, who are also David Brooks' bobos or bourgeois bohemians, Richard Florida's creative class, John Kenneth Galbraith's New Class. (Writers spend a lot of time making up cute names for what used to be called the upper middle class.)

It's not clear to me why a group of people, largely self-made, doing satisfying work, and living at one of the highest standards the world has ever known, should not be satisfied and seeking to preserve their position. They would be crazy not to.[29] And I believe that this class has always been complacent, probably more so in the past than today. Just read, from a century ago, Sinclair Lewis' *Babbitt* and H. L. Mencken's rantings about the *booboisie*.

Yet the predictable and understandable complacency of the professional class is the subject of Cowen's principal complaint and, in his reckoning, the source of our current malaise. What would Cowen have them do differently?

He doesn't really say, but one can infer from the context: start businesses, move far from home, marry outside one's class or one's nationality. If you're a prospective businesswoman, become a backpacker for a year; if you're headed for a life of adventure, try working in a bank. Work with your hands. Live for a while with someone much older; they already know what you will someday know.

Cowen himself is a Renaissance man. Perhaps he thinks of his own wildly varied interests as a model for others.

These are good ideas (and they are just my wild guesses). But they will not raise economic growth by a couple of percentage points. Only policy-level changes in incentives can do that, and, even then, results are not guaranteed.

The Productivity Riddle

But maybe we don't need a radical cure because, just maybe, we don't have all that serious a problem.

Headline U.S. productivity statistics continue to disappoint, with labor

---

[28] Jim Manzi, in "Keeping America's Edge," *National Affairs*, Winter 2010 (republished Spring 2017), http://www.nationalaffairs.com/publications/detail/keeping-americas-edge, does a nice job on digging in.

[29] I wonder, however, whether there ever was a time when the upper middle class was not complacent. When it was small, before the 1960s explosion in public higher education, it was probably even more complacent and dug in.

productivity per hour, a key measure, rising at 1.1% per year over 2007-2016, compared to 2.3% per year over 1947-2007 as shown in Exhibit4.1. Of course, this is just a growth rate; the *level* of productivity is the highest it's ever been. But slow growth for a long time is a legitimate concern, and has a large opportunity cost.

Some distinguished economists, however, including the Berkeley professor and blogger[30] Bradford DeLong and former Council of Economic Advisers chairman Martin Feldstein, believe that official productivity statistics materially understate growth in the standard of living.

Exhibit 4.1 Productivity Growth Rates in the United States

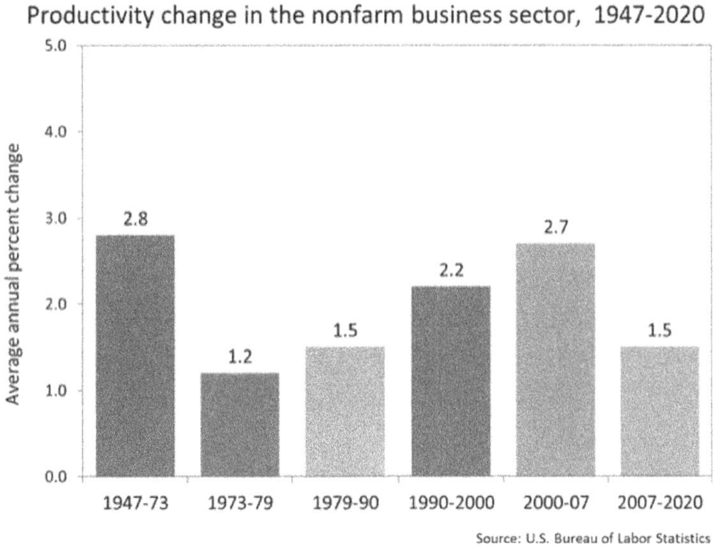

Productivity change in the nonfarm business sector, 1947-2020

Source: U.S. Bureau of Labor Statistics

Source: https://www.bls.gov/lpc/prodybar.htm

The Macbeth Effect

DeLong's argument begins with the observation that the global economy produces about 20 times as much, per capita, as it did before the Industrial Revolution when a typical worker could afford to consume 2000 calories of grains per day. But, he notes, "[40,000]...calories a day in basic grains wouldn't do anyone much good." The amount of money needed to purchase 20 days' food supply can, today, instead buy a set of goods that are much more varied and valuable than a big pile of grain. For example,

---

[30] http://delong.typepad.com

In 1606, there was only one person who could sit at home and watch a bloody audiovisual drama about witches. His name was James Stuart, the king of England and Scotland. He had William Shakespeare and the King's Men on retainer. Today, more than four billion people with smartphones, tablets, and televisions enjoy a form of on-demand entertainment that was once reserved for absolute monarchs.[31]

DeLong also notes that the richest man of the early nineteenth century, Nathan Rothschild, died of an infection that, today, would be cured by one dose of antibiotics. Few of these quality-of-life improvements show up in the productivity data, which assume that the dose of antibiotics is worth what you pay for it, about a dollar. In fact, Rothschild would probably have given his entire fortune, estimated in the hundreds of billions in today's money, to get the medication.

Thus, official productivity statistics greatly understate economic growth over long periods of time. At present, people benefit from easy and cheap access to the world's libraries through the Internet, as I did while writing this article on the beach. Only a quarter-century ago I would have had to camp out at a serious academic library, pay library tuition, hire research assistants to chase down background material and make photocopies, and limit my research to the publications that my local university could afford to buy. Thus, the spread between growth-as-measured and true growth persists into the present day.

The Cholesterol Effect

This spread is, of course, a global phenomenon: almost everyone benefits from the Internet, from medical advances, from improvements in the food supply. In contrast, Marty Feldstein offers an argument that the U.S. in particular is enjoying a growth rate higher than that captured by official measures. The reason (caution: geeky) has to do with the way that price indices are calculated:

> When a new product is developed and sold to the public, its market value enters into *nominal* GDP [my italics]. These nominal values of GDP are converted to *real* values using price indices that don't reflect the new product at all. Why? Because the new product is too small in the beginning to be worth changing the weights in the GDP price index. But over time, if the new product eventually represents a large

---

[31] https://www.project-syndicate.org/commentary/rethinking-productivity-growth-by-j--bradford-delong-2017-03

enough amount of spending, the BLS [does include] the changes in its price...in the price index...[32]

The result is that, even if the nominal GDP measure is just right, the inflation rate used to convert it to the real GDP measure is too high, so the real GDP measure itself is too low. Thus, continues Feldstein, "when new products are introduced, [the real GDP statistics do not] reflect the extra value to consumers created by those products."

The end result of all this math, taking statins (Feldstein's example) as a proto-typical improvement in technology, is that GDP-as-measured went *down* due to statins becoming less expensive as they became widely adopted. But GDP-as-measured didn't rise due to statins being introduced in the first place because they were not in the market basket! Thus, the tremendous benefit of the new drug never showed up in the data.

This effect is much more important for countries on the technological frontier, such as the U.S., where innovations are high-priced at first, than for countries off the frontier where innovations enter the economy once they have become cheap. So the spread between GDP or productivity as measured, on one hand, and the true standard of living, on the other, is wider for the United States than for other countries.[33] This observation is important and is missed by most econ-omists.

This long digression is a way of saying that the problem to which Cowen has devoted his book may be overstated. If the problem of slow growth is sufficiently overstated, we may not need a solution – although some Americans have terrible problems, a topic to which I now turn.

The Mysterious Dying of Middle-Aged White Males

Meanwhile, in parts of the industrial heartland and in rural areas across the country, we are not doing well.

The economist Anne Case, and her husband Angus Deaton, who won the 2015 Nobel economics prize, recently presented evidence that, in contrast to the

---

[32] Feldstein, Martin S. 2017. "Why Is Growth Better in The United States than in Other Industrial Countries?" http://www.nber.org/papers/w23221.

[33] This is my observation, not Feldstein's.

sharply falling mortality rates of most segments of the population in the U.S. and elsewhere, middle- aged white males were dying younger. Exhibit 4.2 summarizes the Case and Deaton finding, which has been widely publicized:[34]

Exhibit 4.2 is for both sexes but, disaggregating the data, the big increase in mortality is for white, non-Hispanic men. The chief reasons, according to Case and Deaton, are "suicide, drug and alcohol poisoning (accidental and intent undetermined), and chronic liver diseases and cirrhosis." Not good, and the picture is almost certainly even worse once you take out the upper-middle and upper classes.[35]

Exhibit 4.2 Mortality from All Causes (Deaths Per 100,000), Age 45-54, for Various Groups

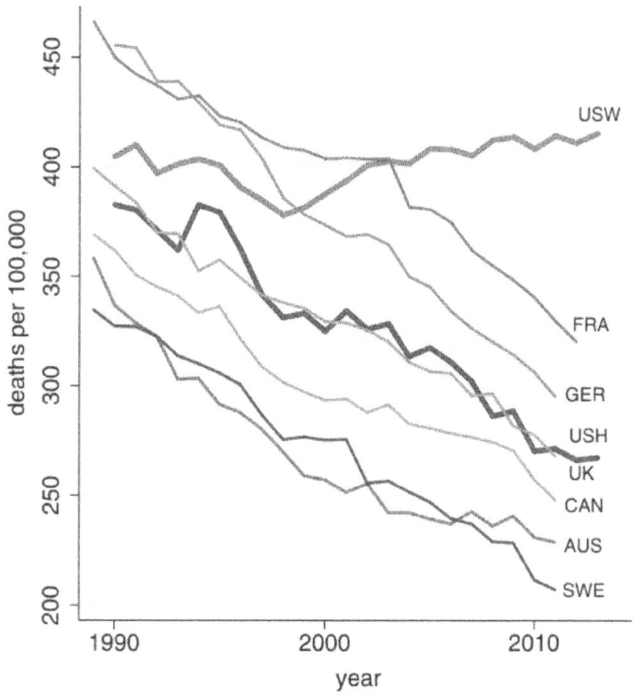

All-cause mortality, ages 45-54 for US White non-Hispanics (USW), US Hispanics (USH), and six comparison countries: France (FRA), Germany (GER), the United Kingdom (UK). Canada (CAN), Australia (AUS), and Sweden (SWE). Source: Case and Deaton [2015].

---

[34] Case, Anne and Angus Deaton. 2015. "Rising Morbidity and Mortality in Midlife among White Non-Hispanic Americans in the 21st Century." *Proceedings of the National Academy of Sciences,* Vol. 112, no. 49 (December 8). A later paper by the authors, https://www.brookings.edu/wp-content/uploads/2017/03/6_casedeaton.pdf, goes into further detail and corrects earlier errors.

[35] Case and Deaton's work has been criticized. The authors failed to correct for increasing age within the 45-54 category; when that correction is made, mortality levels off after 2005. The period

Even if the broad measures of economic health that I cited earlier are favorable, we cannot overlook these indicators of social and medical pathology in such a large segment of the population. Although the timing is not precise, the connection to economic dislocation seems obvious. In the light of Case and Deaton's work, Cowen is right to be critical of our economic performance.

I now summarize and comment on some of the specific issues raised by Cowen in *The Complacent Class*.

The New Segregation

As Ana Swanson of the Washington *Post*, who interviewed Cowen, summarized his observations, "the U.S. population has sorted out not only along political lines, but also by education, race, income, social status and even technological ability. Along the way, the country has become more polarized, less dynamic and less fair."[36]

But, instead of seeking out ethnic enclaves as in the past, the complacent class has achieved this self-sorting by cramming themselves into the best school districts.

Elizabeth Warren on the left, and Charles Murray on the right, have both confirmed Cowen's observation the high price of real estate in these districts is one reason for the decline – real or apparent – in social mobility. This process leaves the less desirable school districts and less well-polished neighborhoods for the next class down, and so on until all the social positions have been filled, from élite to ghetto.[37]

I like the following explanation for the apparent reduction in social mobility

---

of greatest increase in mortality, 2000-2005, was well before the 2008 crash and was economically relatively benign, making cause and effect unclear. But poisonings (including from drugs), suicides, and liver disease continued to rise after 2005, no matter how you slice the data. Hidden within the fairly prosperous U.S. population, it seems there is a community of the very miserable. See, for example, http://andrewgelman.com/2015/11/06/what-happened-to-mortality-among-45-54-year-old-white-non-hispanic-men-it-declined-from-1989-to-1999-increased-from-1999-to-2005-and-held-steady-after-that.

[36] Swanson, Ana. 2017. "Upper class elites might hate Trump, but they were key to his success," Washington Post (February 28). https://www.washingtonpost.com/news/wonk/wp/2017/02/28/upper-class-elites-might-hate-trump-but-they-were-key-to-his-success/?aspoinz&utm_term=.e926652418af

[37] Of course, in a country as complex as the U.S. there are even elite ghettos, such as Palmer Woods in Detroit and Sugar Hill in Harlem, New York. African-American society is as stratified as any other.

better (it's my own idea): upward mobility depends in part on raw talent. If the lower and working classes have been stripped of their most talented members by the well-meaning effort to give everyone a college education who can do college-level work, no wonder those left behind seem a little dull! And no wonder they are having a tough time. Of course, all we've done is replace upward mobility through luck and pluck with upward mobility through college admissions testing. Overall social mobility has probably not changed.

The democratization of higher education has not, of course, plucked every single talented member out of the lower classes and placed him or her in the professional class. But sometimes it seems that way. I remember having discussions about the stock market, stereo equipment, and astronomical telescopes with my plumber.[38] Would that happen today?

Nimby and Banana

A group of successful people who are mostly concerned with preserving their own status does not, of course, take kindly to letting strangers and strivers in. This attitude reveals itself in NIMBY (Not In My Back Yard), a political posture that begins with a good-hearted effort to preserve one's hard-won neighborhood ambience and the natural environment but that ends up creating barriers to entry through astronomical real estate prices.

The Mecca of the new complacent class is San Francisco. Old-timers can remember when a new house, in a desirable part of the city, could be bought for around $15,000,[39] because the dockworkers and fishermen who lived there in the 1950s had very little money. Today the same house sells for upwards of $2 million, the highest rate of appreciation in the country. If San Francisco had been allowed to develop along free-market principles it would look like Manhattan and would be dramatically less expensive. But it would not be "San Francisco."

NIMBY has been so successful at keeping the riff-raff out, in Complacent Class cloisters from San Francisco to Ann Arbor to Boston, that it has morphed into what Cowen calls BANANA, "Build Absolutely Nothing Anywhere Near Anything." This is effectively the program of the environmental and anti-growth movements, which turn out to be powerful forces for stasis. Of course, we need to protect the environment, but we should also recognize the social and human costs of doing so, and achieve balance.

---

[38] All right, I'm cheating a little. The plumber was my uncle. Genetics matter.

[39] http://www.outsidelands.org/midtown-terrace.php

Matching

In a society where we've sorted ourselves out into residential communities by educational level, industry (tech in California, finance in New York), taste for urban, suburban, or rural living, and political and sexual preference, we tend to marry those who are much like us and produce children who are even more like us. Instead of seeking mates who belong to the same church, go to the same (economically diverse small-town) school, or are pleasing to the eye, we use social networks and software to search for partners who match us very closely in a whole array of deeply personal characteristics and desires. Some of us even look for sex partners on Tinder.

The results are not impressive: marital happiness is not visibly improving, divorce rates are down only a little, and many people choose to forgo marriage altogether.

Due to some of the same software, we are also more closely matched in other ways, for example to our music. There are 1371 music categories on Spotify, including black sludge, solipsynthm, and skweee. These compare with about five (rock-and-pop, jazz, country, folk, classical) in the record stores of my youth. This blizzard of choices has not made music noticeably better — we are just better matched to it, and spend less time listening to music we don't like. But we also don't often discover something delightfully new. We are musically complacent.

Cowen argues that this intense matching creates communities that are anti-civic, pursuing their own parochial interests instead of the national interest. I think this concern is justified. The hipsters of Portland, the former coal miners of eastern Kentucky, and African American strivers in the Atlanta suburbs all have something in common: they're Americans, and human beings. But how often do they think of each other as members of one giant, embracing national community?

Casual Friday Every Day

Cowen even finds a downside in the uniquely American, and mostly salutary, habit of not dressing up. Of course, once Cowen explains it, it's obvious:

> The less strict the dress code, in fact the harder it is to look good and to fit in, and that disadvantages those who are not from well-educated

and successful backgrounds... If everything is casual, what do you do to show your seriousness?

Fashion is but one example of how the American wealthy have been redefining social status through...countersignaling [that is, signaling one's virtue through displays of modesty]. Bill Gates...can countersignal all he wants, and he is still Bill Gates and obviously so... If you're twenty-four years old and looking to get ahead, it can be tougher.

It's a sign of Cowen's intellectual inventiveness that he can identify the social cost of dressing casually, a practice that on first glance is leveling. That's what economists do — in any situation they're trained to ask, "what are the costs?" — but only in the afterglow of Gary Becker's Nobel prize-winning work do economists think to apply this principle broadly to include khakis and blue jeans. (Becker's gift to economics was to apply it to all sorts of non-economic questions.) Cowen, a Becker acolyte, is ideally suited to making these connections, and all of his books benefit from such unconventional thinking.

Rooted or Stuck?

Did you know that Americans have (almost) stopped moving house? "The interstate migration rate has fallen [to a level] 51% below its 1948-1971 average," Cowen writes. During the peak years, about 20% of households moved each year. Now, it's fewer than 10%.

A group of Germans with whom Cowen spoke thought he was kidding or exaggerating when he quoted the 20% number. In Germany, buying and moving into a house, often one's parents' house or a house nearby, is usually a lifetime decision. But Americans, in search of opportunity, a change of scenery, or better weather — or to escape from bad conditions — really did move at the rate described.

The new, more sluggish rate of relocation keeps many people from getting ahead. A quarter-century ago, Michigan residents who had lost their jobs in the auto industry migrated quite aggressively to Texas. Today, they tend to stay behind, adjusting to the lower pay of new jobs or to disability payments. It's hard for the economy to grow that way, and it's not healthy to have a resentful and dependent population concentrated in one area. Today, there are many such areas.

People who rarely move can be rooted or stuck. Cowen suggests they are mostly stuck, although they may be comfortable in communities to which they are economically and culturally matched. Staying put, matching, and segregation are all related. NIMBYism is also related, because high-growth areas can be numbingly expensive, reducing the incentive to move for better pay.[40]

Sclerotic Government

One does not have to be a partisan of one side or another to think that we are poorly governed. Our acrimonious political debates resolve fewer and fewer issues, and the overall quality of government is questionable. How did this happen to a country that produced Washington, Jefferson, Lincoln, and Roosevelt?

Cowen provocatively argues that it's because of entitlement spending, which now consumes 50% of tax revenues, headed toward 80% as entitlements grow due to the aging of the population. (The biggest entitlements are Social Security, Medicare, and Medicaid.) Thus political fights, which are mostly about discretionary spending, resolve a smaller and smaller part of the total budget.

A government that is stuck in this way cannot be of much help to a population that is also stuck. Interest groups trying to preserve their special privileges find themselves playing a zero-sum game with other interest groups in similar positions. It isn't pretty.

Compare this situation with 1960s California, which supported the largest expansion of public higher education in history while building a magnificent highway system and greatly expanding welfare payments — all without sparking a tax rebellion. How did they do it? Massive economic growth due to a technological boom that included civilian aviation, defense, and the space program and spurred migration from other states in pursuit of the big paychecks on offer.

Through aggressively pro-growth policies and continued immigration at all skill levels, the U.S. can, and I believe will someday, recapture the energy of that unique time. It could be a long wait — an aging society has some disadvantages relative to a young one — but we will not be an aging society forever, and the goal is worth striving for.

---

[40] It can be hard to distinguish complacency from a rational response to incentives. Casey Mulligan, in *The Redistribution Recession*, Oxford University Press, 2012, argues that much of what appears to be the former is in fact the latter, and argues for reform of policies that have the effect, intended or unintended, of reducing job mobility.

The Great Reset

How does all this complacency end? Cowen suggests that it is through a "great reset" analogous to the Reformation: pressures silently build until it becomes obvious that we have a problem. Campus unrest, a pause in the decline of crime, and political chaos are the early first signs that have already occurred.

In "one scenario" of Cowen's future, the chaos does not last forever and, as the term "reset" implies, we eventually reach a new equilibrium in which birth rates begin once again to rise, the U.S. population is refreshed with entrepreneurial immigration from Africa (not as farfetched as it sounds), and the benefits of technology become more obvious and more widespread.

I wish that Cowen had put more effort into his visions of the future, because speculative thinking is his great comparative advantage. The world is full of social critics, but visionaries are rare and he can make a serious claim to being one.

Conclusion

It seems almost unpatriotic to give one of Tyler Cowen's books a middling review. Here is journalist Ezra Klein on Cowen's mind:

> We discuss[ed] everything from New Jersey to high school sports to finding love to smoked trout to noötropics to Thomas Schelling to Ayn Rand to social media to speed reading strategies to happy relationships to the disadvantages of growing up in Manhattan. [T]hat is a small sampling of the topics we cover[ed].[41]

Thus, it's unsurprising that Cowen is at his almost magical best when noting the profound relevance of an apparently trivial fact, finding markets operating in the oddest places, and uncovering connections between seemingly unrelated ideas and events. Read his blog — I do so every day. But this book is not particularly compelling. *The Complacent Class* is for readers who want to go that extra mile in their search for insight into contemporary social dilemmas. The basics are better covered elsewhere.

---

[41] http://marginalrevolution.com/marginalrevolution/2017/03/new-podcast-ezra-klein.html. Noötropics are purportedly cognition-enhancing drugs.

In *The Complacent Class,* Cowen sets forth a one-sided, deeply gloomy, and essentially unfair view of America's current troubles. Keynes was right about one thing: animal spirits are crucial to the dynamism of an economy. We could talk ourselves into an economic depression by allowing our animal spirits to flag — by concluding, incorrectly in advance, that few if any undertakings are likely to be fruitful. Let's not do that.

The United States has plenty of faults, but complacency among the leadership class is not one of the major ones; lack of opportunity for the less able is. Let's educate our less fortunate and provide practical incentives to work so they can participate and compete in global markets and enjoy the opportunities and pleasures that Cowen's so-called complacent class has created.

Steve Sexauer provided many helpful comments.

Investing

This is home turf for Larry. This is where he learned to analyze, to think, and to write.

Larry didn't start college or even graduate school thinking of a career in finance, but research assistant positions and coursework pulled him in the direction of economics and then investment management. Decades later, he is well known for his wide-ranging, provocative thinking on the subject.

Wayne's personal favorite: Is it science or is it baloney?

—WHW

Chapter 5. Is It Science or Is It Baloney?

September 2016[42]

Which currently popular investment fads are flashes in the pan, and which are actually worthy innovations? Which are somewhere in between?

Because the theoretical or academic pedigree of an investment strategy helps mightily to sell it, marketers often represent whatever they're selling as "real science," with roots in the work of Nobel Prize-winning financial economists. Some of these claims are entirely justified. Some are almost entirely hype. More often, they're in between — good investment ideas that, sooner or later, take on the shape of fads and become crowded trades that lose their effectiveness.

Let's look, through this lens, at some strategies that are currently receiving attention from investors. Before starting, I'll state my biases: indexing is usually a very good way for investors to obtain access to an asset class, because it is hard to pick successful active managers and active strategies — but active management is *not* useless.[43] Far from it! Many strategies, especially value strategies, have delivered superior returns over long periods of time. Given the behavioral biases and information asymmetries that we observe almost everywhere, value investing can be expected to continue to perform well on average over time (although not all the time!). The effort to distinguish good active strategies from doubtful ones is well worth one's while.

Because most strategies start out as plausibly good ideas, at least in a backtest, and because no active strategy can "work" everywhere and always, most of the

---

[42] This article is based on a panel discussion in which I participated at the Commonfund Forum, Orlando, Florida, March 16, 2015. I am greatly indebted to AJO (Philadelphia, PA) for its financial, moral, and practical support of this article and of my work in general; to Paul Kaplan (Morningstar Canada), Stephen Sexauer (San Diego County Employees Retirement Association), Rodney Sullivan (Richard A. Mayo Center for Asset Management, University of Virginia), and Barton Waring (Barclays Global Investors, retired) for their critical and always helpful comments; and, especially, to Thomas Idzorek of Morningstar for allowing me to recycle some of the ideas in his great article, "Caveat Emptor!" [Idzorek 2014], in the present work. A slightly abridged version of this article appeared in Morningstar Magazine, December/January 2017.

[43] There are some strategies, such as private equity, private real estate, and certain natural resources investments, for which an index fund cannot realistically be constructed (mostly because positions, or deals, have to be individually negotiated and there is not enough liquidity to rebalance the index). In these asset classes one must select active managers.

investment ideas covered in this article are in-betweeners. They are neither exact science nor pure baloney. But, as practiced and marketed, they sometimes lean to one side or the other.

For each strategy, several questions should be asked:

- Is it grounded in real theory?

- Is it scalable, that is, will it still work more often than not after it becomes popular? It is not necessarily bad to pursue a strategy that fails as more and more people attempt it, but at least you should know that a strategy has that characteristic, and you should have some indication of when to stop.

- Does it work (have a reasonable prospect of producing alpha) after all transaction costs and reasonable fees have been subtracted?

Let's go through a few of the major currently popular strategies.

Capitalization-Weighted Indexing

Cap-weighted indexing is the base case to which all active strategies must be compared. For a strategy to be considered active, it is necessary to define what is not active. A number of passive strategies can be imagined, including buy-and-hold-forever-without-rebalancing. But the only passive strategy — in fact, the only strategy of any kind — that *everyone* can follow without any stocks or bonds or other assets being "left over" is cap-weighted indexing. Cap-weighted indexing is *macroconsistent*.[44]

5-1 John C. (Jack) Bogle
(1929-2019)
Index fund pioneer
Source: BogleCenter.net Reprinted with permission.

---

[44] See my book, *Benchmarks and Investment Management* [Siegel 2003], for an extended discussion of cap-weighted indexes (benchmarks), indexing, and macroconsistency.

Cap-weighted indexing has been criticized mightily by proponents of the active, non-cap-weighted strategies discussed below. One author said it was worse than Marxism.[45] (It's not.) The primary criticism is that one can do better by observing the fundamental values of securities. Cap-weighted indexing is said to overweight the stocks that are the most overpriced, to bet on momentum or the "greater fool theory," or to be demonstrably inefficient. (This last criticism usually involves some sort of look-back to see what would have been a better investment.)

Of course it's always possible to find an investment better than the cap-weighted benchmark with the benefit of hindsight! But we do not select securities for future holding periods with that kind of foreknowledge. So the cap-weighted index, demonstrably *efficient* when we use neutral return, risk, and correlation forecasts that do not embody any special foreknowledge, is the benchmark for evaluating all other (that is, all *active*) strategies.

But indexing has recently become massively popular, not just as a benchmark but as a portfolio to be held for long-term investment. Is this trend hazardous? Someone has to set the prices of securities on the margin, and that "someone" has to be the community of active managers. They need to be paid for their work and risk. Are we at the point where there's so much indexing that no one is setting the prices?

Not nearly. If not enough people are setting security prices, active management should be easy and alphas should be huge.[46] The difficulty that both traditional active managers and hedge funds in the 21st century are having in extracting alpha is testimony to the fact that indexing is at least fairly efficient and active management is not easy. (We'd also note that we do not know the optimal amount of effort to devote to alpha production, if the objective is allocating resources so as to maximize long-term economic growth. This is a worthy topic for future research.)

Cliff Asness argues that index fund investors, free-riding on the price discovery efforts of their active brethren, are taking advantage of capitalism's greatest gift — the information in prices.[47] This is exactly what they should be doing. The

---

[45] Fraser-Jenkins et al. [2016]. See http://www.bloomberg.com/news/articles/2016-08-23/bernstein-passive-investing-is-worse-for-society-than-marxism for a discussion.

[46] To be completely clear, even in a very inefficient market alphas are huge only for those with above-average skill; active management still a zero-sum game, no matter how efficient or inefficient the market. See Sharpe [1991], which, by the way, has the great virtue of being only two pages long, with no math. A must read.

[47] https://www.bloomberg.com/view/articles/2016-09-02/indexing-is-capitalism-at-its-best

ability to use this information without paying for it, Asness concludes, is not a defect of capitalism, but one of its most valuable features. That's where I come out too.[48]

In extremis, the world doesn't need conventional active managers at all. As Rex Sinquefield pointed out a generation ago, corporations can set the prices of their own securities by deciding whether to issue more stock, buy some back, or leave well enough alone. (They know more about the value of their stock than managers do.)

But don't worry, this is not about to happen. There is no shortage of active managers or of active management ideas.

> *Science or baloney? Cap-weighted indexing is firmly rooted in science.*

Fundamental Indexing

Fundamental indexing (of equities) is just like cap-weighted indexing except that you don't use cap weights; you use other data about the sizes of companies as the weights. These other data can be sales, earnings, dividends, number of employees, book value, or a combination of these. What is not used is the market's own assessment of the stock's value, in the hope that stocks which are overpriced by the market (relative to their fundamental value) get a smaller allocation than they do in a cap-weighted index.

5-2 Robert D. Arnott
Inventor of Fundamental
Indexing™
Source: By Gage Skidmore from Peoria, AZ, USA. CC BY-SA 2.0.

What an appealing idea for beating benchmarks! We all know that markets are not perfect at pricing securities, and avoiding those that are overpriced, while giving generous weights to those that are underpriced, would seem to be an almost surefire formula for success.

---

[48] Consider a hardware store owner who is trying to figure out how to price an item, say, a power saw. He can perform fundamental analysis, studying his cost for the saw, labor costs, rent, the normal rate of profit in the hardware business, and so forth, and repeat this process for each item in the store; good luck with that. Or he can see what other stores are charging and charge a dollar less, or try to provide slightly better customer service. The strategy of using price information that has already been generated by others is obviously better and more efficient.

It's not a bad strategy, but *it's just value investing.* As Paul Kaplan, of Morningstar, shows, a fundamental index is just a yield tilt applied to a cap-weighted index: "the fundamentally weighted index underweights stocks that have lower yields than the market-cap-weighted portfolio and overweights stocks that have higher yields than the market-cap-weighted portfolio."[49]

What is good about fundamental indexing, relative to most other value indexes, is that it does not segment the market into two halves (value and growth) and throw away the growth stocks. It reweights them just like it does the value stocks. This practice reflects an appropriate degree of humility about which stocks are really growth and which are value — it is impossible to know for sure.

> *Science or baloney? Fundamental indexing is science in an elegant marketing wrapper. But the wrapper doesn't tell the full story that it is just a tilt to value and, like any other value strategy, it won't work in every period.*

Low Volatility

Back in 1972, the great finance professor Fischer Black said that if investors cannot leverage or sell short, the security market line (the line expressing the relationship between beta and expected return) should be flatter than predicted by the Capital Asset Pricing Model (CAPM), so that low-beta stocks will generate a positive alpha.[50] (The reason is that investors wanting to increase their returns will buy high-beta stocks as a substitute for leveraging up their portfolios, leaving low-beta stocks undersubscribed and underpriced.) Robert Haugen, another professor, made a career out of studying this phenomenon. Many firms now manage low-volatility portfolios, and the low-volatility or low-beta anomaly has produced good results up through the present day.

But why hasn't it been arbitraged away? Now that hedge funds, ETF managers, and other investors *can* use leverage and sell short, why don't investors just hold portfolios that are efficiently balanced between low- and high-volatility stocks, and leverage them up if they want higher risk and higher expected returns?

One reason may be that the leveraged fund industry (including hedge funds) manages "only" a couple of trillion dollars, tiny compared to the overall size of

---

[49] Kaplan [2008], p. 36. At least, that is the case if yield (dividend yield or earnings yield) is the sole variable used by the fundamental indexer. If the fundamental indexer uses a different variable, such as book value, or a combination of variables, the same principle applies.

[50] See Black [1972].

markets and not enough to bring the prices of low-volatility stocks into parity with the rest of the market. A careful analysis by Ilmanen *et al.* [2015] shows that, as recently as two years ago, there was little sign of overpricing or crowding in low-volatility U.S. equities. The limits of arbitrage — the fact that smart investors rarely have enough capital to correct large market mispricings — make it possible for factors that everybody knows about, such as value and low-volatility, to deliver positive excess returns for a very long time.[51]

But another possibility is that the anomaly *is* being arbitraged away; we just can't see it yet in the data. When Bloomberg Markets calls low-volatility investing a "craze," it just might be too late.[52]

> *Science or baloney? Low volatility has been a winning factor bet for a very long time. There is a scientific basis for it. Still, with large capital flows into the strategy, there is legitimate concern that it can't work indefinitely.*

Risk Parity

Risk parity is just "low volatility" for asset classes. But consider how it's typically implemented: you borrow short (that is, at short-term interest rates) and lend long (by buying bonds and other long-dated assets)...what could possibly go wrong?

Joking aside, risk parity has a bit of a scientific pedigree. With risk parity, each asset class is held in a weight that causes it to make the same contribution to total portfolio risk (standard deviation) as every other asset. The portfolio may then be — but does not have to be — leveraged up or down to the volatility level that the client prefers.

5-3 Ray Dalio
Risk parity investor
Source: CC BY-SA 2.0.

According to Kaplan [2015], the risk parity portfolio "sit[s]...between the

---

minimum variance portfolio and the equally weighted portfolio in that it is the solution to an optimization program that assigns equal weight to...two diversification measures... [namely] the standard deviation [and the] average log-weight."[53] If you're still following this, I can simplify by saying that the risk parity portfolio is optimal under a carefully defined set of conditions.

Here is the analogy to low-volatility investing within an asset class: it works if assets (or asset classes) are mispriced relative to one another because investors can't or don't want to use leverage. In the absence of leverage, investors overweight high-risk asset classes to increase their expected return. Investors who *can* leverage take the other side of this trade through risk parity, which overweights low-risk assets such as bonds, then leverages the whole portfolio.

So, is risk parity a sensible strategy? Yes, for the same reason as low volatility within equities — safer assets have tended to outperform on a risk-adjusted basis — but, like low volatility within equities, it has a *peso problem*.

A peso problem has nothing to do with the feeling you get when you've drunk too much tequila, or spent too many pesos. It is the economist's term for a risk that is present in an asset but that cannot be found in the historical data. It comes from the Mexican peso's behavior around the time of the 1982 crisis: the yield on peso-denominated assets was very high, but the peso had never crashed, so the high yield appeared to deliver a free lunch (presumably with *pico de gallo* on the side). After the peso had provided a high yield for a while, however, it did crash — just as the market had predicted.

With risk parity, the peso problem occurs if long rates spike up and one's fat position in bonds loses value, or if the yield curve inverts, raising borrowing costs. (Risk parity can perform well when rates rise slowly, because the gain from leveraging higher-yielding assets outweighs the capital loss from the overall rise in yields. However, when yields rise quickly, risk parity can be expected to lose.[54]) To this "peso" risk one must add leverage, liquidity, and counterparty risks. These are the risks for which risk parity's apparent return premium is compensation.

Leverage only presents a serious risk if used carelessly. Many well-designed investment products include leverage. But we have heard of risk-parity products that had an unleveraged volatility of 3% being leveraged to a volatility target of 15% — that's five-to-one, a disaster waiting to happen. Careful risk management is essential to the success of risk parity or, for that matter, any leveraged strategy.

---

[53] Kaplan credits Maillard, Roncalli, and Teiletche [2010] with this insight.

[54] See Hurst, Mendelson, and Ooi [2013].

Science or baloney? Using leverage when other investors cannot is science, but it's risky unless risks are managed very carefully. Do it if you're confident that bond yields won't spike up during your intended holding period. However, claims that risk parity portfolios are structurally or inherently better than other portfolios are mostly baloney. You also need to decide whether the use of leverage presents a risk that you cannot tolerate.

Factor Investing and Smart Beta

Quant is dead, long live the quant.

When quantitative investing — as then practiced — hit a very rough patch starting around 2007, quants didn't die; they became factor investors, assembling factor-based index funds and ETFs (fundamental indexing is one) and marketing them, in some firms, as "smart beta." (A quant, after all, is just someone who is skilled in math; presumably some, or most, of them are general-purpose soldiers who can be redeployed in solving a new problem when an old one goes away.) The factors include the usual suspects — size, value, and momentum — as well as some new ones, such as "carry" (yield), quality, and low volatility.

5-4 The Q Group

Discussion group for quantitative investment managers

Source: Laurence B. Siegel

Old fogeys will remember when yield was the only factor anyone knew about — as John Burr Williams said in his 1938 attempt at writing poetry, "A cow for her milk / A hen for her eggs / And a stock, by heck, for her dividends." (He should be glad he kept his day job at Harvard.) Everything old is new again.

As practiced by the more naïve managers, factor investing is chasing your tail, betting on past factor performance; it is data mining. But if you can make at least partially accurate forecasts of factor returns, it's much better. At bottom, factor investing is just a claim that you can add alpha, but at the factor level rather than the security level.

Stephen Sexauer, the CIO of the San Diego County pension fund, has pointed out that most quantitative active strategies can be thought of as a highly intelligent "bot" wandering through the securities markets.[55] There is also a mother bot, or perhaps a committee of human beings, constantly monitoring the bot to see if it is doing anything useful. The criteria for usefulness are whether it's making a profit and whether its success is attracting a swarm of competing bots big enough to take the profits away. If the latter, or if it's not producing a profit, the bot gets retired and replaced.

This isn't a bad way to try to make money; it just has its limits. Investment managers — being human — tend to pursue each quant active opportunity identified by the bot well past its limits, as we saw from the "quant crash" of August 2007.

Factors and "quant" investing, then, are just active management, subject to Barton Waring's Two Conditions needed for justifying active management. These are: (1) you have to believe that managers skillful at adding alpha exist, in the future and not just in past performance data; and (2) you have to, yourself, have the skill needed to select them from among a population of managers that underperforms on average.[56]

> *Science or baloney? Factor investing is science if there is fair reason to believe the manager can identify factors with a positive expected alpha — until the factor becomes a crowded trade and the expected excess return flips to negative. Then, unless you change your factor bets, it's baloney. It's hard to see how any factor can work forever.*

Unconstrained Investing:
Hedge Funds, Absolute Return, Market Neutral, Long/Short, and Portable Alpha

Thomas Idzorek [2014] beautifully characterizes these strategies as ways to "enable managers to maximize the benefit of their skill." He also discusses the differences among them in some detail, so I don't have to. Please refer to his article,

---

[55] Personal communication.

[56] See Waring, Whitney, Pirone, and Castille [2000], Appendix C on pp. 101-103.

entitled "Caveat Emptor!"[57]

Most of these strategies increase the impact of manager skill by relaxing the long-only constraint and/or the no-leverage constraint (where security positions have to add to 100% and no more). In the case of portable alpha, the convention is relaxed that says alpha has to be delivered to the investor in the asset class in which it was produced by the manager. Note that these strategies aren't fully unconstrained, but the relaxing of traditional constraints is the distinguishing feature that they have in common.

The catch, as always, is that you have to have skill in the first place. Managers who are lousy at alpha production in traditional (long-only, unleveraged) investing are unlikely to become better at it when the constraints are removed. Given the small number of traditional active managers who consistently beat their benchmarks over time, there are way too many nontraditional active managers claiming that they'll do so now that they've been liberated from the long-only constraint...after all, they're the same guys (and girls). Removing a constraint does not make you smarter.

But constraints do reduce the potential for earning return. So why are they there? For risk control. They protect the investor from the manager's mistakes, some of which, as enough time accumulates, are likely to be big enough to destroy a completely unconstrained portfolio.

If investors didn't care about risk, unconstrained investing would be the bee's knees. But, as Harry Markowitz said more than 60 years ago, "That afternoon in the library, I was struck by the notion that you should be interested in risk as well as return."[58] Thank goodness for Markowitz's afternoon in the library, and for constraints.

> *Science or baloney? If you truly can add alpha after transaction costs and fees, in the future when you are managing real money and not just in a backtest, then unconstrained investing is science. If your active process is really just a random number generator, then it's baloney. But the fees can be spectacular...for the manager.*

---

[57]https://www.nxtbook.com/nxtbooks/morningstar/magazine_20140405/index.php?startid=9#/p/8

[58] Quoted in Bernstein [1993].

The Endowment Model

In the 1990s the great investment managers Jack Meyer at the Harvard Management Company and David Swensen at the Yale University investment office became famous and popular for earning very high returns for their institutions. Their secret was large allocations to unconventional investments such as venture capital, private equity (buyout) funds, hedge funds, timber, and commodities. In Meyer's case these were supplemented by aggressive internal management of conventional asset classes, conducted by highly paid specialists.

5-5 David Swensen
Endowment management leader

Source: Yale.edu. Reprinted with permission.

The word quickly got out that top universities, and some other institutions such as charitable foundations, had discovered a new model of investing, focused on alternatives. Many smaller endowments and foundations, and some pension funds, tried to copy the Harvard and Yale models. This first met with some success, but later — especially after the crash of 2008 — these institutions found that the new strategies consumed a lot of liquidity (due to capital calls from venture and private equity firms), required hiring expensive and finicky staffs, and sometimes lost dramatic amounts of money.

By June 2008, about the peak of the alternatives craze, 60% of the total assets of a group of eight top universities were invested in hedge funds and nonmarketable securities (mostly private equity). Including expected capital calls as well as hedge funds and nonmarketable securities, the number rises to a stunning 91%.

This could not end well. As I wrote in 2013, "We don't have data on exactly how these endowment funds performed in the crash or how hard they had to scramble for liquidity in 2009. The anecdotal evidence is that the results weren't pretty. A number of universities had to go to the capital markets to borrow, while others made drastic adjustments to spending. Liquidity is more than just a theoretical concern!"[59]

Crashes and liquidity crises aside, we can't all earn huge alphas at the expense of each other. If the endowment model is implemented successfully on a large

---

[59] See Siegel [2013].

scale by many investors, that means there has to also be a large population of investors willing to earn negative alphas relative to the world's overall capital market benchmark. In this age of accurate performance measurement and hypercompetitive investment organizations, it is more of a stretch than it used to be to assume that such a population of willing losers will always be there. For all but the most skilled investors, endowment-model investing may be a good idea whose time has passed.

> *Science or baloney? The endowment model is science if you're Jack Meyer or David Swensen; otherwise, beware. (Just ask Harvard after the last few years of underperformance.) It also helps to have friendly markets, with low prices and glaring inefficiencies. If you can start 25 years ago, you'll be way ahead.*

Environmental, Social, and Governance Investing (ESG)

I am reluctant to address this topic because I am swimming against the tide. However, my conscience is gnawing at me. I know, as do most investors deep down, that ESG investing is almost always suboptimal from a pure investment, or risk-adjusted return, standpoint. In fact, Elroy Dimson, Paul Marsh, and Mike Staunton, a celebrated trio of British economists and financial historians, show that an anti-ESG strategy, buying the stocks shunned by ESG investors, delivered superior returns over 2002-2014.[60] Such a "bad guy" strategy does make some sense. All other things equal, divestment lowers a stock's price, raising its expected return to those who do not participate in the divestment.

Moreover, ESG investing is unlikely to achieve the social goals it purports to promote. The stock doesn't know you don't own it. On a massive scale, divestment could raise the cost of capital for an issuer, but not if there are enough bad-guy investors taking the other side of the trade. And, at some level of enhanced return, the bad-guy investors will come out of the woodwork.

Why is ESG investing likely to be suboptimal? Businesses always try to externalize — that is, to get third parties to pay part of their costs if they can. An example is pollution, where a business and its customers impose a cost on other users of the atmosphere, water, and so forth. That may not be very nice, but it is what

---

[60] See Dimson, Marsh, and Staunton [2015].

the business' competitors are allowed to do — so, in an economic sense, it's fair, because one business should not have to pay costs that its competitors can legally avoid. That is why we need laws and regulations that all businesses are equally required to comply with.

Thus, companies that voluntarily do not pollute, or that operate in other ways deemed desirable by ESG investors, will make less money and be less desirable investments.[61]

If you think it's immoral to buy a security, don't buy it, at least not with your own money — it's your conscience that you have to live with. But, if you're a fiduciary, remember that it's other people's money you're using to assuage your conscience. You have to live with the consequences of that too.

Science or baloney? ESG investing is mostly baloney.

Other Strategies

Investment innovations and fads come and go, but a few seem to stick around through thick and thin: All Equities All The Time, liability-driven investing, the free lunch in diversification, global investing, and dividend growth. We'll slay these dragons — or show how they're supported by real science — in future articles.

---

[61] If you want to use ESG indicators as an input to fundamental analysis — for example, if you think well-governed companies deliver higher profits — you may be onto something, but that is not what most people think of as ESG.

Conclusion

The investment management industry has made a great many managers rich beyond imagining. Many of them have earned their riches, but investors would be well served to understand better the difference between science and baloney in investment management. Science, applied to markets to generate superior returns, is worth its weight in gold. Baloney is worth its weight in baloney.

By distinguishing science from baloney, one can deal better with the vast asymmetry between the interests of the manager, who needs to get it right once to become very rich, and those of the investor, who needs sustained and repeatable successes to build wealth over time.[62] Where are the customers' yachts?

---

[62] This asymmetry is especially large for high-fee, high-active-risk managers. It is much less for index fund managers and for low-fee active managers who build diversified portfolios intended to be held for the long run.

REFERENCES

Asness, Clifford S. 2015. "How Can A Strategy Still Work if Everyone Knows About It?" *Cliff's Perspective* (August 31), AQR Capital Management, https://www.aqr.com/cliffs-perspective/how-can-a-strategy-still-work-if-everyone-knows-about-it

Bernstein, Peter L. 1993. *Capital Ideas: The Improbable Origins of Modern Wall Street.* New York: Simon & Schuster.

Black, Fischer. 1972. "Capital Market Equilibrium with Restricted Borrowing." *Journal of Business*, Volume 45, Number 3 (July), pp. 444-454.

Dimson, Elroy, Paul Marsh, and Mike Staunton. 2015. "Responsible Investing: Does it pay to be bad?" *Credit Suisse Global Investment Returns Yearbook 2015*, pp. 17-28, http://publications.credit-suisse.com/tasks/render/file/index.cfm?fileid=AE924F44-E396-A4E5-11E63B09CFE37CCB

Fraser-Jenkins, Inigo, *et al.* "The Silent Road to Serfdom: Why Passive Investing is Worse Than Marxism," Sanford C. Bernstein & Co., LLC. Privately circulated.

Hurst, Brian, Michael Mendelson, and Yao Hua Ooi. 2013. "Can Risk Parity Outperform If Yields Rise?" (July), AQR Capital Management, https://www.aqr.com/Insights/Research/White-Papers/Can-Risk-Parity-Outperform-If-Yields-Rise

Idzorek, Thomas. 2014. "Caveat Emptor!" *Morningstar* Magazine (April/May), http://www.nxtbook.com/nxtbooks/morningstar/magazine_20140405_global/index.php?startid=5

Ilmanen, Antti, Nielsen, Lars N., and Chandra, Swati. 2015. "Are Defensive Stocks Expensive? A Closer Look at Value Spreads" (November), AQR Capital Management, https://www.aqr.com/library/aqr-publications/are-defensive-stocks-expensive-a-closer-look-at-value-spreads

Kaplan, Paul D. 2008. "Why Fundamental Indexation Might—or Might Not—Work." *Financial Analysts Journal*, Volume 64, Issue 1 (January/February).

Kaplan, Paul D. 2015. "Which Portfolio Is the Most Diversified?" *Morningstar* Magazine (June/July)

Maillard, Sébastien, Thierry Roncalli, and Jérôme Teiletche. 2010. "The Properties of Equally Weighted Risk Contribution Portfolios," *Journal of Portfolio Management* (Summer).

Sharpe, William F. 1991. "The Arithmetic of Active Management." *Financial Analysts' Journal*, Vol. 47, No. 1 (January/February), pp. 7-9.

Siegel, Laurence B. 2003. *Benchmarks and Investment Management.* Charlottesville, VA: CFA Institute Research Foundation, http://www.cfapubs.org/doi/pdf/10.2470/rf.v2003.n1.3922

Siegel, Laurence B. 2013. "The 'new finance': Illiquidity, the liquidity premium, and liquidity-preserving strategies." *Ounavarra Review* (now *OCP Capital Review*) (Winter). Privately circulated; available from the author.

Siegel, Laurence B., and M. Barton Waring. "TIPS, the Dual Duration, and the Pension Plan." *Financial Analysts Journal*, Volume 60, Issue 5 (September/October).

Waring, M. Barton. 2004. "Liability-Relative Investing." *Journal of Portfolio Management*, Volume 30, Number 4 (Summer).

Waring, M. Barton. 2011. *Pension Finance: Putting the Risks and Costs of Defined Benefit Plans Back Under Your Control.* Hoboken, NJ: John Wiley & Sons.

Waring, M. Barton, Duane Whitney, John Pirone, and Charles Castille. 2000. "Optimizing Manager Structure and Budgeting Manager Risk." *Journal of Portfolio Management,* Vol. 26, No. 3 (Spring), pp. 90–104

Williams, John Burr. 1938. *The Theory of Investment Value.* Cambridge, MA: Harvard University Press.

Chapter 6. Debunking Nine *and a Half* Myths of Investing

Pre-coronavirus edition, written March 4, 2020 when the S&P 500 was at 3130.

March 2020

A reader asked if I had updated my Debunking Nine Myths of Investing, which I wrote up in 2011 and 2016, for this strange new decade.[63] (It's a sobering thought that the long-awaited 21st century is one-fifth over.) I had not, so I'm doing so now, in the light of the profound changes that have taken place since 2016 when I wrote my last Debunking article: soaring then plunging markets, peculiar governments around the world, once obscure central bankers as masters of our universe, diseases of mysterious origin, and two middle-aged ladies upstaging the Super Bowl with their halftime show.

And, as the decades roll on, we're still wondering what kind of world we're going to leave for Keith Richards.

Despite recent extreme volatility, the U.S. public equity market continues to outperform everything else. Private equity, private debt, private infrastructure, private investment in public equity, and public investment in private equity were the flavors of the decade just ended; beware of their future performance. Hedge funds were the flavor of the previous decade, tech stocks the decade before, and leveraged buyouts the decade before that. What goes up does not always come down, but it's a thought worth considering. While stock market prices have risen, the number of stocks has *shrunk* so that the Wilshire 5000, intended to comprise the entire U.S. market, has 3473 constituents. I told you the decade was strange.

---

[63] 2011 article summarized at: http://allaboutalpha.com/blog/2010/05/02/ordem-e-progresso/ 2016 article: https://larrysiegel.org/debunking-nine-myths-of-investing/

Looking Back on My Nine Myths of 2016 with a Byron Wien-Type Self-Criticism Session

The score: five wins to three losses, with one "no decision." My 63% win rate sure beat active management, which at the last report scored 12% over the past ten years.[64]

Here were my nine myths of 2016 (and 2011, when I first started this series, on a trip to the delightful country of Brazil), along with my self-scoring — remember that these are *myths*, so the statement turning out to be wrong is a win for me:

Myth 1.   "We will be in a low-return environment for the foreseeable future."

WIN: returns on investable assets have been excellent.

Myth 2.   "The endowment model is broken."

PARTIAL WIN: while endowments and their exotic investments have underperformed conventional equity and bond investing, most endowments are doing fine.

Myth 3.   "Diversification doesn't work anymore."

LOSS-to-draw: the S&P 500, with a total return of 13.4% per year over 2010-2019, has beaten every other asset class in the world. But the Original Alternative Asset, U.S. Treasury bonds, also had a great decade, up 4.2% per year. Diversification is still a good and necessary idea; ignore at your peril.

Myth 4.   "Alternatives are where the return is, so these managers deserve their high fees."

WIN: alternatives were not where the return was, and many managers have stopped collecting those high fees. Yet, many still are: we can't tell if it's rent-seeking as investors pursue the unattainable high returns they crave, or if there truly is something special about "alts" managers as a class. We know a few are genuinely special (Jim Simons comes to mind); the idea that there are thousands of managers in that category is hard to swallow.

---

[64] S&P Dow Jones Indexes. SPIVA ® U.S. Scorecard, Mid-Year 2019 Update.

Myth 5.   "You should try to minimize fees."

LOSS: near-zero-fee index funds were the star performers. I said that you should try to maximize return after fees, which allows for active management; I'd still say that. But minimizing fees was the way to go in the time period since the last "Myths" article.

Myth 6.   "Active management only makes sense in markets that are ineffi-cient."

WIN, active management didn't help in emerging or frontier mar-kets any more than it did in U.S. large cap. In fact, most investors seem to have bought into the idea, now approaching its 70th birthday, that indexing is a good idea. (I credit Jack Bogle's 1951 senior thesis at Princeton, not the later work of the estimable Bill Sharpe, with the first thoughts on this topic. Sharpe is probably the greatest financial thinker of our time, but Bogle scooped him on this one.)

Myth 7.   "It is a good thing to be an absolute return investor."

WIN, it's a good thing to participate in markets ("beta"). Other than the rare example of truly market-neutral long-short funds with a cash benchmark, there's no such thing as an absolute-re-turn investor anyway.

Myth 8.   "Liability-relative investing is good in theory, but interest rates are too low."

UNCLEAR, but interest rates have declined even further (reaching an all-time low of 0.91% on the 10-year Treasury bond on March 2, 2020), and defined benefit pension fund liabilities have conse-quently soared, so maybe the funds should have paid more atten-tion to their liabilities when allocating assets. The same applies to defined contribution funds, endowments, savers, and other classes of investors, since all asset pools are gathered to pay some sort of liability or expense stream.

Myth 9.   "All you need is alpha. Alpha makes the difference between a suc-cessful and a failed investment program."

WIN, reliable and consistent alpha seems to have gone the way of the dodo. Asset allocation is what has made the difference be-tween a successful and a failed investment program, as Roger Ib-botson and many others told us 40 years ago.

How did I do? Not badly, but I didn't make any specific market forecasts, so I don't exactly deserve a medal for bravery. Byron does. He's quite good, and is the first to admit when he's made a mistake. Read his work, not mine, if you want to see the future. I just like being a mythbuster.

Nine and a Half Myths for 2020 and Beyond

There are a few repeats, but mostly they're new.

Myth #1: There is so much indexing that the market must be getting more inefficient, because there is not enough money managed by people who analyze securities.

Fat chance. About half the assets in the U.S. equity market are actively managed. That represents trillions of dollars overseen by analysts who diligently try to beat the market. While their success ratio is not great, they do engage in price discovery, enabling index funds to "free ride" on their efforts. And corporations can price their own securities, as Rex Sinquefield pointed out decades ago.[65] They issue stock when they think the price is high and buy stock back when they think it's low. This activity is a major contributor to price discovery.

At any rate, if the market were becoming "deliciously inefficient," in Jeremy Grantham's memorable phrase, we'd see it in the alphas. We don't.

Myth #2. There's no inflation, so the government can borrow all it wants.

About a decade ago, Carmen Reinhart and Kenneth Rogoff came out with a masterly study showing that highly indebted nations get into trouble when their debt/GDP ratio exceeds 90%. They did not literally say that this was a tipping point beyond which recovery was impossible without an inflation that destroys the real value of the debt, but a reader could be forgiven for thinking that's what they meant.

Later, a group of researchers found that Reinhart and Rogoff had made a data error. Some people ridiculed their work, and came to the astonishing conclusion that, because R&R had been a little careless, debt doesn't matter. Borrow away!

Debt does matter, because you have to pay it back. Or, if you're a government

---

[65] Personal communication.

or a certain type of private borrower, you can just "roll over" the principal but you have to pay the "debt service" (interest and possibly a portion of the principal). We don't know where the tipping point is, and it may be different for each country and in each time period, but at some debt level you can't pay the interest, much less the principal.

So, at some level of indebtedness, we *will* have problems! More than two hundred years ago, David Ricardo noted that there are only three ways the government can raise revenue: (1) current taxation, (2) borrowing (which necessitates future taxation), and (3) inflating away the real value of existing debt (which is a tax on capital). (Ricardo omitted asset sales, but he was English and maybe the Crown selling off its property to raise revenue was not an option; at any rate, asset sales are not a repeatable strategy.)

Nothing has changed since Ricardo to make his observation less valid. So we will either get higher taxes now, much higher taxes in the future, or inflation. Which do you think it will be?

In a forthcoming article, Wylie Tollette and Gene Podkaminer, of Franklin Templeton, and I wrote,[66]

> Inflation is a ninja. A shock to global growth will flatten you, but you will see it coming... [But] inflation will kill you in stealth. It can creep up on you year after year. While inflation does not seem like a threat to portfolio values at this time, that is when investors should be most vigilant. Beware the ninja.

Myth #3. We are in a new era of technological change at breakneck speed where growth outperforms value permanently, or at least out as far as the eye can see.

In an excellent 2019 white paper, Charles Dalziell and Graeme Shaw, of Orbis, an investment firm in Australia, argue that value and growth follow cycles that are more or less predictable from valuation levels (not from the duration of the cycle), and that the cycle has not been repealed.[67] Thus they believe we are on the verge of a period of substantial outperformance for value. Because I'm

---

[66] Tollette, Wylie, Eugene Podkaminer, and Laurence B. Siegel. 2019. "Protecting Portfolios Against Inflation." Submitted to the *Journal of Investing*. Available at https://www.ftinstitutional.com/download/ftinstitutional-us/common/k5teiwzr/protecting-portfolios-against-inflation.pdf

[67] Dalziell, Charles, and Graeme Shaw. 2019. "Complacency Kills: The Party is Over for Growth Investing." Orbis Investment Advisory, Sydney, Australia, https://portfolioconstructionforum.edu.au/perspectives/complacency-kills-the-party-is-over-for-growth-investing/

contemplating writing my own paper on the topic, with similar findings, I'll just cut to the chase and quote their conclusion:

> Value has a long history of outperforming growth and while this has not happened since 2006, investors should require a strong argument before accepting [this] unusual performance...as a permanent fixture. Falling interest rates and unusually rapid technological development are often cited as reasons for a paradigm shift to a world where growth stocks will permanently outperform value shares. [But,] when you look at the data, you find that *technology has not achieved a growth rate faster than what was achieved historically, and that historical return differences between value and growth have not been sensitive to large changes in interest rates.*[68]

Thus our conclusion is that "this time it's not different." A far simpler explanation is that growth stock outperformance began with the justifiable support of attractive valuations in 2006, but momentum has now carried this trend to a point where growth stocks look expensive and value stocks look cheap. This pattern is a recurring theme in the stock market: what begins in truth ends in farce. That is why we have cycles and this time around we believe the cycle is offering investors a real opportunity in value stocks.

The authors find that, in the eight previous periods of growth outperformance relative to value, the cumulative advantage of growth was 32%, *which is exactly the same as it was over 2006-2020.* The difference is that this period lasted 148 months while the others averaged only 26 and the longest, before the current one, lasted 56. But, remarkably, the subsequent value performance in excess of growth was 34% over one year, 52% over two years, and 54% over three years. Food for thought.

An old investment aphorism says that there is no successful investment strategy that can't be destroyed by a wall of money. The growth of sales and earnings of big tech have been very high, reflecting the "breakneck" speed of the changes, but the valuations have moved at even more of a breakneck speed. Nothing grows at a high rate forever.

---

[68] Italics added.

Myth #4. We are in a new "bipolar" world of U.S. and Chinese dominance where those two economies are the only ones anyone should care about. Since it's hard to invest in China, a very large weight in the U.S. is a good idea, as it was in the 2010s.

The U.S. had an equity market capitalization of $30,436 billion (that is, $30.4 trillion) as of the end of 2018, and China $6,325 billion.[69] Here are the next 20 countries by market cap:

Exhibit 6.1 Next 20 largest countries by market cap (2018 data)

Rank	Country	Market cap	Rank	Country	Market cap
3	Japan	5,297	13	Netherlands	1,100
4	Hong Kong	3,819	14	Brazil	917
5	France	2,366	15	South Africa	865
6	India	2,083	16	Spain	724
7	Canada	1,938	17	Singapore	687
8	U.K.	1,868	18	Russia	576
9	Germany	1,755	19	Italy	522
10	Switzerland	1,441	20	Thailand	501
11	Korea	1,414	21	Saudi Arabia	496
12	Australia	1,263	22	Indonesia	487

These "next 20" total $30,120 billion — almost exactly the same as the United States. Japan's market cap is almost as big as China's. And Taiwan, which is somehow "not a country," had a market cap of $1,202 billion, which would cause it to rank between Australia and the Netherlands and which would push the market cap of the "next 20" above that of the United States.[70]

Don't you think there are some stocks in those 20 or 21 countries that someone would want?

And let's not forget the fastest-growing economies in the world, according to nasdaq.com: Guyana, Ethiopia, Rwanda, Bangladesh, and India.[71] It might be hard to get stocks in the first three, but that won't always be the case, and Bangladesh is already in the MSCI Frontier index. India is a well-established emerging market and the case for investing there is well-known. And then there's booming Vietnam.

There are many enticing investment opportunities in the world, and the farther

---

[69] 2018 is the latest date for which we have market caps for all countries. Source: https://www.indexmundi.com/facts/indicators/CM.MKT.LCAP.CD/rankings

[70] The $1,202 billion market cap for Taiwan is a 2019 data point, not 2018.

[71] https://www.nasdaq.com/articles/the-5-fastest-growing-economies-in-the-world-2019-06-27

afield you go from the mainstream, the more likely you are to find overlooked companies. In the unlikely event that you have no views on any of these countries or companies, the efficient or Markowitz-optimal equity portfolio is the cap-weighted all-country portfolio of world equities. A number of index funds and ETFs offer this portfolio in pre-built form.[72]

Myth #5. Big data and AI/ML are the next big thing in active management.

One of my most valued (and most brilliant) clients does this for a living, so I'll be careful. But Bryan Kelly, of Yale (formerly of the University of Chicago) and AQR, correctly points out that machine learning (ML), sometimes mislabeled artificial intelligence (AI), is just applied statistics. It is what you learned when you read Thomas Bayes (1702-1761) and Carl Friedrich Gauss (1777-1855) in your advanced statistics class in business school. But statistical inference feels different, and works differently, when you apply it to really large amounts of data with really fast and cheap computers, hence the new terminology and media hoopla.

Kelly writes (caution—geeky),

> [The] canon of methods [comprises those] one would encounter in a graduate level machine learning textbook. This includes linear regression, generalized linear models with penalization, dimension reduction via principal components regression (PCR) and partial least squares (PLS), regression trees (including boosted trees and random forests), and neural networks.[73]

This sounds a lot — well, *exactly* — like what I learned (not very well) in a graduate level Statistical Methods in Economics course *in 1977*, except for the last two items, which were not in the course. What is new, again, is the speed of the computers, the sophistication of the programmers (the "trainers" of the "intelligent" machine), and the unprecedented abundance of data — not the thinking behind the methods.

---

[72] More formally, there's a large literature on "home bias," the phenomenon where investors in a particular country overweight equities in that country. It's particularly prevalent in the U.S., which has a rich and varied domestic market, but is found everywhere. *Pace* the great Jack Bogle, who periodically objected to global investing (beyond a small, say 20%, non-U.S. allocation) on the ground that U.S. equities provide enough international profit exposure without the currency and sovereign risks, home bias is mostly irrational and investors should resist it.

[73] Gu, Shihao, Bryan Kelly, and Dacheng Xiu. 2018. "Empirical Asset Pricing via Machine Learning." Presented by Bryan Kelly at the Q Group, Laguna Beach, CA (October 16), https://www.q-group.org/wp-content/uploads/2018/10/Kelly_MachineLearning_paper.pdf

Big data and AI/ML are a really big deal if you are a credit card company using applied statistics and endless computing power to mine the 369 billion transactions last year (on a planet with only 7.8 billion people) for information about consumers. But if you are humble stock picker mining the 300,000 monthly returns on 5,000 stocks for 5 years, or worse, an asset allocator with 772 independent 5-year returns across 39 markets from 1921 to 2019, your data set is small by Big Data standards and is matched to small incremental gains, relative to what you can accomplish using traditional analysis.

This is not to say that Professor Kelly is against machine learning. He's a major advocate of it. He just wants you to know the limitations and be able to cut through the hype.

Myth #6. Central bankers can get us out of any kind of scrape we get ourselves into. A flood of money into the economy is the pill that cures all ills.

When you're a fireman, you benefit from an abundance of fires. When you're a central banker, which is a boring job except in economic emergencies, you benefit from emergencies. If you are always running to the rescue and perceived as successful, you become a rock star, asked for advice by kings and presidents, invited to the best parties, and feted in Michelin 3-star restaurants.

This does not make for good policy. Looking at the fiscal side, John Maynard Keynes said that governments should engage in deficit spending *during downturns*, and build up a surplus or reserve during periods of growth, that is, most of the time; but today's so-called Keynesians think it's always an emergency, even though we haven't had an economic downturn in 11 years, so they are always trying to stimulate.[74] On the monetary side we have something similar: the cure for every real or imagined threat to economic growth is lower interest rates and "easy money."

You could call this view of the world a "crisis crisis." Everything that happens is a justification for expensive intervention. This benefits the intervenors.

The first central bank intervention during the 2007-2008 meltdown was right and necessary. The continuing policy of quantitative easing was not. There is no evidence that it did any good — the recovery was slower than normal — yet unwinding the policy has the potential to do substantial harm. Central bankers should stop trying to be rock stars and should manage the money supply to a

---

[74] This was written before the COVID pandemic.

steady and predictable rate of growth.

Central bankers would do well to be more humble about what they can do, as Luis de Guindos, vice president of the European Central Bank, said at a Global Interdependence Center/Fundacion Rafael de Pino conference in Madrid. He noted that

> central banks are not almighty. We cannot address all the problems in the world... because...there are other actors in [the economy]... If we are humble and if we believe we are not the saviors of the world, there are other people [who] will start to take decisions in other areas of economic policy.... Central bank policy needs to respect the roles of fiscal policies, regulation, and labor market flexibility."[75]

We've argued elsewhere that the money supply is less tightly controlled by central banks that it used to be.[76] There are other providers of money and money-like instruments, including private lenders, money market funds, hedge funds, and cryptocurrency issuers. But the fact that central bankers have limited influence means that they should do less, not more, because of the law of unintended consequences. Their interventions have the same costs as before — the encouragement of borrowing, the penalizing of thrift, uncertainty about long-run inflation — but fewer benefits. Stop already.

Myth #7. The endowment model is still broken.

It's still a myth. Most endowments are doing fine: not walking above us, or crashing in illiquid investments. Their performance has been workmanlike, just normal for what they set out to do. Endowment returns should not be compared to the S&P 500, which bears no resemblance to any benchmark that a perpetual endowment should have, but to the world market wealth portfolio or to their goal of earning enough to meet payout requirements and still remain whole in real terms.

The Nobel Prize-winning economist James Tobin said that "the trustees of endowed institutions are the guardians of the future against the claims of the

---

[75] https://www.interdependence.org/resources/central-banking-series-madrid-morning-session/# at 1:23:25 to 1:25:30. Quoted in an AJO communication, https://larrysiegel.org/conference-roundup-negative-interest-rates-and-the-end-of-the-age-of-experts/

[76] Siegel, Laurence B., and Stephen C. Sexauer. 2017. "Five Mysteries Surrounding Low and Negative Interest Rates." *Journal of Portfolio Management* (Spring). See, especially, "mystery #1."

present."[77] As such, they should pursue conservatory strategies, not maximally aggressive ones, and should be judged against the Tobin criterion. Thus, the (correct) statement that endowed institutions, as a class, have underperformed during the 2009-2020 bull market is misleading. They have, by and large, done what they were supposed to do. (Note that the world equity market delivered much lower returns than the U.S. market; moreover, long-term bonds far outperformed any conceivable expectation, so that endowments would have been irresponsible in taking the risk of holding them.)

We'd do well to remind ourselves that liquidity matters. As numerous market sages have said, "Liquidity is a coward. It runs at the first sight of trouble." Harvard and the University of Chicago painfully relearned this lesson in 2008-2009. But endowed institutions have developed technologies — mostly consisting of an Excel spreadsheet — for managing liquidity requirements in the face of significant allocations to illiquid assets. One large endowment, the Helmsley Trust, is led by Roz Hewsenian, who spoke at the Foundation Financial Officers Group in San Francisco in May 2019. She said, tongue firmly in cheek for the first part,[78]

> We classify assets into four liquidity categories. Now get ready — *this took a lot of thinking*: Safe, Liquid, Semi-Liquid, Illiquid. We define them literally in terms of how quickly we can get the money, regardless of whether that liquidity impairment is caused by the underlying illiquidity of the investment or by legal encumbrances such as gates and notification periods that affect how quickly you get your money back.

She went on to describe each category, then concluded that "by defining risk in terms of liquidity…, all the levers within an asset category were open to us." They did not have to limit exposure to illiquid assets out of fear; they were able to manage the process and achieve the desired balance between liquidity and other investment characteristics, such as expected return.

Myth #8. The global economy can add 4 billion-plus people to the middle class and at the same time stop using carbon-based energy to support the quality of life as we know it.

In the rich west we may be using too much energy, but an awfully large number

[77] Tobin, James. 1974. "What Is Permanent Endowment Income?" *American Economic Review*, Vol. 64, No. 2, (May), pp. 427-432.

[78] AJO communication, at https://larrysiegel.org/conference-roundup-you-must-have-a-very-successful-dentist-a-conversation-with-cios-linda-strumpf-and-roz-hewsenian/

of people in the world use too little. Mercy Njima, a Kenyan doctoral student, explains:[79]

> Consider the women and children who spend hours every day searching for...energy resources... [O]nce they start burning biomass [e.g., wood], the acrid smoke causes serious lung disease... More people die from smoke inhalation than from malaria. [And,] because children have to help collect fuel during school hours, time spent on their education is severely reduced.

You want to *take away* energy from these people?

As Vaclav Smil, probably the world's leading energy expert, points out, energy transitions — wood to coal, coal to oil, and so forth – take a long time, because of the size of the installed base and the capital required to create a new energy infrastructure.[80] Sixty years is a typical transition time, but if we have a head start, as we do with nuclear power because much of the technology already exists, we may be able to speed that up some. But, in the meantime, developing countries will use more carbon, not less.

Developed countries have already started to cut their carbon usage, with energy efficiency improving at about 1.5% per year globally. That rate compounds up pretty quickly, adding to a very substantial energy savings over time.

The alternative, a carbon sudden stop, would condemn the 4 billion to eternal poverty and ourselves to something similar but not quite as bad. Energy is the master resource; carbon stores an awful lot of it very efficiently; and renewables such as solar and wind power are attenuated, pose serious storage problems, and use a lot of carbon in mining and transporting the needed materials.

There's no easy answer. While we should most certainly try to mitigate carbon emissions, we should also devote resources to climate adaptation. And we shouldn't punish the world's poorest people for wanting to live a little more like we do.

---

[79] Siegel (2019 – see footnote 89), quoting Diamandis, Peter, and Steven Kotler. 2012. *Abundance: The Future Is Better Than You Think*. New York: Free Press/Simon & Schuster. Diamandis and Kotler interviewed Ms. Njima.

[80] Smil, Vaclav. 2014. "The Long, Slow Rise of Solar and Wind Energy: The Great Hope for a Quick and Sweeping Transition to Renewable Energy is Wishful Thinking." *Scientific American* (January). http://www.vaclavsmil.com/wp-content/uploads/scientificamerican0114-521.pdf.

Myth #9. We will be in a low-return environment in the near future.

Not a myth, but reality based on the numbers.

It depends, of course, on what you mean by the near future. Truly short-term forecasts are worthless, but we can make generalizations about the next five or ten years. The 10-year real Treasury bond (TIPS) yield tells you exactly what market participants collectively expect the real riskless return to be over the next 10 years: -0.44% per year.[81] That's a low return environment. It reminds me of Will Rogers' wisecrack that "I am not so much concerned with the return *on* capital as I am with the return *of* capital." Today, what he said is not that funny: in riskless bonds, you will not get all your capital back, in real terms.

In the equity markets, the expected real total return (including dividends) is given roughly by the inverse of the P/E — not the CAPE, but the current P/E. With the S&P around 3000 and current (average of trailing and forecast) S&P earnings around $169, the P/E is 17.8. Taking the reciprocal of the number, that's a real total return of 5.6%. Not too shabby in a zero real interest rate environment, but appreciably lower than the historical average return on equities.

Myth #9½. We will be in a low-return environment for the *indefinite* future.

This is completely wrong, and totally a myth. Look at the diagram below, from my book, *Fewer, Richer, Greener* (the exhibit originally appeared on Max Roser's wonderful website, OurWorldInData.com).[82] Over the last 200 years, U.S. GDP per capita has mushroomed from around $3000, in today's money, to a little more than $60,000. Global GDP per capita has grown, over a somewhat shorter period (because the global data start later), from a little over $1000 to about $18,000.Remarkably, the world average is now approximately what the U.S. average was in 1949, when the U.S. was incontestably a first world country.

---

[81] As of March 4, 2020. This volatile number will be out of date by the time you read it, but it is unlikely to have risen to anything resembling a decent return.

[82] Siegel, Laurence B. 2019. Fewer, Richer, Greener: Prospects for Humanity in an Age of Abundance. Hoboken, NJ: John Wiley & Sons.

Can you think of any reason why this growth should suddenly stop, or slow dramatically? While there are fluctuations in the growth rate — the U.S. has been a laggard since about 2007 — the overall trend should continue along the path that it has followed in the past, because people keep innovating in an effort to do more with less. And innovation is what causes incomes, and thus corporate profits and stock prices (which follow incomes pretty closely in the very long run), to rise.

Exhibit 6.2 Real GDP per capita, United States and World

GDP per capita

Real GDP per capita is measured using US$, inflation adjusted at prices of 2011. Multiple benchmarks allow cross-country income comparisons.

Our World in Data

United States

World

$10,000

$1,000

| 1820 | 1850 | 1900 | 1950 | 2000 2016 |

Source: Maddison Project Database (2018)

CC BY

Betting against human ingenuity and the desire to better one's condition is a fool's game. The democratization of wealth in the last half century — with some of the world's poorest countries emerging as big success stories (Bangladesh and Vietnam come to mind) — has been amazing. Africa has started along this path too, mostly just in this new century. It is the first big break the world's poor have ever gotten, and I don't think it will stop. This broadening of the culture of prosperity will take a lot of capital, and will reward risk-takers on average over the long run. Investors should look beyond the United States for opportunity in the rest of this century.

But don't write off the United States either. In the U.S., where we have a deep store of human and physical capital as well as the long-established rule of law, we'd look to several ways of bringing about a sustained jump in productivity and labor force growth, with its associated gains in GDP, sales, and profits. These include a much-needed fix to our immigration policies, a better balance on regulation, and exploiting the new technologies of genomic engineering, ecoengineering, and AI/ML (even if the last is really just applied statistics). The future will be fascinating — as investors, let's think creatively about profiting from it.

Larry wishes to express special thanks to Stephen Sexauer, CIO of the San Diego County Employees Retirement Association, for his extensive contributions to and comments on this article.

Chapter 7. "Uneasy lies the head that wears a crown": A Conversation with Jack Bogle

January 22, 2018

7-1 John C. "Jack" Bogle, 1929-2019

On January 8, 2018, I interviewed John C. (Jack) Bogle, the founder of Vanguard, the largest manager of U.S. index funds and the second largest investment management organization in the world. Bogle, born in 1929, founded Vanguard in 1974 and launched the first index mutual fund, designed to track the S&P 500, in 1975. He served as chairman and CEO of Vanguard until 1996 and senior chairman until 2000. He now runs the Bogle Financial Markets Research Center and remains actively engaged in the investment industry.

Jack Bogle's Early Years and the First Index Fund

Larry Siegel: Let's begin at the beginning, not of your life but of the index fund revolution, which I date to Bill Sharpe's 1964 article on the Capital Asset Pricing Model. A few years after that, you began to set up a firm that had an index fund at its core. What were you thinking? What evidence did you have that anybody would want it, and what were the steps by which you came to where you are now?

Jack Bogle: I talked about the idea of an index fund in my senior thesis at Princeton in 1951. The idea had always intrigued me, but I had never thought about following up much with it. But I did point out, at that time, that mutual funds can make no claim to superiority over the market averages. If my involvement with index funds began anywhere, it began there.

Larry: When did you begin to implement the idea?

Jack: A couple of decades after Princeton, there I was in mid-career at Wellington Management with the index fund idea going nowhere in an industry that doesn't innovate very much. I was fired as Wellington's CEO in 1974. A few months later, I created Vanguard. After a long struggle, Vanguard finally succeeded in making its funds independent of Wellington Management Company, which was at that time the manager of its funds. The key to launching an index fund was in the Vanguard structure. We created a novel, truly mutual structure in which the fund manager would be owned by its fund shareholders, rather than by insider executives or outside stockholders. Because Vanguard's interests are closely aligned with those of our fund shareholders, we were interested in seeking fee reductions rather than higher fees and higher revenues. The whole idea was to reduce fees, not maintain or increase them. In those early years, we reduced the fees paid by our funds some 205 times.

We also made the fee reductions prospective, so they would only apply to assets not yet gathered. Therefore, the negotiations with Wellington Management Company were not very difficult. We would say, "let's reduce the fee to 15 basis points on fund assets over $10 billion." When you do that on a fund that manages $500 million, no one much cares.

The idea of a fee reduction led, all of a sudden, to the idea of a fund that would pay no fees whatsoever. If you have a mutual company, this is something you want to do. As with a crime, you need both the opportunity and the motive; everybody had the opportunity, but we alone had both the opportunity and the motive to start what was, in fact, the first index mutual fund.

At that time, of course, there was a lot of activity surrounding recent academic advances, including the idea of an index fund. We are all familiar with the work that was being done at Wells Fargo on behalf of the Samsonite pension plan.

Larry: What was the dynamic between you and the Wells Fargo index or quantitative group led by John McQuown?

Jack: I think that the Wells Fargo effort failed at the beginning because they picked an equally-weighted index that wasn't easy to manage. The execution was a nightmare. After we had started our fund, they moved over to the S&P 500, which is, of course, capitalization-weighted. In that very important way, we are even older than they are.

Since then, Samsonite has gone through bankruptcy. God knows whether the pension plan even exists any more; I do not. But that little germ of an idea back in 1974 turned into the first index fund, which was approved by the Vanguard board in September 1975. After a flop of an IPO (the fund raised only $11 million, not even enough to buy round lots of all 500 stocks in the index), the fund now holds assets of some $625 billion in the two series of the 500 Index Fund.

Larry: Why you? When an idea is "in the wind" like that, it is there for the taking by whoever is most enterprising, by what we now call the first mover. How did you come to be that person?

Jack: I'd experienced the worst part of investment management during my career. I was on the Wellington Fund Investment Committee. I did a merger with a "go-go" firm called Thorndike, Doran, Paine, and Lewis, which managed the Ivest Fund, among others. They were abject failures. To make matters worse, Wellington brought in a guy named Walter Cabot (who eventually became treasurer of Harvard and president of Harvard Management Company) to run the Wellington fund. Over 10 years he ran it into the ground. The fund managed $1.9 billion when he started, and $685 million when he got through, the worst performance record of any balanced fund in the industry.

Larry: Nothing like a little failure to get the juices moving.

Jack: I was fed up with investment management. I could see what a tough business it was. I'd been on the investment committee. It's hard to win on performance, so why not just rely on cost savings to win over the long term, a logical proposition that couldn't be rebutted. In the very long run, he who has the lowest costs has the highest returns.

Index Funds Go into High Gear

Larry: What events began to catapult index funds toward the prominent or even dominant position they occupy today?

Jack: What I've told you so far was the genesis. Thereafter, I became the passionate advocate of the index strategy. My books have been a huge accelerator for the index idea. I wrote my first book, *Bogle on Mutual Funds,* in 1994 in which the index fund was first of the *New Perspectives for the Intelligent Investor.* It sold 250,000 copies. My *Little Book of Common Sense Investing,* now in its 10th anniversary edition, almost entirely on the topic of indexing, also sold 250,000 copies.

Those two books were read, then, by 500,000 people, and were commented on favorably. Investor acceptance became a meme, and was a big part of what would follow after what was a dismal start. Skeptics said, "Index funds are un-American," "Help stamp out index funds," and "If you had a brain tumor would you go to an average brain surgeon?" We took a lot of criticism.

Larry: How did the growth of indexing affect your venture, Vanguard?

Jack: Vanguard's growth began to accelerate concurrently with the growth of the index fund, which took off during the late 1980s. By the 1990s, our cash flow was coming in mostly to index funds. Vanguard's rolling 5-year growth rate was running at 20% to 25% a year during the late 1980s and early 1990s. That's a remarkable rate of cash-flow growth; it doesn't take the rise in the market into account. Even today's 8.5% growth in cash flow is pretty remarkable, but it's only one-third of what it was in those days, albeit from a much larger base.

Year after year, the index fund became more and more important to Vanguard. It was less than 5% of our assets in 1980, about 25% in 1995, 40% in 1998, 50% in 2005, 60% in 2010, and now index funds are 77% of our assets. Indexing has been the key to Vanguard's growth. The cause of our success is not just indexing taken alone, but — I emphasize — the pairing of the index strategy with the mutual structure, the idea of running funds for the shareholders.

In those early days we had no ability to finance new funds. So I had to put up $100,000 to get that tiny underwriting kicked off. I wouldn't have dreamed it would grow to what it is now.

Is There Too Much Indexing?

Larry: With all this indexing, how much can the economy and the market absorb? Many critics of indexing have pointed out that if everyone does it, then there will be no one analyzing securities and the markets will be profoundly inefficient. Does this critique resonate with you? And, if not, why not?

Jack: It doesn't resonate; let's take the easy part first. There are two categories of index funds. The traditional index fund (TIF) I started back in 1975 was broadly diversified, low-cost and designed to be bought and held forever. TIFs now holds about 5% of the shares in each company in the U.S. The TIF has been to some degree superseded by the exchange-traded fund (ETF), whose initial tag line was, "Now you can trade the S&P 500 all day long in real time." When Nathan Most, the creator of the first U.S. ETF, came to talk to me about it, I asked him, "What kind of a nut would want to do that?" As we now know, a lot of nuts would like to do that, and not just with the S&P as the trading vehicle.

The largest ETF is the State Street SPDR or "Spider," Standard and Poor's Depository Receipts (SPY), which turns over around 2000% a year. It seems there are few true investors in it. They are largely traders and speculators. I look at that as, at best, a benign business that is not very interesting and has little investment implications or corporate governance consequences.

If we are talking about broad market indexing, meaning people who are trying to capture the market return over the long term, I'm going to guess that maybe $2 trillion is in broad market indexes, less than half the index fund total. Indexing's true share of mutual funds, the share that represents passive ownership of the broad market, is something much less than the 40% that is frequently cited. However, it's true that index funds in-the-large, including specialized or undiversified index funds, are 40% of U.S. equity mutual fund assets.

To estimate the total in broad-market, buy-and-hold index funds, you'd probably take out the specialized funds as well as index funds that are traded, like the SPDRs. That would get you down to a core of maybe $1.5 trillion, out of a total index fund capitalization of almost $4 trillion.

The economic impact of indexing is overstated. A little later on, I'll discuss exchange-traded funds, which are, for me, a real problem.

Larry: What is wrong with trading in and out of funds? I think I know, but I want to hear it from you.

Jack: One of the hidden, unseen advantages of an index fund is its performance predictability. There is a syndrome in the fund management business that when funds have very good records of beating the market, more money pours in. The better the record, the worse the syndrome. Then, because there is an inevitable reversion to the mean in returns relative to the market, when funds start to do badly, as they inevitably do, the money pours out. The fund's return may look all right, but, according to Morningstar, the investor's return typically lags the fund's return by 1.5 percentage points per year, and that's a huge lag. Investors are their own worst enemy.

Larry: That is a huge lag, all right. I once wrote an article, mercifully unpublished but written up by Jason Zweig who at the time was at *Money* Magazine, saying the lag was 4%. However, that was in 1997-2001 when the market was exceptionally volatile. Maybe the lag is less now — still very large.

Jack: But I would ask, are they really their own worst enemy? Aren't brokers telling them to do things? Aren't advisors telling them to do things? Don't we all pay far too much attention to exceptional past performance, despite the knowledge that it doesn't recur? Past performance reverts to the mean. We ignore that. Yet the questions investors ask are: How many stars do you have from Morningstar? What percentile are you in, based on your competitive peer group or whatever the universe may be?

There is too much emphasis on the past and that hurts you in the future.

One of the great merits of traditional index funds is that you don't switch back and forth. When you cut through all this, the power of indexing in the marketplace is greatly overstated by the popularity of ETFs, including those invested in the S&P 500. They may have shareholder turnover of a couple of thousand percent a year because of their heavy trading by financial institutions.

Larry: Bottom line – is there too much indexing?

Jack: When Cliff Asness of AQR, one of the more notable money managers, writes an article that says, "No, there's not too much indexing, there is still too much active management," I take him at his word. He and I have been very close. We share a lot of ideas. It is possible for us to find a remarkable mutual respect and admiration. I think Cliff would say the same thing about me. I'm a great admirer of his brain, his ability to produce research, and his writing skills. I've written 16 papers for the *Journal of Portfolio Management*, but he's written 23.

Larry: You are making me feel inadequate. I only have 10 — one of those was an editorial — and Cliff is younger than me.

Jack: I also have had 11 papers published in the *Financial Analysts Journal*. I love the academic side of the business. You must be able to intuit that.

Where do we start to worry? It depends on how you define indexing — I'm not trying to be cute– but all this junk that is going on with betting whether the market will go up or down today using triple leverage, or creating a new ETF that is long electronic retail and short traditional retail — that is not indexing. It is speculation, which is not a very good idea.

Would I be troubled if traditional indexing got to 70% or 80% of stock ownership (which would imply a substantial drop in stock market turnover)? True, indexing may never get there, but if true indexing got to 50%, the market would continue to function. There wouldn't be a problem. The problem only occurs when indexing gets to be 100%, and that is never going to happen. It would mean no quotes and no activity in the marketplace. Indexing accounts for only about 5% of the trading in the stock market anyway, because traditional index funds don't trade much. Even ETF portfolios (as distinct from their investors) tend to have low turnover.

Private Versus Public Ownership of Fund Companies

Larry: Well, that's where I come out too; there's still too much active management. Let's now consider the question of fund company ownership, about which you have been very outspoken. You've said that publicly traded fund companies cannot serve two masters, the investors and the shareholders. But what is unique about fund companies in that respect? Doesn't every public company have a fiduciary obligation to its shareholders and a commercial obligation to its customers to deliver the best possible products at a fair, competitive price?

Jack: First, a little bit of background. Publicly held companies are a small minority in the mutual fund industry. Of the 50 largest fund companies, one is mutual. That, of course, is Vanguard. Eight firms remain private. Fourteen companies are held by the public, and 27 are held by financial conglomerates.

While the public owners are not able to inflict their will on the manager very easily — typical publicly held companies have widely dispersed investors — the conglomerate gets its way. The conglomerate owners can say, "Pal, we bought this thing for $1 billion, we want to take out $200 million a year, and if you can't earn us the $200 million we will get somebody who can." The conglomerate owner has absolute power; that's more of a problem than the mere fact of public ownership.

Yes, every public company has a fiduciary obligation to its shareholders. However, it does not have an obligation to deliver the best possible product at a fair, competitive price. That's the way we'd like to think the world works. But, as you well know, there is a lot of shoddy and overpriced merchandise in the fund business. Every public company does have an obligation to its shareholders, but the mutual fund manager's obligation to provide the best possible product at a fair price is completely overwhelmed and lost in the shuffle of the emphasis on past fund performance. Moreover, investors think past performance is more important than future cost; it is not.

Managers want to provide the best possible product, meaning the best performance. Given good performance, variations in cost don't make a great deal of difference. If you have great performance, it is not going to matter much in any given year or short-term cycle whether you are charging 0.5% or 1.5%. Thus, we have lost sight of what is a fair competitive price. However, we at Vanguard have brought the cost factor up towards the importance that it truly deserves in the field of finance and investment management.

Larry: How has Vanguard's attention to cost affected the industry, or how will it affect the industry going forward?

Jack: We've made it much more difficult to raise costs or to bring out funds with very high costs. But there isn't going to be very much price-cutting. Let's say an index fund can operate at 4 basis points and you've got somebody like Fidelity operating at, say, 70 basis points.[83] If Fidelity cut its expenses from 70 to 50, that would have a staggering impact on the firm's operations. It would eliminate their profits. It would be a mess, for the want of a better word. Yet even that lower cost would still be 12 times as high as the going rate for index funds. There's really not much point in shaving prices in the world of active management.

Larry: Have fees come down?

Jack: Fees charged by active managers have come down a little bit, but not a lot. But, over a long, long period, the economies of scale have been shared inadequately, if at all, with mutual fund shareholders. This is the industry's Achilles' heel in terms of fiduciary duty. Back in the early years, roughly 1951 to 1961, the industry's costs dropped from about a 62 basis point asset-weighted expense ratio to 56 basis points, according to the early studies I performed.

In those days, it was about a $3 billion industry. Now it is a $20 trillion industry, and the overall expense ratio is about 65 basis points weighted by size. Costs have actually gone up! Zero economies of scale have been shared with the shareholders, and that's because of the dominance of the manager that controls the fund and the monetary incentives sought by the manager, whether public or private. The private manager can deal pretty well with the issue of cost, because the cost reduction is out of his own pocket . . . if he wants to do that.

Larry: How does the difference between private and public ownership play out in practice?

Jack: For example, early in my career at Wellington, which was a privately held

---

[83] A basis point is 1/100 of one percent.

company at that time, we reduced the fee on assets over about $100 million from 50 basis points to 37.5, that is, three-eighths of 1%. An individual owner or possibly a management group owner can afford to do those kinds of things without wondering if that is the right thing to do for public shareholders.

Nonetheless, as many fund managers did after a decision in the Ninth Circuit Court of Appeals, Wellington Management Company went public in 1960. Fifteen or 20 other companies went public as well. Their owners got huge windfall gains. But then the transition was over and the companies were actually traded, often sold to financial conglomerates. There was trafficking in investment management contracts, just what the SEC had opposed.

The whole question of public ownership, the difference between publicly held and conglomerate held and, for that matter, privately held, all comes out in the wash. I certainly accept your point that publicly held companies have better disclosure; at least the idea of it is there.

This brings me to the point that, whatever their ownership structure, all fund managers should have to make those disclosures, whether public, private, conglomerate or even mutual. They should all be required to make the same broad disclosures. They should all show their P&Ls. They should all be disclosing their management compensation. That's just the way the world should work. Disclosure is always the sunlight that we need to keep us on the right side of the scales of fairness.

"Money Is a Demanding Mistress"

Larry: We both know a number of people who became billionaires in the fund management industry. They earned it fair and square. Yet, there is something quaint and sweet about the old-fashioned idea of a person who becomes moderately rich, and no more, by managing people's money for a living. Like a doctor or a lawyer, an investment manager could think of himself or herself as engaged in a profession. How did we get so far away from that?

Jack: Money is a demanding mistress. Executive compensation in our country has gotten totally out of hand. Compensation consultants have introduced a process of "ratchet, ratchet, and bingo," to use Warren Buffett's felicitous phrase. Nobody wants their CEO to be in the fourth quartile of compensation, for God's sake, so they bump them up to the first or second. As a consequence, another CEO else falls into the fourth quartile. It has to be that way. That board says,

"Not our man, not good old Harry over there. He is definitely a second quartile or first quartile guy." And so the process iterates. Bingo!

This process has become the basis of executive compensation in the U.S., and it is an outrage — a moral outrage, a social outrage. It's just the wrong way to run a fair compensation plan.

I don't know exactly what to do about it. I would hope that, in this new era that we are moving into where funds are going to be much more transparent — and Vanguard has made huge strides in that area – we will set up a whole new basis for executive compensation. It would ideally have to do with return on total capital. If an industry in total earns an 11% return on total capital, you don't get paid until you earn 11% on your company's capital — nothing. You can get a salary, but no incentives until you can produce a return on capital to your investors in excess of the industry's return on capital. The compensation criterion should not be the price of the stock. A stock price is the most misleading thing in the world, for it so often strays from a firm's intrinsic value.

Compensation is one of the big issues that has been at the center of corporate governance discussions in the period since Berle and Means wrote their classic book, *The Modern Corporation and Private Property*, in 1932.[84]

Value, Growth, and Smart Beta

Larry: If you were to cross an index fund with an active manager, and breed them, you would get something that today is called smart beta. As far as I'm concerned, that is just factor investing, something that emerged from the academic world in the late 1970s and early 1980s with small caps, which was the first factor to emerge, and then value investing. Is factor investing a good idea? I'm a value-oriented investor myself, but I haven't beaten the market with it. The value premium comes and goes, and sometimes it goes negative for a long time, as it has recently. Where do you come out on this? Are you a value investor, or do you believe holding the broad market, including growth stocks, is the right thing to do?

Jack: The total market is so much better for just about every investor for one significant reason: The relationship between growth and value changes. Exhibit 7.1 below shows, all the way back to 1928, the relationship between a dollar

---

[84] Berle, Adolf A., and Gardiner C. Means, *The Modern Corporation and Private Property* (New York: Harcourt, Brace & World, [1932] 1968).

invested at the outset in growth stocks and value stocks. (The growth and value indexes are from CRSP.) I used this chart in a presentation at the 2017 JOIM seminar in Boston last September.

At the end of this period, value had produced 5.5 times as many dollars as growth. That is essentially where the thesis that value beats growth comes from.

Larry: But wasn't most of the gain in the distant past?

Jack: Yes. The trick here is that, if you go back to 1983, the ratio was also about 5.5. In other words, value and growth have been equal for the last 34 years. Something changed in the early 1980s – likely the fact that value was repriced to reflect its past superiority.

If you look at Exhibit 7.1 you can see what changed. There was a general upward trend through 1972 where value returned 10.7% and growth 8.8%. Then the picture became choppy and unpredictable. Value soared from 1972 to 1988, 15.8% per year versus 7.3% per year, and then growth did better from 1988 to 1999, 21.3% versus 15.9%. Value then had a huge run up that ended in 2006, and growth has done better since 2007.

Exhibit 7.1 Ratio of Cumulative Returns of Value Index to Growth Index, July 1928-August 2017

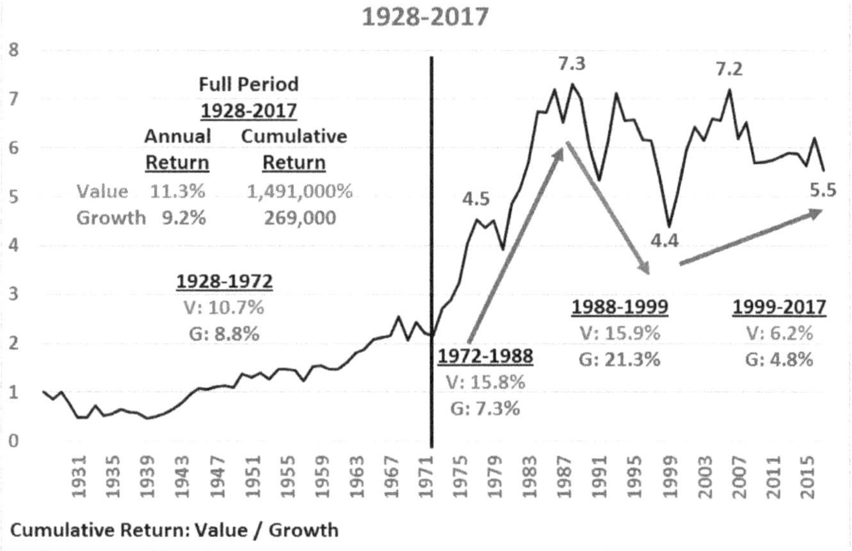

Source: John C. Bogle, based on Center for Research in Security Prices (University of Chicago) data.

You have all these fluctuations and it's very befuddling to an investor who picks value. Investors should have no confidence at all that value will win in the long run, for the obvious reason. Once everybody "knows" that value does better than growth, the prices of value stocks consequently go up relative to growth, driving down the subsequent value return; and the prices of growth stocks go down relative to value, driving up the subsequent growth return. The market seems too often unaware of this pattern.

When you look at Exhibit 7.1, 1928 to 1972 had a gradual upward slope in favor of value. Then the chart is all over the place, up, down, and sideways, big drops, small drops, uneven. Just as factor investing, by and large value investing, became popular a couple of years ago, value fell on its face. Last year growth was up 21%, and value 14%.

Value could be the right approach for the future, but why gamble? Nonetheless, back in 1993, I decided investors should be entitled to a choice between growth and value. It had nothing to do with factor investing.

Larry: How could growth and value index funds have nothing to do with factor investing? They are two of the most basic factors.

Jack: My idea at that time was if you accumulated money in growth, you have a higher percentage of your return without taxes; and a lower percentage of your return in income, which is highly taxed. Then, when you got to retirement, you'd move over to value where you'd have less volatility, and a higher income component in your return. I warned in those early annual reports that you shouldn't trade back and forth between the two funds. Nobody knows which is going to do better over the next 25 years. If I had to guess, I'd say they will do the same.

What happened over those 25 years, since 1993? Both the growth and value funds themselves had a 9% return. These are the Vanguard growth and value index funds, which differ somewhat from the CRSP indexes in Exhibit 7.1. However, the average investor in our growth index fund earned 5%, and the average investor in our value index fund earned 5%. By comparison, if the two funds were used from the beginning to accumulate, you would have gotten a 9% return from either one. By switching back and forth you got a 5% return, and imagine what the difference is from compounding at 5% versus 9% is for 25 years.

Larry: To what do you attribute the terrible performance of investors versus the funds they own? How could investors be such bad market or factor timers?

Jack: The temptation to "do something" is one of the worst temptations that investors face. There is always some bluebird on the horizon. Maybe it's bitcoin or some other kind of coin. These things come and go. In an investor's lifetime he's going to be so much better off owning American businesses in the S&P 500 or the total stock market, and never trading it. He is guaranteed to have the same non-manager the day he starts as the day he retires. In contrast, with the counter-productivity of swapping from one expensive fund to another the odds are about 0% that an average investor can outpace the stock market over that long a time period. People are going to tell you there's a certain chance, a 1% chance or a 2% chance. That's the chance that a given fund will beat the market, not a given investor. I don't happen to think even that's right.

Should We Be Global Investors?

Larry: You've made the point before, many times in many places, that investors should own American businesses. What's wrong with Japanese, European, or Chinese businesses? The U.S. is 4.5% of the world population, and a larger but not overwhelming percentage of its economy. Aren't there opportunities that are missed by just being a U.S. market investor?

Jack: People misunderstood my position on this question. In my first book in 1993, *Bogle on Mutual Funds,* I said that U.S. companies had, at that time, 40% of their revenues and 40% of their profits coming from abroad. You shouldn't think that the S&P 500 is not internationally diversified. Yes, fluctuations in the value of the dollar — nominal returns in foreign markets, and dollar-adjusted returns — can vary. But in the long run, I would expect them to iron out.

Then, look at what is in the global market index. The largest investment is the U.K. I'm not happy about that, with Brexit and all. This is a personal judgment. Japan is next, and France is next after that. I don't think those countries can do better than the U.S., and they are the three largest holdings.

I could be wrong, but what I said then was, you don't need non-U.S. stocks because you already have non-U.S. exposure in the S&P 500. In any event, because of the risks — sovereign risk, dollar risk — you don't need more than, say, a 20% holding in non-U.S. equities. Avoiding your home currency, in which you spend and save money, carries its own risk.

In the period since then, since 1993, the U.S. market is up approximately 800%, and the non-U.S. market is up about 250%, not even close. I was right. Does that say anything about the next 10 years? No! If you believe strongly enough in reversion to the mean, you ought to go into non-U.S. stocks. But I don't like timing. You are almost always better buying and then holding a given position in non-U.S. stocks, but no more than 20%, because of the risks. But I do not have any special knowledge. It's just the way I invest my own assets. That strategy has been right for the right reasons.

Will it continue? God alone knows, and he is not telling me.

Index Fund Proliferation

Larry: Let me move toward the conclusion. If everything you say is correct, then only the index funds representing the broad market are passive investing. Everything else — value, growth, small and large cap, auto stocks, tech stocks, all the other choices the index fund industry offers are active investing. If the virtues of passive, low-cost, low-trading investing are the philosophical premise behind Vanguard, why offer investors so many non-market choices? Is that a commercial decision, or is there something else behind it that I am not understanding?

Jack: The mutual fund business used to be a business in which we sold what we made, and now we are business in which we make what we sell. The marketing pressures are substantial. Someone brings out a new fund and you think you have to have one too. The reality is that, generally speaking, funds that are good marketing ideas are bad investment ideas.

You see this clearly with exchange-traded funds. Since 2004 the average TIF investor return has been 7.4% a year. The average ETF investor return has been 4.6% a year, which means a 70% gain versus a 135% gain for the TIF. Even the active funds' investor return has been 6.2% a year, better than the ETF investor has done. Creating things to meet market demand has not been a profitable enterprise except for the people who start them, the entrepreneurs, the financial buccaneers, and for that matter legitimate people who just want to be more competitive in the market place and don't dare miss something.

There are 9,000 funds in our industry. We at Vanguard have 370 funds. But the one thing that distinguishes our company, which I said earlier, is that index funds are 75% of Vanguard's total assets, now almost $5 trillion. That huge number is one that doesn't actually warm my soul. But the reality is that our indexed assets are much, much, much higher than 75%, probably more like 97%, 98%.

Larry: Why is that?

Jack: Take a fund like the Wellington Fund. It has a 98% R-squared, or coefficient of determination, with the two indexes it tracks – 65% S&P 500 and 35% Barclays/Bloomberg corporate bond index. Ninety-eight percent! Is that an actively managed fund? Well, 2% of it is. But does it go in the actively managed category when it is 98% tracking its benchmark? This is what people forget about in the mutual fund industry. We are all heavily influenced and our performance is determined by the action of the market. The average Vanguard actively managed fund has an R-squared of 95%, but even the average equity fund in the industry has an R-squared of 88%.

We talk about the difference between indexing and active, but the difference can be as small as the difference between a 98% R-squared and 100%, or as large as maybe an 80% R-squared, which leaves 20% of variation that is not explained by the market; very few funds fall outside that range.

There's a misunderstanding about managers operating in the abstract. They are all tied to the market. If you are a closet index fund, you can get to a 98% or 99% R-squared very easily. You would be amazed at the number of funds that have over 95% of their returns explained by the S&P 500.

In many ways, index versus active is not a clear distinction, because many of the big funds have their return 92% to 96% explained by the market's fluctuation. When you look at Vanguard in total, we can't completely differentiate our index funds from our other funds — all, finally, earn returns that are heavily market-determined.

Larry: Why not? Don't you know when you are actively managing a portfolio?

Jack: A good example is that I was never able to create a true municipal bond index fund. There are too many bonds to try to track all of them. We therefore created index funds for municipal bonds but they were not called index funds. They all have 93% to 97% correlations with the comparable municipal bond index. We are now actually starting an index fund in that sector. It will be interesting to see how it does, but it won't be easy to run.

I was determined to provide returns that were solid compared to their competitive market indexes, have a high R-squared, and then win on cost. Winning on cost doesn't make much of a difference in a year, but if you can pick up 50 basis points on expense ratio; if you can pick up another 50 basis points on low turnover (a key part of our advisor selection process); and another 50 or even 100 basis points on no-load, the low-cost fund can earn 20% more than the average fund over a decade at no extra risk.

It's basically guaranteed to be a great investment strategy. It also happens to be, I'm embarrassed to say, a great marketing strategy, as Vanguard's growth certainly attests.

The Growth of Vanguard and the Competitive Pressures of the Fund Industry

Larry: And Vanguard's growth has been...what, numerically?

Jack: We are at a 25% market share of long-term mutual fund assets. No one has ever been over 15% before. Massachusetts Investors Trust was the largest firm for 30 years. (it is now part of Massachusetts Financial Services.) They were the largest starting in 1932, and by 1952 they got to a 15% market share. They were succeeded by the old Investors Diversified Services, now Columbia Threadneedle, which was the leader for 30 years, also rising to a 15% share of assets. They were succeeded by Fidelity, which also got to a 15% market share. So 15% was a stopping point, yet here we are at a 25% market share.

What flows from that unprecedented dominance? A lot of competitive challenges, regulatory challenges, percentage ownership challenges, and other challenges that no fund firm has ever faced before. I'm a little sorry about our present status as a colossus; I loved the years of challenge that I faced at the beginning — the greatest challenge of all . . . to survive. We really didn't know whether we'd be in business at the end of the week or not. Then we got into the years of momentum, beginning in the early 1980s, and we've been thriving on momentum ever since. I would not know how to run today's Vanguard. I have to entrust that task to our new management.

Larry: This has been a lot of fun just for me to sit here and listen. I really appreciate your time and effort. My last question is: is there a question that you wish I had asked that I did not?

Jack: I wanted to talk about, "Uneasy lies the head that wears a crown." The head that wears a crown is indexing's 25% market share of mutual fund assets – that's the true share, not including index funds used as trading vehicles – and that share continues to grow. It's amazing.

Larry: Uneasy lies the head that wears a crown?

Jack: *Henry the Fourth, Part Two.* Vanguard's share of total mutual fund assets grew by almost 500 basis points over the past two years. That's amazing. Most firms in this industry are not growing market share at all. But we have several rivals. The rivalry between ETFs and TIFs is going to be an important factor in the future. But, given the known failure of ETFs to deliver to investors the returns they might have expected, the winning course is a TIF – a broad market index bought and held forever at low cost. Passive management with passive investors is what I would do. The ETF business, in contrast, is passive management (sort of) with active investors. There, the activity returns, the trading costs return, and the emotions return. By chasing performance, investor returns go down. The traditional route will be the winning route in the long run.

By the way, over the last 10 years, index funds have taken in $3.3 trillion in net cash flow, and active funds have taken in just $150 billion. Active funds have taken in only 5% of total industry cash flow.

Larry: A lot of people were selling their active funds to buy index funds.

Jack: That's right, and there is also a lot of new money being drawn into them from new investors. I hear from these investors every day.

But still, active managers run a pretty vibrant business when you realize that, in the last 10 years, assets of active managers have gone from $7.3 trillion to $11.4 trillion. That's about a 60% gain. Since there is not much net new money coming in, almost all of that gain comes from market appreciation.

They are sitting on very profitable businesses, and I don't think they yet feel the pressure to make changes or make some kind of strategic adjustments. When they do — I think it's almost predictable as the night that follows day — they will go into ETFs and not the TIF route. As it has been in the past, that will be a loser's game.

Larry: Why are ETFs a loser's game?

Jack: With all the cash flows into ETFs, $840 billion in the last 10 years, compared to $400 billion into TIFs, I wondered how TIFs could have kept up in terms of their asset growth. The answer is that ETFs have had $504 billion in market appreciation, and TIFs have had $800 billion. Two-thirds of the growth in TIF assets has been in the form of investment returns, and only one-third of the growth in exchange-traded funds has been investment returns. That's where the performance differential that I cited earlier comes from. The investor return for TIFs average 7.4%, for ETFs it was 4.6%, even less than the 6.2% investor return in active funds.

Those numbers are not ready for a *Financial Analysts Journal* article, but if you average them they do cross check closely against the known returns we have for all the ETFs and all the TIFs (Strategic Insight data). It's a pretty good indication of where things are going.

The mutual fund industry faces a lot of challenges. With $20 trillion in assets, we are America's largest financial institution. The indexing business is highly concentrated, with BlackRock (which is growing well) Vanguard, and State

Street, which is by far the smallest of the three.

But, ultimately, BlackRock faces a real challenge, and this goes back to the publicly held versus privately held issue. Their business is essentially an index fund business, so there is no investment management component that can improve returns for their fund investors. If they want to reduce fees on their ETFs, or they are required to for competitive reasons, that will hurt the earnings of the management company, the other master. If they want their earnings to go up, they'll have to create funds with higher fees. That is going to be a very tough conflict in the years ahead for a publicly held company like BlackRock, a giant conglomerate interested in making its corporate owners rich, which is the job of modern capitalism. They are going to have to deal with this challenge in a price-competitive business.

Larry: I want to thank you profusely for this generous contribution of time.

Jack: You're most welcome.

Chapter 8. Black Swan or Black Turkey?

The State of Economic Knowledge and the Crash of 2007–2009

Financial Analysts Journal, July/August 2010.
Reprinted with permission.

Nassim Nicholas Taleb has an elegant explanation for the global financial crisis of 2007-2009: It's a black swan.[85] A black swan is a very bad event that is not easily foreseeable—because prior examples of it are not in the historical data record—but that happens anyway.

Exhibit 8.1 Black Turkeys All Over the Place

Asset Class	Period	Peak-to-Trough Decline
U.S. stocks (real total return)	1911–1920	51 %
U.S. stocks (DJIA, daily)	1929–1932	89
Long U.S. Treasury bonds (real total return)	1941–1981	67
U.S. stocks	1973–1974	49
U.K. stocks (real total return)	1972–1974	74
Gold	1980–1985	62
Oil	1980–1986	71
Japanese stocks	1990–2009	82
U.S. stocks (S&P 500)	2000–2002	49
U.S. stocks (NASDAQ)	2000–2002	78
U.S. stocks (S&P 500)	2007–2009	57

Note: All returns are nominal price returns unless otherwise specified.

---

[85] Taleb, Nassim Nicholas. 2007. *The Black Swan: The Impact of the Highly Improbable*. New York: Random House.

My explanation is more prosaic: The crisis was a black turkey, an event that is everywhere in the data—it happens all the time—but to which one is willfully blind. Exhibit 8.1 presents large negative returns on major asset classes around the world over roughly the last century; from that perspective, the 57 percent decline in the S&P 500 Index is hardly unique. There is no mystery to be explained: Markets fluctuate, often violently, and sometimes assets are worth a fraction of what you paid for them.

Yet the market declines of 2007-2009 are sometimes accused of overturning various bodies of more or less established knowledge in financial economics and macroeconomics. Let's examine these accusations.

Efficient Market Hypothesis

The efficient market hypothesis (EMH) is a specific proposition about market prices (that they always reflect all available information) and not an assertion that a market economy is an efficient way to organize society (an entirely separate question). The EMH is not realistic, but it is a starting point that enables us to derive many valuable insights in finance, including the capital asset pricing model and the Black-Scholes option pricing model. Although a few diehards may still assert that markets are efficient, the contrary evidence of more than 40 years is overwhelming.

Most financial economists consider the EMH valuable because it places the burden of proof on the analyst who would beat the market. The test of the analyst's ability to make forecasts superior to the market-consensus forecasts is the subsequent alpha, correctly calculated to remove all beta influences.

Thus, the EMH resembles the presumption of the defendant's innocence in a criminal trial. Nobody really thinks that all or even most criminal defendants are innocent, yet it is hard to imagine a fair starting point other than the presumption of innocence. The burden of proof must be on the prosecutor to "prove" the defendant guilty

As a realistic description of nature, the EMH has long been subject to serious challenges. Perhaps the most vivid is the crash of October 19, 1987, when the U.S. equity market fell by 22 percent in one day and some non-U.S. markets fell even more — for example, Hong Kong declined by 45 percent. In the language of the EMH, only two explanations for such a decline are possible:

1. The price was fair (reflecting all available information) before, during, and after the crash; that is, the fundamental value of U.S. stocks declined by 22 percent in one day.

2. The price was unfair at some point in time — either before the crash (the price was too high), after the crash (the price was too low), or throughout the entire episode except, perhaps, at one instant when the price was just right.

The first explanation defies belief. No "new" news emerged on or shortly before October 19, 1987. Interest rates had been rising, some unwelcome regulation of mergers was progressing in the U.S. Congress, and there was tension in the U.S.-Iran relationship. All these factors were presumably "in the price" before the one-day 22 percent decline. The most plausible, and still not entirely convincing, explanation for the crash is the supply-demand imbalance caused by program trading associated with portfolio insurance — an inefficient-market argument. So, prices were unfair at one time or another.

By 2007-2009, you had to be a fanatic to believe in the literal truth of the EMH. The market was awash in hedge fund assets, trillions of dollars of which were leveraged to exploit market inefficiencies in a frenetic attempt to earn alpha. Such effort has the effect of making the market more, not less, efficient; but if the market were perfectly efficient, the effort would be all for naught — a conclusion defied by the successful track records of many hedge funds and other active managers.

That stocks fell by 57 percent and some financially engineered mortgage pools (as well as individual stocks) fell by 100 percent did not overturn the EMH. The EMH had been downgraded from a testable hypothesis to an unrealistic but convenient working assumption (known to be false) decades earlier.

Optimization

Harry Markowitz's mean-variance optimization, sometimes mislabeled modern portfolio theory (MPT), has also been accused of failing during the recent crash.[86] These assailants misinterpret optimization and diversification as somehow promising to eliminate investment risk.

---

[86] As I see it, the term MPT, correctly used, signifies a real theory in a philosophical sense and embraces the work of not only Harry Markowitz but also William Sharpe, Merton Miller, Franco Modigliani, Jack Treynor, Fischer Black, and many others. Markowitz's normative algorithm should be called optimization or mean–variance optimization.

But optimization is just a technique for manipulating numbers! It is not a theory. It does say, by way of theoretical justification, that "investors should be concerned with risk as well as return."[87] Optimization then goes on to say how, exactly, to do that by producing a portfolio that is optimal (to investors with certain carefully specified utility functions) *given* a set of correct inputs. The required inputs are the expected return and variance of each asset and the covariance (or correlation) of each asset with every other asset. Markowitz and his successors never suggested that optimization or other aspects of MPT eliminated market risk—on the contrary, they emphasized that expected risk rises with expected return.

What today's critics of optimization are implicitly saying is that they did not have correct inputs. Their estimates of expected return were too high, or their estimates of variance were much too low. Alternatively, their estimates of both expected return and variance may have been correct, but the return distributions of certain investments (say, collateralized debt obligations backed by subprime mortgage pools) may have been so fat-tailed as to render simple mean-variance optimization useless and require more sophisticated models that take fat tails into account. These more sophisticated models substantially predate the crash and should have been used.

Some critics of optimization have a simpler tale to tell. They say that "MPT told you to diversify and diversification didn't work." Baloney. Diversifying among 50 kinds of equities isn't diversifying—and in bad times, corporate credit and even mortgage credit are forms of equity! Diversifying into government bonds and cash *did* work, and investors who held substantial positions in those asset classes did well in the crash. "Buy, hold, and diversify" is perhaps the best short piece of investment advice ever given, but you have to define your terms—diversify into what?

Capital Asset Pricing Model and Equity Risk Premium

The recent crash has also called into question the relevance of the capital asset pricing model (CAPM), not so much because anything is wrong with asserting a linear relationship between market-related risk and expected return — for that is all the CAPM does — but because the slope of the CAPM line, which links the

---

[87] Markowitz, Harry M. 1959. Portfolio Selection: Efficient Diversification of Investments. New York: John Wiley & Sons.

return on riskless cash with the expected return on the market for risky assets, might be negative. In other words, the expected equity risk premium might be negative.

From January 1, 1969 through February 28, 2009, the S&P 500, including rein-vested dividends, had a slightly lower total return than the Ibbotson index of long-term U.S. Treasury bonds, according to data from Ibbotson Associates (now Morningstar). Forty years and two months is a long time to wait for the equity risk premium to be realized, only to be disappointed with a realization marginally below zero. (Because of the subsequent fast recovery in the stock market, this condition did not last long; but stocks are still underperforming the long bond over historical time horizons lasting decades.)

Is the expected, future, forward-looking equity risk premium negative?

Let's begin at the beginning. If a company with a given stream of expected cash flows issues two securities — one a fixed-interest bond or senior claim and the other a residual interest or share of equity stock — which has the higher ex-pected return? Clearly, no one would buy the stock if it were not priced to have a higher expected return than the bond. That's the equity risk premium — it's that simple.

Or I can make it even simpler. Every day, corporate managers go to work. They have the option to liquidate the company, put the proceeds into Treasury bills, and then go home. Or they can stay at work and operate the company. The fact that they (usually) do the latter implies that they think they can earn a higher return for shareholders that way. That, too, is the equity risk premium, reduced to the simplest form I can think of.

Despite the occurrence of long periods when bonds outperformed stocks, it is hard to imagine a world in which equities are not priced — on average, over time, if not always — to have higher *expected* returns than bonds. (And I have been more than a little unfair to equities by comparing them with the *long* Treasury bond, a risky strategy that almost no one pursues.) That the periods of equity underperformance can be so long means that we may have underesti-mated the long-run risk of equities, for which investors require compensation in the form of an expected risk premium. Why do you think it is called *risk*?

Macroeconomics and the Crash

Another thread in the literature of macroeconomics either criticizes other economists for not having forecasted or prevented the crash or apologizes for the failure of the profession. This thread reveals a profound confusion about what economics and other sciences can and should do.

Paul Krugman, whose Nobel Prize–winning work was in economic geography, not macroeconomic policy, has nevertheless become a highly visible social critic who focuses on macroeconomic questions. His salvo on economics and the crash has been widely quoted:

> Few economists saw our current crisis coming, but this predictive failure was the least of the field's problems. More important was the profession's blindness to the very possibility of catastrophic failures in a market economy. During the golden years, financial economists came to believe that markets were inherently stable—indeed, that stocks and other assets were always priced just right. There was nothing in the prevailing models suggesting the possibility of the kind of collapse that happened last year.

> Meanwhile, macroeconomists were divided in their views. But the main division was between those who insisted that free-market economies never go astray and those who believed that economies may stray now and then but that any major deviations from the path of prosperity can and will be corrected by the all-powerful Fed. Neither side was prepared to cope with an economy that went off the rails despite the Fed's best efforts.[88]

Actually, many economists were vocal about what they saw as an unfolding crisis. Some focused on subprime mortgages themselves, others on the role of a housing bubble in the real economy, others on the vulnerabilities of the banking system, still others on the potential contagion to other industries and countries. In reply to Krugman, the University of Chicago's John Cochrane argued that no serious economist ever said that markets couldn't fluctuate widely or even crash:

> The case for free markets never was that markets are perfect. The case for free markets is that government control of markets, especially asset

---

[88] Krugman, Paul. 2009. "How Did Economists Get It So Wrong?" *New York Times* (September 2), http://www.nytimes.com/2009/09/06/magazine/06Economic-t.html, accessed September 27, 2020.

markets, has always been much worse. Free markets are the worst system ever devised — except for all of the others.

Krugman at bottom is arguing that the government should massively intervene in financial markets, and take charge of the allocation of capital. To reach this conclusion, you need theory, evidence, experience, or any realistic hope that the alternative will be better.[89]

Cochrane goes on to cite a large number of instances in which government completely failed at such tasks. In essence, he argues that the attack on economics and its relationship to the crash is political — and collectivist in its politics.

I am sympathetic to Cochrane's explanation, but I prefer a simpler one. People expect too much of experts. Blaming economics for the crash is only slightly more sensible than blaming geology for the eruption of the Icelandic volcano Eyjafjallajökull. Economics and geology are both inexact sciences. Their goal is, first and foremost, to make sense of data. That is what science does. A side benefit of studying either economics or geology is that we might be able to learn when to move away from impending danger. Because economics is a science of the human, it might also tell us how to prevent the dangerous event in the first place. But more likely it will not, because free human beings do not typically do what economists tell them to do.

In a related vein, Narayana Kocherlakota, president of the Federal Reserve Bank of Minneapolis, has offered a beautifully written but sadly mistaken apology for the failure of macroeconomics itself:

I believe that during the last financial crisis, macroeconomists (and I include myself among them) failed the country, and indeed the world. In September 2008, central bankers were in desperate need of a playbook that offered a systematic plan of attack to deal with fast-evolving circumstances. Macroeconomics should have been able to provide that playbook. It could not.[90]

A playbook? Economics is that part of the human drama that is concerned with how we make a living and allocate scarce resources. *We* write the playbook.

---

[89] Cochrane, John H. "How Did Paul Krugman Get It So Wrong?" (2009): https://www.johnhcochrane.com/news-op-eds-all/how-did-paulkrugmanget-it-so-wrong, accessed September 27, 2020.

[90] Kocherlakota, Narayana R. 2010. "Modern Macroeconomic Models as Tools for Economic Policy." https://www.minneapolisfed.org/article/2010/modern-macroeconomic-models-as-tools-for-economic-policy, accessed September 27, 2020.

Macroeconomists set themselves too difficult a task if they would rewrite it for us. No wonder some of them think they failed.

By and large, macroeconomists have nothing to apologize for. Like other scientists, their job is to make sense out of seemingly chaotic data from nature. Their hypotheses are constantly being tested, rejected, and refreshed with new hypotheses. Only when macroeconomists stop testing the limits of their knowledge and start proclaiming received wisdom to policymakers do they risk having a reason to apologize. Those macroeconomists and policymakers who promised us a glorious new age of high growth and low volatility — through monetary policy or other means, such as countercyclical government spending — may be justified in feeling sheepish (and their followers may be justified in feeling sheeplike!).[91]

I am pretty sure that global growth will continue to surprise on the upside, but not with low volatility and not because of macroeconomic policies but despite them. Growth will happen because people, left to their own devices, will do almost anything they can to make better lives for themselves and their children.

---

[91] Even the low measured volatility of the two decades preceding the crash is suspect. Christina Romer, chair of President Obama's Council of Economic Advisers, studied modern macroeconomic data using methods from the more volatile pre–World War II period and concluded that the "Great Moderation" was essentially a data error: Rather than reflecting any actual change, it arose from the changing methods used to measure the volatility of the real economy. See Romer, Christina D. 1980. "Is the Stabilization of the Postwar Economy a Figment of the Data?" *American Economic Review*, vol. 76, no. 3 (June): 314–334.

Finance

This section goes beyond the practical ideas covered in the Investing section, and dips gently into the stream of evolving thought that began when Harry Markowitz and Bill Sharpe figured out how investment managers can think about risk as well as return. Larry keeps up to speed on all the latest ideas by studying the most provocative thinking of the best minds in the field.

Wayne's personal favorite: What We Can Learn from Andrew Lo's Adaptive Markets, or the Trouble with Tribbles

—WHW

Chapter 9. Bubbles for Fama

May 2018

At the Q Group in Palm Beach, Florida, on May 7, 2018, Robin Greenwood, a Harvard finance professor, presented a paper, "Bubbles for Fama," that he co-authored with Andrei Shleifer and Yang You.[92] The Q Group is a discussion group where directors of research and other senior investment professionals interact with finance academics. Founded in 1966, and conducting two seminars per year, the group's full name is the Institute for Quantitative Research in Finance.

Who is Eugene Fama and why does he need bubbles? Fama is the Nobel Prize-winning University of Chicago finance professor who first developed the Efficient Market Hypothesis (EMH) in the 1960s. A *wunderkind* who reportedly finished the Ph.D. program at that university's business school faster than any other candidate before or since, Fama was also one of the few authors ever to have his whole Ph.D. dissertation reproduced in a major journal.[93]

The Efficient Market Hypothesis

In a story that's familiar to most readers, the EMH says that stock prices reflect either all available information (the strong form of the EMH), all *publicly* available information (the semi-strong form), or all past price movements (the weak form). If that is the case, then stock prices are fair and it is impossible to beat the market other than by luck or random variation. As an early finance professor put it in his classroom, "the price is right," a phrase that he repeated by waving his hands wildly and shouting, a practice that I'm sure drove his students to distraction (but also convinced many of them).

The EMH was so logically sound, and Fama's presentation of it so persuasive, that for decades (roughly 1965-1985) it was difficult for academics to get evidence against the EMH published. It was thought that the evidence had to be wrong because the theory was so self-evidently right. Opponents of the EMH

---

[92] Greenwood, Robin, Andrei Shleifer, and Yang You. 2017. "Bubbles for Fama," https://scholar.harvard.edu/files/shleifer/files/bffs_20170217.pdf. The article was also published in the *Journal of Financial Economics*, 2019, vol. 131, no. 1.

[93] Fama, Eugene F. 1965. "The Behavior of Stock-Market Prices." *The Journal of Business*, Vol. 38, No. 1 (January), pp. 34-105.

were treated as flat-earthers. Attitudes toward the EMH have softened as behavioral finance, which admits of the possibility that the price isn't always right and active management isn't always fruitless, became respectable in the 1990s and later.[94]

Three Hundred Years of Bubbles — Or Maybe Not

Observers have thought they could perceive bubbles in markets since the 1720s, when the South Sea Bubble, so named at the time, was followed by a Bubble Act passed by Parliament to prevent bubbles from reoccurring. A bubble is a situation where a large increase in the price of something implies the *expectation*, although perhaps not the guarantee, of a large subsequent price decline. Researchers have identified hundreds of possible bubbles since then, including the U.S. stock market in 1929, the Japanese stock market in 1989, the NASDAQ in 1999, commodity prices at various times, and U.S. housing in 2006-2008.

But if prices are fair, there cannot be such a thing as a bubble. And that is the position that Fama has taken:

> For bubbles, I want a systematic way of identifying them. It's a simple proposition. You have to be able to predict that there is some end to [the bubble, when the price trend reverses]. All the tests people have done trying to do that don't work. Statistically, people have not come up with ways of identifying bubbles.[95]

Bursting Fama's Bubble

Greenwood and his co-authors sought to test this proposition. If large price increases in an asset are typically followed by large declines, then it makes sense

---

[94] The increased respectability of non-EMH views was certified by the Nobel committee in its awarding of the 2002 prize to Daniel Kahneman, a psychologist whose work greatly influenced behavioral finance, and the 2017 prize to Richard Thaler, a behavioral finance pioneer. Fama did not win the prize until 2013. See my articles on Kahneman at https://larrysiegel.org/the-bromance-that-turned-economics-upside-down-2/and Thaler at https://larrysiegel.org/the-inventor-of-behavioral-finance-looks-back/.

[95] Fama, Eugene F. 2016. "Are markets efficient?" (video), *Chicago Booth Review* (June 30). Available at http://review.chicagobooth.edu/economics/2016/video/are-markets-efficient

to talk about the existence of bubbles, and to try to identify them to avoid participating in the large subsequent decline. If that is not the case, we need to do something else.

"People get angry," reported Greenwood, when faced with the claim that a particular market is in a bubble. Which people? Academics, who are still in thrall to Fama's EMH of 1965, which strongly implies that bubbles can't exist. (Academics are an odd bunch. I get angry — well, a little — for the opposite reason: when I have to pay what appears to be a bubbly price for a stock or fund that, as a result, has little hope of producing a profit over any reasonable time frame. So I don't buy it.)

Greenwood reports being told that "it's easy after the fact to say there was a price rise then a decline, so it's a 'bubble' — or it's a bubble if the current price, or price history, suggests a crash in the future." But, *a priori,* Greenwood perceived some merit in the idea that bubbles exist. So, with his co-authors, he designed a series of tests, which are the topic of "Bubbles for Fama."

Design of the Study

The authors catalogue all of the episodes since 1928 in which stock prices in a U.S. industry have increased by over 100%, either in raw terms (absolute return) or in excess of the market's returns, over a period of two years or less. They used the industry criterion because "most bubbles have a strong industry component" — dot coms in the 1990s; new-economy industries of the time such as utilities and radio in the 1920s.

They identified 40 such episodes in U.S. data, and analyzed:

- Average returns post price run-up

- The likelihood of a crash after a large price run-up

- Whether other features of the price run-up can help forecast a crash, and in doing so, help an investor earn abnormal returns from "timing the bubble"

After conducting this analysis, the authors repeated it on international sector returns in 34 countries, developed and emerging, going back to the 1980s.

Greenwood's Results

"Fama is right about *average* returns," Greenwood reported. "After a price run-up, the price is about right; excess returns are mediocre but not sharply negative." He noted that returns were typically negative after large run-ups, but even those negative returns did not, on average, constitute crashes.

However, high past returns are associated with a dramatically higher *probability* of a crash (defined as a 40% decline or more). In other words, if there is a large run-up in a given industry, the industry is more likely to crash but also more likely to continue its price rise, averaging out to performance that is more or less normal, but much worse or much better than normal in the individual instances. In fact, starting at the moment the "bubble" or large past price rise is identified, the price went up another 30% on average — even for episodes identified *ex post* as resulting in a crash. Momentum is powerful.

Exhibit 9.1 shows Greenwood *et al.*'s results for U.S. markets. Over 1928-2012, there were 40 qualifying price run-ups and 21 of them crashed. Thus, the probability of a crash after a price run-up is slightly over 50%, while the unconditional probability of an industry crash (irrespective of whether there was a price

Exhibit 9.1 Returns for Industries Following Stock Price Run-Ups of 100% or More in Two Years, International Markets, 38 Countries, 1987-2012

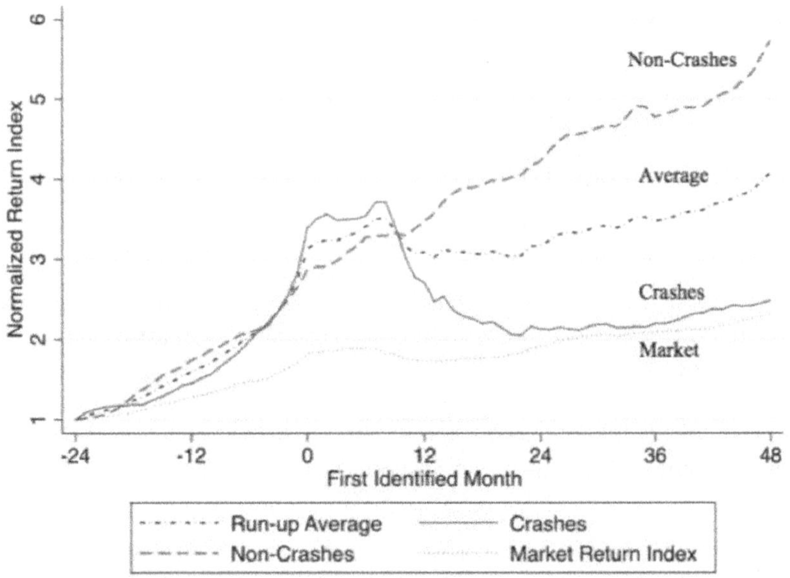

Source: Greenwood et al. (2017).

run-up) is only 14%.

Exhibit 9.2 shows the results for international markets. Over 1987-2012, there were 107 qualifying price run-ups in 31 countries; 53 of these, again about 50%, crashed.

Exhibit 9.2 Returns for Industries Following Stock Price Run-Ups of 100% or More in Two Years, United States, 1928-2012

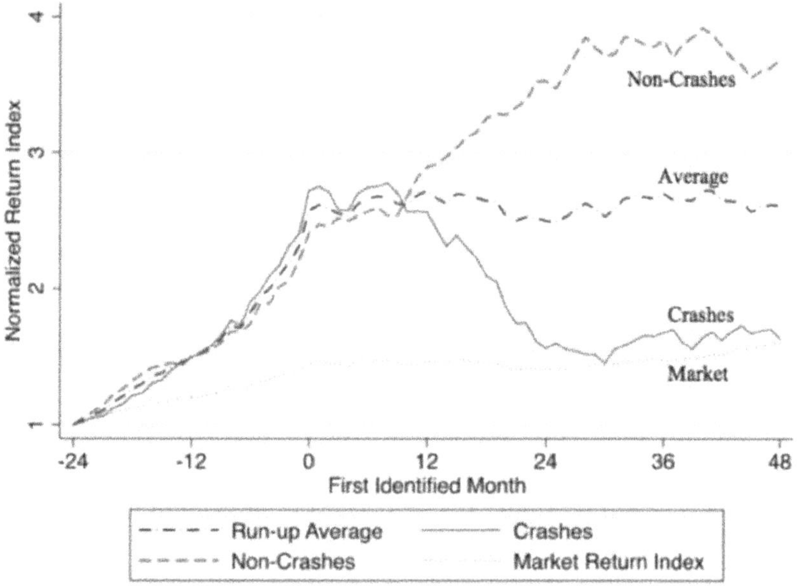

Forecasting Crashes After a Price Run-Up

So there is something qualitatively different about performance after a large price run-up: it's much more likely to be very good or very bad, like the little girl with the little curl. This is a potentially very profitable finding if we can identify the characteristics that distinguish price run-ups that crash from those that don't.

The authors tested various characteristics:

- Volatility and change in volatility

- Sales growth

- Book-to-market ratio

- Turnover

- New issue and secondary issue activity in the industry

- Firm age and "age tilt" (age tilt describes whether the price run-up oc-curred disproportionately among the younger firms in the industry)

- Acceleration (convexity of the price path)

- CAPE (modified P/E) ratio of the industry

- Stock price increases among newer firms (relative to older ones)

For the U.S. data, the authors found significant ($t > 2$) effects for past 2-year re-turn, one-year change in volatility, firm age, age tilt, new issuance, and return acceleration. The CAPE ratio was almost significant. The results were almost exactly the same for the international sample.

Making Money from Crash Avoidance

Greenwood then described a hypothetical trading strategy that could take ad-vantage of the research findings. The strategy is to hold all industries (as in an index fund) until a given industry exhibits a characteristic "greater than the cor-responding mean [from] among crashed price run-ups" in the study sample. Then sell the industry, and never buy it back after selling.

Greenwood commented that the study is subject to various critiques regarding data mining. He further cautioned, "there is a tradeoff between false positives and false negatives: setting higher thresholds tends to reduce false positives but at the expense of more false negatives."

Greenwood vs. Goetzmann

It was interesting to hear Greenwood's presentation in the light of Will Goetzmann's similarly motivated study, "Bubble Investing: Learning from His-tory," which he presented at the Financial Market History Workshop conducted by the Cambridge (UK) Judge Business School on July 23-24, 2015.[96] Goetzmann,

---

[96] In Chambers, David, and Elroy Dimson, editors. 2016. *Financial Market History: Reflections on the Past for Investors Today*. Charlottesville, VA: CFA Institute Research Foundation, https://www.cfainstitute.org/en/research/foundation/2016/financial-market-history

one of the most distinguished financial historians, traced bubbles, and rumors of bubbles, back even farther than 1720, to the late 1400s when *kuxe*, German mining shares, were all the rage – even Martin Luther knew about them! (He didn't buy any.[97])

Focusing on more modern times, Goetzmann found that price rises perceived to be bubbles were not, *on average,* followed by uncommonly bad returns. He wrote, "Crashes that gave back prior gains happened only 10% of the time. Market prices were more likely to double again following a 100% price boom." Thus, what appear to be bubbles may not be. This finding is consistent with "Bubbles for Fama." But Goetzmann did not take the important last step of trying to determine what characteristics separated true bubble episodes from those that merely appeared to be (but were large price rises followed by normal or good returns).

Conclusion

To sum up, it is "perfectly obvious" that there are asset-price bubbles. But a few (not many) things that seem perfectly obvious turn out to be wrong. The Earth is not flat; the sun and stars do not revolve around it; and it's not easy to beat low-cost index funds by analyzing securities.

In this case, however, Greenwood, Shleifer, and You have shown that the obvious conclusion is right: bubbles exist. But not all large price rises are bubbles. On average, large price rises are followed by roughly normal returns. But a much larger percentage of them are followed by crashes than one would expect in an ordinary sample without the price rises. And it is possible to distinguish, with some predictive accuracy, between price rises that are bubbles and those that are not.

---

[97] Luther, in 1554, said, "Ich will kein Kuks haben! Es is Spielgeld und will nicht wuddeln das selbig Geld." "This," writes Goetzmann [2016], "(roughly) translates as the following: I want no shares! It is play [speculative] money, and I will not make this kind of money multiply."

"MR. HARLOW, LET ME GIVE YOU A PIECE OF ADVICE: EVERYTHING IS A BUBBLE."

Chapter 10. The Inventor of Behavioral Finance Looks Back

June 23, 2015

> "Economics is...a branch of...animal behavior."
> — Walter L. Battaglia[98]

Behavioral finance is one of the great discoveries of our time, and the University of Chicago professor and investment manager Richard Thaler is one of its principal discoverers. *Misbehaving* is Thaler's personal account of his discoveries, which influence the way assets are managed, policy is conducted, and economic theory is understood and taught.

Behavioral finance is the idea that investors do not act like the rational optimizers and profit maximizers that neoclassical economics assumes them to be. (Behavioral economics, a related field also closely linked to Thaler, studies irrational behavior in the real economy.)

Misbehaving is not an exceptional read. Thaler is not Michael Lewis or Peter Bernstein, weaving dry concepts into magical prose. His book, constructed as a memoir, is workmanlike and informative with much to recommend it. But the reader is unlikely to come away with a changed view of the world. Those interested in revolutionizing their thinking on human behavior as it relates to investing should start with Daniel Kahneman's *Thinking, Fast and Slow* — a psychology book — and Hersh Shefrin's *Beyond Greed and Fear*, which delves deeply into the investment issues raised by behavioral finance.[99] Read those and add Thaler's book as enrichment.

Misbehaving is one part personal history, one part brief against neoclassical economics, one part primer on behavioral economics and finance, and one part guide to practical applications. (The main applications are active investment management, where investors' predictable errors provide a framework for

---

[98] Battaglia, Walter L. 2005. *The Graduate Student's Question: Before the Last Tree*, self-published, p.177. Let it never be said that I do not cite left-wing authors.

[99] Kahneman, Daniel. 2011. *Thinking, Fast and Slow*. Random House, New York. Shefrin, Hersh. 2002. *Beyond Greed and Fear: Understanding Behavioral Finance and the Psychology of Investing*. Oxford University Press, Oxford, UK.

beating the market; and "nudge" policies, which are behavioral tricks intended to help people help themselves, for example by saving more.) While *Misbehaving* does not hold together as a unitary book, it combines different aspects of Thaler's work into a single, accessible volume, and in that regard it succeeds.

A Personal Victory

Thaler's journey through the economics profession was a curious one. As a young Ph.D. student, he attacked head-on one of the most fundamental principles of conventional economics, the assumption that economic agents (people) act rationally. Others who had taken this path did not get far. The late labor economist Sherwin Rosen, unimpressed with the young Thaler, said, "We did not expect much of him."[100] Yet, some decades later, Thaler ended up as president of the American Economics Association, the field's most prestigious group. In that sense behavioral economists have won — it has become socially acceptable to be one — despite the persistence of the rationality assumption as the foundation of economic analysis.

Cognitive Biases

Behavioral economics and behavioral finance are based on the observation that people do not process information rationally. Instead, they suffer from cognitive biases, are laden with imperfections in processing that cause them to believe things that aren't true, misunderstand the consequences of even simple decisions, and act against their own interest. Thaler devotes several chapters to documenting these often amusing foibles.

For example, a plurality of people surveyed think that if they paid $20 for a bottle of wine, but it is now worth $75, drinking the bottle costs them nothing (because they already paid for it), but dropping and breaking the bottle costs them $75. If that is the best that people can do in assessing the costs and benefits of an action, no wonder they misprice securities, invest in funds that have already gone up, and fail to save enough for retirement! The behavioral critique of rationality in economics and finance certainly has strong intuitive appeal.

---

[100] *Misbehaving*, p. 12.

Humans and Econs

Thaler draws a sharp distinction between real people, who make mistakes — "humans" — and the fictional agents of economic models, whom he calls econs.[101] Econs are lightning-fast calculators who have access to complete information about every situation, understand all of the ramifications of their decisions and make each decision with an eye to maximizing utility, invoking a kind of enlightened selfishness.[102] People don't behave like that, so it's sensible to question what would happen to economic theories and predictions if one drops the assumption that they do. That is the essence of Thaler's contribution to economics, and it's a valuable one.

Yet Thaler overstates the faults of conventional economics. There may have been (and there still may be) economists who believe that humans act like utility-maximizing genius robots, but I haven't met one. More realistically, economists tend to believe that economic models can be constructed *as if* people behave like econs, and that such models are much more useful and accurately predictive than they would be if one had to drop the rationality assumption. Without the rational-agent assumption, economics would be lost at sea, unable to make a prediction or a policy recommendation — but that doesn't mean the assumption is, or should be, realistic. A half-century ago Milton Friedman famously argued that the test of a theory is the accuracy of its predictions, not the realism of its assumptions, and that principle still holds.[103]

---

[101] Or Homo economicus in the classic literature (see the discussion of John Stuart Mill at http://en.wikipedia.org/wiki/Homo_economicus). However, the H. economicus of Mill (he did not use the phrase, but it is used in discussions of his work) is the economically rational component of the human animal, the part that counts for economic analysis; he is not the same as Thaler's econ. For Thaler's take on this question (which contrasts with mine), see Thaler, Richard H., 2000, "From Homo Economicus to Homo Sapiens," *Journal of Economic Perspectives,* Vol. 14, no. 1 (Winter), pp. 133-141.

[102] In an earlier work, *Nudge* (co-authored with Cass R. Sunstein, Yale, 2008), Thaler really lets fly at conventional economists and their imaginary friends, the econs. He is shocked that some people think of their fellow human beings in such robotic, dehumanized terms. He is at peace only when wandering over to the psychology department, where (he thinks) a more realistic view of human nature prevails. All this drama is kind of cute; I'm wondering why he chose to leave it out of *Misbehaving.* One possible reason is that he now knows economists aren't that rigid in their thinking.

[103] Friedman, Milton. 1953. "The Methodology of Positive Economics," in *Essays in Positive Economics,* University of Chicago Press, 1970 edition, pp. 3-43 (first published in 1953).

The "As If" Critique, Dismissed by Thaler, Is Actually Relevant

Thaler, noting that he encountered the "as if" critique often in his early effort to persuade colleagues of the behavioral view, is dismissive of it:[104]

> One of the most prominent of the putdowns had only two words: "as if." [T]he argument is that even if people are not capable of...solving the complex problems that economists assume they can handle, they behave "as if" they can... Even today, grunts of "as if" crop up in economics workshops to dismiss results that do not support standard theoretical predictions.

While Thaler is dismissive of this concept, it deserves a fair hearing.

It is hard to overstate the beauty and power of neoclassical, rationality-based economics as an explanation for the world as we see it (or "theory of everything"). Once you've grasped the importance of tradeoffs, incentives, competition, cooperation, decision-making on the margin and so forth, you see these principles in everything, including non-human realms such as biological evolution.[105] Yet behavioral economics says that the founding principles of conventional economics, especially the assumption of rationality, are, in some sense, wrong. If that is the case, we can't rely on the intuition provided by conventional economics, about the real economy, financial markets, or much of anything else.

For example, conventional (neoclassical) economics says that companies increase their production until the marginal cost of a unit of production equals marginal revenue. By asking corporate managers, Thaler found that many companies don't even know that their marginal cost varies with the amount produced, nor do they maximize profits by setting output at the optimal level. Instead, they try to sell the greatest number of units they possibly can.

Does behavioral economics, then, overturn this foundational idea, that companies set marginal cost equal to marginal revenue? Yes and no. "Sell as much as you can" is a pretty good – not perfect – heuristic for getting close to the profit-

---

[104] *Misbehaving*, p. 44-46.

[105] I include cooperation as part of neoclassical economics because the Nobel Prize-winning economist Ronald Coase's [1937] theory of the firm ("The Nature of the Firm," *Economica*, vol. 4, no. 16, pp. 386-405), which shows how people within firms cooperate in order to compete, has been incorporated into conventional economics over time and is based on neoclassical principles. During his heyday, Coase, an early advocate of incorporating behavior into economics, was critical of conventional economics as it was then taught.

maximizing level of output because of the limits placed on "as much as you can" by competitors' production and pricing, alternative uses for the money, and consumers' limited ability to pay. There will be some waste, some unsold goods, but not a lot! And there will be some waste with the marginal-cost method, too, because of error in estimating the proper level of output.

At any rate, companies will learn pretty quickly not to make massive, repeated mistakes in determining output because, if they do, investors will allocate capital elsewhere, driving the poorly run company's stock price down or running the company out of business (which is exactly as it should be; markets are a machine for allocating capital to its best use, unforgiving of poor management). The economy functions *as if* conventional economics is its set of operating instructions, even if that isn't precisely true.

From Behavioral Economics to Behavioral Finance

As Thaler points out, finance is the branch of economics where behavior is most likely to be rational because financial markets tend to be liquid, transparent, deep, continuous, and subject to arbitrage. Thus, it was in finance that the discovery of behavioral anomalies was most surprising and most vigorously resisted.

Still, the anomalies are there, and there are many of them. Thaler recounts many anecdotes familiar to readers of other behavioral finance literature. Among them are the stocks of 3Com and Palm, linked by crossholding, which were priced in such a way that, by using a long-short strategy, 3Com could theoretically be purchased at a negative price; the inconsistency of the prices of Royal Dutch and Shell, which are claims on the same corporate assets; the existence and persistence of value and small-cap anomalies that violate the CAPM; and many others. By the time Thaler is done, you would have to be a real hardass to believe that market prices, always and everywhere, reflect fundamental value.

The Dogmatism of (Some) Academics

But today's investors are unlikely to appreciate the extent to which academics in the 1970s, when Thaler began his quest, shut out all attempts to show how or why markets might be inefficient. As Thaler notes, most papers that challenged efficient markets were rejected outright by prestigious journals, and the few that were accepted were accompanied by "abject apologies [from the authors] for the results."[106] It was as though the authors had announced to their preachers that they had ceased to believe in God.

It is right for the proponents of a good theory to defend it from flaky, flat-Earth attackers. But, in the case of efficient versus inefficient markets, there were good arguments on both sides. The academic community should be embarrassed by the long delay between Fama's groundbreaking 1964 study showing that markets are likely to be efficient and the wide acceptance of market efficiencies in the 1990s; it was one of the worst examples of groupthink ever.[107]

Thaler and his behavioral compatriots, of course, had much to do with this shift in attitudes. Part of the shift came from the persistence of well-trained academics, such as Thaler, in poking holes in efficient markets — and part of it came from the obvious success of practitioners in exploiting inefficiencies, culminating in the hedge-fund craze of the last 20 years.[108] Readers interested in the history of financial thinking will find Thaler's account of this transition, and of his role in it, valuable.

---

[106] *Misbehaving*, p. 221.

[107] The small-cap and value anomalies were discovered as early as 1978-1979 (although Fama and French took credit for them in 1992) but most academics (including Fama and French) explained these away as compensation for hidden risks, not true inefficiencies (alpha opportunities). Meanwhile, DFA and other managers made fortunes exploiting these anomalies. Benjamin Graham, with and without co-authors David Dodd and others, had advocated value investing two generations earlier (see, especially, Graham [1963], a brilliant and prophetic speech recently rediscovered by Jason Zweig and re-published, along with Zweig's commentary).

[108] Despite this success, William Sharpe's [1991] "Arithmetic of Active Management" (*Financial Analysts Journal*, vol. 47, no.1 [January/February]) still holds, so there were just as many dollars lost as won, relative to market benchmarks, over this period.

Beating the Market

The beginnings of behavioral finance, and of Thaler's story, rely heavily on Shiller's [1981] finding that stock indices fluctuate much more than can be justified by subsequent changes in fundamental value.[109] (See Exhibit 10.1, created by Shiller but reprinted in *Misbehaving*, comparing actual levels of the S&P 500 with hypothetical fair values calculated by discounting all future dividend payments, where the calculation is done as if those future dividends had been known with perfect foresight.[110])

Exhibit 10.1 Do Stock Prices Move Too Much? Comparison of Detrended Real Stock Prices with Hypothetical Perfect-Foresight Prices Based on Future Dividends, 1871-1979

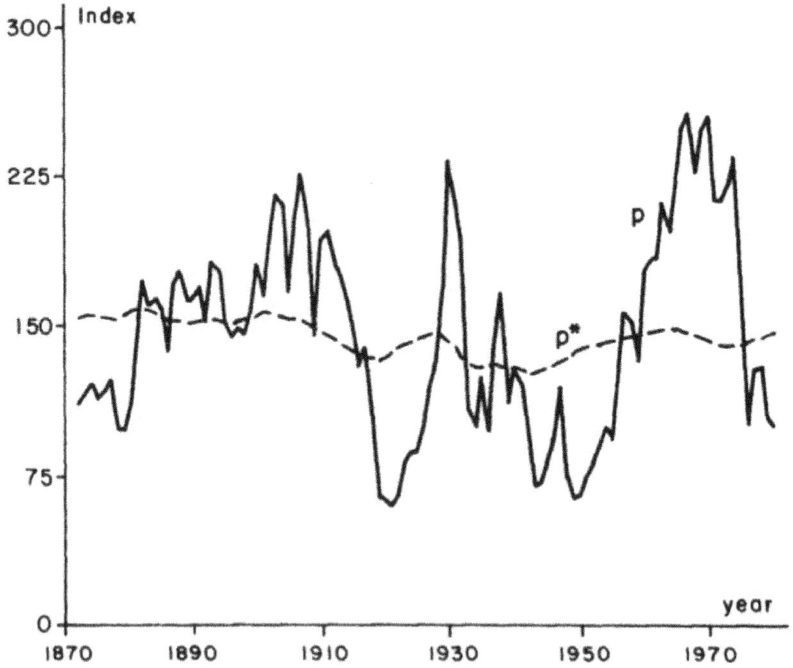

Source: Shiller (1981), p. 422.

---

[109] Shiller, Robert J. 1981. "Do Stock Prices Move Too Much to be Justified by Subsequent Changes in Dividends?" *American Economic Review* (June).

[110] In the original article, Shiller describes the diagram as follows: "Real Standard and Poor's Composite Stock Price Index (solid line p) and ex post rational price (dotted line p*), 1871-1979, both detrended by dividing a long-run exponential growth factor. The variable p* is the present value of actual subsequent real detrended dividends, subject to an assumption about the present value in 1979 of dividends thereafter." (p. 422).

I believe that stocks fluctuate more than is justified by changes in fundamentals — the crash of 1987 is a case in point — but Shiller's argument is not a fully convincing one. Stock prices are present values and, as such, are exquisitely sensitive to changes in both the discount rate (which Shiller's study takes into account) and the expected long-term growth rate (which it does not take into account). In the 1930s and, to some extent, the 1970s, it looked as though economic and earnings growth would be permanently much lower than before. In the 1960s and 1990s, growth was expected to be much higher than before. Nobody had perfect forecasts or even tolerably good ones. Of course stock prices fluctuated more than they would have if good long-term growth forecasts had been available!

Today, stock prices are fairly high while growth is widely expected to be slow. Should equity owners sell? I did, prior to the crash of 2008, and I now regret my decision every time the market hits a new high. I'm also afraid to get back in. It's difficult to time the market, even if behavioral finance teaches us that the price is not always right.

Value Versus Growth

If stock prices overreact to changes in information — a hypothesis strongly supported by Thaler — then one should be a value investor. Good news causes a stock to become overpriced, even after taking into account the increase in fundamental value caused by the news, and you should sell the stock; likewise, bad news causes a stock to become underpriced and you should buy it. A value strategy will take advantage of this effect.

But Thaler also indicates that stock prices can underreact. If that is the case, then you should be a momentum investor! The reason is that good news, not fully incorporated in the stock price, will cause the stock to rise further after you've bought it.

So...which is it? The verdict seems to be that stock prices both overreact and underreact, and it's hard to tell which is which in any given situation. Stock prices, instead of being right all the time (the efficient market hypothesis), will be wrong much of the time. If that is the case, you should mostly be a value investor since wrong prices are a mixture of too high and too low, and value strategies overweight the low ones.

This intuition has been vindicated by decades of value-stock outperformance, although the value effect is highly variable and cannot be relied on in any short or even medium-length time period. Nor is there any assurance that the value advantage will not be arbitraged away as more capital flows into such strategies.

Nudge

The last chapters of *Misbehaving* recap Thaler's effort, with co-author Cass Sunstein, to help people achieve their savings goals and otherwise improve their lives.[111] This effort, labeled "libertarian paternalism" by the authors, has begun to transform defined-contribution retirement savings. The idea is counter to the top-down, regulatory impulse of government and seeks to improve people's behavior *as judged according to their own criteria*. This last part is important.

Behavioral scientists have discovered that small influences or "nudges" can have big results. An example is Thaler and Benartzi's [2004] "Save More Tomorrow™" plan which, in a test site, increased employee savings for retirement from 3.5% to 13.6% in just four years by asking employees to commit to save part of their future raises.[112] Since the normal cost of a traditional pension is only 15% of payroll, this plan could achieve the savings needed to help make DC plans work as well as DB plans (although the needed investment return at a savings rate of 15% is higher than one can reasonably expect under current market conditions).

Other "nudges" are having similar success in other areas, such as getting taxpayers in the U.K. to pay their taxes more promptly to avoid penalties. The idea is not new; the speed limit is basically a nudge, rarely enforced but widely followed within a standard error of about 9 miles per hour. But libertarian paternalism, in an era when government is not widely trusted but people desperately need help in achieving many different goals, is a concept with promise.

Conclusion

Misbehaving is a welcome addition to the literature on behavioral economics and finance. Its benefit to investors is indirect because it is a book on economic concepts, not investment strategy. Moreover, as a memoirist telling a tale of scientific discovery, it helps to be a natural raconteur like the great Richard

---

[111] Thaler, Richard H., and Cass R. Sunstein. 2008. *Nudge: Improving Decisions about Health, Wealth, and Happiness*, Yale University Press, New Haven, CT.

[112] Thaler, Richard H., and Shlomo Benartzi. 2004. "Save More Tomorrow™: Using Behavioral Economics to Increase Employee Saving," *Journal of Political Economy*, Vol. 112, No. 1, pp. S164-S187 (February).

Feynman.[113] Thaler's storytelling is drier and more matter-of-fact. But those wishing to round out their general knowledge of important topics that affect investors will benefit from reading *Misbehaving*.

---

[113] Feynman, Richard P., and Ralph Leighton. 1985. *Surely You're Joking, Mr. Feynman!* W. W. Norton, New York.

Chapter 11. What We Can Learn from Andrew Lo's Adaptive Markets

...or the Trouble with Tribbles

June 2017

Is the market efficient? Of course not – not exactly, or not even close, depending on your point of view. However, the efficient market hypothesis (EMH), while self-evidently not quite correct, has remained surprisingly resistant to overturning. The reason is that, as MIT professor Andrew W. Lo says repeatedly in his new book, *Adaptive Markets*, "it takes a theory to beat a theory." And, up to this point, there has been no alternative theory that can substitute for the EMH if the latter is found wanting.

In the modern study of capital markets there have been two kinds of innovation: (1) insights that contribute to our ability to make better judgments, as found in the brilliant work of Fischer Black, Peter Bernstein, Marty Leibowitz, and many others; and (2) true hypotheses and theories, which are testable and, as I'll explain shortly, falsifiable. The latter are few and far between. Andrew Lo's book aims to present a new theory of capital markets, but, while it does not really do so, it is full of brilliant insights into behavior, evolution and the ways in which these factors help us to better understand how capital markets work.

What is a hypothesis?

Karl Popper, the great 20th century philosopher of science, said that a hypothesis is a statement, intended to explain a set of observations, which can be *falsified*. It only takes one exception to a supposedly universal rule to prove it wrong: the existence of one black swan, Popper said, proves that the rule "all swans are white" is incorrect.[114]

---

[114] Popper, Karl. *The Logic of Scientific Discovery* (1959). Popper's statement, above, is the origin of the concept of the "black swan" that Nassim Nicholas Taleb used to great effect – but Taleb uses it to mean a highly improbable event with a large impact, while Popper uses it to mean a single observation that invalidates or falsifies a generalization (quite a different meaning). Taleb, Nassim N. 2007. *The Black Swan: The Impact of the Highly Improbable*, New York: Random House.

By this standard, Lo's adaptive markets hypothesis (AMH), despite its name, is not a theory or hypothesis. It is a set of observations about human nature and, by extension, the behavior of markets. Lo delivers a detailed and thoughtful critique of the EMH in particular and modern finance in general, but no new theory and no revolution in financial thinking. Along the way, however, he introduces a great deal of challenging and informative material, and for that reason the book is worth reading.

The EMH in context

The EMH, in contrast, is a proper hypothesis or theory. It is a theory of *price*. It says that the price of a security reflects all available information. (If this is true, you cannot beat the market on a risk-adjusted basis except through pure luck, but that is a consequence of the EMH, not an essential element of it.) If all available information can be reduced to a set of period-by-period – say, annual – cash-flow forecasts, then the price of the security is the discounted present value of those cash flows, where the discount rate reflects the amount of risk inherent in the forecasts.

The EMH says that the market performs this task correctly. It does not say that every individual does it properly, only that in aggregate the answer is correct: "the price is right."

The EMH can be falsified by finding *even one* example of an abnormal profit opportunity in the market that is not arbitraged away. There are so many such examples that no one considers the EMH to be literally true anymore.

Spoiler Alert: Here's the Adaptive Markets Hypothesis

The only thing that is lacking, then, is an alternative to the EMH. It is not good enough to say "the market is not efficient." How, then, are security prices formed if not by market participants collecting all available information and agreeing on a price so they can trade? Do they ignore certain types of information? Do they disagree on the importance of each piece? Of course they do, but what is the mechanism?

Here is Lo's presentation of the AMH:

> The basic idea can be summarized in just five key principles:

1. We are neither always rational nor irrational, but we are biological entities whose features and behaviors are shaped by the forces of evolution.

2. We display behavioral biases and make apparently suboptimal decisions, but we can learn from past experience and revise our heuristics in response to negative feedback.

3. We have the capacity for abstract thinking... predictions...based on past experience; and preparation for changes in our environment. This is evolution at the speed of thought, which is different from but related to biological evolution.

4. Financial market dynamics are driven by our interactions as we behave, learn, and adapt to each other, and to the social, cultural, political, economic, and natural environments in which we live.

5. Survival is the ultimate force driving competition, innovation, and adaptation.

These are generalizations that describe life in the real world, but they do not constitute a theory. A scientific theory or hypothesis (there's a difference but I'm ignoring it for the moment) can usually be reduced to a statement something like, "If we perform experiment A, we expect outcome B to be the result, because of thus-and-such." The "because," the mechanism, is important; it cannot be a mystery process.

In the sciences, if we drop a ball from a tower near the surface of the Earth we expect it to accelerate at a rate of 32 feet per second each second. In the social sciences, if we subsidize a good we expect to get more of it, and if we tax a good we expect the economy will produce less of it. The predictions are less precise in the social sciences – after all, it's people whose behavior we're trying to predict – but there must be some predictive ability for the theory to have any use at all.

Classical finance and behavioral or evolutionary finance

From Markowitz's 1952 discovery of portfolio optimization to 1979, when Daniel Kahneman and Amos Tversky published their seminal work, "Prospect Theory: An Analysis of Decision Under Risk," we were on a path that used neoclassical economics, including its assumption of rationality, along with the new and powerful tool set of data and computers, to understand capital markets.[115] We made great progress, and we had insights worthy of Nobel Prizes – those of Harry Markowitz, William Sharpe, and Eugene Fama.

But, in 1979, Kahneman and Tversky opened a parallel door by asserting the obvious: that we are not balls dropping from a tower, but organisms. As such, we are fallible and prone to biases and misunderstandings. Their parallel door leads to a different set of insights and that is what this book is about – it's a compendium of what we've learned about finance in the 38 years since Kahneman and Tversky published their landmark work, augmented by Lo's unique take on the way that evolution and survival fit into the behavioral story.

Evolution and Adaptation

How, then, does the AMH translate information in the economy to a *security price*? After all, that is the question we seek to answer when forming and testing hypotheses about the way financial markets work. Lo replies,

> Prices reflect as much information as dictated by the combination of environmental conditions and the number and nature of 'species' in the economy. (Lo [2005], p. 36)[116]

What he calls "species" are the various market participants in the financial zoo: issuers, market makers, security analysts, long-term investors, and so forth. Each struggles, not to maximize profits, but to survive, as real species do in an ecosystem.

The bottom line – the prediction that AMH makes – is that the prices of some securities are more efficient than others. Nearly everyone can agree on what the price of a 10-year Treasury bond should be: all the species use the same bond math. Fewer people will agree on what the price of an ancient Greek vase should be; the "issuer" has been dead for thousands of years, there are only a few potential buyers, and "market makers" – dealers, museums, and so forth – have their own agendas. So there should be more alpha or profit opportunities in assets that resemble the vase than in those that resemble the Treasury bond.

---

[115] Kahneman, Daniel, and Amos Tversky. 1979. "Prospect Theory: An Analysis of Decision Making under Risk." *Econometrica*, Vol. 47, no. 2 (March), pp. 263-291.

[116] Lo, Andrew W. 2005. "Reconciling Efficient Markets With Behavioral Finance: The Adaptive Markets Hypothesis." *Journal of Investment Consulting*, Vol. 7, no. 2, http://alo.mit.edu/wp-content/uploads/2015/06/ReconcilingEffMarkets2005.pdf.

This assertion is not directly testable in the way that the EMH is, but it is certainly more realistic.

The Arithmetic of Active Management

The bad news (this is my interpretation, not Lo's): Because William Sharpe's "Arithmetic of Active Management" [1991] applies always and everywhere,[117] if there are more profit opportunities in less efficiently priced asset classes then there are also more loss opportunities. No matter how inefficiently priced an asset class, simply being an active manager does not guarantee you a profit. You have to extract the profit from other active managers who are trying just as hard, are likely to be just as smart, and need the money just as badly as you do.[118]

Evolution and the origin of behavior

Now that I've gotten that off my chest – there's no theory! – I feel obliged to emphasize that there's a whole lot of fascinating material in *Adaptive Markets*. Let's focus on one topic, the evolutionary origin of human behavior. (Lo has no small ambitions.)

"Probability matching" is betting on an event in proportion to the likelihood of it occurring, instead of betting on the most likely event every time. For example, if an urn contains three-quarters red balls and one-quarter black balls, most people will bet on the ball being red three-quarters of the time instead of all the time (the latter strategy being the one most likely to win).

Although probability matching seems irrational, people do it all the time. So, writes Lo, do "ants, fish, pigeons, rats, and [non-human] primates." What's wrong with them?

---

[117] Sharpe, William F. "The Arithmetic of Active Management." *Financial Analysts Journal*, Vol. 47, No. 1 (January/February), pp. 7-9, https://web.stanford.edu/~wfsharpe/art/active/active.htm.

[118] Some observers try to evade the arithmetic of active management by saying that, for less homogeneous and less liquid asset classes, there's no benchmark. While that may be technically true, there's still an opportunity cost of capital that you have to exceed to make an economic profit – that is, there are alternative uses for the money, and that's the "benchmark."

The Trouble with Tribbles

Lo, with a co-author (Tom Brennan), wrote an ingenious paper in 2009, summarized in *Adaptive Markets*, that answered this question.[119] Brennan and Lo set up a simulation in which tribbles, mythical furry creatures from Star Trek, live or die according to geography and the weather. Each tribble has three offspring.[120]

Tribbles can choose to live in a valley or on a mountain. If they nest in a valley and the weather is sunny, all their offspring survive; if it rains, they drown. Conversely, if they live on a mountain and it rains, their offspring survive; if it is sunny, they die of sunburn (I guess). It is sunny 75% of the time, it rains the other 25% of the time, and tribbles do not know how to predict the weather.

Now, how should a tribble decide where to live? If it simply wants to maximize the number of surviving offspring, it lives in the valley – an undiversified bet that is right 75% of the time. There is no strategy that is right more often.

But if the *community* of tribbles wants to maximize the number of *its* surviving offspring, the best strategy is a surprising one: it diversifies its bets, with some tribbles settling in the valley and others on the mountain. Exhibit 11.1 shows the number of surviving tribbles, generation by generation, for various diversification strategies (values of f, shown across the top of the exhibit, ranging from f = 0.20, where 20% of the tribbles settle in the valley, through f = 1, where all of them do.

At first, valley tribbles multiply faster than any of the other populations, because it rarely rains. This success reflects the optimality of their decision, made in a single-period framework by individuals trying to maximize their own reproductive success. But, in the 14th generation, it rains and the entire valley tribble population is wiped out.

---

[119] Brennan, Thomas J., and Andrew W. Lo. 2011. "The Origin of Behavior." *Quarterly Journal of Finance*, Vol. 1: 55–108.

[120] The number of offspring is important because individual tribbles can decide to "move house," so more offspring means the potential for greater diversification (in this case, in exposure to both mountain and valley conditions). Tribbles reproduce asexually, removing the need to model their mating behavior. Making up stories like this is what economists do...really. The Star Trek episode in which tribbles were introduced was also called "The Trouble with Tribbles." It aired on December 29, 1967 and was written by David Gerrold.

Exhibit 11.1 Number of Tribbles in Each Generation for Tribble
Populations with Various Diversification Strategies (f-values)

Generation	$f = .20$	$f = .50$	$f^* = .75$	$f = .90$	$f = 1$
1	21	6	12	24	30
2	12	6	6	57	90
3	6	12	12	144	270
4	18	9	24	387	810
5	45	18	48	1,020	2,430
6	96	21	108	2,766	7,290
7	60	42	240	834	21,870
8	45	54	528	2,292	65,610
9	18	87	1,233	690	196,830
10	9	138	2,712	204	590,490
11	12	204	6,123	555	1,771,470
12	36	294	13,824	159	5,314,410
13	87	462	31,149	435	15,943,230
14	42	768	69,954	1,155	0
15	27	1,161	157,122	3,114	0
16	15	1,668	353,712	8,448	0
17	3	2,451	795,171	22,860	0
18	3	3,648	1,787,613	61,734	0
19	9	5,469	4,020,045	166,878	0
20	21	8,022	9,047,583	450,672	0
21	6	12,213	6,786,657	1,215,723	0
22	0	18,306	15,272,328	366,051	0
23	0	27,429	34,366,023	987,813	0
24	0	41,019	77,323,623	2,667,984	0
25	0	61,131	173,996,290	7,203,495	0

Note: f is the proportion of a given tribble population that locates in a valley.
Source: Lo [2013], p. 274.

After 25 generations, only the communities with diversified strategies have survived at all. The tribble community with the most survivors is the one that allocates 75% of its population to the valley and 25% to the mountain – matching the probability of sunshine, also 75%.

Probability matching! Remarkably, from this little thought experiment, Brennan and Lo derive not only probability matching, but also portfolio diversification and kin altruism – all complex behaviors widely observed throughout the animal and plant kingdoms – from the most basic principles of natural selection, or evolution. (Kin altruism is the tendency of individuals to sacrifice their personal interest to help others who are genetically related, with the degree of sacrifice typically proportionate to the degree of relatedness.)

Bounded rationality and "satisficing"

In another *tour de force*, mercifully shorter and easier to explain, Lo – this time without a co-author – studied "The Origin of Bounded Rationality and Intelligence."[121] Bounded rationality is the human tendency to limit the amount of effort spent in trying to behave rationally. While Lo's bounded-rationality paper is quite extensive, an example from *Adaptive Markets* provides the gist of it. Each morning, Lo chooses an outfit to wear to work. With five jackets, ten pairs of pants (five of which match the jackets), 10 shirts, 20 ties, and a number of accessory items, Lo has 2,016,000 possible outfits to choose from each morning.

Does he optimize by estimating the utility of each of the two million outfits, perhaps decrementing the utility of a potential outfit if he's recently worn it, and choose the single best one? No – if he did that, he'd never get dressed. Instead, he "satisfices," the Nobel Prize-winning economist Herbert Simon's term for figuring out what solutions are good enough, as opposed to formally optimal.[122] "I use a variety of heuristics," Lo writes, "to balance the cost of evaluating different combinations against the desire to get to work on time." One of Lo's heuristics is to avoid wearing a yellow striped tie with a red striped shirt: a colleague thought he looked ridiculous.

How do you know when your solution is good enough?

> You don't. You develop rules of thumb by trial and error. You usually don't know whether a decision is truly optimal. Over time, though, you experience positive and negative feedback from those decisions, and you alter your decisions in response to this feedback. In other words, you learn and adapt to the current environment.

That's what investors do too, and it's one reason why the market is not perfectly efficient – but not grossly inefficient either (with easy profit opportunities everywhere).

---

[121] Lo, Andrew W. 2013. "The Origin of Bounded Rationality and Intelligence," *Proceedings of the American Philosophical Society*, Vol. 157, no. 3 (September). https://www.semanticscholar.org/paper/The-origin-of-bounded-rationality-and-intelligence.-Lo/fef36b46653b831181056d2149adb6e3dd261553 (click on "View PDF")

[122] Simon, Herbert. "A Behavioral Theory of Rational Choice." 1955. *Quarterly Journal of Economics*, vol. 69, no. 1: pp. 99-118.

An intellectual adventure

Puzzles like this, along with highly creative and sophisticated solutions to them, make up much of *Adaptive Markets*. It's an intellectual adventure – a very long one – for people whose interest in markets and behavior has led them to pursue a liberal arts self-education strategy. Readers who are undaunted by Richard Bookstaber's *Demon of our Own Design* and Nassim Taleb's *Fooled by Randomness* will love it. More practical minds may have some difficulty with it.

Andrew Lo is well prepared to lead such an adventure. He is sufficiently well read that his work on just one topic – the evolutionary origins of behavior – brings together five quite separate threads of scientific literature, all but one outside finance:

- Behavioral economics and finance;

- The psychology and cognitive science of Amos Tversky and Daniel Kahneman;

- Evolutionary psychology and sociobiology;

- The evolutionary game theory of John Maynard Smith; and

- Behavioral ecology, which derives from the work of Charles Darwin, R. A. Fisher, J.B.S. Haldane, and other intellectual giants of the last century and the one before.

Lo's conclusions are also suitably lofty, given this list of influences: "We derive risk aversion, loss aversion, probability matching, and randomization from evolution."[123]

So that's where human behavior comes from. We might have guessed that, but it's nice to have a proof, or what passes for proof in the social sciences.

Practical Applications

Does Lo provide anything practical? I've emphasized some of Lo's more exotic ideas, partly to show how good his work is, but also because his flights of fancy regarding tribbles and tie-wearing are more fun than his financial advice. But the intellectual virtuosity with which he addresses practical concerns is just as impressive.

---

[123] From a class slide deck, http://web.mit.edu/9.s915/www/classes/slides_lo.pdf.

He discusses financial fraud, ways to "fix" finance, hedge funds ("the Galapagos Islands of finance," where speciation takes place at warp speed) and events such as the bizarre "quant crash" of August 2007. (The quant crash was, it turns out, a temporary failure of statistical arbitrage, an under-the-radar momentum strategy that had grown huge as large banks and hedge funds adopted it.)

Adaptive Markets is encyclopedic, and any attempt to summarize it in a brief review will fall short.

Conclusion

At half the length, and with the claim of having created a new theory left out, *Adaptive Markets* had the potential to be a classic of the literature of science. Richard Dawkins' *The Selfish Gene* is the archetype of this genre. In finance, Peter Bernstein's *Against the Gods* and Nassim Taleb's *Fooled by Randomness* are fine examples.

Lo is not quite as vivid a writer as these exemplars but he has a keen sense of what might interest thoughtful readers. The ideas in this capstone volume, summarizing an extraordinary career, may be better conveyed in the journal articles, speeches and classes from which the book has been constructed; at least, in those they are separated into manageable pieces.

Fans of Lo's thinking should hear his speeches – his delivery is truly exceptional.[124]

By reading *Adaptive Markets*, investors and their advisors will benefit from a better understanding of the reasons, based in biology and human nature, that the market is not efficient. In fact, the market is so full of gross inefficiencies that active management should be like shooting fish in a barrel. But it's not, because of competition and arbitrage. However, competition and arbitrage do not eliminate all profit opportunities. Keep analyzing securities, managers, asset classes, or whatever enables you to take advantage of your expertise.

Steve Sexauer provided extensive comments.

---

[124] See, for example, his TEDx talk, "Can Financial Engineering Cure Cancer?" [2015], https://www.youtube.com/watch?v=xu86bYKVmRE

Savings and Retirement

Charley Ellis, CFA, a well-known deep thinker on investment issues, wrote recently in the *Financial Analysts Journal*:

> One of the consequences of the shift in corporate retirement plans from defined benefit to defined contribution is widespread retirement insecurity. Although most people in the top one third of economic affluence will be fine, for the other two-thirds – particularly the bottom one third – the problem is a serious threat. We can prevent this painful future if we act sensibly and soon by raising the alarm with our corporate and government leaders.[125]

Big problems are addressed here, both in the macro sense of what needs to be done to mitigate the national problem of overpromising and underfunding, and at the micro level of providing practical insights relevant to individual savers and retirees.

Wayne's personal favorite: After 70 Years of Fruitful Research, Why Is There Still a Retirement Crisis?

—WHW

---

[125] "Our #1 Challenge: Retirement Insecurity," by Charles D. Ellis, Financial Analysts Journal, Fourth Quarter, 2018

Chapter 12. After 70 Years of Fruitful Research, Why Is There Still a Retirement Crisis?

Financial Analysts Journal, January/February 2015.
Reprinted by permission.[126]

"A hundred a year would make [my sisters] all perfectly comfortable."

His wife hesitated: . . . "It is better than [giving them] fifteen hundred pounds at once."

"But then, if Mrs. Dashwood should live fifteen years, we shall be completely taken in."

"Fifteen years! my dear Fanny; her life cannot be worth half that purchase!"

"Certainly not; but if you observe, people always live forever when there is any annuity to be paid them; and she is very stout and healthy, and hardly forty. An annuity is a very serious business; it comes over and over every year, and there is no getting rid of it. I am sure I would not pin myself down to the payment of one for all the world."

—Jane Austen, Sense and Sensibility[127]

Even in 1797, the 22-year-old author Jane Austen, patron saint of annuitants, understood why *issuers* of lifelong income promises might be unhappy about their side of the deal and why *beneficiaries* of such income guarantees are presumably happier. Austen understood time risk and longevity risk — the principal risks that individuals saving for retirement should be concerned about — better than most of today's would-be retirees and some of today's economists. Clearly, the problem of saving and investing for retirement is not new; neither are some of the solutions.

---

[126] This article was originally the lead article in a special issue of the *Financial Analysts Journal* (January/February 2015), which I edited for that one issue only, on the topic of retirement investing.

[127] Set in England in the 1790s, when the author wrote it, *Sense and Sensibility* was first published in 1811; this excerpt is from page 13 of the 1908 edition published by Cassell & Company, London.

Yet, today — more than two centuries later and despite thousands of scholarly and practical articles (many of which have appeared in the *Financial Analysts Journal* over the years) and much earnest effort by researchers, financial product designers, pension plan sponsors, advisers, legislators, regulators, and individual investors — we still have a retirement crisis. Retirees and those saving for retirement continue to struggle with the same challenge as in Austen's time: funding lifetime income. How can this be?

The contents of this special retrospective issue on retirement strongly suggest that we have both the intellectual tools to avoid a retirement crisis and many (not all) of the needed institutional arrangements. But there is a broad consensus that many of today's retirees and those saving for retirement have seldom been in worse shape, with abandoned defined benefit (DB) plans, low savings or low defined contribution (DC) plan balances, poor investment returns, and no workable strategy for converting assets into income.

Causes of the retirement crisis

What went wrong? We can locate the most important causes of the retirement crisis in human nature:

- Low saving rates: Many people prefer living for today over saving for tomorrow.

- Agency costs: Some of the people entrusted with other people's money keep as much as possible for themselves or simply do not know how to do their jobs.

- Lack of knowledge: Accustomed to having employers save on their behalf, employees who must now provide for themselves do not know how much to save, how to invest, or how much to spend.

- Longevity: People are living longer but not necessarily working longer. Most of the other causes of the retirement crisis concern market circumstances and policy errors:

- Poor market returns: Since 2000, markets have mostly disappointed, but those responsible for pension and retirement planning have generally assumed strong returns and have budgeted their contributions accordingly.

- Ordinary costs: Conventional investment management and advice are expensive, and indexing has only recently caught on as a near-majority strategy.

- Unskillful investing: Many investors buy when asset prices are high, after market gains, and then, in a panic, sell low in the next downturn to avoid further losses. They also chase manager alpha unsuccessfully, buying funds after they have performed well and experiencing the inevitable deterioration.

- Ill-advised regulations and taxes: In the United States, for example, tax laws favor DB plans, which allow a large fraction of income to be tax deferred. Meanwhile, caps on DC plan tax deferrals are set so low that most participants cannot realistically retire on tax-deferred balances alone. US tax laws also favor certain types of employee benefits over others, regardless of what is best for the employee, and thus many individual investors face high marginal taxes on savings.

- Poorly defined property rights: With DB pension assets and liabilities (benefits) not clearly belonging to anyone, they become a political football and an object of financial maneuvering.

That's quite a gauntlet for workers seeking retirement security, through either DB plans or individual investing, to run! It's no wonder that a sufficient and reliable retirement income is elusive.

A historical perspective

The modern problem of retirement income generation is very new in human history. In Jane Austen's time, life expectancy was around 40 (as her narrative suggests) and, for the lucky few who lived to an old age, retirement resources were provided through such private channels as living with one's children. A few wealthy people consumed assets or received annuities.

By 1889, when the German chancellor Otto von Bismarck established the first public retirement system, wealth had increased greatly because of the Industrial Revolution and because life expectancies were rising, but few people lived long enough to collect benefits. Even in 1935, when President Franklin Roosevelt's Social Security system was adopted in the United States, life expectancy was only 62, and so those surviving to collect payments were a minority.

Since then, medical advances and economic growth have enabled many to live past 100 (with life expectancy around 80), but the ability and incentive structures to work longer have not increased correspondingly. So, retirement saving and investing have become a challenge for which few are prepared. Fortunately, sustained economic growth has increased the amount of wealth available to devote to retirement, making it easier, at least conceptually, to provide for consumption 40 or more years in the future.

The main reason that 70 years of retirement research have not produced easy and generally accepted solutions is the newness and difficulty of the challenge we face. But we are making progress.

70 years of research relevant to retirement investing

In scouring hundreds of issues of the *Financial Analysts Journal* from the last 70 years for articles germane to the challenges facing today's investors saving for retirement, I found that an astonishingly wide variety of articles had at least some relevance. This is because individual investing for retirement is perhaps the most general and the most challenging investment problem. It requires understanding of long-run rates of return, diversification, time risk, longevity risk and annuities, demographics, taxes, DB plans, laws and regulations, and investor behavior. In choosing articles for this retrospective issue, I tried to cover most of these topics. Still, the number of important and valuable articles left out is many times the number included.

Bookstaber and Gold: Equities in the liability

I decided to begin in the late 1980s, a time when the literature on DB pension management was extraordinarily rich. (Although there are important *FAJ* articles before then, I omitted them from this issue to save trees.) It looked as though the retirement problem had been solved, at least in principle. Employers made pension promises to their employees on the basis of salary and length of service. The challenges were to expand the DB system to include the roughly half of workers who were uncovered, to protect against inflation, and to achieve greater portability (benefit formulas greatly favored long-service employees over those who moved from job to job).

Against this backdrop, Richard Bookstaber and Jeremy Gold's 1988 article "In Search of the Liability Asset"[128] shows that the pension liability contains not only bonds (the obvious choice) but also equities. The presence of equity in the

---

[128] Richard Bookstaber and Jeremy Gold's "In Search of the Liability Asset" was originally published in the *Financial Analysts Journal*, vol. 44, no. 1 (January/February 1988): 70–80, 62.

liability comes from the sensitivity of the liability to economic growth and wage growth in the long term. This sensitivity arises because as workers become more productive and earn higher real wages in the future (trust me, they will), retirees need to be able to compete with workers to buy the same goods.

Since the early 1800s, US productivity, as measured by real GDP *per capita*, has grown at nearly a 2% annual rate. So, over a 20-year retirement, real *per capita* wealth can be expected to rise by almost 50%! Thus, if retirement incomes rise only with consumer price inflation, retirees' relative standard of living will fall. Their incomes need to rise at roughly the rate of productivity and wage growth. And equities are the only asset class that moves with long-run changes in productivity.

Bookstaber and Gold's article was originally intended to apply to DB plans, but in that context, their argument applies to a plan's full economic liability — particularly the part in excess of the accumulated benefit obligation (ABO) or benefit security portion of the liability (which can be hedged, in principle, with bonds).[129] So, it is debatable whether their recognition of the equity component in the larger liability is relevant to setting the DB plan sponsor's investment policy. In the new DC world, however, the authors' argument becomes central, because the saver's portfolio is set against her whole economic liability and thus should usually contain equities as well as "safe" assets.

Kritzman: Pros and cons (but mostly cons) of time diversification

In his 1994 article,[130] Mark Kritzman solves a riddle that had pitted thinkers as distinguished as Paul Samuelson, Zvi Bodie, and Jeremy Siegel against one another for years. Time diversification is the idea that risky assets, such as stocks, are less risky if held for a long time than if held for a short time. If time diversification exists, then retirement investors, who don't need their money back for a long time, can engage in a kind of time horizon arbitrage against short-term investors, whose aversion to price fluctuations causes the equity risk premium to be high. By this logic, long-term investors can ignore the fluctuations and safely capture the premium.

Kritzman shows that under simplified conditions, this arbitrage does not exist.

---

[129] The economic liability is the present value of all benefit payments expected to be made by the plan, including benefits for future service.

[130] Mark Kritzman's "What Practitioners Need to Know . . . About Time Diversification" was originally published in the *Financial Analysts Journal*, vol. 50, no. 1 (January/February 1994): 14–18.

Long-term investors face at least as much risk from risky assets as do short-term investors.

However, if stock returns are mean reverting, with good returns followed by bad ones and vice versa, there may be some benefit to time diversification. In a related article,[131] Zvi Bodie, Robert Merton, and William Samuelson pointed out that young investors have more human capital than do old investors, enabling them to take more risk because they can make up for investment losses by working harder or longer. Kritzman agrees with this position. Investors should consider these arguments carefully, because so many of them invest large amounts in equities, behaving as though time diversification is a "real thing" when, under most circumstances, it isn't.

Bernstein: The repeatable return to equities and bonds

Knowing what returns to expect from each major asset class is critical to deciding how much to save, what assets to invest in, and how much to spend. The legendary author and historian Peter Bernstein spent much of his career studying this question.

Writing near the peak of the bull market in the late 1990s, Bernstein studied past returns and valuation levels to determine what "basic" or repeatable rate of return would have been earned in the stock and bond markets if valuation levels had not changed.[132] He showed that stocks earned an arithmetic mean real annual "basic" return of 5.7% whereas bonds earned a "basic" return of 2.7%.

Bernstein thus concluded that the equity risk premium (over bonds, not cash) is 3%, lower than the estimate reached by many other authors but still positive to an economically significant degree. Bernstein's 3% realized equity premium is the market's reflection of long-term real economic growth, consisting of the productivity growth of 2% mentioned earlier plus labor force growth of around 1%. Although an optimist, Bernstein cautioned that "there is a difference between an optimist and a believer in the tooth fairy." "Tooth fairy" pension calculations and assumptions have ruined DB plans and now threaten individual savers.

---

[131] Zvi Bodie, Robert C. Merton, and William Samuelson, "Labor Supply Flexibility and Portfolio Choice in a Life-Cycle Model," *Journal of Economic Dynamics and Control*, vol. 16, no. 3–4 (July–October 1992): 427–449.

[132] Peter L. Bernstein's "What Rate of Return Can You Reasonably Expect . . . or What Can the Long Run Tell Us about the Short Run?" was originally published in the *Financial Analysts Journal*, vol. 53, no. 2 (March/April 1997): 20–28.

Bodie: Putting lifecycle finance into practice

A formal theory of lifecycle finance has been part of the literature of economics since 1930, when Irving Fisher observed that people smooth their consumption relative to their income, borrowing and saving as needed to do so.[133] Zvi Bodie has been a key contributor to this literature, which has become normative (how to choose an investment policy so as to smooth consumption) as well as positive (whether people smooth consumption). Bodie's sometime co-author, the Nobel Prize–winning economist Robert Merton, made key contributions to lifecycle finance as early as the late 1960s and early 1970s.[134] Bodie's 2003 article,[135] reprinted in this issue, simplifies Merton's work for the practitioner and introduces several new types of financial instruments intended to help in financial planning.

Bodie's main point, which has influenced almost all subsequent retirement research, is that "lifetime consumption of goods and leisure," not "end-of-period wealth," is what retirement savers care about. Consequently, for those saving for retirement, the riskless asset is not cash — as William Sharpe would have it — but, rather, a portfolio of laddered bonds or TIPS (Treasury Inflation-Protected Securities), with each cash flow from the portfolio matched to a consumption need. Two articles in the issue of the *Financial Analysts Journal* in which this article originally appeared (January/February 2015) — one by Stephen Sexauer, Michael Peskin, and Daniel Cassidy and one that I co-authored with Barton Waring — build on this idea.

In his article, Bodie also suggests two financial products that, if properly developed, would make the provision of retirement income easier. The first product, an escalating life annuity, tracks the performance of a portfolio of equity call options. This suggestion fits well with Bookstaber and Gold's observation that there is equity in a retirement liability.

---

[133] Irving Fisher, *The Theory of Interest: As Determined by Impatience to Spend Income and Opportunity to Invest It* (New York: Macmillan, 1930). For further discussion, see Waring and Siegel's "The Only Spending Rule Article You Will Ever Need" in this issue.

[134] Robert C. Merton, "Lifetime Portfolio Selection under Uncertainty: The Continuous-Time Case," *Review of Economics and Statistics*, vol. 51, no. 3 (August 1969): 247–257; Merton, "Optimum Consumption and Portfolio Rules in a Continuous-Time Model," *Journal of Economic Theory*, vol. 3, no. 4 (December 1971): 373–413.

[135] Zvi Bodie's "Thoughts on the Future: Life-Cycle Investing in Theory and Practice" was originally published in the *Financial Analysts Journal*, vol. 59, no. 1 (January/February 2003): 24–29.

The second product, also described by Mark Warshawsky,[136] bundles together longevity annuities,[137] which appeal to the healthy, and nursing home insurance, which appeals to the sick. By offering both types of protection in one product, the adverse selection that affects both products is mitigated and many more people are covered (and at lower cost).

I now turn to some policy articles by Keith Ambachtsheer and Don Ezra, originally published in the January/February 2007 special pension issue of the *Financial Analysts Journal*.

Ambachtsheer: Calling for a pension revolution

In a brief and farsighted polemic,[138] Keith Ambachtsheer suggests that the "DB or DC" dilemma is misstated and that "neither DB nor DC" is the path to a better pension system. The system he favors, modestly called TOPS (The Optimal Pension System), involves DC-like contributions that are used preferentially to buy life annuities but that can also be used to make non-annuitizing investments. If this sounds a lot like TIAA-CREF, the US private pension plan for college teachers, it's intentional: Ambachtsheer proposes that organization as a model, with some modifications, for a universal retirement system. (Later in this editorial, I argue that there is no single optimal solution but that if we must agree on one, TIAA-CREF is a very good solution.)

Ambachtsheer also brings other countries' pension systems into the discussion. He admires the Dutch and Australian systems and notes that at the time of writing (2007), the United Kingdom was considering enrolling the entire uncovered part of its work force (i.e., not covered by a traditional pension scheme) in a TOPS-like plan.[139]

---

[136] Mark J. Warshawsky, "The Life Care Annuity," in *The Future of Life-Cycle Saving and Investing*, edited by Zvi Bodie, Dennis McLeavey, and Laurence B. Siegel (Charlottesville, VA: CFA Institute Research Foundation, 2007): 103–106.

[137] For further discussion of the longevity annuity, also called a deferred income annuity (DIA) or advanced life deferred annuity (ALDA), see the article by Sexauer *et al.* and the article by Waring and Siegel, both in the January/February 2015 issue of the *Financial Analysts Journal*.

[138] Keith Ambachtsheer's "Why We Need a Pension Revolution" was originally published in the *Financial Analysts Journal*, vol. 63, no. 1 (January/February 2007): 21–25.

[139] Much of the UK plan as described by Ambachtsheer was adopted in the Pensions Act of 2008. Unfortunately, withdrawals under all circumstances at ordinary tax rates became permissible in 2014, making it that much harder to get people to leave their money alone until they retire.

Ezra: How pensions were destroyed, and how to bring them back

Don Ezra begins by telling the true story of how the DB system was destroyed.[140] Funding targets were originally set *above* the economic present value of the pension liability, providing a cushion in case of bear markets. However, "in the 1980s, when inflation subsided, actuaries lowered the salary assumption but left the return assumption high" so that pensions could be legally (but not economically) funded with "70-cent dollars." That is, every 70 cents in the pension fund was deemed to offset a dollar of liability, because every 70 cents, invested in stocks, was expected to grow to $1 over time. What economic folly! Yet, this practice persisted and enabled corporate raiders in the 1980s and afterward to "buy" pension assets at a discount, often closing the plans.

As one might guess, the near demise of the DB system was not intentional; it was the consequence of a set of historical accidents, coincidences, and misbehaviors.

Arguing in a footnote (he and I disagree on this point) that the US Pension Protection Act of 2006 eliminates the ability to say that 70 cents is worth a dollar, Ezra presents an intriguing DB plan design for the future.[141] Fully funded by law, Ezra's plan is "nonpenalizing" in the sense that short-service employees get as large a pension benefit per employer-contributed dollar as do long-service employees. Thus, the system is portable — and fairer than in current practice.

Ezra also suggests a fix for DC plans: They should use auto-enrollment, auto-escalation (the "Save More Tomorrow" plan of Thaler and Benartzi),[142] and auto-conversion into annuities, either at retirement or upon achieving one's life expectancy. The latter choice makes it possible to capture much of the benefit of annuitization without losing all of one's liquidity at retirement.

Scott: An annuity for everyone

Annuities! Everybody loves them on paper — they replace DB income streams and capture the huge gains from pooling longevity risk — but nobody buys them. Even Jane Austen would probably shun annuities today, given their

---

[140] Don Ezra's "Defined-Benefit and Defined-Contribution Plans of the Future" was originally published in the *Financial Analysts Journal*, vol. 63, no. 1 (January/February 2007): 26–30.

[141] By stipulating a discount rate formed from stale (not current) Aa rated corporate bond yields, the Pension Protection Act continues to allow 70 cents to be called a dollar.

[142] Richard H. Thaler and Shlomo Benartzi, "Save More Tomorrow: Using Behavioral Economics to Increase Employee Saving," *Journal of Political Economy*, vol. 112, no. S1 (February 2004): S164–S187.

inflexibility, high fees, adverse selection, and lack of a transparent market.

Observing that almost no one puts all his wealth into annuities — nor should he — Jason Scott has developed an optimization method for deciding what annuities to buy and how much.[143] The answer is shockingly simple. The key is to break up an annuity promise into year-by-year promises: income in one's 65th year, 66th year, and so forth.

Let's say that an investor believes the longest she might possibly live is 107 years. Then, working backward, she should buy a deferred income annuity for years 107, 106, 105, and so forth, until she runs out of money that she is willing to commit to an annuity portfolio. Aggregating the different years, the investor buys a deferred income (longevity) annuity that starts its payout somewhat late in life — say, age 85 — and that continues until death.[144] Only the rare investor willing to commit her *entire* wealth to annuities should buy an immediate annuity, one that covers all the years of planned retirement.

Reichenstein, Horan, and Jennings: After-tax returns are what count

Although much advice to investors is rendered without considering taxes, "taxes exist," as William Reichenstein, Stephen Horan, and William Jennings remind us, and can consume a huge slice of retirement savings.[145] This concern especially affects savers who have most of their assets in tax-deferred accounts, because they have not yet paid any tax on the amount saved. A retirement plan or benefits structure that minimizes taxes thus adds a significant "alpha," one that does not require a beat-the-market strategy and that is, from the retiree's perspective, a needless waste of money if *not* achieved.

The authors' analysis produces an asset allocation that does not ignore taxes. Moreover, the analysis produces a substantially different *asset location*, the practice of holding each asset in the type of account that produces the highest after-tax present value. Investors, advisers, and plan sponsors who are not paying attention to asset location had better start.

---

[143] Jason S. Scott's "The Longevity Annuity: An Annuity for Everyone?" was originally published in the *Financial Analysts Journal*, vol. 64, no. 1 (January/February 2008): 40–48.

[144] I hope that a more complete, transparent, and fairly priced market in deferred annuities develops so that investors can put Scott's advice into practice more easily. Investors also need to be able to hedge against inflation, making deferred real annuities highly desirable.

[145] William Reichenstein, Stephen M. Horan, and William W. Jennings's "Two Key Concepts for Wealth Management and Beyond" was originally published in the Financial Analysts Journal, vol. 68, no. 1 (January/February 2012): 14–22.

Sexauer, Peskin, and Cassidy: More savings, More annuitization, less risk.

How much do you need to save for retirement? Many would-be retirees seem baffled by this question, because it's hard — or impossible — to forecast market returns. By assuming riskless investing, Stephen Sexauer, Michael Peskin, and Daniel Cassidy have eliminated the need to make such a forecast and have arrived at a "retirement multiple" that enables investors to set an asset accumulation target.[146] To keep the multiple from growing unmanageably large, the authors assume that retirement income after age 85 will be funded by a deferred income annuity.

In a world where inflation is an ongoing risk, riskless investing means building a ladder of TIPS, which currently offer very low interest rates. In fact, at the time of writing (2012), the authors assumed a *zero* real rate, so the first 20 years of retirement (65 to 85) would need to be funded by 20 years' required post-retirement income. The deferred income annuity, however, is surprisingly cheap — an additional 1.5 years' income — so one needs to save only 21.5 times the yearly real income requirement (over and above Social Security benefits) to guarantee one's income for life.

The authors acknowledge that few investors will want to invest entirely risklessly, with most preferring to hold stocks and other risky investments to get to their "retirement multiple" with less savings and more investment return. But investors who don't mind taking risk need a benchmark. The TIPS-plus-deferred-annuities strategy can thus be regarded as a benchmark against which other retirement investment strategies (those that include risky investments, such as stocks) can be judged — a benchmark easily used by practitioners as well as individual investors for their own portfolios or to judge a pension promise made by an employer.

Waring and Siegel: How much to spend so you never run out

I co-authored (with Barton Waring) the new article "The Only Spending Rule Article You Will Ever Need"[147] and will keep my summary of it here brief. Each year, one should spend (at most) the amount that a freshly purchased annuity — at then-current portfolio values, interest rates, and number of years of

---

[146] Stephen C. Sexauer, Michael W. Peskin, and Daniel Cassidy's "Making Retirement Income Last a Lifetime" was originally published in the Financial Analysts Journal, vol. 68, no. 1 (January/February 2012): 74–84.

[147] See footnote 137.

required cash flow remaining — would pay out in that year.[148] Investors who behave in this way will experience consumption that fluctuates with asset values, but they can never run out of money.

A retirement template for the future

With the benefit of 70 years of research, what conclusions can we draw — what recommendations should we make — about the future of retirement saving and investing?

Unlike some researchers, I don't believe the retirement puzzle has One True Solution. As with most economic arrangements in a free society, different people will want, and should have access to, different retirement solutions or (this is key) combinations of solutions. We can begin with Robert Merton's observation that would-be retirees should seek to build income guarantees — not to accumulate assets.[149] Assets are just a steppingstone or type of financial intermediation between income earned from work and consumption many decades later in retirement.

Keeping in mind the DB/DC distinction — best re-characterized as a distinction between income promises and guarantees (DB) and asset accumulation and decumulation (DC) — let us review some of the options.

DB only

DB plans "work" — that is, provide a secure retirement without bankrupting the provider — if the plan is fully funded by design, sponsors have resources to "top up" plans that become less than fully funded, plans are portable (or people don't leave their jobs), plan assets are not subject to capture, and benefits are sufficiently generous that people don't need to save separately.[150] Those are a lot of conditions, and they are expensive to comply with, but they are essential to obtaining the tremendous benefit of lifetime income guarantees.[151] DB plans also achieve longevity-risk pooling through their inherent structure, an advantage

---

[148] Instead of using a life annuity, we use a fixed-term annuity — say, one designed to make payouts for 30 years — to illustrate this principle, but it also works with life annuities.

[149] Robert C. Merton, "The Crisis in Retirement Planning," *Harvard Business Review*, vol. 92, no. 7–8 (July–August 2014): 43–50.

[150] See M. Barton Waring, *Pension Finance* (Hoboken, NJ: John Wiley & Sons, 2011).

[151] See Don Ezra, "Retirement Income Guarantees Are Expensive," *Financial Analysts Journal*, vol. 61, no. 6 (November/December 2005): 74–77.

that is costly to replicate in non-DB environments.

In the United States, Social Security, a type of DB plan, is widely criticized, but its flaws can be repaired. Meanwhile, it serves as a template for what can be accomplished using a DB structure: People over 65, once the poorest Americans, are now among the richest, and Social Security has cut off the left tail of the distribution, virtually eliminating extreme poverty in retirement.

Following this logic, William Goetzmann has proposed "More Social Security, Not Less" — the idea that the government should sell Social Security–like guaranteed income streams at actuarially fair prices.[152] Retirement savers could then buy their own DB plans much more easily. Insurance companies, nonprofit organizations, and mutual benefit societies could also offer DB plans so long as they followed relatively simple hedging and full-funding rules, and traditional DB plan sponsors could offer retirement benefits to people outside their current beneficiary population. It's an engineering problem — not a profound economic challenge — and the solutions already exist, many of them documented in the *Financial Analysts Journal.*

DC only

Asset accumulation/decumulation works well for people who save enough, invest at low risk (or take risk successfully), don't spend the money before retirement, and withdraw using a sensible spending rule. Bequests are possible. To expand the population for whom DC-only plans work well, saving rates could be mandatorily high or other strategies could be used to incentivize high voluntary savings.[153]

Neither DB nor DC

Here, I'm echoing Keith Ambachtsheer in saying that a hybrid program combining the best aspects of DB and DC plans can be very effective. Contributions — which are high, consistent, and pretax to the extent permitted by law — are used

---

[152] William N. Goetzmann, "More Social Security, Not Less," *Journal of Portfolio Management,* vol. 35, no. 1 (Fall 2008): 115–123.

[153] Because most Americans, and many in other countries, are probably stuck with DC-only plans (plus Social Security) while these problems are being worked on, we might as well figure out how to use DC effectively to generate desirable levels of retirement income. For a discussion of how to replace 70% (or any desired number) of pre-retirement income with a DC-only program and low-risk investing (the key is high saving rates), see Stephen C. Sexauer and Laurence B. Siegel, "A Pension Promise to Oneself," *Financial Analysts Journal,* vol. 69, no. 6 (November/December 2013): 13–32.

to buy life-annuity units. The participant has some discretion over the shape of the annuity — individual or spousal, some resources saved for a bequest, and so forth. TIAA-CREF is the best example. Under current US law, the provider of such an arrangement must be an insurance company.

Both DB and DC

This is the best solution. Counting Social Security as a DB plan, it is what most people have, but they don't have enough of it. By "both DB and DC," I mean that it is highly desirable to have a DB plan *in addition to* Social Security, as well as a DC plan: a three-legged stool. This is the direction I hope retirement investing will take. Adding a DB plan, even if modest in size, to a DC benefit makes the participant's retirement income less reliant on strong markets, takes some of the burden of saving away from the participant, and brings longevity-risk pooling directly and costlessly back into the retiree's arsenal of tools. Institutional incentives and legal structures need to be revised so that employers will again be motivated to undertake the planning and management tasks involved in converting every worker's current income into lifetime income.

Conclusion

If the future of retirement evolves as I hope it will, employees will be able to choose from among these structures, weighing the size and "shape" of the retirement benefits of a given job or business activity against its other characteristics. Employers will innovate to attract and retain talented workers. Retirement arrangements that are unrelated to employment should also be encouraged. Most people will find a combination of DB and DC benefits to be more attractive than other choices. However, because the combination is more expensive to provide, employees will have to sacrifice more of their current income than they do for other retirement deals. They should also be able to change their minds (e.g., leave a job with a DB plan for one with a DC plan) without losing the benefits they have already earned.

The challenge of providing retirement income over a very long period is not trivial, and we have understandably stumbled in trying to create the best system or combination of systems for doing so. Let us sincerely hope, however, that we won't still be experiencing a retirement crisis 70 years from now. Given the resources in this [January/February 2015] issue of the *Financial Analysts Journal* and elsewhere, there's really no excuse for one.

Chapter 13. The Pension Crisis: Six Lessons Learned and a Way Forward

Laurence B. Siegel and Stephen Sexauer[154]

Retirement Management Journal®, Fall 2015

What have we learned from the seemingly endless recent run of pension crises, which have lasted some seven years and have encompassed both DB and DC plans?

Having lost assets and then regained them, both kinds of pension plans should be on a path to being healthy, yet they are not. For many plans, liabilities still exceed assets, some by vast amounts. In many cases there is no feasible plan for making up the difference — even the generally prosperous state of Illinois is near bankruptcy because of pension shortfalls. In the eurozone, concerns about the solvency of Greece pivot on pension liabilities.

Lesson 1: Liabilities Matter. Savings Matter.

When pensions and pension-like retirement income programs were first implemented — privately at American Express in 1875, then by governments starting with Bismarck's system in Prussia in 1889 and progressing to Social Security in the U.S. in 1935 — the liability was small because life expectancy at retirement was short. More than a century of economic growth later, we are richer, we are healthier, and we live much longer.[155]

---

[154] Stephen C. Sexauer is Chief Investment Officer of the San Diego County Employee Retirement Association. The views expressed here are those of the authors and not those of either author's employer. The authors thank François Gadenne, Chairman and Executive Director of the Retirement Income Industry Association (RIIA), as well as Robert Powell, Editor and Publisher of the Retirement Management Journal, for their encouragement and support. Minor updates to this article were made in September 2020.

[155] For some basic data on changes in incomes and life expectancies over roughly the last 200 years, see Siegel, Laurence B. 2012. "Fewer, Richer, Greener: The End of the Population Explosion and the

In addition to living longer without the associated adjustment to the amount saved, the current pension crisis episode has seen both DB and DC pension plan liabilities grow rapidly because interest rates have declined to all-time low levels.

By liabilities we mean, of course, the amount one has to save in order to be able to generate the desired level of lifetime income. For DB plans, these are the present value of the pension benefit promises made by the plan. For DC plans, while the equivalent liabilities are not recognized on conventional balance sheets, they are just as real as if accounting conventions required them to be recorded on one's personal balance sheet. Pension promises, by a formal pension plan or to oneself, are the *economic liability* of the plan, and they must be matched by assets or the plan will fail — ignoring the liabilities or making wishful assumptions about them will not make them go away.

Lesson 2: Investment Skill Is Not a Panacea.

The second lesson is: investment skill matters less than you think. One reason we have a crisis is that we think we can solve the pension problem by being the smartest investors in the room.

It would be nice if skillful investing could generate huge excess returns relative to average investing. But that is not today's reality. Most DB portfolios are pretty well diversified and close to the efficient frontier, and target-date funds have moved a great many DC-plan investors toward the efficient frontier as well. The search for the Perfect Portfolio is less likely to be fruitful than the search for behavioral, institutional, and policy changes designed to help the pension beneficiary. Such changes are the focus of this article.

Lesson 3: Agency Costs Matter.

When one group of people makes a promise that a different group has to keep, that structure creates incentives for poor decision-making and a potential crisis. Economics categorizes this friction or inefficiency as an *agency cost,* analogous to the friction created when business owners hire professional managers, who do not own the business, to run it for them.

Future for Investors," *Financial Analysts Journal*, Vol. 68, No. 6 (November/December); and Siegel, Laurence B. 2019. *Fewer, Richer, Greener: Prospects for Humanity in an Age of Abundance*, Hoboken, NJ: John Wiley & Sons.

In the public pension sector, this agency problem is made worse by a double agency relationship. Those who make the pension promise in one period are no longer in office when the bulk of the pension payments must be made. In addition, the officials making the pension promises are, in many cases, elected by those who benefit from the payments. In all these situations, the agents are spending other people's money — the taxpayers' money — and not their own. No wonder there is a public pension crisis![156] Agency costs can do great damage to what should be, and can be, a very valuable benefit to workers: a well-run public pension plan.[157]

Lesson 4: People Respond to Incentives. Behavior Matters.

The University of Rochester professor Steven Landsburg, author of *The Armchair Economist,* wrote, "Most of economics can be summarized in four words: 'People respond to incentives.'" Although everyone knows this at some level, good economics is distinguished, Landsburg wrote, by taking it seriously all the time.

The idea that incentives matter — a lot — is closely related to the observation, made famous by the Nobel Prize-winning psychologist Daniel Kahneman and his collaborator Amos Tversky, that human behavior differs considerably from what is predicted by conventional economics. These principles apply to saving and investing as well as to almost every other aspect of life. In retirement investing, for example, auto-enrollment, auto-escalation, and qualified default investment alternatives (QDIAs), are effective "nudges" — small, subtle influences that convey big behavioral benefits.

Here are some economic and behavioral-based incentives that will increase savings and retirement income:

---

[156] The private DB pension situation is not much better, but at least corporate managers are spending money over which they have unambiguous authority. And they are supposed to be motivated by the knowledge they can put their employer out of business if the decisions they make are bad enough. The fact that we don't have a healthy private DB system is evidence that agency costs are very destructive.

[157] For a discussion of the virtues of a well-run DB plan and what is lost when DC plans are substituted for it, see, for example, Waring, M. Barton, and Laurence B. Siegel. 2007. "Don't Kill the Golden Goose: Saving Pension Plans," *Financial Analysts Journal,* Vol. 63, No. 1 (January/February). One important point the authors make is that longevity-risk pooling makes it possible to pay benefits much more cheaply than if every retiree has to save to his or her maximum life span.

- To qualify as a DC plan, require the sponsor to implement auto-enrollment, auto-escalation, and qualified default investment alternatives (QDIAs).

- Remove the IRA and 401(k) contribution caps and let people save as much as they can for retirement on a tax-deferred basis, with the possible exception of the very wealthiest taxpayers. (SEP-IRA contribution caps, which apply to the self-employed, have already been raised to realistic levels, around $50,000 per year.) Because of required minimum distributions, taxes will eventually be paid on these balances, so the net cost to the government is not large.

- To qualify as a DC plan, require the sponsor to default all participants within ten years of retirement into a Qualified Life Annuity Contract (QLAC) with a significant part of their savings. By doing so, the participants gain access to longevity pooling—lifetime income—at institutional pricing, with administrative efficiency and ERISA protection[158].

- Legislation should require a certain percentage of U.S. government debt to be issued in inflation-adjusted form, that is, as TIPS bonds. A TIPS bond with a duration matched to that of the pension promise is the ideal hedge for the risks of that promise. While TIPS with maturities up to 30 years have been issued, that is not long enough – a pension promise can extend over 80 years (age 25 to 105). Moreover, there is not much depth to the TIPS market even at 30 years. The market should be both deepened and lengthened. Maintaining a deep, long-horizon market in TIPS also has the secondary benefit of limiting the government's incentive and ability to debase its own promises to bondholders and helping to keep a stable price level.

- A nationally regulated and standardized market for life-annuity insurance contracts should be established. Currently, insurance companies are legally allowed to offer individual annuity contracts and each state sets its own regulations with its own insurance commissioner and regulatory structures. The inefficiency of having 50 separate sets of regulations, the associated agency costs, and challenges of portability can be removed with a regulatory structure parallel to that of banking, where a bank can be nationally chartered or state chartered

---

[158] Under ERISA, the plan sponsor would be responsible for hiring and monitoring the QLAC suppliers. After leaving the plan, the participant can stay with that provider, switch to another, or opt out. They could also opt out beforehand, when they are employees.

Lesson 5: Longevity Pooling Is Second in Importance Only to the Savings Rate.

It does not take a PhD or Nobel Prize in economics to understand the benefits of longevity-risk pooling. With longevity pooling, one needs to save only to one's life expectancy, or average age at death, say 85; that's 20 years of payments if they start at age 65.[159] Without longevity pooling, each retiree needs to save enough to pay for his or her maximum possible life span, say 105 or 40 years of payments. Thus the pension liability is potentially twice as big when savers cannot pool their longevity risk.

How can individuals get institutional quality access to longevity pooling, or annuities? QLACs (mentioned above), nationally regulated insurance markets, deep TIPS markets enabling suppliers to reliably hedge their promises, and two-way market making in annuity contracts are structural changes that can reduce the magnitude of the challenge faced by the individual in managing his or her retirement liability, and by DB plans in providing more options to economically and reliably fulfill lifetime income promises.

Lesson 6: Start Now.

While we have outlined some proposals for a much better set of institutions and practices, today's investors cannot wait for these proposals to be implemented. They need help now.

Savings rates can be increased using auto-enrollment, auto-escalation, and investor education. Inflation hedging can be achieved using a laddered TIPS portfolio up to the maturity of the longest existing TIPS, and to some extent through proxy hedges such as equities. Longevity pooling can be arranged in the private market for deferred annuities. (Deferred annuities can be combined with conventional investing to achieve lifetime income protection without transferring most or all of one's wealth to the annuity provider, as one is required to do when purchasing an immediate annuity.[160])

---

[159] What's relevant is the life expectancy at age 65, when payments to the retiree begin — not life expectancy at birth, which is lower.

[160] See Totten, Thomas L., and Laurence B. Siegel. 2019. "Combining Conventional Investing with a Lifetime Income Guarantee: A Blueprint for Retirement Security," *Journal of Retirement,* vol. 6, no. 4 (Spring), pp. 45-59; Sexauer, Stephen C., and Laurence B. Siegel. 2013. "A Pension Promise to Oneself," *Financial Analysts Journal,* Vol. 69, No. 6 (November/December); Scott, Jason. 2015. "The

In other words, don't wait for a perfect world to do what is best for yourself and your employees. Many of the tools and technologies needed for effective pension and retirement-savings management already exist, some in well-engineered and fairly priced packages and others more roughly. While working toward a more complete and efficient market in pension and retirement tools, the existing ones should be used vigorously and enthusiastically.

Conclusion

A reliable pension is very valuable — to the employee, the employer, and society. While each of us has unique circumstances and needs, we all have a common interest in making both DB and DC pensions work. This task includes saving more to match our ever-lengthening lives, gaining access to efficient longevity pooling, and demanding legislative and regulatory policies — from ERISA to insurance regulation to employment rules — that create employee and employer incentives to make these valuable pension promises last a lifetime.

Longevity Annuity: An Annuity for Everyone?" *Financial Analysts Journal*, Vol. 71, No. 1 (January/February). Scott shows that deferred annuities are almost always preferable to immediate annuities.

Chapter 14. A Pension Promise to Oneself

Stephen Sexauer and Laurence Siegel

Financial Analysts Journal, **November/December 2013.**
Reprinted with permission.[161]

Overview

"Don't have a pension? Don't worry. Most people don't. They will get to retire, and so will you.

What you and almost everybody else do have is the ability to *make a pension promise to yourself* that is the economic equivalent of the promise that an employer could make. With your employer's help, or possibly without it (it helps, but isn't really required), you also have the ability to deliver on that promise. You will make pension payments to yourself from the moment you retire until the end of your life, or your spouse's life, whichever comes later.

"You don't know that you have this ability, but you do. You are about to receive the basic components of a tool kit for making this happen, and over time you will receive the rest of the tool kit. The strategy for making this happen involves a lot of saving, but almost no risk. When you do face risk, you will have been provided with the tools necessary for managing it. You'll be just fine."

- - -

Why aren't these words spoken to every employee who begins to work at a company, government agency, or nonprofit organization? Why aren't they taught in school? Why aren't they part of the advice lovingly given by fathers to their sons, and by mothers to their daughters, as adulthood looms?

The reason is that many of the people who should be delivering this message

---

[161] This article has been slightly revised to reflect changes in markets since it was published (it is not a full update), and to reflect moving the Appendices in the article to a web site.

don't even know that it's true. Yet every word of it is true. There is nothing magical about the pension promise that an employer with a traditional defined benefit (DB) pension plan makes to an employee. The employer saves and invests money on the employee's behalf, according to a set of rules that are designed to make sure that enough money is available to pay the promised benefit, then pays it to the employee as a post-retirement income stream. Failures do occur, but that's because people — employers and employees — don't stick to the rules.

The individual can provide a pension for himself almost as easily. There's no magic in this either. It requires saving a lot of money – almost exactly the same amount, if opportunities to pool longevity risk are taken advantage of, as is needed to fully fund and pay out a DB promise. Hence, a powerful point: if the amount of money needed to fund a DB plan can be made available to DC-plan investors, that amount is also enough to make the DC plan work.[162]

We say "*almost* as easily" because there are some economies of scale involved in providing a pension for a large group of people. These economies can mostly be replicated by the individual.[163] It's not that hard, and anyone who makes a pension promise to herself, and who does what is needed over time to keep that promise, is made vastly better off by doing so. He or she will be able to sleep well at night.

The Pension Setting

Much ink has already been spilled on the pension catastrophe we're facing, so we won't go into the details. It suffices to say that private sector DB plans are all but extinct, mostly because sponsors hoped against evidence that stock market profits would substitute for adequate contributions. Public-sector DB plans were, until recently, propped up by the ability to tap a growing tax base, but

---

[162] The same contributions would provide the same average benefit across employees, rather than the same exact benefit for each employee, because many DB plans contain a redistributive feature (with, for example, short-service employees subsidizing long-service employees). The same contributions would provide the same exact benefit for each employee if longevity pooling can be achieved at no cost, any redistributive aspect of DB plans is ignored, and individuals can invest at institutional (that is, low) fee schedules and with institutional-quality performance. See Waring, Siegel, and Kohn (2007).

[163] Since one big advantage that DB plans have is economies of scale for longevity pooling, what would help individuals would be a federal charter, much like that used for national banks, that would allow insurance companies to offer and administer longevity pooling contracts on a national basis, thus providing individuals economical access to longevity pooling. At present, the private life-annuity market offers some access to longevity pooling, but it is not especially economical nor are the various offers from insurance companies easy to evaluate.

when tax revenues turned sharply downward in 2008-2009, the plans fell on hard times, with some defaults already experienced and many more threatened. The inability or unwillingness to control benefit growth is a secondary reason for both private and public DB-plan failures.

In addition, long-term interest rates have plunged to historic lows, so that the present value of long-dated future liabilities has mushroomed. This, not poor market performance, is the proximate cause of the pension crisis – markets have, in fact, performed well enough in this century.[164]

The defined-contribution (DC) plans that have almost universally replaced DB plans suffer from even worse outcomes: Waring, Siegel, and Kohn (2007) reported a few years ago that the median DC-plan participant was retiring with an investment balance of $44,000; the mean balance of $150,000, skewed by a few affluent retirees, isn't much better. The 2010 Federal Reserve's Survey of Consumer Finances (SCF) shows little improvement, with households approaching retirement having median DC balances of $63,000; when IRAs are included the median balance is $120,000. Assuming a 4% withdrawal rate, the SCF balances, as of 2010, support monthly spending of $210 and $400 respectively. These aren't pensions at all, but "beer money" savings plans. We simply have to do better for our valued employees and for ourselves.[165]

We concede that the battle to save DB plans in their original form is almost entirely lost. This essay is about using DB-plan thinking to achieve better DC-plan outcomes. The thinking behind DB and DC plans is the same: the task at hand is *to spread the earnings from one's working life over one's whole life*, and one can only consume what one has. Thus, contributions to a hypothetical fully funded DB plan are also enough to fully fund a DC plan in the sense of providing an average benefit across employees that is as good as the DB-plan benefit.

---

[164] This paragraph was added on September 28, 2020.

[165] Because of the bull market, these numbers have risen somewhat since the original date of this article but not by nearly enough to make them "wine money" instead of beer money. In 2012, The Boston College Center for Retirement Research calculated that a worker with pre-retirement earnings of $65,000 who contributed 6% with an employer match of 3% should reasonably have accumulated about $363,000 at retirement, well above the Survey of Consumer Finances 2010 balances. We show here that, to make a pension promise to oneself, the savings goal for this $65,000 per year worker needs to be higher, about $565,000 for a 70% income replacement ratio if he expects to receive $1598 in monthly Social Security benefits, the amount shown (as of the original date of this article) on the Social Security quick calculator page for a 66-year-old worker retiring at that income level and at that time. See Munnell (2012).

Why DB and DC Plans Require the Same Amount of Money

We noted earlier that the amount of money needed to fully fund a pay out a DB plan promise is also sufficient to fund a DC plan that is equally beneficial to the participant. What exactly does this mean?

The function of any pension or savings plan (DB or DC) is to shift cash flows over time. There is only one way to do that, which is to participate in the investment markets.[166] A DB plan sponsor first uses actuarial information to project what benefits it will need to pay out. Then, it invests an amount of money sufficient, when the projected investment return on those assets is taken into account, to pay out those benefits.[167] As investment gains or losses become apparent, and as other changes in the environment occur (say, life expectancies lengthen), the sponsor adjusts the contributions to the fund accordingly. Finally, the sponsor pays out benefits as promised.

A DC plan does exactly the same thing, except that you, the investor, are the "sponsor." You first project the cash flows you are going to need in retirement. Then, you develop and execute a savings plan in an amount sufficient, when investment returns are taken into account, to fund the retirement income requirement. (Savings or contributions into the DC plan, whether by the participant or from an employer match, are analogous to the sponsor's contributions to the DB pension fund.) Next, and this is a key concept, the DC plan participant makes adjustments along the way, for investment gains and losses and for other changes in the environment. Finally, the participant uses the money when she is retired.

Note that these two stories are very similar. Money is not created or destroyed in either one. What you get is what you put in, plus or minus investment returns after fees. The only differences are: (1) who is making the contributions, and (2) who is managing the process. And any economist will tell you there is no difference, in terms of total compensation, between the employer making the

---

[166] Or to hire a financial intermediary, such an insurance company, to participate in the investment markets for you.

[167] If the sponsor sets aside less than the required amount, the plan is considered underfunded, which means that it is implicitly funded by a debt owed by the sponsor to the beneficiaries (which can also be seen as an involuntary loan by the beneficiaries to the sponsor). If this debt is not paid off in the interim through extra contributions to the fund, it is paid off when the sponsor pays out the benefits in full. If the beneficiaries receive anything less than a full payout, the sponsor is considered to have defaulted.

contributions directly (in a DB plan) and the employer giving the money to the employee to invest himself (in a DC plan).

A Three-Part Rule Set for a Personal Pension Plan

Count Leo Tolstoy could be forgiven — and might be considered more up-to-date — if he had begun *Anna Karenina* with the lines, "All successful DB and DC plans are alike. Each failure is unique." Plans that understand and play by the rules succeed. Those that do not, whether DB or DC and no matter what rule they think they can break, fail.

Since our point is that a well-run DC plan can and should use the same principles that big institutions have used for managing a DB plan on an economically sound basis, we identify the three basic steps that a DB plan or a DC plan needs to take.

1. Liabilities must be appraised, and discounted back to a present value. This is what actuarial firms do for DB plans: they estimate the combined pension promise the company has made to all its employees, and then discount this liability to a present value. An individual can do the same, and we will show how this is done and set forth a shortcut (the Retirement Multiple) for arriving at the amount of money that needs to be saved.

2. Assets must be accumulated according to an economically sound plan, with wishful thinking about markets not allowed to substitute for rational savings rates. While not all DB sponsors are this virtuous, the successful ones play by the rules and have close to fully funded pension plans. This is what DC-plan investors must do too. Hope is neither an investment strategy nor a retirement plan; this principle applies to both DB and DC structures.[168]

3. Assets must be decumulated (spent, paid out) in a sensible manner that preserves the tremendous value of longevity pooling. While decumulation is not the main point of this essay, Waring, Siegel, and Kohn (2007) and Sexauer, Peskin, and Cassidy (2012) have described ways that a stable

---

[168] The general framework around which asset accumulation for retirement has developed — manifesting itself today in "target date funds," "lifecycle funds," and other products that adjust the asset mix for the participant's age or time to retirement — originates with Merton (1969) and Bodie, Merton, and Samuelson (1992). The framing of "hope" in contrast to prudent and responsible investment solutions comes from Brent Harris at PIMCO in his 2009 Project M essay entitled "Hope Is Not A Retirement Strategy" (Harris [2009].) (Project M was a service of Allianz Global Investors; unfortunately the service, and the article, are no longer available.)

income lasting for the rest of one's life can be generated from an asset pool.[169]

DB plans can make adjustments over time when its estimates are off due to economic events that materially change the value of the promises (the liability) or of the matching assets. They can do this by increasing pension contributions and lowering profits, decreasing future compensation and benefits, or both. But this flexibility is not limited to DB plans! Individuals also have the ability to make adjustments, and they do this all the time. We call this concept a personal fiscal adjustment, or PFA, regarding it as the "dark matter" that, over time, enables resources needed to be made equal to resources available.

Personal fiscal adjustments — decisions to increase or decrease consumption or production, or to shift the time period in which consumption or production occurs — will be made as surprises arrive. For example, in an extreme case, personal fiscal adjustment can include moving in with family (typically children, the millennia-old retirement plan). It can also include working almost full time in "retirement." The key point is that people can and do make the required adjustments to match needs and resources. This is the same thing that DB-plan sponsors do: they adjust to changing circumstances, by contributing more to the plan, taking a contribution holiday, or renegotiating benefits.

The retirement decision-making framework set forth in this essay is usable by the vast majority of the U.S. working population. Those in, say, the top 7% or so when ranked by income (or assets) can afford professional financial planning and often have access to institutional-quality investment management. While our approach applies to the top 7%, many of these investors are already doing fine and need little additional help.[170] Our goal is to bring the needed technologies and resources to everyone, especially the other 93%.[171]

---

[169] See also Totten and Siegel (2019), written after this article and, unfortunately, not available for reprint in this book. A draft circulated by AJO is at https://larrysiegel.org/combining-conventional-investing-with-a-lifetime-income-guarantee-a-blueprint-for-retirement-security/. Totten and Siegel incorporate equities into the pension-promise-to-oneself framework.

[170] We don't want to overstate the quality of investment decisions made by the affluent. Many such investors have concentrated positions, large equity allocations at an advanced age, fat fee arrangements, and other portfolio quirks. One of us has a neighbor, whose assets are in seven figures, who says that she lost half her money in the crash of 2008 — in money market funds. She is not alone in confusing money market funds with stock funds, and at any rate has no business being mostly in stock funds at her age (sixty-something). No investment professional who has heard this story is the least bit surprised by it.

[171] Typically those in the fifth (bottom) quintile of income find that their post-retirement income needs are for the most part met by Social Security. But even these individuals will be helped by the framework we are setting forth. It provides a purpose for savings, a structure that works, and they may place great value on even a modest addition to Social Security payments if it is reliably always

Why Is This So Hard? Why Are There Failures?

In part because we have been conditioned by employer-provided pensions to think narrowly about the retirement question, and in part because there is much lazy or misleading writing about the topic even among those who recognize that employer-provided pensions are a rarity, most thinking about pensions and retirement savings is anchored in a static and oversimplified world. In this world, people work from age 20 to 65, and then magically transition to a state called "retirement" wherein they live for another 20 to 40 years with a minimal, or at worst a modest, drop in consumption.

Let's see how many holes we can find in this story without filling an encyclopedia. When was the last time you met a 20-year-old who was working at what would become his or her life occupation? Who works for 45 years without quitting, getting fired, or becoming ill or disabled? Don't quite a few people these days live to 100 or 105, potentially making a mockery of the idea that saving for 20 or 30 years of retirement is adequate? Don't some people run up medical bills in the hundreds of thousands of dollars? Aren't we all afraid that we'll end up in a nursing home?

OK, enough doom and gloom. Let's look on the bright side. Don't quite a few people experience lucrative careers and comfortable retirements, either through a series of promotions or career changes, or through successful saving and investing, or both? Don't most people, when setbacks arrive, adjust and go forward, some even being prudently prepared with low-cost but valuable disability insurance? Are not many employers careful and responsible, offering a prudent combination of current wages and future income, *and* fully funding the pension promises; or, if they offer a DC plan, do they not work with employees to help them accumulate a DC plan balance that is at least adequate? What might we learn from the success stories that can be used to build the toolkit for everyone?

The retirement problem — what we propose to help solve through a pension promise to oneself — needs to be understood as follows. We are trying to distribute the income from one's work years over one's whole life. Life is long and getting longer, and work years are short (due to increasing educational requirements at the beginning as well as the desire for a long and comfortable retirement at the end). We face the unprecedented challenge of dealing with 80 or

---

there. The high adoption rate of the Save-More-Tomorrow[tm] program developed by Thaler and Benartzi (2004), where future raises are saved, indicates that a Pension Promise to Oneself can work for all income levels.

more years of uncertainty, beginning as one reaches adulthood and potentially ending as late as age 105. Yet we are charged with creating some sense of certainty or security in old age, which we define as the part of life when the option to materially change one's financial well-being through work is mostly gone, and which could last for 40 of those 80 or more years.

No wonder retirement planning seems hard! We are now going to make it very simple. Like dieting, however, it is simple to understand but not easy to do, because it involves saving a very large fraction of income.

The Personal Pension Plan: Simplicity Is Paramount

The most important principle in building a framework, a personal pension plan, is to keep it simple. K-I-S-S. It is hard to generalize about human beings, but it's a pretty safe bet that nurses, airplane mechanics, lawyers, and restaurant workers are not crying out to become experts in portfolio theory. In our experience, many investors do not fully grasp the difference between a stock and a bond, much less the difference between an expected return and a return one can count on. Even experienced investment professionals suffer from an illusion of precision regarding return expectations, overweighting the likelihood of attaining the expected return and materially underestimating the variance of real-life outcomes. We write this not to be demeaning but to be realistic: a complex strategy involving fancy math and beautiful statistical simulations simply will not be widely adopted, or else it will be adopted incorrectly and hurt the investor.

There is an additional reason to keep the pension promise simple: In the mid-to-late retirement years our cognitive skills leave us, and do so at an increasing rate. So, you do not want to match this almost assured fall in clear thinking with a retirement plan full of complexity and risk taking. It should be simple, and as we get older it should become more automatic.

What Is the Personal Pension Plan?

Thus the Personal Pension Plan that we set forth in this essay is strikingly, even childishly, elementary:

1. We determine the income stream that the investor will need in retirement; that's the liability. It can be as simple as an educated guess, a rule of thumb such as 70% of what I am earning today. We then subtract

expected Social Security payments to determine the yearly amount the investor will have to generate from personal savings.

2. We then determine the *multiple* of that number that the saver needs to accumulate (this number is called the retirement multiple), and

3. We determine a savings rate that will produce that amount of money when invested in low-risk assets.[172]

That's all. We're done. It comes down to two numbers: how much income I would like in retirement, and the retirement multiple. Investing for retirement really is that simple.

The Personal Fiscal Adjustment or PFA

OK, we're not *quite* done. We noted earlier that all successful DB plans adjust to changing circumstances. We also said that DB and DC plans involve the same thinking and essentially the same operational steps. We now discuss what individual people, including DC plan participants, do to adapt to changing circumstances. When such an adaptation relates to one's financial affairs we call it a "personal fiscal adjustment," PFA, in homage to the currently popular term, "fiscal adjustment," used to describe similar behavior by governments. Thus, when either the asset or the liability side of the investor's balance sheet changes in an unexpected way, he or she undertakes a PFA to bring it back into balance.

Continuous adaptation to changing circumstances is a good start at fixing what's wrong with any financial arrangement. If DB pension plans had reacted to poor market returns and rising liabilities by upping contributions and limiting the growth of benefits, they'd still be the dominant retirement program. The PFA is the most natural behavior imaginable and we see it in every aspect of life. When you have less, spend less. When you have more, you can spend more or save more, with the tradeoff between current and future consumption determined by the usual factors — the extent to which one's liability is unfunded, the attractiveness of various investment options, and so forth.

Let's apply the PFA to managing DC plans. Without such adaptive behavior, the

---

[172] All this has to be done on an after-tax basis. Taxes are typically lower in retirement than before retirement, not just because the tax bracket is likely to be lower but because retirement income is not subject to the payroll tax. In addition, in some states retirement income is untaxed while labor income is taxed.

pension promise to oneself is almost doomed; with it, the promise can be kept, in most cases easily.

Why is the PFA so crucial to success? Human life is far too long, too uncertain, and too leptokurtic for the standard finance models to apply. ("Leptokurtic" means fat-tailed, with the left, or downside, tail the troublesome one; you might get a bonus equal to 10% or 20% of salary, but when you lose your job, you lose the whole job, not 10% or 20% of it.) One of us heard Paul Samuelson, the originator of much of the standard model, say, at a conference, "Assume that a school teacher saves $10,000 a year for 50 years." (This was some years ago, when the price level was lower.) Where we live, school teachers have to retire at 66 so this imaginary teacher must have started working at age 16 — and she must be a genius, since school teachers are also required to have a college degree. This particular rendition of the standard model does not account for marriage, children, strikes, layoffs, illness, disability, the desire not to do the same thing for 50 years, or for that matter good fortune (her husband succeeds in business and she no longer wants or has to work).

Investment planning must conform to reality, not pretend that reality can be forced to conform to the model. The real, flesh-and-blood version of Samuelson's idealized schoolteacher-saver makes PFAs all the time, in all aspects of her life.

PFAs differ between the short and the long run. In the short run, the main adjustment is to consumption. In the long run, however, one can work harder, increase the number of workers in the family, work smarter (by pursuing strategies to enhance one's human capital), or plan to work longer. Large changes in one's consumption plans can be accomplished by relocating, moving in with relatives, and through other means.[173] People are far more dynamic and adaptive than any planner thinks they are!

Everyone makes PFAs at some point. Some do this throughout their lifetime, some only when a crisis begins to be perceived around age 50 or 55. Our objective is to encourage PFAs sooner in life — not waiting until the crisis — and to make PFAs better thought-out and better executed.

The concept of the PFA enables us to understand how anyone gets by at all in a

---

[173] For example, families can pool, or share, their resources. The co-housing movement is a baby step in that direction. While thinking about these possibilities, it's occurred to us that the vast amount of perfectly serviceable housing in every well-preserved working-class neighborhood in the country is a resource crying out to be used by retirees who need a safe, pleasant environment but who place little value on school systems and other amenities that drive housing prices upward.

world where DB pension plans are failing and DC plan participants are saving way too little and investing poorly. The answer is that people make do with available resources, and sometimes make more resources available. They muddle through. They do what has distinguished the human species since it began its time on earth: they adapt.

A lot of energy is going into looking for bulletproof systems and turn-key solutions that will make retirement "work" without the ability to make ongoing adjustments. There aren't any. The retirement establishment acknowledges this *by calculating the probability of failure*. Most income solutions are framed exactly this way, as though failure were an acceptable outcome. We know that an adult lifetime can encompass 80 years, which is such a long time that forecasts are almost completely useless. However, what we always do have is the ability to make adjustments, adapt, and go forward. This is an invariant component of human behavior and is the hidden option on the personal balance sheet that keeps it in balance, thus making the Personal Pension Plan work when other methods do not.

The Retirement Multiple

The Retirement Multiple, or RM, figures prominently in the Personal Pension Plan. What is it? It's the number of years' income you need to save, where "income" is not your current pay but the amount of income you need to generate, over and above Social Security benefits, in retirement. This simple heuristic reduces the retirement calculation to a multiplication problem that a fifth grader can solve. For most investors, the RM itself will have to be provided externally, that is, by a data provider who calculates the relevant RM based on interest rates and other market data.

The Investment Return Assumption

Our simplified method assumes that you invest at the riskless rate and use longevity pooling so that retirement savings only need to last to a certain age, say 85. This rate can be calculated as a blend of the TIPS yield, covering the first 20 years of retirement, and an average of deferred annuity rates, covering the rest

of retirement. Unfortunately these rates are now extremely close to zero in real (inflation-adjusted) terms. We expect them to rise in the future.[174]

The DCDB strategy assumes that you actually hold 100% of the amount needed for consumption between ages 65 and 85 in a laddered portfolio of TIPS bonds, with an additional amount reserved for purchase of a deferred life annuity. The portfolio pays out inflation-indexed principal and interest until the age of 85. After 85 the annuity pays a fixed annual payment that is not inflation protected. While almost no one invests this way, and we are not suggesting that you do, we are using the almost-riskless-rate strategy as a base case, which can also be understood as a benchmark (measuring stick) by which the investor can gauge her progress in a riskier strategy. An investor who wants to avoid as much risk as possible does have the option to create a DCDB portfolio, demonstrating a key point: the strategy should be, and is, executable by a typical investor using standard investments.

Suppose you do want to take investment risk? Let's confine this discussion to risk-taking before retirement, and investing risklessly to generate income afterward. (Since by definition you cannot work longer or save more if you are truly retired, the only PFA that is available if post-retirement risk doesn't work out is to cut consumption, an uncomfortable decision.) With a risky pre-retirement portfolio, *you still need the same amount of money upon retiring as with a riskless one,* but accumulating it may require less saving. Specifically, the expected value of the amount you should plan to save is lower in each period, but instead of being able to map out the entire savings schedule in advance, you have to adjust it in each period for realizations (the difference between the return you achieved and the return you expected or planned for).

As we said earlier, DB and DC plans face the same underlying dynamic. You can only get out what you put in, plus market returns. Most DB plan failures have occurred because the sponsor took risk (with the beneficiaries' deferred wages) and were unprepared for shortfall risk at a scale that overwhelmed the sponsor's ability or willingness to pay up the difference.[175] DC failures happen the

---

[174] The real rate has gone negative since this article was originally written. Sorry, we're lousy interest-rate forecasters. There is a body of so-called natural rate theory that attempts to say what riskless interest rates would be, on average over the long term, in the absence of Fed intervention and other distortions to markets. One estimate is that it should be equal to the long-run compound annual rate of productivity growth. While very long-term data for productivity growth do not exist, it is well proxied by per capita GDP growth, which has been 1.8% in the U.S. over 1790-2019. But it could be a long wait before real rate rise to 1.8%.

[175] There is a long and well documented history of pension failures. As recently as 2012, a federal bankruptcy court ruled that the bankrupt city of Central Falls, Rhode Island could decrease its pension payments to police and fire retirees, some by as much as 50%. Central Falls both overpromised — allowing full retirement after twenty years of work — and underfunded those promises.

same way.

Therefore we use a riskless rate as the investment assumption in the accumulation period because we need a clean reference point. We realize that, in practice, investors will choose other portfolios. Now, let's look at our two variables, how much retirement income do I want and what is the Retirement Multiple, using an example.

The Columbus Teacher's Pension Promise to Himself: A Numerical Example

We consider a public high school teacher in a large U.S. city (Columbus, Ohio, because as of 2013 it was one of the largest cities that offered either a DB or DC plan at the employee's choice) to be the prototype for a middle-income worker.[176] Let's say our teacher is early in his career and is earning $37,328 per year.[177] We need our teacher to do three things: First, take a guess at what he will want for retirement income. One easy way is to look at what senior

---

This combination, of overpromising and underfunding, goes back a long time. For example, on March 28, 1980, after 75 years of making steel for International Harvester tractors and equipment, Wisconsin Steel closed its doors and 3,400 steel workers lost their jobs. On May 31, 1980, the steelworkers' pension plan ended in "termination." On December 31, 1981, the Pension Benefit Guarantee Corporation (PBGC) assumed responsibility for the plan, with a maximum monthly pension payment of $1,261 for those age 65, well below the pension promises made by the now-defunct Wisconsin Steel.

In contrast, just a few miles away, the fully funded pension plan of Inland Steel (now part of ArcelorMittal) is still making full pension payments. While employment at both companies shrank dramatically after the 1979-1980 recession and productivity-driven recovery, Inland had fully funded its pension plan. In 1998, when Inland Steel was purchased by Ispat International N.V., the fair value of its pension assets was $1,991 million and its projected benefits obligation (PBO), a measure of the liability, was $1,967 million. Equally important, Inland made the decision to immunize its liabilities by buying U.S. Treasury bonds that matched its expected future pension payments. Hence, Inland made the funding of its pension promise to its workers independent of Inland's future economic prospects or the prospects of the returns from higher risk-return assets.

[176] Only Alaska and the District of Columbia have DC-only retirement plans for teachers, and these two jurisdictions are too unrepresentative to use in a general example. Ohio, Florida, and South Carolina allow teachers to select either a DB or DC plan. Ohio is close to the national average in a large number of demographic and economic dimensions, and Columbus is Ohio's largest city (incorporated city, not metropolitan area). This information was correct in 2013 when this article was written.

[177] We proxy the salary of the beginning teacher using the 10th percentile salary for Columbus high school teachers, that of the mid-career teacher (with 20 years' experience) with the 75th percentile salary, and that of the about-to-retire teacher (with 40 years' experience and a master's degree) with the 90th percentile. It is appropriate to use a well above median salary for the mid-career teacher because the teacher population is skewed toward short service (that is, many young teachers drop out of the profession). Data are in 2011 dollars and are were accessed on January 8, 2013.

colleagues earn, say a teacher who is about to retire with 40 years' experience and a master's degree, which for the city of Columbus is $79,904, and multiply by a number, say 70%, representing the percentage of pre-retirement income that he will need in retirement. For our Columbus teacher, this would be $55,933.[178] Of this amount, Social Security will provide $24,912, so he will have to generate the difference, $31,021, from savings and investments.[179]

The second step is to apply the market-based Retirement Multiple to the annual retirement income

number. The Retirement Multiple is based on the real returns on low-risk investments that exist in the market at that point in time. We use the DCDB rate, which is currently 4.657%.[180] The multiple is thus or (rounding) 21.5.

$$\frac{1}{DCDB\ rate} = 21.47$$

The required savings amount, or savings target, is the expected or target

[178] The entire analysis is in 2011 dollars, meaning that the teacher could expect inflation-related increases beyond the increase from $37,328 to $79,904 — and that retirement income requirements will increase correspondingly. In addition, bringing the analysis up to date by restating the amounts in 2019-2021 dollars would increase all the numbers by about 16%. A retirement income replacement ratio of 70% is considered low by some commentators but is entirely consistent with the requirement to save more than 30% of late-career income; someone who can live on less than 70% of income before retiring can live on 70% of the same number when retired.

[179] The Social Security quick calculator was accessed at http://www.socialsecurity.gov/OACT/quickcalc/index.html on February 23, 2013. Because of the quirks of the Social Security quick calculator, we use inputs that reflect a 65-year-old with the following characteristics: date of birth 12/31/1948, date of retirement 12/2013, and "current" pay equal to our worker's final pay.
     The quick calculator then backfills prior earnings using various assumptions, including wage growth 2 percentage points faster than the national average; because the backfill starts with final pay and works back in time, fast wage growth means low pay in earlier years. We override this default input with a wage growth rate equal to the national average, in other words a excess-over-the-average wage growth rate of 0.
     While the workers in our example have specific wage growth rates that differ from one another, the output of the Social Security quick calculator is unpredictable and, for this particular purpose, it is better to use a single wage growth rate for all worker categories. The calculator is particularly inaccurate for high income earners, whose year-by-year wages are backfilled as if final pay were equal to the Social Security withholding maximum, which was $113,700 in 2013; thus early-year wages are higher in fact than in our examples, and the Social Security benefit for high earners, likewise, will be higher in fact than in our examples unless benefits are cut in the future.

[180] 2013 data.

retirement income times the Retirement Multiple.[181] This, then, $21.47 \times \$31,021 = \$666,111$, is the savings goal.

The third step is to spread the required savings amount (net of already accumulated balances) over the remaining years of work. For our teacher, we assume that he is 25 years old and will work for 40 years, through age 65.[182]

That's it. From here our young teacher will behave as an experienced and practiced Bayesian. As time goes on and more information unfolds — updated needs or desires, wage levels, asset levels, and so forth — our teacher will simply adjust the retirement income number, something that can be done without computers, models, or simulations. While the specific amounts will be updated over time as conditions change, the power of the approach is that it's a simple rule that (1) works and (2) allows people to compress 40 to 80 years of dynamic complexity into something that they can manage and understand. In table form, it looks like this:

Exhibit 14.1 Retirement planning basics for Columbus high school teacher (based on minimum-risk investing)

Initial salary	$37,328
20th year salary	$68,897
Final (40th year) salary	$79,904
Retirement income replacement ratio	70%
Retirement income goal	$55,933
Expected Social Security	$24,912
Personal Pension Plan income	$31,021
Retirement Multiple	21.47
Lifetime savings accumulation goal	$666,111

Our teacher's goal for accumulated savings, $666,111, is a pretty good slug of cash. Shocked by these numbers? Think they are unrealistic? Maybe unattainable? Well, they are reality. They are what a DB plan would need to save, on the

[181] The DCDB rate is a blended low-risk rate (as close to the riskless rate as practical), consisting of (1) the nominal interest rate on a portfolio of laddered Treasury Inflation-Protected Securities (TIPS) held to match cash flow requirements for the first 20 years of retirement, and (2) the implied interest rate on a nominal deferred annuity that begins its payout in the 21st year of retirement and continues until the retiree's death. See Sexauer, Cassidy, and Peskin (2012).

[182] We assume that the worker retires at age 65, earlier than the Social Security full-benefit retirement age. This is for two reasons: (1) it makes the math easier, since the DCDB rate of return (for post-retirement investing at the lowest achievable level of risk) assumes retirement at age 65; and (2) retirement at age 65 or even earlier has become customary, even though benefits are somewhat reduced.

employee's behalf, if it didn't accept shortfall risk by investing in equities and other risky assets. And because the calculation is transparent and easy, both the goal and the reality are clear — one either saves the amount shown, or one makes a personal fiscal adjustment and decreases expectations for retirement income.

The Retirement Multiple heuristic is powerful. It informs and shapes behavior. Basic economic theory teaches us that knowledge and incentives are two of the most powerful forces in human behavior. Behavioral finance teaches us the importance and power of framing. A pension promise to oneself is a toolkit with the knowledge, incentives, and framing for making a lifelong series of high-utility decisions about one's retirement.

We also believe that the economics "work," even with such a high required savings rate. Remember that if the goal could have been attained in a DB plan by the employer withholding the money from the employee and investing it on his behalf, then it's attainable by the individual making a pension promise to himself.

Let's look at an example of both the overall savings level and the pattern of change in the savings level over time that gets to the goal of a pension promise to oneself. Note three things. First, the growth in human capital and the associated higher wages is explicit: if wages grow from $37,328 to $68,897 over the first 20 years of the teacher's career, that is a growth rate of 3.11% per year. Second, to meet the savings goal, we apply a key successful concept from behavioral finance, called auto-escalation: our teacher saves a large portion, 52%, of the real (inflation-adjusted) portion of his *raises*. Third, the expected return is what can be earned in risk-free inflation-indexed bonds, which today is effectively zero.[183] Given a starting savings rate of 10%, here is what the accumulation plan looks like.

---

[183] In this example, we assume that the real riskless rate of return is exactly zero. We recognize that our teacher's life may not be smooth like these assumptions, and that rates of income growth will change over time. But what matters here is the basic framework, a framework that works and that provides a usable frame of reference for making savings, investment, and consumption decisions as circumstances change.

Exhibit 14.2 Asset accumulation plan for Columbus high school teacher
(based on minimum-risk investing)

Number of work years	40
Real investment returns	0.00%
Human capital growth (years 0-20)	3.11%
Human capital growth (years 21-40	0.74%
Human capital growth (whole period)	1.92%
Initial savings rate	10.00%
Percentage of raise saved	52%
Savings goal	$666,111
Total saved under accumulation plan	$666,419

Year	Income	Savings rate	Annual savings	Accumulated savings
1	37,328	10.0%	3,733	3,733
2	38,490	11.3%	4,333	8,066
3	39,687	12.5%	4,951	13,017
4	40,922	13.7%	5,589	18,606
5	42,196	14.8%	6,247	24,853
6	43,509	15.9%	6,925	31,778
7	44,863	17.0%	7,624	39,403
8	46,259	18.0%	8,345	47,748
9	47,698	19.1%	9,089	56,837
10	49,182	20.0%	9,856	66,693
11	50,713	21.0%	10,646	77,339
12	52,291	21.9%	11,461	88,800
13	53,918	22.8%	12,302	101,101
14	55,596	23.7%	13,168	114,269
15	57,326	24.5%	14,062	128,331
16	59,110	25.3%	14,983	143,314
17	60,949	26.1%	15,933	159,247
18	62,846	26.9%	16,913	176,160
19	64,801	27.7%	17,923	194,083
20	66,818	28.4%	18,964	213,047
21	68,897	29.1%	20,038	233,085
22	69,409	29.3%	20,303	253,388
23	69,926	29.4%	20,570	273,958
24	70,446	29.6%	20,838	294,796
25	70,970	29.7%	21,109	315,905
26	71,498	29.9%	21,381	337,286
27	72,030	30.1%	21,656	358,942
28	72,565	30.2%	21,933	380,875
29	73,105	30.4%	22,212	403,087
30	73,649	30.5%	22,493	425,579
31	74,197	30.7%	22,775	448,355
32	74,749	30.9%	23,061	471,415
33	75,305	31.0%	23,348	494,763
34	75,865	31.2%	23,637	518,400
35	76,429	31.3%	23,928	542,328
36	76,997	31.5%	24,222	566,551
37	77,570	31.6%	24,518	591,068
38	78,147	31.8%	24,816	615,884
39	78,728	31.9%	25,116	641,001
40	79,314	32.0%	25,419	666,419

Our teacher thus begins his career saving only 10% of income, but by the 20th year he is saving 28% of income, and by the 40th year, a robust 32%. While these savings rates and levels appear high, even unattainable, we have evidence that large increases in saving can be achieved. One of the biggest and most encouraging revolutions in DC plans has been the success of the Save More Tomorrow[tm] (SMarT) program introduced by Thaler and Benartzi (2004). Exhibit 14.3 shows the large success of this program at a Midwest manufacturing company. When a DC plan has the right structures and incentives, people can and do save more.

Exhibit 14.3 Effectiveness of Auto-Escalation Plan

Increases in Savings Rates from Adoption of Save More Tomorrow™
at a Midwest U.S. Manufacturing Company over 1998-2002

Source: Thaler and Benartzi (2004), Table 2, page S174.

Before SMarT was introduced, the savings rate was low and the strong belief of both the employees and the company was that at the employees' (generally low) income levels they did not have the ability to save more. Clearly this was not the case: People can and do save more when the information, structures, and incentives to do so exist. The data in Exhibit 14.3 show that adoption of SMarT can boost savings rates into a realistic range for the first part of an employee's pension promise to himself. Whether, over decades, SMarT can achieve the savings rates upwards of 30% that are required in the later years remains to be seen, but the early-year results suggest that it can.

We have been conservative and strict with our assumptions, including the use of today's real risk-free rate of zero instead of a long-term average rate, which is positive. These assumptions establish a base case to build upon. We believe the risk-free rate is likely to be positive in the future.[184]

We also know that most investors will wish to take shortfall risk (say, by holding

---

[184] We warned you once already: we're terrible forecasters.

equities) to *try to* reduce the savings burden; if the risk does not pay off, the investor has increased rather than reduced the burden, but the expectation is to reduce it. The calculations can be adjusted to reflect these variations on our base-case theme of essentially riskless investing.

Investing in Risky Assets During the Accumulation Phase

Here is an example where our teacher is willing to accept shortfall risk by investing during his working years to earn an expected real return of 2%. We start with the same retirement income goal and expected Social Security benefit as before, and thus the same income goal from the Personal Pension Plan, $31,189. We still use the DCDB rate — a version of the real riskless rate — to discount the post-retirement liability because we assume that our teacher will want to invest risklessly to generate income *after* retirement. We thus arrive at the same savings goal, $666,111.

While saving during his working years, however, the teacher takes risk and expects to earn a real rate of 2%, changing the savings schedule. If the 2% annual real returns were spread evenly over time, only 27% of the real part of raises would need to be saved, and the savings rate (savings as a percentage of income) climbs less steeply, to 20% by the 20th year and 22% by the 40th year. Thus the 2% real investment return assumption makes the accumulation plan much easier and provides a big boost to consumption during the teacher's working years. The accumulation plan at a 2% real return in the accumulation period is in Exhibit 14.4.

But what is the downside? Because the 2% real rate is a risky rate, the return might not be realized. Any investment disappointments would have to be met with a PFA — either an increase in the savings rate or a decrease in post-retirement consumption.[185] The PFA will be large if market returns are much less than expected.

---

[185] If we knew that riskless rates would be higher than zero, say 2%, in the retirement years, foreknowledge of that would raise the DCDB yield, reduce the Retirement Multiple, and thus reduce the savings requirement. (The historical real riskless rate is about 2%.) Being able to invest at higher-than-zero real riskless rates during the accumulation phase would also improve the picture.

It is important to amplify a key point that we made regarding the Retirement Multiple: Investing in risky assets during one's working years, and consequently hoping for higher investment returns, does not change the savings goal! It just changes the amount that needs to be saved each year in order to be targeted to the goal, with the understanding that one might not achieve the goal unless one adjusts the savings rate for investment results. The RM is based on riskless investing in retirement, when personal fiscal adjustments are more difficult to implement (because one big lever, the opportunity for additional savings, has been removed). We also note that, even with a 2% real return assumption, achieving

Exhibit 14.4 Asset accumulation plan for Columbus high school teacher at real 2% investment return in accumulation period (some years omitted)

Number of work years	40
Real investment returns	2.00%
Human capital growth (years 0-20)	3.11%
Human capital growth (years 21-40	0.74%
Human capital growth (whole period)	1.92%
Initial savings rate	10.00%
Percentage of raise saved	33%
Savings goal	$666,111
Total saved under accumulation plan	$666,783

Year	Income	Savings rate	Annual savings	Accumulated savings
1	37,328	10.0%	3,733	3,733
2	38,490	10.7%	4,118	7,926
3	39,687	11.4%	4,516	12,600
4	40,922	12.0%	4,926	17,779
5	42,196	12.7%	5,349	23,483
10	49,182	15.6%	7,668	60,761
15	57,326	18.1%	10,372	115,148
20	66,818	20.2%	13,523	190,617
25	70,970	21.0%	14,902	286,173
30	73,649	21.4%	15,791	396,235
35	76,429	21.9%	16,714	522,484
36	76,997	22.0%	16,903	549,837
37	77,570	22.0%	17,093	577,927
38	78,147	22.1%	17,285	606,770
39	78,728	22.2%	17,478	636,383
40	79,314	22.3%	17,672	666,783

the savings goal requires a much higher savings rate than most investors ever achieve. This shows one of our major points: To spread the income from 40 years of work over up to 80 years of consumption takes a lot of savings indeed.

If it is surprising just *how* high the required savings rate is, consider the following: you are trying to work for half of the years in which you're likely to be consuming. At a zero real return and with no help from Social Security or from a lower standard-of-living expectation in retirement, you'd have to save half your income. One more time, just for fun: *save half your income.* Acknowledging that it's very difficult to save half one's income, we should obviously try to get that number down, through annuitization, positive investment returns, PFAs, and anything else that helps.

There exist many variations of these plans, or calculations. Our teacher could save less early on and then more during peak earning years, years when household expenses can be falling. It is beyond our objective in this paper to analyze individual savings plans. Rather, it has been our purpose to provide a framework, a tool kit, to make and keep a pension promise to oneself — a promise that is doable with a low risk of failure, allows for pension payments to yourself from the moment of retirement until the end of life, and can be used to assess and measure the value (utility) higher-risk, higher-return, strategies.

There are many career and income paths one can take, with our teacher representing a relatively successful middle-income earner. Appendices B and C, omitted from this book and available on the Web at https://larrysiegeldotorg.files.wordpress.com/2013/12/siegel_sexauer_a-pension-promise.pdf, show the retirement planning basics and accumulation plan for two other prototypical workers: (1) a San Diego sanitation worker, earning a lower middle income and experiencing limited human capital growth; and (2) a software developer in Austin, whose human capital grows rapidly and who achieves an upper middle income later in her career, as she grows into a management position.

Summary

We have shown that an individual saving for retirement is not facing a hopeless task. Far from it — defined benefit pension plans, equipped with the same underlying resources, have been able to provide the same required level of retirement income for generations, by understanding a basic set of rules for deciding how much to save and how to invest, and then sticking to the rules. When DB plans have failed, it's because, in the hope of not having to pay the true cost of the retirement benefit, they've broken the rules. The same applies to an individual.

Fulfilling a pension promise to oneself requires a lot of saving, more than most people are accustomed to. When one thinks about spending only, say, 70% of income, and saving the rest, it's necessary to ask: "Are there other people who make 70% of what I do, who have perfectly fine lives? What are their consumption patterns?" If the answer is, "No," you should try to improve your human capital position (that is, your income). If the answer is, "Yes," you can make and keep a pension promise to yourself.

The State of Ohio, which sponsors the teacher's savings plan that we used in our main example, implicitly recognizes the high savings rate needed for a pension promise to oneself by setting a starting savings rate of 20% for teachers entering the DC plan. Of this amount, 10 percentage points are contributed by the employer and 10 percentage points by the employee. Thus, the true or economic salary is 10% larger than the headline salary, and the total savings rate is slightly less than 20% (it is 20/110 or 18.2%). We left this wrinkle out of the example because we did not think it was necessary to mention it to make our point. While 20% is not enough as a career average savings rate, it is a great start, while the tiny 6% to 9% rates often seen in employee benefit programs are not even in the right ball park, and will lead to penury in the employees' old age unless supplemented by massive (and tax-disfavored) additional personal savings.

We have also indicated that people can increase their savings rates greatly — by amounts large enough to matter in the present context — through agreements such as Save More Tomorrow™. This is not just an idle speculation. They have already done so in an impressive and growing number of work environments.

Presumably our employees mean enough to us, in terms of the output they produce and the profits they help us generate, that we want them to be enthusiastic and satisfied workers who do not lose sleep over how they can possibly survive in old age. The procedure that people need to follow in order to generate an adequate retirement income exists, and we already know what it is. We owe it to our valued employees to tell them about the procedure, and to help them implement it.

REFERENCES

Bodie, Zvi, Robert C. Merton, and William Samuelson. 1992. "Labor Supply Flexibility and Portfolio Choice in a Life-Cycle Model." *Journal of Economic Dynamics & Control,* vol. 16, nos. 3-4 (July–October): pp. 427–449.

Harris, Brent M. 2009. "Hope is Not an Investment Strategy." *Project M* (September), accessed on February 16, 2013. No longer available.

Merton, Robert C. 1969. "Lifetime Portfolio Selection under Uncertainty: The Continuous-Time Case." *Review of Economics and Statistics,* 51, no.3 (August): 247-257

Munnell, Alicia. 2012. "401(k) Plans in 2010: An Update From The SCF." Center for Retirement Research at Boston College, *Issue Brief* No. 12-13 (July 10).

Samuelson, Paul A. 1969. "Lifetime Portfolio Selection by Dynamic Stochastic Programming." *Review of Economics and Statistics,* 51, no. 3 (August): 239-246.

Sexauer, Stephen C., Michael W. Peskin, and Daniel P. Cassidy. 2012. "Making Retirement Income Last a Lifetime." *Financial Analysts Journal,* vol. 68, no. 1 (January/February).

Thaler, Richard H., and Shlomo Benartzi. 2004. "Save More Tomorrow: Using Behavioral Economics to Increase Employee Saving. *Journal of Political Economy,* vol. 112, no. 1 (February), part 2, pp. S164-S187.

Totten, Thomas L., and Laurence B. Siegel. 2019. "Combining Conventional Investing with a Lifetime Income Guarantee: A Blueprint for Retirement Security." *Journal of Retirement*, Spring 2019, Volume 6, Issue 4 (Spring), pp. 45-59.

Waring, M. Barton, Laurence B. Siegel, and Timothy Kohn. 2007. "Wake Up and Smell the Coffee: DC Plans Aren't Working – Here's How to Fix Them." *Journal of Investing* (Winter).

Money

The price (value) of money is controlled or manipulated by the Federal Reserve System, and by market forces. Congress has directed the Fed to conduct the nation's monetary policy to support three specific goals: maximum sustainable employment, stable prices, and moderate long-term interest rates.

Several problem areas are evident: the three goals are not always in synch, and the tools available are not always effective. Also, Fed policy is influenced by political and social trends that override the stated objectives.

As Claudio Borio, who runs the economic research department for the Bank for International Settlements, laments, "The problem is that politicians have come to rely too heavily on the central banks to stimulate growth since the crisis." Borio describes the institutions as overburdened. "At the same time, central banks are constrained by economic theories that offer little meaningful guidance for how to simulate growth and financial stability." [186]

Wayne's personal favorite: Phooey on Financial Repression
                                            —WHW

---

[186] "Why Central Bankers Missed the Crisis," by Joseph C. Sternberg. Wall Street Journal, November 17-18, 2018.

Chapter 15. Phooey on Financial Repression

Laurence B. Siegel and Thomas S. Coleman[187] [188]

September 2015

Should the Fed raise interest rates? Are ultra-low interest rates good for investors because they drive up the prices of stocks and real estate, fattening household balance sheets? Or are zero rates an insidious tax, rearranging the terms of trade between borrowers and lenders, as well as between individuals and government, and making investors poorer over time?

We think the latter. Zero interest rates — which translate to negative real interest rates after inflation is subtracted — are a massive transfer of wealth from investors to governments and other borrowers around the world. We'll show that the scale of the transfer is nearly $1 trillion per year in the United States alone, and will argue that the zero-interest-rate policy lowers expected returns on stocks and real estate as well.

In the end, low interest rates hurt more than just investors. They hurt almost everyone because they distort consumption and investment decisions, potentially causing economic growth to be slower than it otherwise would be. Initially, in 2008-2009, low interest rates were an element or consequence of a policy of liquidity injection needed to avoid a serious depression. Since then, however, they have become a tool of stimulative macro policy, with limited success. They are disastrous as an ongoing strategy.

In 1973, the economists Ronald McKinnon and Edward Shaw, looking back on the post-World War II period, described the policies of those times as *financial*

---

[187] This article was published under the title "The Hidden Cost of Zero Interest Rate Policies" in *Advisor Perspectives* on September 29, 2015.

[188] Thomas S. Coleman is executive director of the Center for Economic Policy at the Harris School of Public Policy, University of Chicago. The authors may be reached at lbsiegel@uchicago.edu and tscoleman@uchicago.edu.

repression.[189] Inflation was high and accelerating, while interest rates lagged behind. Thus, while the real economy grew strongly, savers and bondholders were devastated. The resulting "capital strike" was one of the reasons that we subsequently experienced a decade of high inflation and high unemployment.

Some current commentators, including the celebrated economist Carmen Reinhart, say that financial repression has returned.[190] But today's version of financial repression is different from that of the postwar period. The voting public will no longer allow governments to inflate away their debt wholesale with bouts of high and unexpected inflation. But low inflation with even lower nominal rates will accomplish much the same over time, by not paying the interest needed to compensate for inflation.

Negative real interest rates are a nefarious tax, punishing savers and depriving the economy of one of its primary sources of income. John Maynard Keynes's words from 1919 still ring true: "By a continuing process of inflation, governments can confiscate, secretly and unobserved, an important part of the wealth of their citizens... [W]hile the process impoverishes many, it actually enriches some."[191] Inflation and financial repression are not very different and have the same effect on real wealth and real investment income.

Every price paid by someone is also a price received by someone. So, when borrowers pay artificially low interest rates, someone else, whom we'd typically call a saver or investor, receives that rate. What is good for one is bad for the other. This is just another way of saying there is no free lunch. And, in a politicized monetary environment, the seemingly free lunch tends to be served to the economic agent who howls the loudest or appears superficially to need it most. That agent's counterparty is, willingly or not, buying the other agent lunch. It is through this lens that we examine, or extreme low interest rates and/or negative real rates – that is, financial repression.

---

[189] McKinnon, Ronald I. 1973. *Money and Capital in Economic Development*, Washington, DC: Brookings Institution. Shaw, Edward. 1973. *Financial Deepening in Economic Development*, New York: Oxford University Press.

[190] Reinhart, Carmen M., Jacob F. Kirkegaard, and M. Belen Sbrancia. 2011. "Financial Repression Redux," *Finance & Development*, Vol. 48, No. 1 (June).

[191] Keynes, John Maynard, *The Economic Consequences of the Peace*, Harcourt, Brace and Howe, 1920, p. 205. We are also reminded of Lenin's comment that the surest way to ruin a nation is to debauch the currency.

First, "Just the facts, Ma'am"

What has the recent experience of interest rates and inflation been? Before discussing rates any further, we need to distinguish carefully between nominal and real rates. The nominal rate is the stated rate, expressed in annual terms; say, an interest rate of 2%. The real rate is the nominal rate minus inflation. For most savings, consumption, and investment decisions, it's the real rate that counts.

Exhibit 15.1 shows how the Fed responded to the unfolding severe recession of 2007-2009 and its aftermath. Nominal rates plunged from 4-5% in 2006-2007 to essentially zero over the last six years. Meanwhile, inflation has fluctuated around a six-year average of just under 2%. The real rate, then, has averaged just above -2% from mid-2009 to mid-2015. Over the very recent past, January 2015 to the present, the real rate has been close to zero because inflation, dominated by falling oil prices, has also been zero.

Exhibit 15.1 Recent Experience: Nominal and Real Short-Term U.S. Treasury Bill Rates and Inflation, January 2006-July 2015

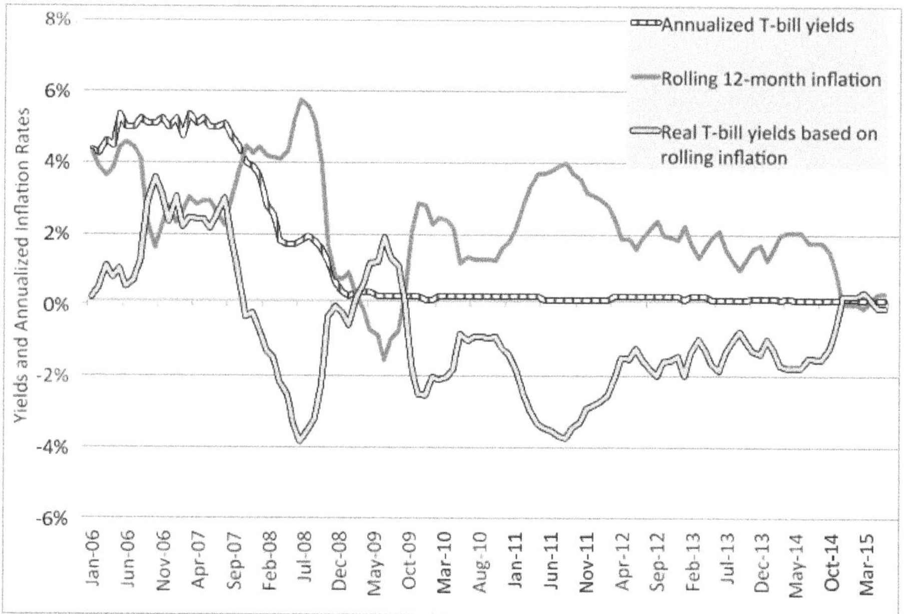

Constructed by the authors using data from Morningstar, FRED (the Federal Reserve), and the Bureau of Labor Statistics. Inflation is represented by the CPI-U-NSA.

Financial repression in this century is thus represented by the space between the zero axis and the green real-rate line. That is the "tax" paid by savers due to the zero interest-rate policy. Actually, that is a low estimate of the tax because real interest rates are usually positive, representing a reward to the investor for deferring consumption.

Exhibit 15.2 Long-Term Experience: Nominal and Real Short-Term U.S. Treasury Bills and Inflation, Annually 1872-1926 and Monthly 1927-July 2015

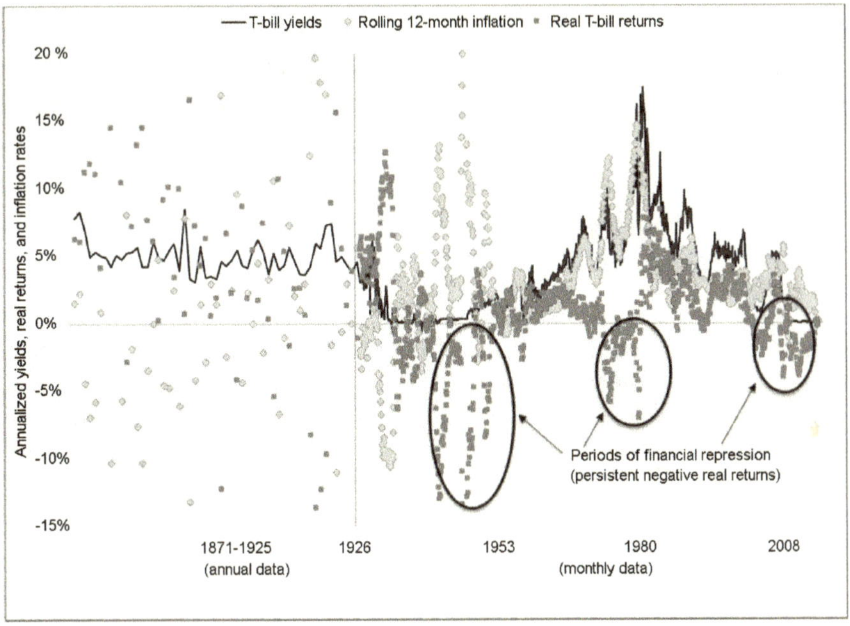

Source: Constructed by the authors using data from Morningstar, FRED (the Federal Reserve), the Bureau of Labor Statistics, and Robert J. Shiller. One-year bond yields are substituted for short-term (30-day and 90-day) yields over 1871-1926. Inflation rates are the CPI (CPI-U-NSA where available).

How positive are real rates historically? Exhibit 15.2 shows the same variables — nominal rates, real rates, and inflation, back to 1871, when Robert Shiller's data series begin.

The exhibit looks complex, but a few words of explanation will help:

- As in Exhibit 15.1, blue is the nominal Treasury bill rate, red is rolling 12-month inflation, and green is the real Treasury bill return.[192]

---

[192] The real Treasury bill return is calculated as the nominal Treasury bill rate (yield), minus the rolling 12-month inflation rate (that is, the average of the current month's and previous 11 months' inflation rates). The result is called a real return, not a real yield, because the real yield is the

- The chart shows annual data from 1871 to 1925, then monthly data from 1927 to the present.

- Real Treasury bill returns averaged 1.02% over 1950-2006, 0.31% over 1927-2015 (the period covered by the Ibbotson studies), and 1.74% over the whole 1871-2015 period.[193] Nominal rates were much higher, consisting of the real return plus inflation.

- The ovals show periods of financial repression (green dots persistently and significantly below zero) during World War II and the immediate postwar period, the Great Inflation years of the 1970s and early 1980s, and recently.

- Between 1871 and 1926, the large amount of green above the zero axis shows that financial repression was rare during that early period, and when it occurred it was due to high and unexpected wartime inflation, not low nominal interest rates. In fact, inflation was negative over most of the period, excepting World War I, which had high inflation, so fixed-income investors did extremely well in real terms.

Financial repression and equities

When we estimate the effect of financial repression on the overall savings of the American public, it's important to remember that equities and real estate make up quite a large fraction of these savings — probably a majority, if equity in one's home is counted. While it's easy to calculate the loss from receiving, say, -2% instead of 0% in real return on one's cash-type savings (money market funds and bank deposits), the effect on equities and real estate is more difficult to estimate.

First, the period of ultra-low interest rates has seen a large increase in equity prices and a healthy recovery in home prices. This doesn't feel like repression — it's more like a gift from the gods. Where's the repression?

High prices mean low expected returns. What investors got over 2009-2015 in capital gains on equities, they'll slowly give back (in whole or in part) through lower *future* returns. This principle applies to houses too. It doesn't matter if

---

expected real return and we do not have expected inflation data with which to calculate an expected real return. All of these numbers are presented in annualized form.

[193] The Ibbotson studies cover 1926 to the present, but it takes 12 months of data to calculate a rolling 12-month inflation rate, so the nominal T-bill data cover 1926 to the present but the other series (inflation and real returns) cover 1927 to the present.

you are buying the equities or houses afresh today or you've held them through the last six years — low interest rates do little or nothing to boost the truly long-term returns of these assets, and with high returns already captured in the recent past, future returns have to be lower.[194]

If we assume (for lack of a better estimate) that the loss from financial repression in fixed-income assets is 2% per year, relative to what it would be with a more typical and benign policy, and that an amount half that large (1% per year) is lost by equity holders due to rich current pricing, we can estimate the size of the implied "tax" on savings. We leave out real estate.

Size of transfer from savers to borrowers

We multiply the "tax base" (the stock of financial assets owned by households) by the "tax rate" (our estimate of the annual percentage loss from financial repression) to arrive at an estimate of the annual dollar loss to savers, as shown in Exhibit 15.3.

"Tax" base. The amount of savings is taken from Federal Reserve data. We assume that the "other" category, consisting of equities, mutual funds, and pensions, is invested 60% in equities and 40% in fixed income. Deposits, credit market investments, and liabilities are assumed to be 100% fixed income.

Exhibit 15.3 Household and Nonprofit Balance Sheet of the United States as of 1Q2015, Showing Estimated Annual Income Loss from Financial Repression

	Dollar amount ($ trillions)	Assumed annual loss from financial repression	Annual dollar loss ($ billions)
Financial assets			
Deposits	$ 10.3	2%	$ 206.0
Credit market	$ 3.3	2%	$ 66.0
Other (equities, mutual funds, pensions)	$ 55.8	1.4%	$ 781.2
Total financial assets	$ 69.4		$ 1,053.2
Liabilities	$ (14.2)	2%	$ (284.0)

Source: Fed's "Financial Accounts" (z---1) table B101, Q1 2015 (households + nonprofits)
Note: Liabilities decline by 2%, so the holder of an asset-liability portfolio *gains* from financial repression on the liability side.

---

[194] One could debate endlessly, and there is a great deal of literature doing so, how much lower. We assume that future equity returns are 1% lower, compared to 2% lower for fixed income.

"Tax" rate. We assume a 2% annual loss from financial repression for fixed income and 1% for equities. Thus the blended "tax" rate for the "other" assets category is 1.4%.

Result. Multiplying through and taking the total, we arrive at $1,053.2 billion per year — rounded, a trillion dollars a year taken out of household balance sheets and transferred to others. That's more than 5% of GDP! Note that this estimate is for the United States alone. Moreover, the U.S. is not an island of financial repression. In fact, there is financial-repression contagion. The total loss for the world is much larger.

What are we to make of this transfer? We look at the assets of the household sector because households consist of actual people; non-household agents in the economy, chiefly businesses and governments, exist to serve households. Thus, it is households that ultimately matter in measuring the magnitude of financial repression.

Where does this transfer go? When we look back at Exhibit 15.3 we see that roughly

$284 billion goes right back to households, mainly due to mortgage debt. We might think this should be netted out, giving only $769 billion as the size of the transfer from households. But this ignores the critical fact that much of the $284 billion *is* a transfer, from one set of households to another. Wealth and income transfers may or may not be an appropriate policy goal, but opaque transfers as a consequence of monetary policy are exceedingly bad public policy.

Some of the transfer is effectively a tax in that it is transferred to the government, the result of low rates for federal, state and local, and agency securities. We estimate this at very roughly $190 billion.[195]

A part of the transfer is an effective subsidy to banks that hold deposits paying interest below inflation. In fact, one could argue that, after the financial crisis, zero interest rates were one method, whether intentional or unintentional, whereby the government aided bank recapitalization.

---

[195] We estimate, very roughly, that the U.S. public holds (directly and indirectly) $3,850 billion of federal debt, $2,370 billion of state and local debt, and $3,200 billion of agency and GSE debt; a total of $9,430 billion. The estimates for Q1 2015 are calculated by the authors from Federal Reserve Z.1, tables L.209, L.210, and L.211. We assume that households hold (mostly indirectly through intermediaries) any securities not held by banks, the monetary authority, or the rest of the world. This may somewhat overestimate the household holdings, but we do not think dramatically. Further, the number for state and local is somewhat underestimated (since the amounts held by banks and the rest of the world include municipal securities issued by corporations).

The most important thing to remember, however, is that this transfer from sav-ers to borrowers represents a distortion of a price that is critical for the effective functioning of our economy: the price of goods and services today versus the future. On this price rests some of the most important decisions we all make as consumers, workers, investors — decisions about whether and how much to in-vest in education, work, leisure, retirement, or productive businesses. When this price is distorted then we are all pushed to behave in inappropriate ways.

What a mess. It will take teams of PhD's, working for years, to unravel all the distorted incentives, capital misallocations, and foregone savings opportunities that emerge from the financial repression of the early 21st century.

The case against raising interest rates

Any recommendation to raise interest rates needs to acknowledge that many well-informed people are against raising rates.[196] We need to understand the ar-guments behind that opposition and assess the costs and benefits of lower ver-sus higher rates.

We have seen that there are costs to the current zero interest rate regime. Con-ventional economic wisdom says that these costs are the necessary burden we bear to enjoy the benefits of low rates and avoid the calamity brought by higher rates. The claimed benefits of low rate are twofold: first, low rates generate in-flation and forestall deflation (the effect of which is purported to be disastrous, through increasing the real value of an already crushing debt burden). Second, low rates stimulate growth and are necessary to repair the economy following the 2007-2009 financial crisis.[197]

---

[196] For example, Larry Summers has recently argued eloquently against higher rates in Op Ed pieces in the *Financial Times*: http://www.ft.com/intl/cms/s/2/f24c9a5c-49e9-11e5-9b5d-89a026fda5c9.html#axzz3lJjapPaw and http://blogs.ft.com/larry-summers/2015/09/09/why-the-fed-must-stand-still-on-rates/

[197] One intriguing part of the case against raising interest rates is that highly indebted governments can't afford to pay higher rates. In this view, low rates are the Fed's contribution to solving the government debt problem — the other side of the effective tax generated by negative real rates. When U.S. entitlement spending is projected through the baby boomers' retirement years without modifying benefit formulae, government debt mushrooms at typical interest rates but is more well-behaved at very low rates. The purpose of monetary policy, however, should not be to support the government, but to support the people.

The Changing Nature of Monetary Economics

The problem with this conventional wisdom, that low rates both generate inflation and stimulate the economy, is that it may not in fact be correct. Some of those economists who have most eloquently advocated for the importance of money in our economy have also warned of the limited power of monetary policy.

Consider Milton Friedman, the prime exponent of monetarism in the 20th century and the economist who, with Anna Schwartz, argued convincingly that "the Fed caused the Great Depression."[198]

Nonetheless Friedman himself said, "[W]e are in danger of assigning to monetary policy a larger role than it can perform, in danger of asking it to accomplish tasks that it cannot achieve, and, as a result, in danger of preventing it from making the contribution that it is capable of making."[199]

John Cochrane, formerly of the University of Chicago, now at the Hoover Institution and a successor to Friedman as a serious monetary theorist, strikes the same tone in a recent blog post: "Monetary policy is a lot less powerful than most people think it is. Bad monetary policy can screw things up. But our growth doldrums are not the result of monetary policy, nor can monetary policy do a lot to change them."[200]

We need to take seriously the words of thinkers such as Friedman and Cochrane because they have thought carefully about money and are themselves strong

---

[198] This is hyperbole, but only slightly. More accurately they argued (in Friedman, Milton, and Anna J. Schwartz, *A Monetary History of the United States*, Princeton University Press, 1963) that mistakes in Federal Reserve monetary policy turned what would have been a severe recession into the Great Depression of the 1930s. Ben Bernanke, when a member of the Board of Governors of the Federal Reserve but before being appointed chairman, went so far as to say: "Let me end my talk by abusing slightly my status as an official representative of the Federal Reserve. I would like to say to Milton and Anna: Regarding the Great Depression. You're right, we did it. We're very sorry. But, thanks to you, we won't do it again." Bernanke, Ben S., "On Milton Friedman's ninetieth birthday," Conference to Honor Milton Friedman, University of Chicago, November 8, 2002, http://www.federalreserve.gov/boarddocs/speeches/2002/20021108/default.htm.

[199] Friedman, Milton, Presidential Address to the American Economic Association, *American Economic Review*, March 1968, vol. 58, no. 1.

[200] Cochrane, John H. "Doctrines Overturned," The Grumpy Economist (blog), February 28, 2015, http://johnhcochrane.blogspot.com/2015/02/doctrines-overturned.html.

advocates of the importance of money in economics. And there are reasons — based on both theory and recent experience — to question the conventional view that low rates can both generate inflation and stimulate growth.

Surprises in the effects of monetary expansion on inflation and growth

Consider our experience over the past five to seven years. Rates have been pegged at zero. Conventional economic theory predicts that such a peg would lead to unstable inflation, but in fact inflation has been remarkably stable, trending slightly downward. Further, conventional wisdom would predict that low rates would produce higher inflation — again not what we have witnessed. Importantly, recent developments in macro theory indicate that raising rates may (at least in some circumstances) generate higher inflation.

Finally, conventional wisdom would predict that zero rates and the resulting negative real rates would be highly stimulative and, while the economy has grown, it has not been spectacular.

If it is the case that low rates are not the macroeconomic panacea we have thought, then the dangers of higher rates may also be less than we have thought and must be weighed against the obvious and present costs of low rates.

Arguing in favor of higher rates, Cochrane has written,

All current macroeconomic theories start with the same basic story: when interest rates are higher, people consume less today, save, and then consume more in the future. Higher real interest rates mean higher consumption growth.[201]

For those who care about the future beyond the next few quarters, then, higher real interest rates are to be desired. Rather than trying to maximize current consumption or production, as measured by quarterly GDP data, we should be trying to maximize wealth, which is (by simple accounting identities) the present value of all future consumption.[202]

---

[201] http://johnhcochrane.blogspot.com/2013/02/three-views-of-consumption-and-slow.html.

[202] What got one of us (Siegel) to think about writing this article in the first place was a comment on Cochrane's blog, at http://johnhcochrane.blogspot.com/2013/03/fun-debt-graphs.html, by a University of Belgrade Ph.D. student, Vladimir Andric:

> Dear Professor Cochrane: You are arguing that growth is a solution to the U.S deficit problem. However, it seems to me that you are treating GDP growth as exogenous. In other words, it is not the spending that is high, but rather the growth that is low.

But our core objection to near-zero interest rates is more basic: it has to do with treating creditors and debtors fairly. If we want healthy levels of saving and investment, and a future that is better than our recent past, we have to have healthy rewards for saving and investment. A permanent bias in favor of debtors (including governments) and against creditors is the wrong way to go.

Conclusion: Growth Is the Answer

Growth profoundly influences everything. It drives stock prices, the debt/GDP ratio, and even bond prices and currency values through the mechanism of the market assessing a government's ability to pay its debt.[203] We are already facing a headwind or decrement to GDP growth from the slowing of population increase.[204] Technological change, which shows little or no sign of slowing, is the main driver of *per capita* GDP growth; but poorly designed incentives and thoughtless policies can interfere with the translation of technological change to economic improvement.

There is every reason to encourage growth and no reason to restrain it.[205]

Growth is also good for democracy and free markets. Good fortune is always unevenly distributed, so when growth is slow, the less fortunate really suffer. And if a large proportion of the population does badly and gets angry, the populist policies they typically demand make growth even slower.

But, maybe, the growth is low because spending is high. A paper by Alesina *et al.* (2002) investigates the impact of fiscal policy on profits and investments in OECD countries. The authors argue that public spending, especially its wage component, has a sizeable negative effect on profits and business investment.
Cochrane replied, "How refreshing. Most of my other commenters seem to be Keynesians who think more spending = more growth. I agree, substantially less spending in the right places could increase growth." Alesina's paper is at https://www.aeaweb.org/articles.php?doi=10.1257/00028280260136255.

[203] See http://johnhcochrane.blogspot.com/2013/03/fun-debt-graphs.html.

[204] One of us has noted elsewhere that this development is welcome for environmental reasons, and that ultimately per capita GDP should be higher because of it; but GDP as measured (not per capita) is lower, all other things being equal, the slower the growth rate of population. See https://larrysiegeldotorg.files.wordpress.com/2012/01/fewer-richer-greener_siegel_2012_03_021.pdf.

[205] See also Sexauer, Stephen C., and Bart Van Ark. 2010. "Escaping the Sovereign-Debt Crisis: Productivity-Driven Growth and Moderate Spending May Offer a Way Out." Executive Action Series, Conference Board, New York. Drawing on the work of the Nobel Prize-winning economist Gary Becker and the University of Chicago professor Kevin Murphy, these authors show that the public-debt problem is greatly ameliorated by rates of long-term economic growth in excess of the growth rate of government spending. Their work was discussed in *Advisor Perspectives*, June 9, 2015.

Investors prosper when the economy prospers. If they are equity investors, they prosper by holding a claim to the change, on the margin, in aggregate wealth.[206] If they are fixed-income investors, they benefit from real interest rates that equilibrate the savings and investment function; rates reflect the net result of the demand and supply of savings and the real returns to capital projects. Investors want both the real interest rate and the equity risk premium to be higher than at present, so they benefit, as we all do, from policies that stimulate long-term growth. We want change. We want adaptation. We don't want the stasis and misallocation that financial repression brings.

We believe that such policies include normal interest rates for normal times. We're close to being in normal times. For some two centuries, the United States has enjoyed 1.8% per year productivity growth (real *per capita* GDP growth). That is our benchmark for normal times. Real overall GDP growth consists simply of productivity growth plus population growth. At the current population growth rate of 0.7% per year, our benchmark for normal times translates to 2.5% real GDP growth.

Exhibit 15.4 shows U.S. real GDP growth, quarterly (but stated as annual growth rates), from 1947 to the most recent quarter.

Look at the last few years in Exhibit 15.4: we're averaging just about 2.5%. The world after 2011 looks a lot like the world before 2007. In terms of monetary policy, let's return to what President Warren Harding liltingly called "normalcy." The right word is normality, but his enthusiasm sometimes got ahead of his vocabulary, and his coinage stuck. Right now, we could use some of Harding's enthusiasm, a big dose of normalcy, and an end to financial repression.

---

[206] This claim is shared with human capital holders (who receive higher wages), governments, and others, but changes in overall wealth flow through to equity holders very directly.

Exhibit 15.4 Real U.S. GDP Growth, Stated as Annual Rate, Quarterly 1947-2015

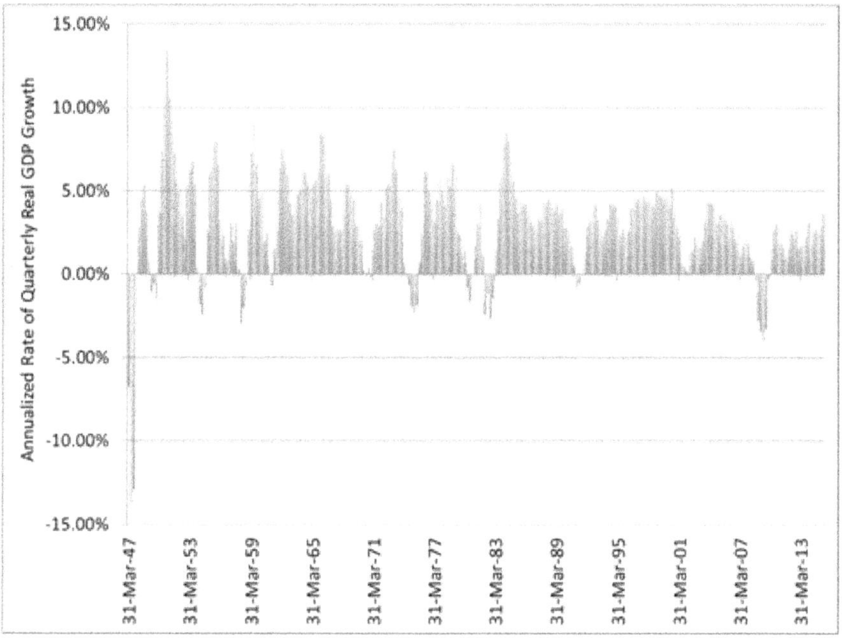

Source: http://www.multpl.com/us-real-gdp-growth-rate/table/by-quarter using U.S. Bureau of Economic Analysis data.

Chapter 16. Milton Friedman and Monetarism Through the Looking Glass

Laurence B. Siegel and Paul D. Kaplan[207]

August 2016

Negative interest rates in Europe and Japan. Itsy-bitsy, teeny-weeny positive interest rates in the United States. One round of quantitative easing after another. An economy that stubbornly refuses to grow. Have we gone through Alice's proverbial looking glass?

In 1946 Henry Hazlitt, the great explainer of economics to the masses, distinguished between good and bad economics:

> The bad economist sees only what immediately strikes the eye; the good economist also looks beyond. The bad economist sees only the direct consequences of a proposed course; the good economist looks also at the longer and indirect consequences. The bad economist sees only what the effect of a given policy has been or will be on one particular group; the good economist inquires also what the effect of the policy will be on all groups.[208]

In thrall to Hazlitt, we distinguished good from bad *monetary* economics in 1997:

Bad [monetary] economics...looks at the initial impact [of an action].

> We see interest rates fall at the time that the Fed buys the Treasuries and conclude that interest rates have fallen. However, the initial fall in interest rates is only the first of a sequence of events that will result in interest rates rising. (2) [Bad monetary economics] assumes that

---

[207] A slightly different version of this article appeared in the October/November 2016 issue of *Morningstar* magazine. Reprinted with permission.

[208] Hazlitt, Henry. *Economics in One Lesson*. New York: Harper & Brothers, 1946.

because the Fed intends or wants to lower interest rates, it will succeed in doing so. There is no reason to expect this. (3) It fails to distinguish between real and nominal interest rates.[209,210]

We told a story in which the Nobel prizewinning economist Milton Friedman was a hero:

> In his presidential address to the American Economic Association in 1967, Friedman showed that the [Keynesian] Depression-era paradigm was bad economics.[211,212] He noted that the theory focused exclusively on short-run effects and confused real and nominal quantities. Through the Fisher effect, he explained, expansionary monetary policy leads to higher rather than lower interest rates. There is no long-run trade-off between inflation and unemployment, as Friedman's contemporary, Edmund Phelps, had recently demonstrated.[213] Expansionary monetary policy can lead to increasing inflation, even if unemployment is rising.

Are our observations from 1997 still valid? Despite massive monetary stimulus, both real economic growth and inflation are as low as they have been over any extended period in our lifetimes. Thus, our first tenet of good monetary economics from 1997, that a policy of lower interest rates leads to higher inflation and, in time, higher interest rates, seems to have gone into reverse. If we can no longer rely on this most basic of tools in the monetarist toolkit, perhaps it is

---

[209] Kaplan, Paul D., and Laurence B. Siegel. "Good and Bad Monetary Economics, and Why Investors Need to Know the Difference." In Kaplan, Paul D., editor (foreword by Laurence B. Siegel), *Frontiers of Modern Asset Allocation*, Hoboken, NJ: John Wiley & Sons, 2012.

[210] It was the great American economist of the early 20th century, Irving Fisher, who first made the key distinction between real and nominal interest rates. Nominal interest rates are what we observe in the market. However, since investors care about real values (how much can be obtained in goods and services), investors care about real interest rates rather than nominal rates. According to Fisher, the difference between nominal and real interest rates is the expected rate of inflation. Hence, the nominal interest rate is the real interest rate plus the expected rate of inflation.

[211] Friedman, Milton. "The Role of Monetary Policy." *American Economic Review*, March 1968.

[212] According to John Maynard Keynes, in his 1936 book *The General Theory of Employment, Interest, and Money*, the level of employment in the economy depends on "aggregate demand," which is the sum of consumer spending, business investment spending, and government spending. If business investment spending is too low, the economy will settle on a low level of employment so that many people will be out of work, as was the case during the Great Depression. The remedy is to expand government spending sufficiently high to get the economy back to full employment. To this day, this is the position of Keynesian economists.

[213] Phelps, Edmund S., "Phillips Curves, Expectations of Inflation and Optimal Unemployment over Time," *Economica*, Vol. 34, No. 135 (August 1967), pp. 254-281, http://www.columbia.edu/~esp2/PhilipsCurvesExpectationsofInflationandOptimalUnemployment OverTime.pdf.

time for monetary economics to get a software update. How could Friedman, who was so right in 1967, appear to be so wrong less than half a century later?

We believe that while Friedman's principles are still correct, the environment in which they operate changed dramatically with the global financial crisis of 2008. This makes it appear that his ideas no longer hold, when in fact they do, but in a different way. In this article, we discuss those principles and how they apply pre-crisis and post-crisis. We look at Friedman's ideas on both sides of Alice's looking glass.

This article asks the easier of two questions: Why has monetary expansion failed to promote growth in the real economy? The short answer, which we develop in detail here, is that monetarism is a theory of the price level; it was never intended as a theory of real economic growth. Friedman emphasized this in his 1967 Presidential address. So we should not be surprised that it doesn't explain real economic growth or give much guidance to policymakers on how to promote such growth.

The much tougher question is: Why has monetary expansion not caused inflation? This is more surprising, exactly because monetarism *is* a theory of the price level, and the price level (inflation) has not responded in the way that traditional monetarism predicts. Leading thinkers are working on a solution.

Here, then, are our new tenets of good monetary economics:

1. Monetarism is a theory of the price level, not of real economic output.

2. The money supply matters mainly when it is broken, as John Stuart Mill said in 1848.[214]

3. Unless the money supply is "broken," the use of monetary techniques to promote real economic growth, what we call Monetary Keynesianism, is likely to fail.

---

[214] John Stuart Mill, in Principles of Political Economy with some of their Applications to Social Philosophy (Longmans, Green & Co. London, 7th edition, 1909), Book III, Chapter 7, section 8, wrote, "There cannot, in short, be intrinsically a more insignificant thing, in the economy of society, than money; except in the character of a contrivance for sparing time and labour. It is a machine for doing quickly and commodiously, what would be done, though less quickly and commodiously, without it: and like many other kinds of machinery, it only exerts a distinct and independent influence of its own when it gets out of order." See http://www.econlib.org/library/Mill/mlP36.html.

The Development of Monetary Theory

It turns out that the best way to describe what monetary policy can and cannot do, in terms of both the price level and real economic growth, is to trace — in simple terms— the development of monetary theory. We'll do so in this section, then move on to the impact of monetary policy on the real economy.

In *A Brief History of Time,* Stephen Hawking, noting that each equation cuts book sales in half, used only one in that book. We use three, so we won't be too upset if our sales are only one-quarter of Hawking's.

The Quantity Theory of Money and the Equation of Exchange

Milton Friedman, who lived from 1912 to 2006, was known as the founder of the monetarist school of macroeconomics, so called because of his emphasis on the impact of money on the economy. He famously declared that "inflation is always and everywhere a monetary phenomenon." This statement is based on his version of Quantity Theory of Money (QTM), which was first set forth by David Ricardo in 1810.[215]

The starting point of the QTM is the equation of exchange:

$$MV = PQ$$

where *M* is the money stock, *V* is the velocity of money, *P* is the price index, and *Q* is real national income (gross domestic product). Note that this equation is just an identity and not a theory. It just tells us that the money in circulation must change hands enough times in a year to account for the purchase (or sale) of all the goodsand services purchased (or sold) in that year. That is, the velocity of money — the number of times it changes hands — is the ratio of nominal national income *(PQ)* to the amount of money in circulation, or "money stock".

Exactly what is meant by "money" in this context is a topic of ongoing contention, but a working definition could be "whatever triggers an exchange of real economic goods." In other words, money is whatever the market says it is.

---

215 Ricardo, David. 1810. "The High Price of Bullion, a Proof of the Depreciation of Bank Notes." John Murray, London.

Friedman's Theory of the Price Level

Many popular discussions of monetary economics go no farther than to state the equation of exchange, but let's push on a bit. To develop a theory of the price level, Friedman recasts the equation of exchange as a market-clearing condition (meaning that markets clear, with goods and services flowing one direction and money the other, only when the equation is "satisfied" or numerically correct).[216] This means that he needs theories for both the supply of and the demand for money.

As other economists did before him, Friedman developed a theory of the demand for money: the amount of money demanded is set by the real value, or purchasing power, of liquid balances that people wish to hold. Real balances are denoted by M/P (money balances adjusted for the price level). The theory proposes that the demand for real balances increases as real income (Q) increases, and also increases as the nominal interest rate (i) decreases, that is, as interest-paying bonds or bills become less attractive compared to money; these relationships are, together, expressed as $M/P = L(i,Q)$, where $L(i,Q)$ is called the *liquidity preference function* because it determines how much "liquidity" (in this case real balances) people want to hold.[217] Because $MV = PQ$, by simple algebra the demand for money is thus related to velocity as follows:

This means that — if the demand for real balances is proportional to real in-

$$V = \frac{Q}{L(i,Q)}$$

come, and logic and evidence suggest that it is — you cannot raise Q (income or real economic output) by lowering interest rates. All you will do is decrease velocity, V.

A Natural Experiment

This proposition was recently tested in a "natural experiment": when interest rates fell dramatically after the global financial crisis of 2008, velocity fell too, as we can see in Exhibit 16.1.

---

[216] Friedman, Milton. "The Quantity Theory of Money: A Restatement" in Milton Friedman, editor, *Studies in the Quantity Theory of Money*, University of Chicago Press, Chicago, 1956.

[217] Friedman discusses other variables in the liquidity preference function including wealth, the division between wealth in human and non-human forms, and the expected return on money and other assets

Exhibit 16.1 The Velocity of U.S. Money (M2), 1959-2016

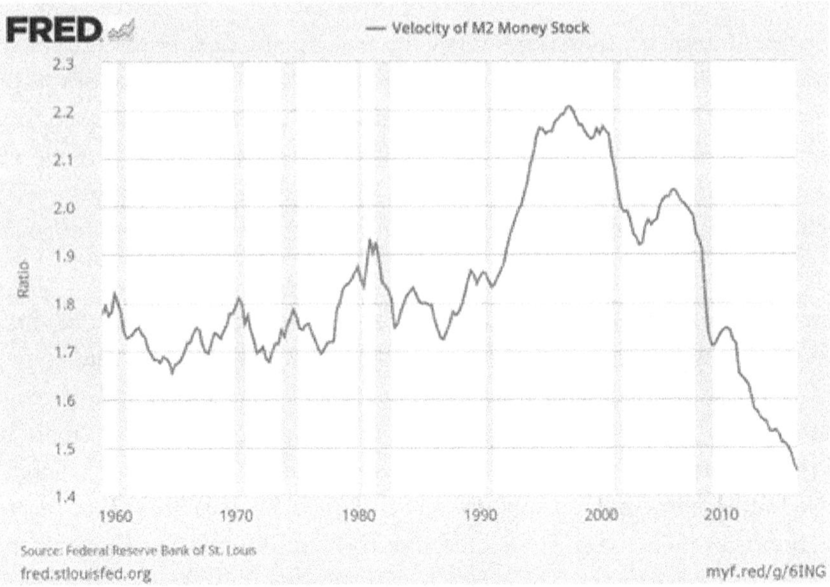

Of course, there are other factors the impact the demand for money and hence velocity, so we cannot claim that we have identified the sole cause of this particular drop in velocity, but the theory appears to be least directionally correct.

What Determines Inflation?

The market-clearing condition — what must be true if markets are to clear — is:

$$M^S = P \cdot L(i, Q)$$

where M^S denotes money supply. In other words, there must be enough money in circulation to satisfy the demand for real balances as described earlier. When this condition holds, at any given level of demand for real balances the price level moves in proportion to the money supply. So, if the money supply were to grow at some rate, that rate would become the rate of inflation.

If there is economic growth, the demand for real balances would grow and, according to monetarism, it would be incumbent on the central bank to grow the money supply at the same rate as the economy to achieve price stability. If the money supply grows at a slower rate, the quantity of money becomes suboptimal and is a restraining factor on economic growth; then, and only then, should central banks increase the rate of money supply growth to enable the real economy to grow.

If, however, the money supply is *not* suboptimal — not a restraining factor — then additional money supply growth will just cause inflation; it will not increase real output. This was Friedman's insight in his 1967 Presidential address and it enabled him to forecast accelerating inflation in the 1970s, a forecast that came true.

Monetary Keynesianism and the Slow-Growth Economy

Now, what does all this theory mean for the ability of central banks or governments to manage the real economy?

Exhibit 16.2 shows the growth of two measures of the U.S. money supply (M2 and the monetary base), as well as of the real output of the U.S. economy (real GDP) and of consumer prices, over 2005-2016. (The monetary base is defined as the sum of currency in circulation and reserve balances held by banks in their accounts at the Fed; M2, a broader measure, also includes checking and savings deposits, certain other deposits, and retail money market funds.) Because the real GDP line is hard to see at the bottom of the graph, we reproduce it on a larger scale in Exhibit 16.3, which also shows annualized quarterly rates of real GDP growth.

The message of Exhibit 16.2 is that, despite massive and unprecedented growth in the monetary base and much less dramatic but still substantial growth in M2, the economy hardly grew and neither did prices. In fact, we need to study Exhibit 16.3 in the context of longer-term data to see just how terrible the performance of the real economy of this period was. After severe recessions, growth usually rebounds sharply; for example, after the 1981-1982 recession, which saw a peak-to-trough decline in real GDP of 2.8%, the real GDP growth rate in the recovery year of 1984 was 7.3%.

Exhibit 16.2 Growth of the Monetary Base, The M2 Money Stock, The Real
Economy, and Consumer Prices Since 2005

Source: FRED, Federal Reserve Bank of St. Louis

This time, however, after a much worse recession, with a peak-to-trough decline
of 4.2% in real GDP, the best recovery year was 2015, with a 2.6% growth rate,
and the average growth rate during the recovery period of 2009-2015 was a miserable 2.1%. What went wrong?

We believe that Monetary Keynesianism is somewhat to blame.[218] Monetary
Keynesianism is the use of monetary techniques, such as low interest rates and
quantitative easing, to achieve the Keynesian goals of full employment of labor
and capital. This is a misuse of monetary theory when the money supply is not
inadequate. Central bankers try to stimulate economic growth by increasing M,
but all they accomplish is to raise P and/or lower V. If they raise P they hope
they will increase Q through the agency of a Phillips curve (which says that more
inflation means less unemployment and consequently more output). However,
as we noted earlier, Edmund Phelps, back in the day of Friedman's Presidential
address, showed that the Phillips curve is highly unstable and essentially unus-
able for policy.

---

[218] To the best of our knowledge, "Monetary Keynesianism" in this sense was first used by Siegel,
Laurence B., and Stephen C. Sexauer, "Five Mysteries Surrounding Low and Negative Interest
Rates," *Journal of Portfolio Management*, Winter 2017. Monetary Keynesianism has a slightly
different meaning in academic economics.

Exhibit 16.3 U.S. Real GDP and Real GDP Growth, 2005-2016

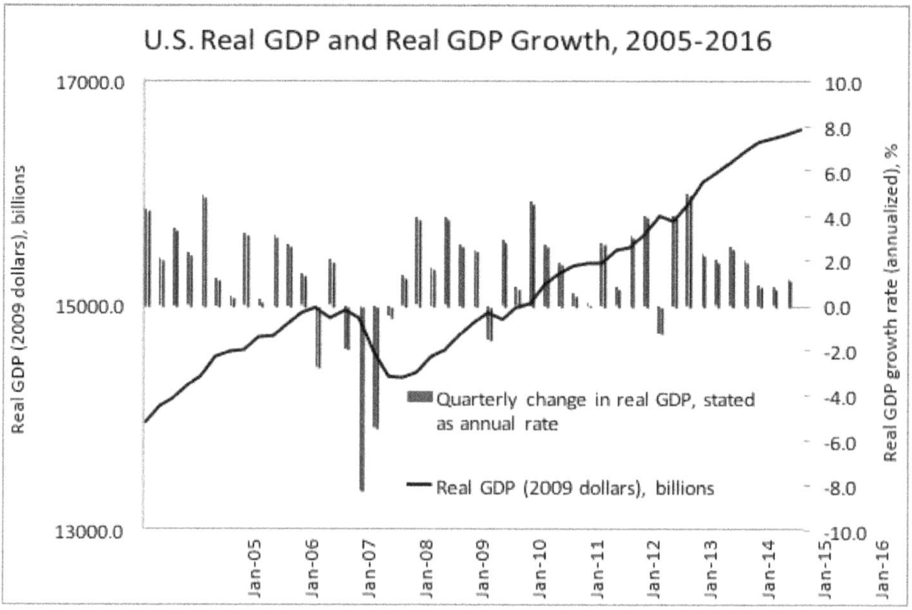

Source: FRED, Federal Reserve Bank of St. Louis

In the post-crisis period, attempts to increase M have raised neither P nor Q; they have lowered V. Monetary Keynesianism has become gospel among central bankers almost everywhere. But it is not effective. Also, it is not monetarism. It isn't even Keynesianism. It is bad monetary economics.

Monetary Policy During and After the Crisis

While monetary easing is not effective at boosting real output in normal times, it does seem to be effective in emergencies. At the worst point of the global financial crisis, in September and October 2008, the money supply was contracting rapidly and the soundness of the global financial system, including the payments system that allows checks and other routine financial transactions to clear, was in question. A massive injection of liquidity by central banks was needed and achieved. This emergency monetary policy measure was successful because the money supply had shrunk to a level that was suboptimal, and was likely to shrink further in the absence of intervention.

After the worst of the crisis was over, however, central banks continued to pursue radically accommodative monetary policies — one quantitative easing (QE) after another — in the pursuit of economic growth. Increasing a nominal value (the monetary base) cannot have a long-run effect on a real value (real GDP). No wonder monetary stimulus, in this case in the form of QE, has produced the lame macroeconomic results shown in Exhibit 16.3. You can't fix a non-monetary problem with a monetary solution.

There you have it. Monetarism offers a very limited toolkit for policy. It basically says that the quantity of money should never grow too slowly, or too quickly, but just right — and that, then, you will get the organic growth that the economy is capable of producing.

Monetary Keynesianism is the use of penicillin as if it were a performance-enhancing drug. It is not, and policymakers will always be disappointed if they act as though it is. Real monetarism is the use of penicillin to cure diseases that respond to penicillin, and not to overuse it lest we breed superbugs that do not. (Continuing our analogy, inflation and recession are among the superbugs that can be produced through unwise use of monetary techniques.).

Policymakers and citizens may be disappointed to hear that monetary theory does not offer a performance-enhancing drug. But economic growth is hard. It comes from innovation. To produce more in a given period than you did last period, you either need more people, more capital, or a way to combine people and capital in a way that is more efficient or creative than the way you did it last period. If people and capital are underemployed, you need to find ways to employ them, but increasing the monetary base will not lead to their employment, except possibly on a temporary basis.

When used properly, monetary policy has had its successes: fighting inflation after Paul Volcker assumed the chairmanship of the Fed in 1979; avoiding a recession after the 1987 stock market crash; and, in 2008, avoiding a financial crisis worse than the one that actually happened. However, ill-conceived monetary policy, based on bad monetary economics, has repeatedly failed to produce the desired results, as we have seen in the long period of very slow growth since the end of the Great Recession.

When you have tried a possible solution to a problem, and it has not worked, you can redouble your efforts — if you are convinced that the solution will eventually be effective — or you can try something else. We are at the point — some would argue long past the point — where it is time to try something else.

Implications for Investors

How should investors react if they accept what we have said? As long as Monetary Keynesianism is being practiced, investors should be on their guard — and it is being practiced almost everywhere. Real growth has been poor; we believe that, all other things being equal, Monetary Keynesianism has caused growth to be poorer than it would otherwise be because it distorts incentives, causes misallocation of resources, and rearranges the tradeoffs between present and future consumption. In other words, growth is poor partly because of Monetary Keynesianism, not in spite of it.

Two observations point to this conclusion. First, Monetary Keynesianism has given us rock-bottom interest rates, just above zero in the United States and negative in many countries, depriving the economy of the income that savers have traditionally earned. This situation, which numerous authors have termed *financial repression*, can't be good for growth.[219]

Second, low interest rates cannot stimulate the economy if businesses and consumers are already borrowing as much as they want (in technical terms, if they are able to fund all positive-net-present-value projects). Borrowers seem to be satiated.

There is nothing in global fundamentals suggesting that growth rates should be this low. Innovation has not stopped and in some fields is accelerating.[220] Emerging markets now produce more in aggregate than the developed world, and this trend will extend further. Even aging populations and societies with slow or negative population growth can continue to improve *per capita* GDP even while total GDP remains stable or falls. (One of us has even suggested that low

---

[219] For a discussion of financial repression and its role in resolving past sovereign debt stresses, see Reinhart, Carmen M., and Kenneth S. Rogoff, "Financial and Sovereign Debt Crises: Some Lessons Learned and Those Forgotten," IMF working paper, December 2013, https://www.imf.org/external/pubs/ft/wp/2013/wp13266.pdf.

[220] Although Robert Gordon, a distinguished Northwestern University professor, has repeatedly argued the opposite: that the unique nature of the second industrial revolution (the "special century" that started around 1870 and the full effects of which were not incorporated into the economy until around 1970) makes it almost impossible for future economic growth to equal that of the past. See, for example, Gordon, Robert J., *The Rise and Fall of American Growth: The U. S. Standard of Living Since the Civil War*, Princeton University Press, 2016. A response by one of us to Gordon's argument, pointing out its flaws and forecasting long-run future growth roughly on par with that of the past, is in Siegel, Laurence B., "Robert Gordon, the Special Century, and the Prospects for Economic Growth," *Advisor Perspectives*, December 22, 2015, http://larrysiegel.org/robert-gordon-the-special-century-and-the-prospects-for-economic-growth/.

population growth makes per capita GDP growth *easier*.[221]) Yet, through Monetary Keynesianism, we in the developed world are engineering a totally unnecessary quasi-recession that goes on and on, seemingly endlessly.

Some day we will look back on this period, as we now do on the 1930s, and wonder how we could have been so foolish as to pursue a policy of Monetary Keynesianism and financial repression in the hope of stimulating growth when a better alternative — a regime of normal interest rates, stable monetary growth, free trade, and low and simple taxes on businesses — was right in front of us. Those remedies, not more monetary madness, are probably what Milton Friedman would prescribe if he were alive today.

---

[221] Siegel, Laurence B. "Fewer, Richer, Greener: The End of the Population Explosion and the Future for Investors," *Financial Analysts Journal*, Vol. 68, No. 6 (November/December 2012).

Chapter 17. A Conversation with Mohamed A. El-Erian

February 22, 2016

Mohamed A. El-Erian is one of the best known and most highly respected investment managers in the world. He is senior economic adviser to Allianz, and was formerly CEO and co-CIO (with Bill Gross) of PIMCO. From 2006 to 2007 he was president of Harvard Management Company. Dr. El-Erian was educated at Cambridge University and received his doctorate from Oxford University. His most recent book, The Only Game in Town, was published in January.

We spoke with Dr. El-Erian on February 16.

17-1 Mohamed A. El-Erian

Larry Siegel: I've read your book, *The Only Game in Town*, which is principally about the Federal Reserve and other central banks. I had an overriding question while reading it: how did we, meaning the American people, let the Fed get so powerful? According to the Fed's own website, the Fed was originally established to prevent banking panics, yet its mandate grew over time to include price stability and full employment and now seems to involve stewardship of the entire economy. What happened, and is this good?

Mohamed El-Erian: We didn't let the Fed get more powerful, nor did the Fed go for a power grab. What happened is that we inadvertently limited our policy responses and created a huge vacuum, and the Fed felt that, in order to buy time for the system, it had a moral and ethical obligation to step in.

Larry: Where did we limit our policy responses? What did we do that was wrong?

Mohamed: It's what we didn't do. We made three basic mistakes. In the run-up to the global financial crisis, we overinvested in the financial services sector as an engine of growth. We wrongly believed as a society that finance was the next level of capitalism. You can see this in the way that countries were competing to become the global financial center; even smaller countries such as Switzerland, Ireland, Iceland, and Dubai opted to grow their financial system to sizes bigger than their GDP. And regulators believed that they could reduce their oversight and regulation of the financial sector because, after all, it was the next level of sophisticated capitalism. So we stopped investing in industries that create growth, and we excessively embraced the financial sector. In fact, we changed its name from financial services to just "finance" – again the notion that it is a stand-alone. So, that was the first mistake.

The second mistake we made was that, when we were coming out of the financial crisis, we didn't understand that it was much more than a cyclical shock. Importantly, it was also structural and secular and, as such, it required a different mindset. Policymakers focused too much on the notion that Western economies operate only in cyclical space and that secular and structural issues were the domain of emerging economies. They didn't understand that we were also facing structural headwinds, so we got an insufficient policy response.

The third mistake was the over-reliance on central banks. And, awaiting a policy handoff that hasn't materialized as yet – to a more comprehensive policy response that deals with the real impediments to growth and genuine financial stability – these institutions had no choice but to venture ever deeper into experimental policy terrain and to stay there a lot longer than they anticipated. As such, the benefits of their policy interventions have come with heightened risks of collateral damage and unintended consequences.

Larry: Let me reflect for a moment on the idea of overinvesting in finance. In retrospect, of course we did, but in a market economy each industry, or each corporation, sees it as their job to grow as big as they can. So, in the 1950s we probably overinvested in cars, and then in the 1990s we overinvested in technology and telecom. I don't think finance is any different. People in financial services companies want big profits and big bonuses, so who is going to stop them from trying to expand?

Mohamed: You're absolutely right. Capitalism has a tendency of going too far on certain activities. The only difference – and this is an important difference – is that overinvesting in cars doesn't mean that you risk the payments and settlement system of an economy, whereas finance *is* an integral part of the payments and settlement system. I think of finance as being the oil in your car. If it breaks down, then no matter how good your engine is, no matter how good your brakes are, you simply are not going to be able to drive the car. Other sectors are different; you can still drive a car if your bumper falls off. Finance, unfortunately or fortunately, speaks to the payments and settlement system, which is a necessity. And what happened in 2008 is that the payments and settlement system was threatened.

Larry: I agree. I think of finance as a type of infrastructure, and it has to function. As John Stuart Mill said about money, it is only important when it doesn't function. Can you elaborate a little on the third mistake we made?

Mohamed: While central banks stepped in to fill a void, they did so based on the understanding that there would be a policy hand-off.

Fed chairman Ben Bernanke's speech in August 2010 at Jackson Hole, Wyoming, really identified the moment when the Fed started using unconventional policies to pursue broad economic objectives, as opposed to pursuing market normalization. He said that it's about "benefits, costs and risks." It was understood that, the longer the Fed remains unconventional, the lower the benefits and the greater the costs and risks. I don't think anybody imagined, at that point, that the Fed wouldn't be able to make the handoff from unconventional monetary policy to a much broader policy response. So the third mistake was the absence of a hand-off, and that speaks to political issues.

Larry: *Advisor Perspectives* operates an online forum that has about 10,000 financial advisors as members.[222] One of those members asks, "You've always maintained that the Federal Reserve is basically a one-tool pony. It only possesses the ability to manage interest rates. However, deliberately or not, it has taken on the public mantle of savior of the economy without revealing to the world how limited its toolbox really is. Do you feel that Janet Yellen, who is now Fed chair, should start to more assertively shift the responsibility for growing the economy to the fiscal side?" After all, hasn't the Fed, almost by definition, reached the limit of what it can do by lowering interest rates? As this member asks, "Don't we need a movement advocating for Congress to fund something like an infrastructure bank to lend to private businesses, who would in turn hire tens of thousands of Americans to rebuild our country" and, in this member's view, "create a new, vital wave of consumer demand?"

Mohamed: That's a really good question. The answer to the first part is that the Fed, the ECB, the Bank of Japan, the Banque de France and the Bank of England

---

[222] The *Advisor Perspectives* web site reaches about 250,000 readers each month. The online forum that had 10,000 members as of the writing of this article is a restricted area of the web site.

have gone out of their way to stress that they cannot be the only game in town. If you look just last week at Fed chair Janet Yellen's testimony, she basically told Congress that you need to do all these things; we, the Fed, can't deliver these things. So I think the central banks have gone out of their way to convey the notion that they cannot be the only game in town.

In fact, Larry, the title of my book comes from a central banker. In November 2014, the outgoing governor of the central bank of France reminded a conference in Paris that central banks were the only game in town and they didn't like it. So I think the central banks have gone out of their way to state that – but it has fallen on deaf ears both in the political process and in markets.

The political system is not in a position right now to deliver the policy responses that are needed. Therefore, it is more than happy to delegate this responsibility to central banks. This is, of course, an excessive burden for central banks. More-over, markets care less about the ultimate economic destination and more about the influence that central banks have on asset prices. And, for a very long time, central banks have been able to decouple asset prices from the underlying fun-damentals. So I would respond to the member that the problem has not been that central banks are not saying the truth. It is about people not listening.

Turning to the question of an infrastructure bank, we definitely need a policy response that includes greater investment in infrastructure. With interest rates so low, and, in the case of Europe, negative, it is absurd that we're not seeing initiatives, including private-public partnerships, to fill obvious infrastructure needs that enable and empower a lot more private sector activity. But I would stress that infrastructure is just one element of a multi-part solution.

Larry: But, as a taxpayer and a citizen, I want to express the other side: we have $18 trillion in explicit debt at the federal level, God knows how much at state and local levels, plus unfunded pension liabilities and other entitlement liabili-ties. From that perspective, I don't want to spend one penny that can't be paid for out of current taxation. I just don't see how we can ask the people to go into debt even further to fund a benefit that may or may not materialize.

Mohamed: I sympathize with that view, but with one qualifier. The level of debt sustainability is rightly expressed as a fraction with a numerator and a denomi-nator. The numerator speaks to the dollar amount of debt and the cost of debt servicing. But there is also a denominator, the amount of income available for servicing the debt, that defines how burdensome that debt is.

Larry: I see where you are going: if we had 4% real growth, the debt would be-come insignificant over time. But there is a real concern that slow growth may not be a result of bad policy, but of an underlying slowing in technological change. If that is the case, there may be nothing you can do to get 4% growth. I don't believe that. I think there's plenty you can do. But many people do believe it.

Mohamed: And I would say to them, do you know what? You are right in saying that there are demographic and structural headwinds to growth. But that doesn't mean we shouldn't be enabling and empowering private sector activity, particularly given how we have underinvested in infrastructure.

Larry: After about six years of near zero interest rates, and now talk about negative rates, it's worth asking what the benefits of low rates are in the first place. Isn't lowering interest rates stimulative only when there are business projects or consumer purchases that are not being done because the rates are too high? Is there any evidence that the rates are too high – in other words, that such forgone projects or consumer purchases exist? Or, is the desire for low or negative rates based on belief in a model, specifically a Keynesian model of aggregate demand, that needs to be tested further and could be wrong?

Mohamed: First, let me tell you what should happen according to people who are pursuing this policy, and then what I think will happen. Note, first, that nominal policy interest rates are now negative in Europe and in Japan, and that around 30% of the stock of government debt around the world is trading at negative yields. This tells you that there is something strange with where we are today.

The theory is that by taking interest rates to a very low – if not negative – level, investors get pushed into higher risk-taking activities, and companies get pushed to deploy the cash that they hold on their balance sheet. As investors take more risk, they push up the stock market. You and I look at our 401(k) statements, we feel that we are richer and we spend more.

This is called the "wealth effect." Meanwhile, companies see that we are spending more, and the companies themselves are being pushed to deploy their cash, so they invest more. Consumption and investment go up, and that promotes economic growth. That is the theory.

In addition, if you can get your interest rates to be very low or negative and others don't follow, you can also weaken your currency. And, the next thing you know, you also promote exports. That is the theory; in practice, it has not worked that way to the extent that central bankers expected.

It does not work for good reasons: companies and households are smarter than that. They want to see genuine growth, not financial engineering. And, increasingly now, people doubt the effectiveness of central banks.

So, for example, when the Bank of Japan took interest rates negative a few weeks ago, it probably didn't anticipate that the currency would strengthen as opposed to weaken or that the stock market would go down as opposed to go up. Yet that is what happened. So, beyond a certain point, lowering interest rates is not just pushing on a string, or unproductive; it can end up being counterproductive. That is why I call it a journey to the end of the road that we were on. That's why I call it the T-junction. We cannot continue like this for much longer before either something gives in a bad way or we transition to a better world.

Larry: What is a T-junction?

Mohamed: It is a British term for the place where a road terminates in another road so that you cannot go forward, only left or right. You have to choose, and the consequences of turning left or right are very different.

My book makes two points about the T-junction. First, I indicate why humans are bad at making good decisions when facing a T-junction; we have lots of science on this. Second, the book argues that there are three characteristics that investors should put front and center when confronting a T-junction. These are resilience, optionality, and agility.

Larry: Regarding the global financial crisis, a member of APViewpoint (the discussion site for *Advisor Perspectives*) writes, "Without central bank intervention I suspect we would have endured a deeper but shorter period of pain, ultimately leaving us in a stronger position than what we are in now. The damage from the intervention still lingers after seven years, including direct bailouts and a massive risk transfer, in the form of mortgage-backed securities, from the banks to the Fed. While market prices are not conclusive evidence, stock prices [of our] financial services companies are saying something." How do you respond to this?

Mohamed: First, counterfactuals are really difficult, so I don't know whether, after the initial shock, the system would have reset quickly. What I do know is that the initial shock would have been massive, that had central banks not intervened in 2008 and the first half of 2009, we would have been in a multi-year global depression. I am pretty confident about that.

What I don't know is whether, once we went through the shock of a global multi-year depression, the system would have reset quickly and if we would have come out as your reader suggests. But I can tell you that very few people will take that risk. Let me give you a parenting analogy. If you let your kid put her hand in the fire, she will not do it again, but how many parents actually allow their kids to burn themselves?

So the intellectual appeal to the idea of having a prolonged and severe crisis so the system will reset is just like the intellectual appeal of your kid learning not to play with fire once she burns herself. Very few people will want to take that risk.

Larry: That's a fair response. You have to go all the way back to 1921 to find a depression that did not provoke a policy response. The results were good, but when 1929 came along, the collapse went way beyond any tolerable limit, and I believe it was correct to have a policy response. No one knew where the bottom would be.

This discussion transitions nicely to the hottest topic of our young century, inequality. Your book indicates that you are deeply concerned about it. Yet there is a very strong thread in growth and development economics saying that inequality in a single country like the United States is an unintended and unavoidable by-product of greater *equality* among countries. Global inequality was greatest around 1950. At that time the First World was already rich, but China and India had lower incomes than they did 500 years earlier. And around 1950, not coincidentally,

U.S. inequality was at a minimum, so we remember it nostalgically as a period of social harmony. But this only makes sense if you care exclusively about people in the United States. Economic growth outside the First World has benefited billions of people while increasing inequality within countries. How, if at all, do these circumstances affect your view of inequality?

Mohamed: There are many aspects to this question. One is that global inequality has come down; that is correct. And, essentially, it is because the developing countries have grown faster than the advanced economies. In the 1990s and most of the 2000s, we had a growing global GDP and we were reducing poverty at the same time because a lot of the poverty was concentrated in the developing world and particularly in China and India.

On top of that, most countries were getting more unequal. So we had less international inequality and more national inequality. Part of that change was structural in nature. Some of it was actually a good thing because inequality is also associated with incentives to work harder.

But then we went too far. Not only did we have structural engines of inequality such as changes in technology, but we made things worse in two ways. One, we relied excessively on central banks. Remember our discussion that central banks can only achieve their objectives by affecting the prices of financial assets. Who owns financial assets but the rich? So we relied on a policy that worsened inequality.

The second problem we created for ourselves was freezing budget policy, fiscal policy. For six years, Congress didn't approve an active annual budget. So we are at a stage where inequality goes from helping the capitalist system to harming it because it goes to far. Inequality harms capitalism in two ways: the demand effect and the opportunity effect.

Larry: What are these?

Mohamed: The demand effect is very simple. When the rich get the vast majority of an increase in income and wealth, which is what has happened over the last few years, they spend less of it. They have a lower marginal propensity to consume. Therefore, you aggravate the economic situation by having insufficient aggregate demand.

Second, you start worrying about inequality of opportunity. In this country we are very proud of having relatively equal opportunity. But, beyond a certain degree of inequality in wealth distribution, that equality of opportunity deteriorates. That is, I think, where we are today. So, in addition to the structural issues you point out, we've made things worse.

Larry: Isn't technology the real source of this inequality? Technology has made it tougher on almost everyone who has an IQ below the median, including those in developing countries. Now that sophisticated machines are available, there just aren't that many jobs for low-skilled people. That is a problem that we are not going to solve through policy adjustments. I just don't know what's going to happen. Can you comment?

Mohamed: Martin Ford has written a very important book on this topic, *Rise of the Robots: Technology and the Threat of a Jobless Future*. He makes your point and says that, with machine learning, it is going to get even worse.

Larry: Yes, it will, at least for the time being while workers adjust by developing new skills – if they can. I am not sure that everyone can. We cannot all be above average.

Mohamed: Okay, so you agree with him, but his policy recommendations are something that, I suspect, you will find rather upsetting.

Larry: To wrap up, how should an individual investor saving for retirement and holding a 60/40 index portfolio of global equities and bonds modify her portfolio to account for the concerns that you raise in your book about liquidity, inequality, stagnation, and the inability of central banks to bear the whole burden of rescuing the economy? What should investors take away from your book in terms of their portfolio construction?

Mohamed: First you have to decide whether you buy into the central hypothesis of my book, which is that the path that we are on right now – one characterized by low, stable growth and the ability of central banks to repress financial volatility – is in the process of ending. The book identifies ten of the underlying contradictions that make this path harder to sustain.

In addition, it should come as no surprise to anybody that market volatility has gone up. Nor should it come as a surprise that improbables are becoming realities. Same for this ridiculous blame game between equity markets and oil markets.

It should also come as no surprise that the narrative about low oil prices has changed. It used to be viewed as a blessing, but it's now being viewed as a curse. All of these anomalies are simply confirmation that we are coming to the end of the road that we have been on.

The second part of the hypothesis of this book is that there is nothing predestined about what comes next. It depends on choices that are made. I talk about the T-junction, this notion that the road you are on ends, but there are two very different roads out of it, or a bimodal distribution of outcomes if you prefer statistical language.

Larry: And if you buy into this two-part hypothesis, then what?

Mohamed: It's a big "if." A lot of people buy into the first part but then say that everything is going to fall apart. And there are many people who don't even buy into the first part – they believe we can just continue as we are by depending on central banks. So I want to stress that, if investors buy into my two-part hypothesis, they should realize that what lies ahead is higher financial volatility. Prices will overshoot on the way up. They will overshoot on the way down.

Second, there will be much less liquidity available for repositioning your portfolios. Third, correlations will break down so that portfolio diversification will be less powerful in mitigating risk. Fourth, once in a while a whole segment of the financial markets will become unhinged. Three of these segments – oil, high-yield bonds and emerging market currencies – are already there.

If this is your outlook, you have to ask yourself certain questions, including some that run counter to conventional wisdom. For example, when you said 60/40, conventional wisdom is that you decide how much to put in equities, put the rest in fixed income, and don't hold cash. Cash is a dead asset in that approach. But in the world that I am talking about, the world of the bimodal distribution, cash has a strategic place in your portfolio, turning conventional wisdom upside down when it comes to asset allocation. Do you know why?

Larry: Because cash is an option to buy something else later, at more favorable prices. It is not a dead asset.

Mohamed: Correct. And the resilience to be able to withstand market volatility is also important.

The second piece of conventional wisdom that gets turned upside down is the advice to be a long-term investor and forget about all these short-term fluctuations.

On the contrary, the short-term fluctuations actually will give you more insights as to how we're going to come out of the T-junction. So pay attention to them because you are going to get information from them. The information may or may not have strategic consequences. But don't dismiss them as noise. They are actually signals in the system. And you may need to get more tactical.

Larry: Thank you. I really appreciate your generosity with your time.

Mohamed: My great pleasure. Thank you very much.

Policy and Governance

Policy and politics can enhance or derail long term growth, stability, and perceptions of risk. Larry reviews and critiques the ideas of some well-known experts.

Wayne's personal favorite: What Is Good Governance, and Why Is It So Rare and Precious?

—WHW

Unknown Knowns

Chapter 18. Michael Lewis on the Hidden Benefits of Competent Government

October 15, 2018

Michael Lewis is such an engaging writer that it's been said he could tell a gripping story about a piece of dirt in the road — beginning with the geological origins, several billion years ago, of the dirt's mineral components. Lewis can write conservative (*The Blind Side*) and he can write liberal ("Obama's Way").[223] He can turn nerdy statistical analysis into an entertaining story about baseball (*Moneyball*) — and the movie version got six Oscar nominations. As you already know, he can write about finance from any perspective you can imagine.

This time, apparently to test his gift for storytelling, Michael Lewis decided to write about *government bureaucracy*. Not at the highest levels of statecraft, which have a certain glamor, but in the weeds where the smaller decisions that affect people directly are made. In the weeds is where data on the weather are collected, stray nuclear material is tracked down, and rural families in poverty are given a leg up. It's also where a royal mess was made of the Hanford nuclear site in Washington state, and where what Lewis describes as the "failure of NASA to heed engineers' warnings about how brittle the rings that sealed the solid rocket boosters could become in the cold" resulted in the destruction of the space shuttle Challenger.

Are you bored yet? If so, read Lewis' book. His account of governance in the age of Donald Trump is frightening, inspiring, and surprisingly lively. Despite some disagreements with its political implications, I cannot recommend it enough.

---

[223] "Obama's Way" was a long-form magazine article that Lewis wrote for *Vanity Fair* (September 2012) after having had six months of access to Obama, who was president at the time.

A Frightening and Inspiring Book

Why is *The Fifth Risk* frightening? Because Donald Trump, unlike his diligent predecessors George W. Bush and Barack Obama (both come out looking good in Lewis' account), is aggressively uninterested in the machinery of government. He didn't think he'd need a transition team: he had to be convinced by Chris Christie that it was against the law not to have one. Christie wound up heading the team until he was summarily fired six months later — by Steve Bannon. Lewis surprises us by saying that "Trump always avoided firing people himself. Mr. You're Fired on TV avoided personal confrontation in real life."

Two years into the Trump presidency, half of the 700 top positions that were supposed to be filled by presidential appointment remain vacant. And the lower-level jobs haven't been handled well either: the Trump team's inability to find people to do them means that about half of those jobs are being done by holdovers from the administration of his nemesis, Barack Obama.

Why is *The Fifth Risk* inspiring? Because it helps us see the expertise and dedication of a large number of modestly paid and technically skilled government employees who work in obscurity to keep the country safe, the machinery of thousands of pieces of the country's infrastructure running, and the laws that protect us and our property enforced. Lewis' biggest contribution in *The Fifth Risk* is to document these functions and explain why we cannot simply eliminate the ones we don't like or would prefer not to fund.

What Is the Purpose of Government?

We have to have a government. Only a nut would advocate for complete anarchy, the dismantling of national defense, or the complete abolition of the social safety net. The Trump administration seems committed, as are many Republicans and conservatives, to reducing the size of government without eliminating it, but Lewis argues convincingly that the president is doing this in the worst possible way. Lewis claims Trump doesn't understand that the most important function of government is to *keep Americans safe*, especially from risks they aren't aware of.

Before reading the book, I saw the government's highest calling as that of a neutral referee in the great game of business, played by what James Madison called "competing private interests." Without government there would be no rules, and cheaters would prosper.

I also embrace the Hobbesian concept of government as holder of the legal monopoly on violence: someone has to catch the criminals, and deter crime and fraud through the threat of punishment. And we have to help those unable to help themselves.

But *The Fifth Risk* provides new appreciation for what Lewis regards as government's central function, which is to ensure public safety. This is a complex task involving a great deal of technical expertise in many different fields.

The Terrorist Attack that Wasn't

An example of the risks against which government protects us was the attack on the electrical grid that took place near San Jose, California in 2013. Almost nobody knew about it (we shall soon see why). Lewis writes:

> At Pacific Gas & Electric's Metcalf substation, a well-informed sniper, using a .30-caliber rifle, had taken out seventeen transformers. Someone had also cut the cables that enabled communication to and from the substation. "They knew exactly what lines to cut," said Tarak Shah, who studied the incident for the DOE [Department of Energy]. "They knew exactly where to shoot. They knew exactly which manhole covers were relevant...These were feeder stations to Apple and Google."

We didn't hear about it because there was enough backup power in the area, the "federal government [having created] a coordinated, intelligent response to threats to the system," according to Lewis. Even with Apple's and Google's sophisticated backup systems, a massive power outage in the tech capital of the United States would have cost millions of work-hours in restoration time, to say nothing of the nuisance caused to residential customers and other, less wealthy businesses.

Yesterday's risks are the ones for which we're well prepared. The likelihood of a repeat of the September 11, 2001 attack is minuscule. But, Lewis writes, "People are less good at imagining a crisis before it happens... For just this reason the DOE...set out to imagine disasters that had never happened before." That is much harder, requires thinkers with imagination and extensive knowledge, and is what many of the people who work in government agencies are charged with doing.

The First Four Risks

By now, you're probably wondering: What are the four risks that governments try to protect us against, and what is the fifth risk about which Lewis is so concerned that he named his book after it? The answers are not specific risks, such as a nuclear attack, a pandemic, a large earthquake, or an unexpectedly rapid increase in sea levels. As DOE Chief Risk Officer John MacWilliams explains, they are *categories* of risks, sorted by probability of occurrence and severity of consequences:

Exhibit 18.1 The Department of Energy's Approach to Categorizing Risks

	Low ← Consequences of an accident → High	
High ↑ Probability of an accident ↓ **Low**	Person hops a security fence at a Department of Energy facility	Nuclear electromagnetic pulse attack disables the power grid, wipes out all bank and securities records, spreads potentially deadly radiation
	Small meteorite lands in a Department of Energy parking lot, destroying a car	Nuclear bomb explodes in assembly plant in Texas Panhandle, with many local fatalities

Consequences of an accident

Low   High

Source: Constructed by the author. The northwest- and southeast-quadrant risks are from Lewis' book. I made up the other two.

This is pretty standard stuff; it's nice to know that government agencies have adopted a framework that has existed for decades in other fields. Maybe it was originally thought up in a government agency — we'll never know. But the matrix provides some insight into what employees of the much-ridiculed Department of Energy actually do.[224] It's a regulatory body, not an actual producer of energy, so it's been on the chopping block in a number of presidential campaigns. Lewis shows why we shouldn't get rid of it.

The Fifth Risk

OK, seriously, folks: "Project management."

I know you were expecting something better, like an attack by space aliens, or a conspiracy by artificially intelligent robots to destroy the people who created them. But, writes Lewis, "When I asked [MacWilliams] for the fifth risk, he had thought about it and then seemed to relax a bit. The fifth risk did not put him at risk of revealing classified information. 'Project management,' was all he said."

At this point, Lewis tells the complex tale, which I briefly mentioned earlier, of the country's first nuclear weapon site, located at Hanford, Washington and open from 1943 to 1987. "In that time," Lewis writes, "it supplied the material for seventy thousand nuclear weapons."

Never mind that there aren't 70,000 Russian cities or military targets; if the bombs had all been deployed, we would have been targeting individual Russians. The importance of the Hanford story is that, three decades after the facility's closure, it is a "monument to mismanagement," riddled with dangerous nuclear waste and costing the DOE $3 billion a year in maintenance and disaster-aversion costs.

Project management is a real risk.

---

[224] For example, George Melloan, reviewing *The Fifth Risk* in *The Wall Street Journal* (October 5, 2018), points out that "the U.S. managed to get along without an Energy Department for 188 years until 1977, when Jimmy Carter created it in response to an 'energy crisis' brought on by federal price controls." He's right, but we did have an Atomic Energy Commission (not Cabinet-level). He's also right to be concerned that agencies tend to grow in size and cost over time. This is because the political constituency for growth of the agency is concentrated and motivated while the constituency for restraint in growth is diffuse and has other concerns. https://www.wsj.com/articles/the-fifth-risk-review-managing-the-unmanageable-1538433119

Feeding the People

In addition to the Department of Energy, Lewis also takes a close look at the sometimes maligned Department of Agriculture (USDA) and the more highly respected National Oceanic and Atmospheric Administration (NOAA, once known as the Weather Bureau — 17 syllables in place of four).

The standard joke about the USDA is that an employee of the agency is seen crying at his desk. Another employee asks him what the matter is and the crying fellow says, "My farmer died." The joke is not *quite* fair — the USDA has 100,000 employees in a country of three million farmers — but the ratio does sound alarming.

What does the agency actually do? A great deal, as Lewis explains in detail. The USDA's largest budget item, 70% of the total, is for what used to be called food stamps; in another syllabic explosion, it's now SNAP, the Supplemental Nutrition Assistance Program, 12 syllables in place of two (and for many people it's not supplemental). That explains a lot: people have to eat.

The USDA also subsumes the Forest Service, which manages 193 million acres of forests and other rural lands — an area 87 times as large as Yellowstone National Park, mostly privately owned but managed under the Forest Service's "wise use" ethic, which contrasts with the competing National Park Service's goal of "preservation forever."[225] Other programs include education (agricultural "extension services" that supply information to farmers) and research.

None of these activities sound particularly labor-intensive to me, and it's not clear that all 100,000 employees are efficiently deployed. Lewis balances his praise for government's heroes with concern about waste and incompetence — he quotes Lillian Salerno, head of rural development for the USDA, as saying that "fewer than 50" of the agency's 100,000 have been trained to create an Excel spreadsheet. Not 50%; 50 *employees*. How do the other 99,950 do their jobs? These days, you can't be a lumberyard worker or a delivery truck driver without knowing how to use a spreadsheet, but you can be responsible for spending your share of the USDA's $151 billion budget. Hmm.

---

[225] This divide goes back to President Theodore Roosevelt, who wanted both approaches implemented. John Muir persuaded Roosevelt to greatly expand the National Park Service and Gifford Pinchot was made head of the newly created Forest Service.

Selling the Weather

The amount of rent-seeking that Lewis documents as taking place between the private sector and the government is enough to make me shudder. (Rent-seeking is an economist's term for a private party using government power to extract unearned profits.)

The example detailed by Lewis involves NOAA. The Trump administration nominated Barry Myers, head of AccuWeather and brother of its founder, to head the agency.

The rub is that AccuWeather's business — its only business — is to repackage publicly available weather data, including that from NOAA, for commercial purposes. AccuWeather does add value, but it gets the data feed from the government for free. In 2005, Pennsylvania Senator Rick Santorum, who had received campaign contributions from Myers, introduced a bill that would have "forbidden...the National Weather Service ...from delivering any weather-related knowledge to any American who might otherwise wind up a paying customer of AccuWeather...[except] when human life and property was at stake," Lewis writes.

Fortunately the bill never made it out of committee. But "pause for a second," continues Lewis, "to consider the audacity of that maneuver." It's bad enough that Myers tried to get Americans to pay again for weather forecasts they had already paid for through their taxes. But Trump nominating him — a lawyer and entrepreneur, not even a weather scientist — to run NOAA is just too much to bear, implies Lewis.

The whole second half of *The Fifth Risk* is about weather, NOAA, and attempts to corrupt or undermine the agency's mission. Weather forecasting is a fascinating and complex affair. It requires intergovernmental cooperation (because weather knows no national boundaries), a network of geosynchronous and polar satellites, and intricate mathematical models that run on some of the world's fastest supercomputers. Chaos theory was invented to help with weather forecasting.

The public safety benefits of making good forecasts and disseminating them effectively are dramatic. Lewis recalls: "'We ran the no-satellite experiment in Galveston in 1900,' says Tim Schmit, a career NOAA researcher who has spent the last twenty-two years creating new and better satellite images of Earth. 'Ten thousand people died.'" Galveston's destruction, still the deadliest natural disaster in American history is vividly described in Erik Larson's fine book, *Isaac's Storm*.[226]

With satellites and supercomputer-based models of the atmosphere, no one needs to die because a monster storm is coming but we can't see it.

Hurricanes, unlike tornadoes, can now be seen to be approaching so far in advance that everyone in its path can theoretically be evacuated. Saving everyone then depends on the efficiency of the evacuation effort and the cooperation of the potential victims. To encourage the latter, NOAA employs behavioral scientists who try to figure out the best ways of convincing people not to ride the storm out, going against the innate human perception that one is safest at home.

There's more to weather forecasting than meets the eye.

The Nonexistent Next Generation of Government Workers

As an employer, the federal government is in trouble. Lewis writes, "there are five times more people working for the government over the age of 60 than under the age of 30." Other than symphony conductors, what other profession can you say that about? Even activities directors at nursing homes are probably younger.

Young, ambitious people don't want to work for the government, and it's not just the money, which, with pensions and health benefits, isn't that bad. It's because the folklore, not entirely incorrect, is that, unless they rise to great heights, their career will consist of writing reports that will go in a file cabinet and never be read.

They want to make a difference, and fear that they won't.

Walking around Washington you see lots of energetic young people, and if you overhear their conversations they sound highly intelligent. But chances are they're working for a lobbying firm, trade association, nonprofit organization, or corporation that sells products or services to the government, rather than for a government agency. Lewis has identified a problem for future administrations to solve. He doesn't have much hope for the current one solving any problem.

---

[226] Larson, Erik. 1999. Isaac's Storm: A Man, a Time, and the Deadliest Hurricane in History. New York: Vintage Books.

Why Immigrants Favor Large Government

I was born American; I did not join this experiment in self-government voluntarily. It just happened to me. So, Lewis argues, I take reasonably competent government for granted, while those who uprooted their lives to come here from poorly governed countries do not. They appreciate a government that is responsible, responsive, and not wholly corrupt. That, and not the accessibility of benefits, is why Lewis says immigrants look upon government with a sympathetic eye, as long as it's a competent and non-corrupt government that protects them and their property, and provides basic services without endless graft. If that is true it bodes well for our future. According to Lewis, immigrants want to be makers, contributors to the public enterprise, not takers. I agree.

Balancing Private and Public Interests

If I have a gripe about *The Fifth Risk* it's that Lewis, like many reporters, has fallen in love with his subject — government. Just because Donald Trump, by Lewis' account an incurious and disengaged administrator, wants to eviscerate parts of the government does not mean that the size and cost of government should go unquestioned.

Actually, Trump's chaotic efforts to shrink government are making rational advocates of smaller government look bad. Some of the activities pursued by "competing private interests" are also inspiring and worthy of a Michael Lewis book: take a look inside Boeing, or Adobe Systems, or a family farm in this age of rapidly changing agricultural technology. Their shareholders and workers need the infrastructure and protection that government provides, but they also need to be able to keep a large fraction of their own money so that they have the incentive to do what they do and reinvest in innovation. With marginal (federal, state, and local) tax rates approaching 50% on people of ordinary means, we need to monitor the balance between public and private interests very carefully.

My other complaint about *The Fifth Risk*, and it's a very mild one, is that the book doesn't have chapters. If you're only interested in, say, Lewis' discussion of nuclear waste at Hanford, you'll have trouble finding it. *The Fifth Risk* reads like a compilation of magazine articles, because that's what it is — but without the usual breaks that make magazines easy to read. Much of it previously appeared in *Vanity Fair*, so its content may seem familiar to voracious news readers.

Missed Opportunities

Instead of 91 pages on the weather and the Agency Formerly Known as the Weather Bureau, I wish Lewis had turned his eye to some other agencies and other problems. It would have been fascinating to hear Lewis' take on the Food and Drug Administration, which shares responsibility for food safety with the USDA. When you eat a cheese pizza, Lewis writes, the FDA tries to make sure it won't kill you. But if it's a pepperoni pizza the USDA has the responsibility. Tell me more!

And I wonder how he would have reacted to Dr. Margaret Hamburg, who regulated one-fifth to one-quarter of the nation's economy as President Obama's FDA chief, being married to Peter Brown, co-CEO of Renaissance Technologies, a massive hedge fund that was and still is in a position to profit from early knowledge of decisions affecting food and drug companies.[227] Rent-seeking is not unique to the current administration.

I also wish Lewis had noticed the little agency that offers the biggest bang for the buck: It used to be called the National Bureau of Standards, but it's now the National Institute for Standards and Technology (14 syllables versus eight). Standards sound boring but they're a good thing. They are the reason why a half-inch pipe bought at a store in Cleveland matches precisely a half-inch pipe from a store in Portland, and why 110-volt electrical appliances manufactured in Taiwan run on the 110-volt electricity supplied to your home in Alabama.

The Internet is also a set of standards, specifying what you can host on a server or build into a browser. The most basic and familiar of these standards is the Internet Protocol (IP), which specifies how your IP address will be generated.

These standards were promulgated not by governments, but predominantly by private organizations such as the Institute of Electrical and Electronic Engineers (IEEE), with some government involvement. Basically, the entire Internet economy was created by setting standards, and relies on them being adhered to precisely. The standards were established by a mix of private and public institutions. As a result, a packet is a packet that is recognized by any router anywhere in the world.[228] Mobile phones work on the same principle — it's the network standards that allow your phone to work on networks from Chicago to London to Beijing.

---

[227] Renaissance Technologies has been, but is no longer, a client of my consulting firm.

[228] It is the TCP-IP 7-layer protocol stack that makes a packet a packet.

The fact that systems such as the packet protocol "work" demonstrates that there are private-sector alternatives to government standards and regulations. In many such cases, however, it is simply more efficient to have the government do it. The reason is simple: negotiations among a myriad of private companies and organizations are hard, and having a central authority is easy. There's a tradeoff between the flexibility of the former and the directness of the latter, and for many decisions the tradeoff works in favor of government. If we all drive 55 miles per hour, there will be fewer accidents.

Conclusion

The Fifth Risk offers the kind of nerdy fun that all Michael Lewis books provide: you learn more about some tiny aspect of life than you thought it was possible. (The U.S. government is not tiny, but Lewis breaks it into suitably small pieces for study.)

All citizens who are concerned that we are not well governed should read it. It will assuage some of their fears: the executive branch of the U.S. government is largely staffed by dedicated experts in their fields. However, it will inflame other fears: the tone at the top is discouraging. We're better than that. In the end, the book will help us better understand what "government" is and does as we engage in the ongoing debate about how big government should be, what it should and should not do, who pays for it, and how much they pay.

The author thanks Steve Sexauer for his generous contribution of editorial time.

"Yeah, we clearly
came at a bad time!
We'll be back in a
few years, and, uh ...
good luck!"

Chapter 19. How Paul Volcker Saved our Country

February 2019

When I had the pleasure of introducing Paul Volcker at a confe ence, I referred to him as "the man who saved the country." This was not hyperbole. It is hard to remember the deep trouble we were in, more than 40 years ago, when inflation reached 13% in 1979.

Times were terrible. A generation's life savings, invested mostly in bonds, had disappeared. In real (inflation-adjusted) terms, the Ibbotson total return index of long-term Treasury bonds, initialized at $100 in 1940, had fallen to $47. That's total return, with all interest reinvested! On a price-only basis, ignoring interest, $100 fell to $8.57 in real terms.[229]

You expect losses like those in countries like Argentina, where monetary folly tipped into hyperinflation and caused growth to come to a halt or go negative for long periods. But a slow-motion version happened in the United States, and it was not obvious we were going to avoid the Argentinian disease.

But we did avoid it, and Volcker deserves the credit.

The basic human will to overcome obstacles and prosper is so strong that even economies badly broken by monetary madness sometimes struggle forward. France, Italy, and Japan all had very high inflation rates either before or during their postwar economic miracles. Having the right individual at the right time in the right institution makes all the difference.

In 1979, in addition to prices spiraling up, trend productivity growth had fallen to 1% (one-half the postwar rate), labor markets were a mess, product quality was low, and you could buy America's best companies for eight times earnings. The part of the economy that could pass price increases along to consumers was doing well; the part that couldn't was collapsing. Consumers...well, they were waiting in gas lines. President Carter gave his famous "malaise" speech, which

---

[229] These are end-of-1979 data. The bond market would go even lower before it recovered in the 1980s. While most bond investors don't hold only the longest bonds, some liability hedgers, such as pension funds, do. Typical bond investors, holding bonds with a shorter duration, lost less money in real terms.

didn't contain the word "malaise" but should have.

Into this nation-sized train wreck rode "Tall Paul," as he was affectionately known — he's six feet seven inches tall, his family of origin is similarly sized, and they all used to live on Longfellow Street — and he cleaned up the town, like Clint Eastwood on his horse. OK, not exactly. In *Keeping At It: The Quest for Sound Money and Good Government*, an autobiography beautifully crafted with the help of the Bloomberg journalist Christine Harper, Volcker recounts the many struggles involved in achieving his aims. And his aims were ambitious: getting inflation down, righting the screwball monetary policy that prevailed when he was appointed, and getting along — or not — with presidents, economists, business leaders, and power brokers of the executive and legislative branches.

A Hinge in History That I Will Never Forget

When President Carter appointed Paul Volcker to the chairmanship of the Federal Reserve on August 6, 1979, the move smacked of desperation. Appointing a hard-money man, a strong monetarist, was not Carter's instinct; the president had previously drawn on the meager talents of G. William Miller, whose tenure as Fed chair was highlighted by his prohibition of smoking during meetings.

Volcker fit the sound-money requirement, although he was not a follower of the leading monetary economist of the time, the University of Chicago's Milton Friedman. Volcker was a Democrat, Friedman a Republican, and Volcker thought Friedman's prescriptions rigid and unrealistic. But the two men were on the same side of the bigger questions. Both thought inflation was a more destructive force that the recession that could potentially result from combating it.

The book informs us of the personal anguish behind Volcker's decision to take the chairmanship position. His wife Barbara was ill and did not move to Washington. Volcker had to take a massive pay cut. Barbara died in 1998. Paul, now remarried, is still alive (but unfortunately ailing) at 91.

Fifteen months into Volcker's term, Ronald Reagan decisively defeated Jimmy Carter in the 1980 presidential election. Volcker was skeptical of his new boss (the Fed is supposed to be independent but the Fed chair serves at the pleasure of the president), and was concerned that the suave Hollywood actor might be a lightweight. But Volcker recalls that Reagan said, "There's good news that the gold price is way down. We may be getting inflation under control."

Volcker adds: "I don't kiss men, but I was tempted."

Surprise! Reagan was not an old fool, but a thinking man with a background in economics and at least an elementary understanding of monetary linkages. (Reagan's economic sophistication was actually much greater than is revealed by this simple comment.) Volcker had a new ally, one who would prove challenging at times but whose overall vision was similar to his own.

Revenge of the Monetarists

I was exactly the right age and in the right position to be profoundly affected by this transition: just young enough to be impressionable, just old enough to know something about the topic. I had recently acquired a degree in finance from the University of Chicago's Booth School of Business. Many of my professors, ignored by Washington for a generation, were suddenly being recruited by the White House. George Shultz, the school's former dean, became Secretary of State. Edward Levi, the university's president, was attorney general. The Booth economist Yale Brozen, who persuaded me to attend the school and who gave me my first job, was on the Reagan transition team. It felt like my teachers and friends had taken over the country.

Brozen advised me to buy some Treasury bonds, which were then yielding 15%. I asked him why he was so sure they wouldn't go to, say, 24%, causing me to lose a bundle. He said, "Paul Volcker is a friend of mine and he won't allow that to happen." It's nice to know people in positions of influence. Unfortunately, I didn't have any money to buy the bonds.

Running of the Bulls

What happened after Volcker was appointed Fed chair? Exhibit 19.1 shows the Ibbotson total-return index for long-term Treasury bonds, expressed in real terms, from 1940 to the date of the Volcker appointment.[230] The stock market (S&P 500 total return, including dividends, and also in real terms) is shown for comparison. Volcker had stepped into a sticky situation, the equivalent of a 40-year Great Depression for bondholders, while equity holders had done spectacularly well for the first two-thirds of the period, only to stumble badly after 1966,

---

[230] To the nearest month-end.

1968, or 1972 (pick your high point; they're all about the same).

The Fed's responsibility is, of course, to keep inflation from getting out of hand and thereby maintain the real value of savers' government bond holdings. It is

Exhibit 19.1 Real Total Returns on U.S. Stocks and Bonds, January 1940 – August 1979

Source: Morningstar Ibbotson SBBI. Used by permission

not supposed to bolster the stock market. So Volcker was essentially taking charge of a failed institution. Since the passage of the U.S. Employment Act of 1946, the government had taken responsibility for a substantial degree of economic management over the previous half-century; it had not been doing its job.

Volcker's radical monetarism got off to a rough start: after he targeted the money supply instead of interest rates, the Federal funds rate soared to 21.5%, unheard of in American history. These sky-high rates drove many credit-dependent enterprises, some of which had survived the real Great Depression, out of business. There were two recessions in the first three years of Volcker's tenure, the second one being particularly severe (and comparable in depth to the Global Financial Crisis of 2007-2009). But was that too high a price to pay for the outcome shown in Exhibit 19.2?

The stock market rose almost as much in the 20 years shown in Exhibit 2 as it

Exhibit 19.2 Real Total Returns on U.S. Stocks and Bonds, September 1979-
December 1999

Source: Morningstar Ibbotson SBBI. Used by permission.

did over 1940-1966. But the really dramatic difference between the two periods
is in the performance of the bond market. Volcker had restored health to the
market for which the Fed is most directly responsible, and those good conditions continue today (the bond market rose further in the new century, not
shown).[231]

Some critics carp that the twin recessions of 1979 and 1981-1982 were too heavy
a burden. However, sustained and accelerating inflation is a much greater threat
to the long-term well-being of a society than a sharp recession (especially when
the latter is followed by an extended recovery, which occurred).

Volcker really did save the country.

---

[231] Exhibit 19.2 goes only through December 1999 because I want to focus on Volcker's impact.

An Overreaching President

Volcker recalls an awkward moment in 1984 when he was called into a meeting with President Reagan and James Baker, his chief of staff (later Secretary of the Treasury and Secretary of State). Reagan "didn't say a word," Mr. Volcker writes. "Instead Baker delivered a message: 'The president is ordering you not to raise interest rates before the election.'"

Ordering him? The Fed chairman was stunned and disappointed. Presidents aren't supposed to tell Fed chairmen what to do. President Nixon had set a negative precedent by pressuring (not ordering) then-chairman Arthur Burns to hold rates steady before the 1972 election. The misstep helped ruin Nixon's reputation. Ronald Reagan was not known for overreaching: Iran-Contra aside, he had a conservative's caution about exercising executive authority. Volcker hadn't intended to raise rates anyway, but he lost some of his respect for the president over this incident.

Today, we see Donald Trump pressuring Fed chairman Jerome Powell not to raise rates, and it isn't even an election year; don't they ever learn? The Fed only has the credibility in the markets that it needs to do its job if it's independent of political influence. It has a Congressional mandate to achieve price stability and maximum employment, not to re-elect presidents.

The Back Story

The Fed chairmanship is, of course, the capstone of any economist's or banker's career, and reflects decades of prior experience. But everyone's basic values come from their childhood.

"They Have a Mortgage and We Don't"

Volcker learned the value of a dollar from his mother. As a child, he went to a summer resort where many people had boats. He asked his mother why so-and-so had a Chris-Craft and they didn't. She said, "They have a mortgage and we don't." Never poor, Volcker had it drummed into him early that you can get poor in a hurry by living beyond one's means.

Imagine his view of trillions of dollars in government debt three-quarters of a century later! He's against it, and was quoted in a New York Times article as seeing "a hell of a mess in every direction."[232] He's exercised not just about the overextended finances of our various levels of government but about the influence of money on politics. And he believes that our main civic institutions have thereby been corrupted to the point that people have lost respect for them: "Respect for government, respect for the Supreme Court, respect for the president, it's all gone...even respect for the Federal Reserve," Volcker said. Only the military, Volcker believes, still commands widespread admiration.

"The Best Job in the World"

Before he was Fed chair, Volcker accumulated a resume that reflected his lifelong attraction to public service. Although he was chairman of the Kennedy for president committee in his home town in 1960, he managed to become one of the two appointed Democrats in the Nixon administration. (The other was Daniel Patrick Moynihan.) Volcker describes his post, undersecretary of the Treasury for monetary affairs, as "for me, the best job in the world." It's nice to love your work.

The tumultuous Nixon years were full of monetary challenges. The dollar was devalued against most leading foreign currencies, the "gold window" (where dollars could be redeemed for gold at a bargain $35 per ounce) was closed, and inflation accelerated from a meow to a roar. President Nixon imposed wage and price controls, which had only previously been attempted in wartime; economists howled; and, in early 1974, Volcker decided he had had enough.

Facing a choice between academia and lucrative private enterprise, he went back to Princeton, where he had been on the faculty. The job did not last long. He was called back to public service as president of the New York Fed, a job he held from May 1975 until President Carter appointed him Fed chair four years later. Of the New York Fed, Volcker writes, "I asked my assistant to dispose of a large plant sitting just outside my office that appeared to be dying. A week or so later, I asked why it was still there. Her dispiriting answer: policy dictated that if I didn't have the plant, none of the officers could have one." No wonder it is hard for governments to get things done!

---

[232] Sorkin, Andrew Ross. 2018. "Paul Volcker, at 91, Sees 'a Hell of a Mess in Every Direction'." New York Times (October 23).

After the Fed, A Private Sector Interlude

Upon leaving the government, Volcker became chairman of Wolfensohn & Company, an investment firm founded by former World Bank chairman Paul Wolfensohn. (Even heroes have to make a living.) He also rejoined Princeton as a professor of economic policy and served as a visiting professor at NYU. That's a pretty good gig for a fellow without a Ph.D., but running the Fed probably provides a better doctoral-level education than researching an obscure topic so as to please a dissertation committee.

During this period in his life, Volcker remained deeply involved with policy issues. He led the Group of Thirty, a consultative club that includes many central bankers and Nobel or near-Nobel-level economists. He was concerned with the risks accumulating in the financial system and suggested substantial reforms, including stricter regulation. Thus, when financial conditions started to deteriorate in 2007, fulfilling a forecast by Volcker, earlier in the decade, of a crisis within five years, he played the role of elder statesman, meeting with figures such as Treasury Secretary Tim Geithner and Fed chair Ben Bernanke periodically as the crisis unfolded.

But Volcker did not always back the consensus. The 2008 rescue of Bear Stearns, accomplished through a government-backed merger with JPMorgan Chase, strained Volcker's patience: "The Fed...had acted at the 'very edge of its lawful and implied powers'," invoking a half-forgotten section of the Federal Reserve Act that allowed it to lend to nonbanks in emergencies. "The point was that the Fed should not be looked to as lender of last resort beyond the banking system," concludes Volcker.

But Volcker did not think that acting at the very edge of its authority was wrong, only of questionable legality. He knew that unfreezing the commercial paper and repo markets, which were collapsing as some of the biggest players in the market, such as Coca-Cola and General Motors, were unable to roll over their short-term obligations, was necessary to prevent a broader economic collapse. Unfortunately, Congress has since taken away the Fed's previously ambiguous power to act as lender of last resort to nonbanks, removing another arrow in the Fed's quiver that could be badly needed in the next emergency.

An Unexpected Role in the Obama Administration

Following the election of Barack Obama, the president called Volcker into public service once more, this time taking the reins of the newly created President's Economic Recovery Advisory Board (PERAB) at the age of 81. Volcker's advocacy of more conservative banking practices led to tussles within the White House, but Obama resolved them by "announcing his administrative support for a ban on speculative activities within commercial banks, 'which we're calling the Volcker Rule, after this tall guy behind me' [Obama said]."

The point of the Volcker rule was to apply "the simple idea that 'thou shall not gamble with the public's money'," he writes. The moral hazard of banks being able to take risk and have potentially huge losses paid by the taxpayer, but keeping gains for themselves, had finally been addressed. Despite rising asset prices and the accumulation of both public and private debt, studies such as a recent effort by the Nobel Prize-winning economist Robert Engle show that financial crisis risk is low. The Volcker Rule seems to be working.

The Paul Volcker and William Sharpe Encounter

Investors will enjoy an anecdote Volcker tells about an encounter he had with William F. Sharpe, who (with some co-discoverers) formulated the Capital Asset Pricing Model, one of the foundations of modern finance. Volcker writes that when both were attending a conference on new techniques in financial engineering,

> I nudged him and asked how much this new financial engineering contributed to economic growth, measured by GNP. "Nothing," he whispered back to me. It was not the answer I anticipated. "So what does it do?" was my response.

> "It just moves around the [economic] rents in the financial system. Besides it's a lot of fun." (Later, at dinner, he suggested the possibility of small ways in which economic welfare could be advanced. But I felt I had already gotten the gist of his thinking.)

The Blunt Skeptic

Volcker spoke as mysteriously as any Fed chair when he was in office — "we did what we did, we didn't do what we didn't do, and the result was what happened" — but afterward he became known for his blunt pronouncements. He said he couldn't think of a financial innovation since the ATM that did any social good.

I'd offer the index fund as one candidate, and using futures and options to hedge tail risk is another. Moreover, some clever financial engineering will be required to create liquid and transparent markets in life annuities, which will be very useful if they arise. The long fellow doth protest too much. Sharpe should have stood up for his profession a little more robustly. But a skeptical attitude is healthy in a policymaker.

Volcker believes the financial system is still vulnerable and that the response to the 2008 crash didn't do much to prevent repeat episodes. The Volcker Rule is not enough; he favors even more regulation, and worries that the Fed and other institutions tasked with overseeing the banking system aren't doing enough to prevent a "too big to fail" situation from recurring.

Evaluating the Book

Readers interested in Volcker's tenure as Fed chairman, as dramatic a period in our economic history as the (fairly) recent crisis, should start at chapter 8. But Volcker's deep experience, his skeptical attitude, and his devotion to the public good are evident on every page. Unfortunately, we'll never known if the luminous writing is his or Christine Harper's; the book is written in the first person, in Volcker's voice. Whoever took the lead oar in the writing is a master of the craft.

Economists, investment managers, and sophisticated advisors would have benefited from more technical detail. Volcker is much more than a political operative; he's an accomplished monetary economist and policy analyst who could have shed more light on our current challenges. His chapter 15, "The New Financial World," addresses these issues, but only in words – no graphics, no math, no data. This is not really a criticism since the book is an autobiography, not an economic treatise, but it's a fact worth noting.

An Inspiring Book

Volcker appeared on the scene as Fed chairman at one of history's critical moments. The United States could have become a monetary basket case on the verge of hyperinflation. Instead, under his leadership, we enjoyed 40 years of disinflation and a bond bull market that impacted the fortunes of equity and bond investors even today. While the twenty-first century has been tumultuous, it is not for monetary policy reasons. In the long tail of Volcker's accomplishments, the dollar is sound and the inflation rate mild.

Investors and advisors who believe understanding history is the key to succeeding in the future — and that should be all of them — should read Volcker's inspiring book.

Chapter 20. What Is Good Government, and Why Is It So Rare and Precious?

January 2020

Navigating between the despotic extreme of authoritarianism and the unbridled liberty of anarchism is the challenge society faces in its quest for good government. A new book looks at the choices facing policymakers to achieve the proper balance and to improve the prospects of those countries outside the "narrow corridor" of effective governance that lies between those extremes.

Before economists were economists, they were called philosophers. (Adam Smith is the best-known example.) And, in that role, they focused not so much on production and consumption as on what John Laughland called "the mystery of state power."[233] They asked, why do people organize governments? How do they manage to collectively agree to give up part of their freedom to achieve some other goal, such as security or cooperation? Does this agreement bubble up from below or is it imposed from above? Does it work? Under what conditions are governments more helpful than harmful, and under what conditions are they the opposite?

Those are big questions, and it takes authors of the stature of Daron Acemoglu, one of the world's leading economists, and James Robinson, held in equal regard in the field of political science, to tackle them. Acemoglu and Robinson have done that in *The Narrow Corridor: States, Societies, and the Fate of Liberty*. It is an encyclopedic, provocative, and sometimes maddening book that is well worth reading — if you have lots of time. Readers with a more modest time budget should focus on specific sections, which I'll summarize individually.

Many of us in the business world fret about the expansive and costly role of government and don't fully appreciate what our lives would be like without it.

---

[233] Laughland, John. 2008. *A History of Political Trials: From Charles I to Saddam Hussein.* Long Hanborough, Witney, Oxfordshire, UK: Peter Lang. Laughland is a British political scientist. The phrase "mystery of state power" has been in the wind for a long time; Laughland's use of it is simply the most accessible.

Thomas Hobbes, the 17th century philosopher (and economist!), said in *Leviathan* that without a strong, effective state, human life would be "solitary, poor, nasty, brutish, and short" and "a war of all against all."[234] (He had a knack for aphorisms.) Readers who have lived in modern failed states, where gangs, rogue soldiers, corrupt policemen, and thugs rule, can relate.

Exhibit 20.1 The Benevolent Despot Rules over a Peaceable Kingdom (Frontispiece of Thomas Hobbes' 1651 Classic, *Leviathan*)

Note: The title is mine; the original artwork is untitled. Note that the ruler's body is depicted as consisting of human faces, representing (I suppose) the body politic that gives him legitimate authority. (Note that the ruler looks a little like Charles I of England. King during Hobbes' lifetime, Charles "lost his head" in 1649.)

Source: Detail of image from frontispiece of Leviathan *by Thomas Hobbes, 1651; engraving by Abraham Bosse.*

What is the optimum role of government — not just the optimum form, about which much has been written, but the right scope of its power? Acemoglu and Robinson argue that, to help more than it harms, it needs to stay within narrow bounds:

---

[234] Hobbes, Thomas. 1651. *Leviathan: or, The Matter, Forme and Power of a Common-Wealth Ecclesiasticall and Civil*. The "war of all against all" is scattered through his works in both English and Latin (bellum omnium contra omnes), but appears in Leviathan in modified form: "a perpetuall warre of every man against his neighbor" (and variations thereof). You get the idea. It's not pretty.

Squeezed between the fear and repression wrought by despotic states and the violence and lawlessness that emerge in their absence is a narrow corridor to liberty. It is in this corridor that the state and society balance each other out.

On first reading, I was reminded of Woody Allen's wisecrack that "mankind faces a crossroads. One path leads to despair and utter hopelessness. The other, to total extinction. Let us pray we have the wisdom to choose correctly."[235]

But it is not that bad, say Acemoglu and Robinson. The corridor is not so narrow as to be unachievable. Liberty has flourished in modern times and has not been totally lacking in any era. The important thing is to be keenly aware of where the boundaries are located and to be on guard when in danger of transgressing them.

In sum, they favor a strong state — not to *oppose* liberty, but as a *prerequisite* for liberty, contrary to the anarchic fever dream of a few radical libertarians. This strong state is not the despotic Leviathan of Hobbes but a "shackled Leviathan," one constrained by rules, checks and balances, and the watchful eye of civil society.

The Red Queen

Originally just a chess piece, the Red Queen is such a vivid character in Lewis Carroll's *Through the Looking-Glass* that she turns up frequently in modern literature, most recently in the estimable Matt Ridley's *The Red Queen* (about evolution and sexual selection) and now in *The Narrow Corridor*. After quoting the familiar passage about Alice's Wonderland being "a slow sort of country... [where] it takes all the running you can do, to keep in the same place," Acemoglu and Robinson write:

> ...[T]he state and society [have to run] fast to maintain the balance between them. In Carroll's book all that running was wasteful. Not so in the struggle of society against the Leviathan. If society slacks off and does not run fast enough to keep up with the state's growing power, the Shackled Leviathan can turn quickly into a despotic one. [But] [w]e need the Leviathan to keep on running too...for breaking down the cage of norms.

The Red Queen, then, represents the race between the state and society, with

---

[235] Allen, Woody. 1979. "My Speech to the Graduates." *New York Times* (August 10), Section A, Page 25.

each seeking to retain and increase its share of power. They need to continue running to stay in the same place (maintain a balance of power and stay in the corridor), but if one or the other runs too fast or too aggressively, it may cause a narrowing of the corridor or an exit from the corridor. That is why the dynamic described by the authors' Red Queen metaphor is such a delicate balance.

What is the cage of norms? "The same norms that have evolved to coordinate action, resolve conflicts, and generate a shared understanding of justice also create a cage...[that] restricts liberty." Among the worst examples of the cage are African slavery in the Americas and the brutal caste system that was traditional in India: these were socially accepted practices that were regarded as proper and necessary (by somebody). They could only be eradicated, and even then only partially in India, by state power.

Defining the Corridor

Acemoglu and Robinson define the Narrow Corridor that supports liberty and innovation using the graphic shown in Exhibit 20.2, which depicts the general model. The Despotic Leviathan seeks total control and the Absent Leviathan allows anarchy, the war of all against all. Only the shackled Leviathan (the narrow and easily breached corridor between them) makes liberty possible.

Prussia moved from within the corridor to the despotic side between the 15th and 19th centuries; Switzerland moved into the corridor in the High Middle Ages and has stayed there ever since; Montenegro, anarchic in the 19th century and then once again after the breakup of the former Yugoslavia, is moving in the right direction but is not quite there.

Exhibit 20.2 The Divergent Effects of an Increase in the Power of the State

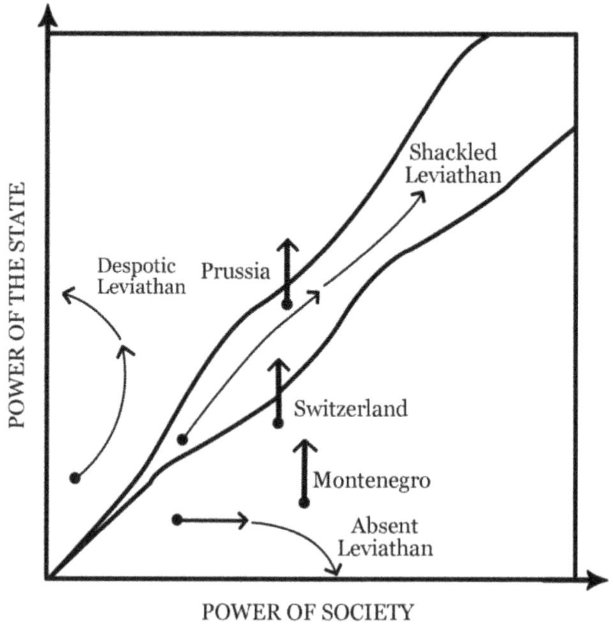

Source: Acemoglu and Robinson, *The Narrow Corridor*, page 268.

This is a helpful framework and can be used to characterize a regime anywhere in the world, in both location and direction. China has remained outside the corridor on the despotic side for eons, but has flirted with the edge of it in recent decades to the extent that economic progress has been strong and personal freedom granted to a limited degree.[236] Still, it is not going to move into the corridor any time soon. Several Central European post-communist nations moved from the despotic side into the corridor and have remained there. Colombia is moving into it from the anarchic side. South Africa moved decisively into the corridor under Nelson Mandela's leadership, but is struggling to remain within it.

---

[236] In *Progress* [2016], Johan Norberg writes, "The Chinese people today can move almost however they like, buy a home, choose an education, pick a job, start a business, belong to a church (as long as they are Buddhists, Taoist, Muslims, Catholics, or Protestants), dress as they like, marry whom they like, be openly gay without ending up in a labor camp, travel abroad freely, and even criticize aspects of the Party's policy (although not its right to rule unopposed). Even 'not free' is not what it used to be." Muslim freedom has suffered recently in Xinjiang, but it is *not* illegal to be a Muslim in China, while it is illegal for a citizen not to be a Muslim in the Maldives.

The United States and United Kingdom represent the balance between society and the state that the authors regard as optimal. (Remember that the next time you're feeling down about the state of either country's government.)

Begin at the Beginning: Ancient and Medieval Times

A book about human nature and the relationship between the citizen and the state is bound to rely on history, although not all such books employ history with as much vigor as Acemoglu and Robinson. They begin at the onset of recorded history, with the Epic of Gilgamesh, Hammurabi, the Greek Bronze Age (the one before the Greek dark age that preceded the golden age of Socrates and Plato), and so on through Roman times and the Middle Ages to modern (post-1500) times. When I said at the outset that the book can be maddening, it is because it provides too much information. Reading it is like reading an encyclopedia; you need to pick the sections that interest you the most and concentrate on those.

By page 152, the authors are up to the dawn of the Middle Ages, with Clovis' ascension to the throne of what is now France — and, a little later in the book and 300 years later in time, Charlemagne. Both kings, the authors claim, led their realms "into the corridor," sowing the seed of the idea that modern liberal democracy is not the only possible recipe for a tolerable amount of human freedom. They make the remarkable claim that modern freedom and prosperity have their origins in the forests of northern Europe at the end of the *fifth century* AD.[237] It's remarkable because the medieval history taught in school portrays this as one of mankind's darkest moments, the descent of the formerly civilized Roman Empire into barbarism, illiteracy, and extreme poverty. The Dark Ages! What if that wasn't so?

It wasn't, Acemoglu and Robinson assure us. To be specific, they write, the "assembly politics of the [Frankish] long-haired kings" were the "first blade of the scissors" that would put early medieval northern Europe into the corridor. "The

---

[237] These assertions by Acemoglu and Robinson give some support to the mythical origin of British liberty as having been introduced by the 5th-century Anglo-Saxon invaders Hengist and Horsa (whose names mean, roughly, "horse" and "horse"), of whom Thomas Keightley wrote in 1837, "[t]he love of liberty was a leading trait in their character; their obedience to their chiefs was free and voluntary; their religion...was no slavish superstition... [They] held the female sex in honour, and nowhere was valour seen to pay homage to beauty as in the forests of Germany" (*History of England*, Part I). I have always thought this view to be silly Anglo-Saxon chauvinism, but maybe there's something to it.

other blade," they write, "came from the Roman Empire," manifesting itself in the "lay institution" of the bureaucratic state and the "hierarchy of the [Roman Catholic] church," which is a legacy of Roman imperial structure that persists to this day. Together, these institutions combined to create an environment that was admittedly short on liberty as we understand it today, but that, "[by] getting a foothold in the corridor, [would start] these societies started on a process that would gradually change all these things": the servitude, feuding, and torture that we associated with medieval times.

If you're not interested in ancient and medieval history, skip to chapters 7 and 8 on China and India, or to "modern" European history in chapter 9. But the early stories are the best parts of the book. Antecedents are always revealing because, in human nature, there is nothing new. Whatever questions we have about our own time and our own problems, someone else has wrestled with the same dilemmas in an earlier and very different time. You think that the ugliness between the supporters of Donald Trump and the far-left Democrats represents a uniquely sharp division in political philosophies? The same social fault lines caused the Wars of the Three Kingdoms in England, Scotland, and Ireland between 1639 and 1651, and for that matter the war between the Maccabees and Hellenists in the second century B.C. that underlies the story of Hanukkah.[238]

The Mandate of Heaven and the Broken People

China: Wealth and Illiberalism

China is one of two dominant countries in the world, and we need to understand it better. Unsurprisingly, Acemoglu and Robinson help us to do that by starting in the 8th century BC, with the era known as the "spring and autumn" period. They write, "Chinese history took a very different path from that of Europe and one that created far less liberty. But it didn't start out that way." They then recount the contributions of Confucius, the leading thinker of that age, and his follower Mencius. The seeds of liberty are present in their works. Yet Chinese society evolved into one where the rulers claimed "that they had been given a mandate to rule from Heaven," an authoritarian concept if ever there was

---

[238] These points were made by Curtis Yarvin (the Three Kingdoms) and Christopher Hitchens (the Maccabees) respectively, not by Acemoglu and Robinson.

one."[239] Within a millennium the warring states of China produced the greatest loss of life from conflict, relative to world population, in all of history. One-fifth of the world's people perished between 184 and 280 A.D.

China is still an autocracy, despite many revolutions and political transitions — and, paradoxically, the country has made great progress, stunning actually, without embracing freedom. One suspects that liberal democracy isn't in their genes (and isn't strictly necessary for robust economic growth). Yet, the authors remind us, "Hong Kong and Taiwan, so close to China and cut from the same cultural cloth, have created societies that have demonstrated the powerful demand for liberty." I concur with Acemoglu and Robinson that this demand for liberty is universally human — but China has not supplied it. After describing the intrusive "social credit" system being imposed in China, which is a social and economic reputation score based on the observed behavior of each individual, as well as the panopticon state that has been developed in Xinjiang (the land of the Uighurs), the authors conclude that "[f]or most, liberty with Chinese characteristics is no liberty at all."[240]

India: Oppression and Enlightenment

In liberal India, ruled until 1947 by the tolerant British and then led by the idealistic and revered Mohandas Gandhi, there are people whose hereditary livelihood is transporting human waste. Really. They are a sub-caste within the large group called Dalits, or untouchables; the meaning of "dalit" in their native language is not "untouchable" but "the broken people." Who broke them? Not a despotic state, but the Absent Leviathan, which cannot protect the people from their own worst instincts and customs. They have been broken by the cage of norms.

India's laws are enlightened. Untouchability is strictly forbidden, and every Indian is a citizen and equal under the law. Yet there are about 200 million Dalits today, more than 15% of the country's population. How could this state of affairs exist? Acemoglu and Robinson are incredulous too: "You may be skeptical that this ancient social [caste] hierarchy could be so rigid as to determine people's occupations in recent times. Who would enforce that?"

---

[239] The European "divine right of kings," asserted not that long ago (by James I of England in the early 1600s), is remarkably similar.

[240] There is a racial component to the oppression of the Uighurs. Basically white, this Turkic ethnic group is visibly distinct from almost all other Chinese, who include nonwhite Muslims who receive much better treatment. Ironically, Uighurs are also much in demand as models, because their partly Caucasian appearance is considered exotically beautiful in Han China.

The answer is *nobody*. The web of ancient social relations, determining the roles and obligations of each group of people to each other, survives — to the extent that it does today — because the Indian state is too weak to destroy it and replace it with the web of voluntary, arm's length, contractual obligations that characterize a free society. A Chinese wag said that China would always beat India in economic competition because China has one ethnic group and India has 40,000. It's an exaggeration, but there is a grain of truth to it. Everything about India is mind-numbingly complex, and steering it into the corridor and keeping it there requires an act of heroism and genius that has only begun to take place.

The Paper Leviathan: Latin America's Curse

One of the most interesting puzzles in world governance is the ongoing struggle of Latin America to achieve real prosperity. The authors call the typical Latin American state, to the extent there is such a thing, a "paper Leviathan" that has the trappings of a proper state apparatus and pretends to function as one but, by and large, does not. (An even more vivid image is the description by Dario Echandía, a mid-20th century Colombian politician, of the country's government as "an orangutan in a tuxedo.")

That sounds right for Argentina, sometimes called the world's only formerly developed country. However, Latin America is a varied place and the failure of the state to function does not apply equally everywhere. The authors go into detail on the divergent paths of Costa Rica and Guatemala,

> ...[which] were initially similar. Both countries were still under the despotic control of the Spanish colonial state until 1821. But in the next hundred years they diverged as sharply as any of [our other] examples... By 1882 Costa Rica was holding regular and peaceful elections...[and] by 1930, two-thirds of all adults could read and write.

In Guatemala, by contrast, the authors describe the brutalized lives of the indigenous people (who form a large majority) in the words of the Nobel Peace Prize winner Rigoberta Menchu, whose grandmother

> ...had to give away her eldest son [Menchu's father]...to another man so he wouldn't go hungry... He lived with the *ladinos* (whites) for nine years but learned no Spanish because he wasn't allowed in the house... They found him repulsive because he had no clothes and was very dirty.

The story gets even worse, ending in civil war, torture, and disfigurement. So, why such divergence between two nearby and physically similar countries? "The answer," Acemoglu and Robinson write, "is related to coffee... The state-building incentives of the coffee boom at the end of the 19th century...created a powerful Despotic Leviathan there. In Costa Rica..., a small coffee-holder economy [instead of vast estates] [was] bolstered by public services and improved property rights in land." What a difference a few twists and turns of history make.

Given its part-European heritage and wealth of natural resources, Latin America has struggled more than one would expect to join the fully developed world. A lack of effective government is the chief reason. Fortunately, that's a problem that can be fixed. Unfortunately, such change comes very slowly, if at all.

Acemoglu and Robinson go into similar detail on the obstinately illiberal Muslim world, which has a glorious ancient history and which began to modernize several times in the recent past, but which has regressed; Nazi Germany; and, oddly, Ferguson, Missouri, where the authors' analysis of recent clashes between blacks and whites reflects their basic theme that state power is only helpful when it remains within the narrow corridor. While the United States is, in their view, an example of the properly shackled Leviathan, sometimes it strays, with tragic consequences.

Once Upon a Time in the West

In this review, I give short shrift to modern Western civilization because it is the aspect of the world that is most familiar to readers, and because Acemoglu and Robinson do not give it a particularly special place in their storytelling — they are more interested in the whole world and the richness of its history. But they do have something to say about our own civilization and time.

In their Chapter 15, "Living with the Leviathan," the authors begin by describing "Hayek's mistake." His mistake, expressed in his influential *Road to Serfdom*, was to regard the move toward a more socialistic society as a one-way street to totalitarianism.[241] What Hayek did not consider was the Red Queen effect, resulting in a pushback from society that keeps the Leviathan shackled as it tries to expand its reach. Thus, the authors, assert, Britain and much of Europe have

---

[241] Hayek, the authors remind us, never opposed "all government intervention or social insurance." Some rigid libertarians, citing Hayek as an influence, thus misrepresent his position. See Hayek, Friedrich A. 1960. "Why I Am Not a Conservative," in his *The Constitution of Liberty*, Chicago: University of Chicago Press. Available at https://fee.org/resources/why-i-am-not-a-conservative/

remained free while adopting substantial aspects of socialism. "And...some of these dynamics played out in the United States as well," they remind us.

We have seen this see-saw effect at work in Sweden, Canada, and many other countries. A large expansion of the state is followed by retrenchment, usually brought about in the name of fiscal responsibility. These countries have retained a very high degree of personal liberty through these transitions.

Acemoglu and Robinson are also concerned about the hot issues of today: inequality, the misbehavior of Wall Street, and the large size of top corporations. Let's focus on inequality. They begin by agreeing with the widespread view that greater inequality in the developed world is due to globalization and technology; a decrease in the wage of low-skilled workers in rich countries is exactly what economic theory predicts. They also acknowledge the tremendous benefits of globalization to those in the developing world.

Their prescription is an interesting, centrist view rooted in their Leviathan analysis. They write:

> [One] challenge is related to trust in institutions. The Shackled Leviathan doesn't just need a balance of power between state and society. It also needs society to trust institutions. Without trust, citizens won't protects these institutions from the state and the elite, and the Red Queen becomes much more zero-sum.

The Red Queen is zero-sum when the state and society are at loggerheads with no moderating influences. What happens in that case? An exit from the corridor, a civil war, Nazism or Communism, or some other "ism" that demeans human life and destroys prosperity.

How are we to avoid this? The authors draw an example from Sweden, not today's Sweden but that of the Great Depression of the 1930s, which

> ...entailed greater involvement and empowerment of the state, while society also became more capable and better organized to control the state. This societal mobilization was bulwarked by a new coalition supporting the new institutional architecture.

These are broad generalities, but helpful in principle: we know what direction to try to go. The authors express concern about

> ...the response of many Western nations today, [which is] closer to Weimar Germany's than Sweden's with the elites fighting to defend their advantages and those in the most precarious positions succumbing to the allure of autocrats, and polarization and intransigence becoming the order of the day.

My concern too! Yet the authors' discussion takes an optimistic turn:

> ...the Red Queen is more likely to get out of control when the corridor is narrower. Here the United States and many other Western nations are in a better situation because their diversified economies built on manufacturing and services, very limited role of coercion..., lack of dominant groups diametrically opposed to democracy (like the Prussian landed elites), and their recent history of uninterrupted democratic politics translate to a wider corridor.

In other words, we have more room for error than, say, Weimar Germany. Still, the authors warn, "the Red Queen can get out of control even in a wide corridor if it turns resolutely zero-sum."

The authors conclude by recounting the three pillars of Swedish recovery from the Great Depression without slipping out of the corridor: (1) "the whole project was built on a broad coalition composed of workers, farmers, and businesses"; (2) the government intervened to stimulate the economy and create a generous welfare state without taking the economy over; and (3) on the political front, "engineer compromise and find ways of building a broad coalition to support the Shackled Leviathan and the new policies."

We can learn from history. While I don't agree with every one of Acemoglu's and Robinson's policy prescriptions, they are well argued and impressively supported with historical knowledge and sophisticated analysis.

Insights for Investors

It's difficult to apply such a broad-based, world-historical theory to investment decision-making, but let's try. Many investors actively allocate assets (hold non-benchmark weights) by country, region, or level of economic development. If one accepts Acemoglu and Robinson's thesis, they should invest more in countries that are moving toward the corridor and less in those that are moving away from it. This information is unlikely to be completed reflected in stock prices or bond yields, so investors may benefit from performing such an analysis.

Countries that are firmly within the corridor are usually considered developed and are priced as such, but there are exceptions. Japan is still in the wake of a 30-year secular bear market and has P/E ratios near the bottom of its own historical range (although high compared to some other countries). Countries such as France and Italy are priced for continued economic hardship although that is by no means a foregone conclusion. All of these countries are in the corridor and have the potential for — but, obviously not the guarantee of — renewed growth.

Countries entirely outside the corridor should not escape investors' notice. Frontier-market funds explore opportunities in places like Bangladesh, Vietnam, and Nigeria, and find some great companies at low prices. It is not impossible to imagine some of these countries moving decisively toward the corridor, as South Korea, Taiwan, and several countries in Eastern Europe did in past decades, and offering very high returns to investors.

Conclusions

The Narrow Corridor provides an effective counterpoint to the bubbly optimism of my own book, *Fewer, Richer, Greener,* in which I predict that continued economic enrichment and a leveling off of world population will produce tremendous human and environmental benefits. Readers need to know both sides of this story. Technological progress may proceed more quickly in states that are within the corridor, but it will proceed at some rate even if the precepts of *The Narrow Corridor* are not followed. Even the stifling atmosphere of medieval Europe and China produced some innovation.

Moral progress is more difficult, but it happens. Jefferson's Enlightenment-inspired America used to practice one of the worst forms of chattel slavery ever known; now slavery is repugnant everywhere, including places where it remains as a relic. The legal status of women in liberal Victorian Britain was appalling: women could not own property, leave their husbands, or even keep the pay from their own labors, which had to be turned over to the man of the house. Such laws seem bizarre today. (The actual lives of 19th-century British women were not as bad as their legal standing suggests.)

Yet the continuing story of man's inhumanity to man, in every age and in every part of the world, leaps from each page of *The Narrow Corridor*. It is only through the careful weaving between the hazard of oppressive government and the trap of anarchy that we can realize our full humanity. And that is such a difficult task that only a few societies have accomplished it, none of them perfectly. We have a great deal more weaving to do.

Chapter 21. The Future of Liberal Democracy

August 2020

Americans enjoy the economic prosperity and freedoms of its liberal democracy. But our elevated stature is threatened. As the U.S. recoils from the world, the era of U.S. dominance appears to be ending.

That is an essential takeaway from Richard Haass' modestly titled new book, *The World: A Brief Introduction.* If investors and their advisors, or ordinary citizens, want to understand the modern world, they should start in 1648. That's what Haass, a richly credentialed diplomat and foreign policy scholar, would have us do. [242] [243]

Haass starts from the premise that most Americans, having received a pitifully inadequate education, don't know enough

21-1 Richard N. Haass

Source: https://twitter.com/richardhaass, accessed on January 21, 2021

---

[242] If there were a Civil Service exam for the presidency, Haass (born 1951) would be in the Oval Office. He is president of the Council on Foreign Relations. During the George W. Bush administration, he was director of policy planning for the State Department and a close advisor to Secretary of State Colin Powell. He has been U.S. coordinator for the future of Afghanistan and U.S. special envoy for Northern Ireland. He is also a lecturer at Harvard University's Kennedy School of Government, a visiting professor at Hamilton (NY) College, vice president and director of foreign policy studies at the Brookings Institution, and a senior associate at the Carnegie Endowment for International Peace. In his spare time, he has written 14 books.

[243] I might have started earlier, in the Middle Ages when the fault lines that define modern life were first established, but there's only so much Haass was able to stuff into a 304-page book. By starting in medieval times, we can see that the fault lines between Western and Eastern Christianity, Protestants and Catholics, Christians and Muslims, Cavaliers and Roundheads, the Union and the Confederacy, and liberals and statists have much in common and are still at work in modern conflicts. One could even go back to Sparta and Athens. (Human nature doesn't change much over time.) And I haven't even mentioned the fault lines outside of greater Europe and the Americas. You cannot understand the present without understanding the past!

about the world to understand the debates and conflicts about international affairs that determine their fates. Having watched the random interviews where strangers are queried about the meaning of July 4 or the role of Abraham Lincoln in American history, he's right. Yet somehow a large fraction of these clueless citizens manages to make it to the voting booth.

Sophisticated readers may be disappointed in the elementary level of the first sections of the book on world history and geography. Those sections of *The World* are a recitation of facts — who, what, where, when — although they are elegantly written and the facts are embellished with a great deal of erudition and nuance, providing a glimpse (but not much more than a glimpse) of Haass's fertile mind. He could have well afforded to provide more analysis and critical thinking in these introductory chapters, but for those wanting a refresher in one of the most important topics imaginable, they are a valuable and accessible resource.

The later sections of the book, on globalization and the political system, are much better. Like most authors, Haass shines most when he is writing about his field of greatest expertise.

What Happened in 1648?

In 1648, the architecture of the modern world of nation-states took shape in Europe. An agreement called the Peace of Westphalia ended the catastrophic Thirty Years' War, a religious and political conflict that cost Germany one-third of its population (possibly a record) and drew in much of the rest of the continent. About this war, the art historian and celebrated author Ernest Gombrich, in a 1936 book called *A Little History of the World* and directed at older children, wrote:

> Whole villages were burned, towns plundered, women and children murdered, robbed and abducted... The soldiers seized the peasants' livestock and trampled their crops. Famine, disease and roaming packs of wolves made wastelands of great stretches of Germany. And after all these years of appalling suffering, the envoys of the various rulers finally met in 1648 and...agreed on a peace which left things more or less as they had been in the first place...What had been Protestant would remain Protestant. The lands the [Habsburg] emperor

controlled — Austria, Hungary, and Bohemia — would remain Catholic.[244]

If this sounds a little like World War I, the war in Vietnam, or the never-ending Middle East conflict, it is. Human beings have made great progress in most areas since 1648, but we have not ended meaningless war.

Exhibit 21.1 Peace of Westphalia or Peace of Exhaustion

Der weſtfäliſche Friede.

Künstler unbekannt

The Peace of Westphalia established the most basic principle of international law, still in force today, although often violated. In Haass' words, it is that "sovereign countries [must] accept...one another's independence and respect...the boundaries separating them."

This peace agreement has done more good than harm. Yet, in modern times, there are hundreds of millions of people living in what the investment manager and my frequent co-author Stephen Sexauer calls a "Peace of Westphalia prison." With Sexauer's input, I wrote in my book, *Fewer, Richer, Greener*:

> This precedent, which still holds and is the basis for much of international law, is the reason Venezuela is...ruled by a butcher who starves his people, while its neighbors, Colombia and Brazil, mostly prosper. Venezuela poses no military threat to any country, so no one can invade it and end the humanitarian catastrophe... The Rwandan genocide of 1994, not so much a civil war as a local hemoclysm, could have easily been stopped...but was not, because it was regarded as a domestic matter... The Chinese could end the misery of North Korea almost instantly.

---

[244] Gombrich, Ernest H. 1936 (English translation, 2005). *A Little History of the World* (Eine kurze Weltgeschichte für junge Leser), p. 195. New Haven: Yale University Press.

This can be changed... International agreements [can be] modified to allow policing by organizations with earned legitimacy... No one should live in a Peace of Westphalia prison.

In the context of describing the world as it evolved after 1648 and as it exists today, Haass spends the next 300 pages explaining how this history, unknown to most people, still haunts us. One of Haass' themes is that little-remembered events of the distant past have left footprints all over our lives, this being but one example.

Structure of the Book

The World is organized into four parts: The essential history, regions of the world, the global era, and order and disorder. The essential history is brief indeed: everything that took place between 1648 and 2019, viewed mostly from a European perspective, is compressed into 58 pages. It is Eurocentric because, as Haass explains, "Europe was the part of the world where the most powerful and influential entities of this era were to be found. A great deal of the world — parts of the Middle East, South Asia, Africa, the Americas, and East Asia — was colonized, mostly by European countries." Fair enough.

Haass emphasizes that the period since 1989, which many people think of as current events, is *history*, as much so as any older span of time. It has been eventful, with the liberation of hundreds of millions, an attack on the United States, a series of small wars, unprecedented economic growth in the developing world, three market crashes, a pandemic, and a regression toward repressive ways of governing.

The enrichment of the world population is one of the most remarkable facts of this short historical period. Haass reminds us of the happy fact that the percentage of people in extreme poverty, currently 9% by the World Bank's standards, is the lowest that it has ever been. As recently as 1981, it was 44%.[245] He also notes that the population explosion is now all but over, except in sub-Saharan Africa. He uses the United Nations Population Division's median estimate of almost four billion (!) people in that region, almost four times the current number, as a warning of what concerns we'll face in 2100. Many demographers think

---

[245] Source: World Bank, at https://www.worldbank.org/en/news/feature/2016/06/08/ending-extreme-poverty

the number will be lower, three billion plus or minus, but that's still a lot of new people.[246]

The Geography Lesson

Haass provides, in the second section, the geography lesson that all of us should have been offered in high school but, in many cases, were not. To someone well-schooled in geography, it will be shocking that some of Haass' material needs to be included in a book for adults, but he persuaded me that it does (see his Introduction).

Some investment professionals and clients are astonishingly worldly and can tell you the differences in food and architecture between Linz and Graz, have visited 15 cities in China, and can distinguish Göttingen, Gothenburg, and Groningen (and recommend the best pub in each). This section of Haass' book is for the rest of us. And some of it is too elementary. We really do know that "the Middle East has been, is, and quite likely will remain the most tumultuous of the world's regions."

Knowing the world is, of course, much more than knowing maps, historical events, and economic and population data. We also need to understand civilizations and cultures, businesses, art and science, wars, "the structures of everyday life" (the French historian Fernand Braudel's brilliant description of what he thought mattered), and power politics.

"The Global Era": Understanding Globalization

This is where the book gets good. While any knowledgeable author can write chapters much like Haass' introductory ones, only someone immersed daily in the world of international relations can produce sections like this and the next one.

The chapters in "The Global Era" cover most of the important issues of today except the COVID-19 pandemic, which started after the book was written. They are: globalization, terrorism and counterterrorism, nuclear proliferation, climate change, migration, the internet and cybersecurity, global health, trade and

---

[246] See the United Nations Population Division estimates at https://population.un.org/wpp/. Demographers persistently overestimated population growth (by underestimating the speed at which total fertility rates would fall) until about 2004, when their estimates began to creep upward.

investment, currency and monetary policy, and development. This sounds less like a table of contents than the course requirements for a two-year master's program in public affairs, and is only one section of the book! *The World* is nothing if not an ambitious effort.

What is Globalization?

Haass begins the section by noting that "globalization...is not — with few exceptions — a policy preference. [I]t is a reality." Hurrah. Unlike many commentators on globalization, Haass acknowledges the fundamental human desire to trade in order to better one's standard of living. Everyone wants to sell what he or she produces to the highest bidder, and wants to buy whatever they need from the lowest-cost seller. But until recently they didn't know that such sellers and buyers existed, or the cost of trading with them was greater than the benefit.

Localism, in other words, is the result of high (or infinite) transportation and communication costs. Globalism is the natural condition of mankind when those cost barriers are lowered by technology. Whether we like it or not, that is the world we live in. We had better take advantage of this profound change in our condition wisely. While globalization conveys tremendous benefits to the commonwealth, it does not benefit everyone equally and may hurt large numbers of individuals. Haass advises us that policies which address this concern will be successful; those that overlook it will spur the kind of unpleasant pushback that we observe in many places, including the United States.

Economic Considerations

Investors and their advisors should be concerned with all of the issues discussed in this section: it makes no sense to try to decide how to allocate assets without understanding the global context in which companies and governments operate. But the last three chapters of the global era section will be of greatest interest to investors. Let's review Haass' coverage of monetary policy, a key issue in this age of central bank overlordship.

Haass unenthusiastically acknowledges that the U.S. dollar is the world's reserve currency and medium of choice for transactions: "[I]n the land of the blind the one-eyed man is king, and for now the dollar is that proverbial one-eyed man." For now. China would like its currency to become the reserve currency, and the euro, cryptocurrencies, and a hypothetical "new international currency" and are also contenders. With its massive debt, poor fiscal position (in this horrible year, the federal deficit is an unprecedented 17.9% of GDP),[247] and low interest rates, the U.S. is not a promising candidate for extending the dominant position of its currency.

I'd note that low interest rates, which may appear beneficial, are actually a problem. With the U.S. government needing to pay a measly 0.6% per year for 10-year money, the temptation to borrow is irresistible. However, interest rates can go up. A $30 trillion debt, refinanced at 5% (close to the historical average rate), would cost the U.S. Treasury $1.5 trillion per year in interest alone. That is not sustainable if we are going to continue to provide government services and avoid punitively high taxes. And, to modify Herbert Stein's aphorism a little, that which is unsustainable will not be sustained.

Haass also comments on economic development in poorer countries, a central concern for investors in emerging markets. He is bullish on the developing countries, but cautions that foreign aid has mostly been unsuccessful and should be directed toward education and infrastructure, not the building of political alliances or the support of a welfare state. And he supports the conventional wisdom that the most important prerequisite of successful development is good government — a goal that can be maddeningly hard to attain.[248,249]

As noted above, there are many other themes in the global era section of the book. I can't summarize all of them in a book review, so I'll discuss one comment about the relationship between NATO and Russia that illuminates Haass' thinking.

Haass asks whether it was a good idea to expand NATO right up to the border of Russia. Most Americans would say, "Yes"; we need as many allies as we can get. But Haass, admitting that his is a minority view even among diplomats, argues that NATO expansion painted Russia into a corner, inducing Putin to pull back from the tendency toward American-style liberalism that had characterized Boris Yeltsin's hopeful interregnum. He writes,

---

[247] https://www.brookings.edu/policy2020/votervital/how-worried-should-you-be-about-the-federal-deficit-and-debt/

[248] See chapter 20 in this book, "What is Good Government, and Why Is It So Rare and Precious?" .

[249] One annoying tendency of non-economists writing about economic issues is to confuse real (purchasing power parity, or PPP, adjusted) GDP with nominal GDP, whether aggregate or per capita. The low GDP per capita numbers cited in, say, Haass's section on East Asia are not reflective of the relatively high standard of living there because they are not PPP-adjusted. Real, or PPP-adjusted, GDP per capita numbers are cited for various countries on page 88 and in the graph on page 89, but a few pages earlier Haass cites nominal (lower) GDP numbers for China, without comment about how to interpret the two different measures. The author could have well afforded to make the use of this basic economic statistic clearer.

Russia under Putin gradually lost interest in joining the liberal world order that had been championed by the U.S. Instead, Putin's Russia increasingly sought to undermine it.

It is too late to do anything about it, but we can only wonder if a less aggressive policy toward Russia would have drawn Putin closer to the Western alliance, an outcome much more favorable than what occurred.

"Order and Disorder": Our Troubled Times

The end of history was supposed to have occurred in 1989, as Francis Fukuyama famously argued. In Fukuyama's defense, he didn't claim that the whole world would embrace liberal democracy, and ended his original article title with a question mark: "The End of History?"[250] Before him, the Peace of Westphalia (1648), the Congress of Vienna (1815), the philosophers G. W. F. Hegel and Karl Marx (in the 1800s), the economist A. A. Cournot (1861), and U.S. president Woodrow Wilson (1918) all proclaimed the end of history, as did the French revolutionaries, the Communists, and various other ideologues.[251]

21-2 Francis Fukuyama
Source: https://moderndiplo-macy.eu/2019/06/22/a-few-words-in-defence-of-francis-fuku-yama/

Yet history marches on. History with a capital "H," the ongoing conflict among visions of an ideal society and the accompanying changes in power relations, is still very much with us. Haass writes:

---

[250] Fukuyama, Francis. 1989. "The End of History?" *The National Interest*, Summer 1989. The question mark came out in the title of his subsequent 1992 book, *The End of History and the Last Man* (New York: Free Press).

[251] Fukuyama (1989) wrote that Hegel (b. 1770-d. 1831) "believed that history culminated in an absolute moment — a moment in which a final, rational form of society and state became victorious." Antoine Cournot, in 1861, was the first to use the term "end of history" to refer to "the end of the historical dynamic with the perfection of civil society," according to the modern British historian Mike Featherstone. (See the Wikipedia "End of History" entry, accessed July 25, 2020.) President Wilson, echoing H. G. Wells, referred to World War I as "the war to end war" (usually misquoted as "the war to end all wars").

Europe...has in a short span of time gone from being the most predictable and stable region — one where history seemed to have truly ended... — to something dramatically different. Democracy, prosperity, and peace seemed truly entrenched. Not anymore. Much of what had been widely assumed to be settled, is not.

This is a bit of an overstatement. Every European country, including economically distressed Greece, has a higher GDP per capita than it did in 1989. The continent is at peace except on the Russian-Ukrainian border; the Balkans, which suffered vicious wars in the 1990s, are peaceful.

But the European peace is an uneasy one, marked by the partial breakup of the European Union, successful right-wing movements in Eastern Europe and elsewhere, a continuing refugee crisis, and an ongoing and unexpected threat from Russia. A similar story can be told about East Asia, parts of Africa, and the always confounding Middle East. We are not a world at war, but there are more flash points than usual. Even the United States is in poor shape relative to its own history.

In an attempt to make sense of this situation, Haass includes chapters on sovereignty, self-determination, and balance of power; alliances and coalitions; international society; war between countries; internal instability and war within countries; and the liberal world order. This, too, sounds like a two-year master's program.

One theme illustrates Haass' approach. While liberal democracy is not the only conceivable way of organizing a successful economy (China is the exception that tests the rule), it is the best way to assure investors of the legal and institutional structure, transparency, and freedom of capital flows that make global investing work. It is also morally right.[252]

What keeps Haass up at night is that the liberal democratic moment since 1945 is in danger despite a fairly consistent increase in the number of people living in freedom over that time. The reason is the weakness of the West, especially the United States:

Effective statecraft is conspicuously lacking. Institutions have failed to adapt. No one today would design a UN Security Council that looked

---

[252] This is a strong claim that needs strong support. A long and interesting discussion of this proposition is in Christiano, Tom. 2006. "Democracy," *Stanford Encyclopedia of Philosophy* (online), https://plato.stanford.edu/entries/democracy/. See also Acemoglu, Daron, and James A. Robinson, 2019, *The Narrow Corridor: States, Societies, and the Fate of Liberty.* New York: Penguin Press; and Riker, William H., 1988, *Liberalism Against Populism: A Confrontation Between the Theory of Democracy and the Theory of Social Choice,* San Francisco: Waveland Press.

like the current one, yet real reform is impossible, because those who would lose influence block any changes... Decisions by European governments or the EU have created a powerful backlash... The United States overreached in trying to remake Afghanistan [and] invading Iraq...[b]ut it has also taken a step back from maintaining global order, and in certain cases it has...done too little.

The rest of the liberal democratic world, he argues, doesn't have the cohesion or collective will *to* do the job. It is up to us:

The United States cannot be an example to others around the world...if it is divided at home...and lacking in resources. The good news for Americans is that their country has the means to do all this and still maintain an active or even leading role in the world...

All of this also requires that the United States get its own house in order — reducing government debt, rebuilding infrastructure, improving public education, investing more in basic research, adapting the social safety net, [and] adopting a smart immigration system that allows talented foreigners to come and stay...

In conclusion, Haass writes:

History...teaches us that [the liberal, rules-based international] order is not the natural state of...affairs...; it requires commitment and concerted effort... The question is whether the governments and those who choose them in this era are prepared to make such a commitment. The answer to this question will tell us...whether the liberal world order and its many benefits will endure.

Sobering but helpful thoughts.

Advice for Investors

Read this book! It does not contain any specific investment advice, but investors need to know the economic, social, political, and historical conditions in which they operate. You are not investing in pieces of paper called "stocks" and "bonds" — you are buying pieces of corporations and lending to governments. These are, of course, just aggregations of people, organized to accomplish some goal.

To succeed at investing, then, you need to know the human context, as shaped by the forces described and analyzed in Haass' *The World*.

Conclusion

As a writer, I've been primarily influenced by other writers whose aim is to make complicated things simple — thus, my admiration of Ernest Gombrich's *Little History "für junge Leser"* (for young readers), and my tendency to judge other popular historical works by that lofty standard. If children can be made to understand the subtleties of history, surely adults can too.

I compare *The World: A Brief Introduction* to Gombrich's elegant 1936 volume. Despite its Eurocentrism and insistent Christianity, which annoy some readers, Gombrich's *Little History* is a powerful personal statement. Everyone who reads it is affected by it.

Haass work has a little of this impact, but it is obvious from his talent that he could have done more to change the reader's world view in a profoundly memorable way. We would all be better off if *The World* were a little less Encyclopedia Britannica and a little more Richard Haass. We know he has it in him. But it is still a very good read and a necessity in today's world.

Provocative

Here, Larry branches out into areas he's only recently begun to explore, including factors that promote or impede economic growth and human progress. He draws on, and reviews, writings of eminent thinkers in various fields including history, technology, philosophy, and biography.

Wayne's personal favorite: Why Nassim Taleb Thinks Leaders Make Poor Decisions

—WHW

Chapter 22. Sam Huntington's Clash of Civilizations 20 Years Later

September 2018

In 2003 I attended a talk by Samuel Huntington, the late Harvard historian who made a big splash with his 1997 bestseller, *The Clash of Civilizations and the Remaking of World Order*.[253] It was an "answer song" to *The End of History and the Last Man*,[254] written by Francis Fukuyama, one of Huntington's former students and protégés.

22-1 Samuel P. Huntington (1927-2009)

Fukuyama's book proposed that liberal democracy was the form of political organization to which all peoples aspired and that they ultimately would achieve, ending ideological conflict once and for all. Huntington disagreed, saying that the world consists of at least nine "civilizations" that are destined to contest one another for power, influence, and allegiance. Sadly, Huntington was the better forecaster.

At the time of the Huntington talk, I wrote it up as a Ford Foundation "Conference Roundup," which I summarize *en passant* while providing my updated view of the issues he raised. First, let's identify Huntington's nine civilizations:

---

[253] Huntington, Samuel P. 1997. *The Clash of Civilizations and the Remaking of World Order*. New York: Simon & Schuster. Image source: https://commons.wikimedia.org/wiki/File:Samuel_P._Huntington_(2004_World_Economic_Forum).jpg

[254] Fukuyama, Francis. 1992. *The End of History and the Last Man*. New York: Free Press.

Exhibit 22.1 The World According to Huntington: Nine Civilizations

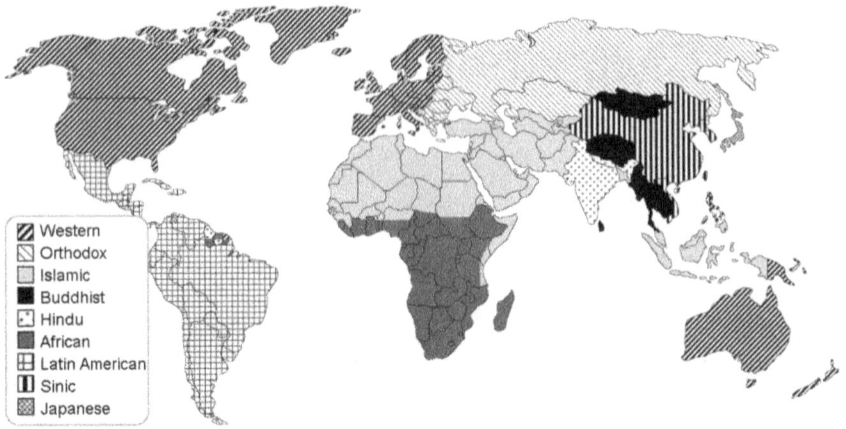

Source: https://commons.wikimedia.org/wiki/File:Clash_of_Civiliza-tions_mapn2.png

Civilizational Fault Lines

In 2003, I wrote:

> In Huntington's view, now that the divide between the "free world" (Western civilization plus Japan) and the Communist world has basically been eliminated, conflicts will tend to be on the geographic "fault lines" between these traditional civilizations, and may spread to involve whole civilizations. Huntington reasons that most non-Western civilizations, while wishing to advance economically, are profoundly threatened by the Westernization that seems to accompany modernization and are seeking ways to develop without compromising traditional values.

> Huntington does not think that the fears [held by] non-Westerners are necessarily irrational. "The collapse of [Communism]," he writes, "does not mean that [non-Western] societies will necessarily import the other Western ideology of liberal democracy. Westerners who assume that it does are likely to be surprised by the creativity, resilience, and individuality of non-Western cultures."[255]

---

[255] Huntington [1997], p. 53.

Where Are the Trouble Spots?

Huntington turned out to be prescient. Most of the world's danger spots are at civilizational boundaries: India and Pakistan; Israel (barely visible in Exhibit 22.1 but designated as Western) and Palestine; Russia and Ukraine; Sudan and South Sudan. There are exceptions, such as the troubles of the two Koreas and Venezuela (caused by Communism), but as a general rule the European Great Powers do not come to blows as they did regularly before 1945, both North and South America are largely peaceful, and so are most of the other civilizational blocs.

There is a schism in Islam (Sunni versus Shi'ite) that is not shown in the diagram, and there are still tribal wars in Africa, but by and large Huntington has been proven right: the main sources of conflict have been civilizational. You might notice that what Huntington calls civilizations correspond pretty closely to religions. Given the large role that religion has historically played in the mind of man, that is not a big surprise.

Islam Versus the West, and Other Conflicts

The biggest geopolitical event of the last 20 years was the transition from the simmering Islam-versus-the-West tension documented in 1990 by Bernard Lewis in his *Atlantic* article, "The Roots of Muslim Rage," into outright war: first, the attack on New York; then, counterattacks by the U.S. and its allies in Iraq and Afghanistan. The counterattack is sometimes portrayed as a six-front war that also included Libya, Somalia, Syria, and Yemen.[256]

But this series of conflicts did not escalate into a major war by the standards of the last century. More Americans were killed in the battle of Iwo Jima, one small part of one of the two principal World War II fronts, than in all American military involvements so far in the 21st century. Our tolerance for battlefield casualties has declined, and that's a good thing.

In fact, with one iffy exception, there have been no major wars in any developed country in the 21st century. The major wars have all been in Africa and the Middle East. The conflict in Ukraine, with about 10,000 dead, where Western and Orthodox civilizations meet (and mix in a small area) would be the exception — and then only if you call Ukraine and Russia developed countries (I do, just barely). On a population-adjusted basis, the 21st century, now about one-fifth

---

[256] Lewis, Bernard. 1990. "The Roots of Muslim Rage." *The Atlantic Monthly* (September).

over, has thus far been the least violent in history.[257]

Fukuyama, then, was not entirely wrong. For example, war brought on by British separation from the European Union is inconceivable. Both sides are arguing, cajoling, whining, begging, and generally acting like children, but they are not deploying their armies and navies. We are making some progress.

The Brighter Future of Western-Islamic Relations

In 2003 I wrote, optimistically,

> The *Newsweek* columns of Fareed Zakaria present a distinctive Muslim, pro-Western voice. Zakaria believes that terrorist acts are the work of "madmen" who could be of any religion. He argues that Islam is going through a "fundamentalist moment" but that the long-term relations between Islam and the West can be friendly and that the clash-of-civilizations theory is irresponsible.[258]

I believe this view, at least the part about Islam, will turn out to be correct. Until the establishment of Israel, the U.S. was regarded as an honest and neutral broker, if not a friend, by the Islamic world. While I support Israel strongly, I understand the reason for the break between Islam and the U.S. under those circumstances. Europe has already made moves to gain Islam's trust.

More importantly, revivals of religious fanaticism don't last forever. The Old Testament is shockingly bloody, but the Jews modernized their practical interpretation of it beginning in the 800s. Christianity and modernity reconciled sometime between Luther's Reformation of 1517 and the last execution of an atheist — by Protestants! — in Scotland in 1697 as the Enlightenment began to take hold.[259] Islam's Reformation is in the future, but it will occur.

I'm a long-term investor.

---

[257] See, also, Pinker, Steven. 2011. The Better Angels of Our Nature: Why Violence Has Declined. New York: Viking; and Pinker, Steven. 2017. Enlightenment Now: The Case for Reason, Science, Humanism, and Progress. New York: Viking. Pinker presents extensive evidence that violence, both state-sponsored (war) and at a personal level, has declined consistently over the centuries.

[258] Zakaria now writes for the Washington Post and is a CNN anchor.

[259] The world did not look upon this atrocity favorably. Even in 1697, world opinion mostly regarded the act as barbaric.

The Structure of Alliances and Rivalries

Huntington began his 2003 talk (based on his 1997 book) by saying that we now live in a *unipolar-multipolar* world. This is Harvard historian talk for saying that the United States is the only superpower ("unipolar") but that there are other Great Powers engaged in (1) a rivalry with one another and (2) a loose alliance against the United States, which would become their master if they did not in some sense band together ("multipolar").

Before World War I, Huntington explained, we lived in a *multipolar* world: the Great Powers were in rough balance with each other. These were Great Britain, France, Germany or Prussia, Austria-Hungary, Russia, the Ottoman Empire, and the United States.

Two World Wars later, all but two of those Great Powers were much reduced, and we lived in a *bipolar* world: the Soviet Union (the successor state to the Russian Empire) and the United States were the only superpowers. In the 1990s, with the Soviet Union having disbanded, the world found itself in the novel power structure described above as unipolar-multipolar.

In this structure, countries are opposed to those one level up in the power hierarchy and allied with those two levels up (because, to put it a little more crudely than Huntington did, the enemy of your enemy is your friend). He diagrammed the relations among the world's major powers as of the turn of the millennium as shown in Exhibit 22.2:

Exhibit 22.2 Huntington's View of the Global Power Structure

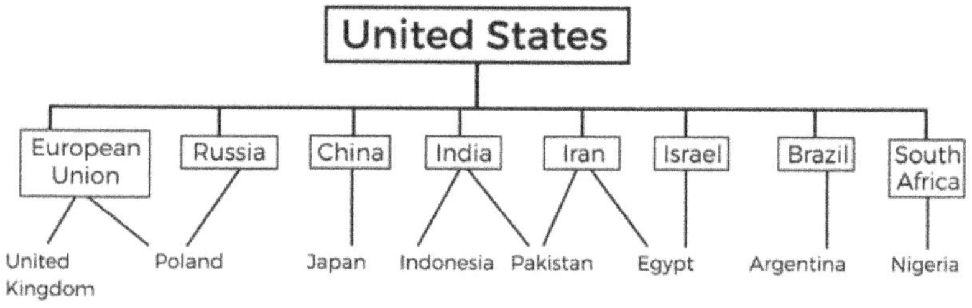

Art credit: Dave Stanwick

The lines, then, represent not alliances but rivalries or, in some cases, domination-submission relations. As I wrote in 2003, describing Huntington's views,

> Western civilization is dominant, and its greatest power, the U.S., is the world's only superpower. However, most of the other civilizations have at least one militarily powerful state, shown on line 2 of the exhibit. The secondary or large regional powers on line 2 are mostly aligned against the United States, since they regard the U.S. as wielding power that must be contained. However, the lesser powers on line 3 are mostly aligned *with* the United States, since they seek protection from the powers in line 2. The U.S. actively cultivates alliances with countries on line 3 while seeking containment of those on line 2.

The diagram explains why the U.K. is allied *with* the United States *against* the "soft empire" ruled from Brussels; why Japan and Poland have been such reliable allies of the United States; why India and Pakistan are perennially at loggerheads; and why Brazilians and Argentines, too hedonistic to actually fight, delight in making insulting jokes about each other.

The New New World Order

But that was 1997 (or 2003, when I heard the speech). Two decades later, things have changed. China is no longer just another Great Power but a superpower, not quite on par with the United States but deserving of a higher position in the hierarchy than shown in Exhibit 22.2. Seemingly natural enemies, Saudi Arabia and Egypt have joined Israel and the United States in a surprising alliance against Iran's Shi'ite ascendancy. India has risen further in prestige. China has acquired some African client states.

So I've drawn Exhibit 22.3, which is my attempt to update Exhibit 22.2 in the light of recent history. I've added, as American allies, Australia and Vietnam (the latter a big surprise considering our mutual history); although the illustration doesn't show it, they serve as a buffer against China. (In Exhibit 22.3, dashed arrows represent alliances rather than rivalries or dominance-submission relationships.) Mexico and Canada are shown as American allies with no intermediate adversary. I've promoted Japan to Great Power status, despite its limited military prowess, because its soft power is significant. I've reversed the positions of Nigeria and South Africa, and I've added Bangladesh with a dashed arrow representing its odd position as an ally, rival, and junior partner of India.

Exhibit 22.3 World Power Relations Today

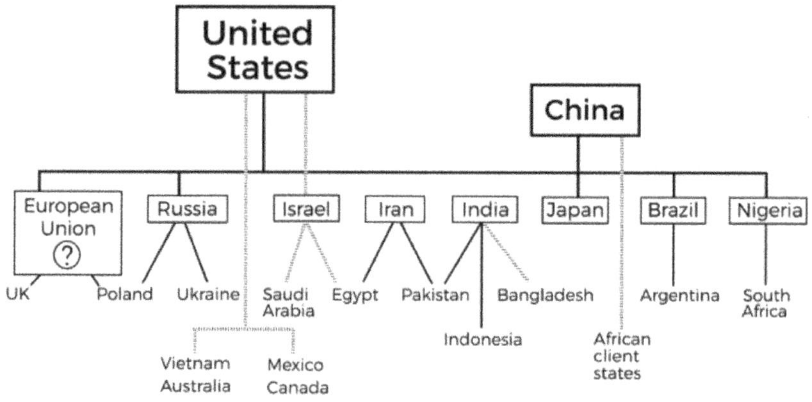

Art credit: Dave Stanwick

I'd like to add the Philippines, with its large population, and Turkey, given its strategic importance, but I don't really know where to put them. And the European Union gets a big question mark reflecting its current, and easily foreseen, instability.

It's become a complicated world. The solid lines still represent rivalry, but the dashed lines indicate alliances, some solid and some reluctant. And the current marriage of convenience between the U.S., Israel, Egypt, and Saudi Arabia is one of the oddest ever.

China and America: Avoiding the Thucydides Trap

Should we be concerned about a war with China?

Graham Allison, a political and military theorist, spoke at the same conference on which I reported in 2003. He believes that the situation in which Athens and Sparta found themselves in the fifth century B.C. is a model for future trouble: when an established power feels threatened by a rising one, war often follows. He is now worried about war between the currently rising world power, China, and the leading or hegemonic power, the United States. Like Huntington a Harvard professor, Allison writes:

[A]s China challenges America's predominance, misunderstand ings about each other's actions and intentions could lead them into a deadly trap first identified by the ancient Greek historian Thucydides. As he explained, "It was the rise of Athens and the fear that this instilled in Sparta that made war inevitable." The past 500 years have seen 16 cases in which a rising power threatened to displace a ruling one. Twelve of these ended in war.[260]

Examples:

- France, then the world's leading power, fought the rising Britain in a series of wars between 1689 and 1763.

- The situation reversed when rising France fought ruling Britain in Napoleon's day, roughly 1803 to 1815.

- A rising Germany fought France in 1870, but avoided war with Britain and the United States until the hellish World Wars of 1914-1918 and 1939-1945.

World War II was the last of the Thucydides-trap wars, so they're not unavoidable. The Cold War, where the rising Soviet Union threatened the hegemonic United States, was relatively bloodless. (At least that was true of the principals, the U.S. and the Soviet Union, with proxy wars fought in Vietnam and Korea.) And, remarkably, the Cold War ended with a whimper instead of a bang.

Interestingly, the rising United States never fought world-ruling Britain after 1815; maybe it's because we're blood brothers who speak the same language, but so were the Athenians and Spartans, who fought "a war like no other."[261] If we're going to avoid war with a rising China, Allison argues, the instances of war averted are well worth studying.

---

[260] Allison, Graham. 2017a. "The Thucydides Trap." *Foreign Policy* (May/June), https://foreignpolicy.com/2017/06/09/the-thucydides-trap/. See also Allison, Graham. 2017b. *Destined for War: Can America and China Escape Thucydides's Trap?* Boston: Houghton Mifflin Harcourt.

[261] As described by the military historian Victor Davis Hanson (2005), in *A War Like No Other: How the Athenians and Spartans Fought the Peloponnesian War*. New York: Random House.

China and the U.S. Will Not Fight a Shooting War

I agree that this historical knowledge is valuable, but China and the United States will not fight a shooting war. The first reason, emphasized by Allison but painfully obvious, is that we are both nuclear powers. Mutually assured destruction (MAD) has proven to be a pretty good formula for avoiding war: whoever strikes first commits suicide. The second reason is that rational people do not blow up their best customer. The U.S. is China's largest trading partner in the sense of exports from China to the United States. The Chinese standard of living would collapse without American purchases. China's leaders and people know that.

In addition, if you care about your standard of living, you also do not blow up your largest supplier — nor do you tax them to death through tariffs and trade restrictions. Not all Americans seem to realize this, but our standard of living depends on foreign trade too. If you want to pay $250 for a toaster and $3000 for a suit, become an autarchy (a country that trades only with itself); I've priced some made-in-U.S.A. goods and those are roughly the correct prices. A trade war is a circular firing squad, and has to stop.

If there is any danger in the U.S.-China relationship, then, it does not come from the Thucydides trap but from domestic political considerations. This kind of trouble can easily be avoided and most of our leaders, although *possibly* not the current president (he has a strange bluffing strategy that scares me but some say is effective),[262] will go to the mat for free trade and a robust and growing standard of living.

Populism, Nationalism, and the Current Dilemma

...which brings us to a topic about which Huntington warned us: populism and nationalism. In a book he wrote just after the 2003 speech, entitled *Who Are We? The Challenges to America's National Identity* (2004),[263] Huntington "argued...that American elites were dangerously out of touch with the American

---

[262] Donald Trump was president at the time this was written.

[263] Huntington, Samuel P. 2004. *Who Are We? The Challenges to America's National Identity*. New York: Simon & Schuster.

public when it came to issues of patriotism, foreign policy, and national iden-tity," writes *Wall Street Journal* editorialist Jason Willick in the centrist *American Interest*.[264] The book was not popular, and "at 77," Willick says, Huntington "was accused in respectable circles of losing his marbles."

Huntington warned that the liberal (in the American sense) elites sought an America that

> ...welcomes the world, its ideas, its goods and, most importantly its people. The ideal would be an open society with open borders, encouraging subnational ethnic, racial and cultural identities, dual citizenship, diasporas, and would be led by elites who increasingly identified with global institutions, norms and rules rather than national ones.[265]

Meanwhile, the conservative (in the American sense, that is, classical liberal) elites sought to give the gift of a bourgeois capitalist paradise to the whole world. West London and the Upper East Side of New York are representative of their idea of paradise. Some of them would spread this vision by force if persuasion failed.

The rub is that the common American would have none of it. Willick, echoing Huntington, argues that neither vision appealed to "the overwhelming patriotism and nationalistic identification of the rest of the American public" and their need for "societal security, which involves sustain[ing]...existing pat-terns of language, culture, association, religion, and national identity."

As Donald Trump governs "on a platform of immigration restriction, trade wars, and Jacksonian foreign policy," Willick concludes, "Huntington's thesis is look-ing more prescient than ever before – not as a prescription, but as a way of de-scribing the divisions running through the heart of American society."

I'm not pleased by Huntington's prophecy appearing to come true. It's not my America, which looks much more like a blend of the liberal and conservative elite visions than the populist, nationalist one. My ancestors came here speaking a funny language that sounds like German but is written in Hebrew letters. While facing discrimination, in one generation they hustled their way into the middle class and in one more generation they were welcomed, sometimes reluc-tantly, into the elite. While they maintained a modicum of separate identity and

---

[264] Willick, Jason. 2016. "How Samuel Huntington Predicted Our Political Moment." *The American Interest* (July 14), https://www.the-american-interest.com/2016/07/14/how-samuel-huntington-predicted-our-political-moment/ (gated).

[265] Quoted in Willick [2016].

customs, they vigorously adopted American values. I welcome anyone who would like to pursue that path today.

Huntington's Prescriptions, Our Successes and Failures

I close by recalling what Huntington said we should do to strengthen Western civilization and our place in it and to improve the prospects for world peace. First, his cautionary words, as reported by me in my 2003 essay:

> Civilizations generally feel triumphant and "universal" right at the time when their influence is beginning to decline. The West, he argues, is at such a juncture. From that point forward, however, decline is not inevitable, since civilizations can renew themselves by applying their economic "surplus" to "new ways of doing things." The problem is when people begin to live off their capital instead of investing in self-renewing enterprises, both private and social; under such circumstances the decline of a civilization is guaranteed.

What to do? Here is his list of recommendations from 2003, along with (in italics) my view of how well we've accomplished them, and a "grade":

> The nations of the West should strive for greater political, economic, and military integration.
>
> > *We are drawing farther apart from Europe. Obama's pivot to Asia and Trump's alienating behavior regarding Europe have done much damage. Trump has even questioned our commitment to defending a NATO ally with which we have a mutual defense pact. D*
>
> The European Union and NATO should include the "Western" (non-Orthodox) states of central Europe.
>
> > *Done. A*
>
> The West should strive for close alignment with Latin America, the non-Western civilization with which it has the most in common.

Relations with Latin America are mixed. Colombia and Peru have become close allies; Chile, despite changes in government, continues to be one. But Brazil and Argentina do not interact much with the United States. Mexico, a historically reliable ally, is understandably upset with our trade and immigration policies. C

The West should try to restrain the "conventional and unconventional" military development of Islamic and Sinic countries (China, Taiwan, Hong Kong, Korea, and Vietnam).

There is not much we can do about it. A further military build-up would strain our finances unacceptably. And China is a rival, not an enemy. B

The West should strengthen ties with Japan, rather than allowing Japan to accept Chinese dominance of the region.

Relations with Japan are good. We cannot protect Japan from hypothetical Chinese aggression involving overwhelming force, but that is extremely unlikely to happen. A–

Russia's role as "the core Orthodox state" should be respected, and its defense of its southern border (against a variety of other civilizations) should be considered legitimate.

We have become perhaps too tolerant of Russian expansionism. But Huntington's recommendation has been followed. B

Conclusion

The world we live in is immeasurably better than the devastated one we inherited from our grandparents at the close of World War II. We are many times more prosperous. More importantly, the prosperity is spreading to countries that were desperately poor not that long ago. In many of those countries, people now have much better lives and hope for even more progress in the future.

But we still live in a dangerous world. I am thankful for people like Samuel Huntington worrying about the dangers and proposing solutions so the rest of us don't always have to. We have much work to do.

The author thanks Dave Stanwick for substantial editorial assistance.

"Super! Now, once you've rebuilt civilization I can do the investment banking."

Chapter 23. Why Nassim Taleb Thinks Leaders Make Poor Decisions

April 2, 2018

Why do experts, CEOs, politicians, and other apparently highly capable people make such terrible decisions so often? Is it because they're ill-intentioned? Or because, despite appearances, they're actually stupid? Nassim Nicholas Taleb, philosopher, businessman, perpetual troublemaker, and author of, among other works, the groundbreaking *Fooled by Randomness*, says it's neither.[266]

It's because these authorities face the wrong incentives.

23-1 Nassim Nicholas Taleb

They are rewarded according to whether they look good to their superiors, not according to whether they are effective. They have no skin in the game.

Seasoned readers of Taleb will be pleased to see the so-called "experts problem" pop up in living color in *Skin in the Game: Hidden Asymmetries in Daily Life*, Taleb's latest collection of essays on risk, rationality, and randomness. According to Taleb, dentists, pilots, plumbers, structural engineers, and "scholars of Portuguese irregular verbs" are real experts; sociologists, policy analysts, "management theorist[s], publishing executive[s], and macroeconomist[s]" are not.

The difference is that, when people from the first list are wrong about something,

---

[266] Photo of Taleb is from https://www.cnbc.com/2018/04/25/black-swan-author-nassim-taleb-has-never-ever-borrowed-a-penny.html

it's obvious from the results and they suffer; they have skin in the game. Bad teeth, crashed planes, and leaky pipes are bad for business. People from the second list cover up their mistakes by substituting a different theory. They were not really wrong but just early, and, if they're lucky, which is to say skillful at apple-polishing, earn promotion after promotion by not failing utterly. (Financial advisors can argue that the fiduciary standard is the most powerful tool for putting them in the first list.) *Skin in the Game* is full of insights like this, some recycled from his earlier work but many of them new. It is well worth the relatively quick read.

Despite the many good qualities of *Skin in the Game*, Taleb's work, including the present volume, is often infuriating. He is too sure of himself, too unkind to his enemies, too full of bluster and obscure humor. Acting on his belief that some kinds of experts are worthless, he has populated the book's dust jacket with anonymous tweets instead of celebrity testimonials. Here's the first tweet: "The problem with Taleb is not that he's an ass—" (spelled out in full on the jacket). "He is an ass—. The problem with Taleb is that he is right." I agree.

I should also admit that, based on my limited dealings with him, I like him. I find his tough-guy persona to be hilarious, like Robert DeNiro's. He is a gentleman, quirky as could be, and masquerading as a holy terror for fun and profit.

Asymmetry, or why we are ruled by the most easily offended

In chapter two of *Skin in the Game*, entitled "The Most Intolerant Wins," Taleb asks why we seem to be governed by the most easily offended. You have to refrain from smoking in the non-smoking section, but you don't have to smoke (that is, refrain from not smoking) in the smoking section, which, by the way, is much smaller. Few people really care whether you say Merry Christmas or Happy Holidays, but the latter has become *de rigueur* in some circles. Almost all soft drinks are kosher.

The reason, Taleb explains, is that, for any given issue, there are a few people who care deeply about it and a great many people who do not. Those who care are spurred to action, even violent action in the case of religious or political passions. The rest of us, wishing to be left alone, rarely fight back with equal vigor. The results of this process include the increasing domination of Taleb's beloved, multi-religious Lebanon by Muslims, for whom conversion to Islam is irreversible. Conversion away from Islam is at least theoretically punishable by death; Christians and Jews don't much care if you leave the faith.[267]

In ancient Roman times, Taleb explains, Christians were the intolerant minority that pushed their views on the Roman majority. That's how Christianity eventually became the official religion of the empire in 323 A.D. Times and players change but the principles of human nature remain the same.

Almost all soft drinks are kosher because it's relatively easy to make a drink kosher. So manufacturers put forth this small effort rather than have two kinds of each drink, one for observant Jews – a fraction of a percent of the total population – and one for everybody else.

If this argument sounds familiar, it's recycled in much more general form from Frédéric Bastiat, the great 19th century French economist. Bastiat wrote that, for any given government action, such as a tax levied to subsidize some activity, there are a few people who will benefit greatly by it and they will work, day and night, to see it enacted. The great many who stand to lose will typically only lose a few pennies and will put forth little or no effort to prevent it. Thus the number of rules, regulations, taxes, handouts, and special favors granted by government grows exponentially with very little acting to restrain the growth.

These are just a few of the asymmetries of daily life to which Taleb's subtitle refers. Once you understand the principle, you'll see it in everything.

Waiter, there's a fly in my soup

The New York deli called Lindy's is famous for its clientele of Broadway actors and comedians, and for having food so bad that it has inspired a bevy of jokes including the one that starts with, "Waiter, there's a fly in my soup." But, Taleb tells us, it is also well-known among mathematicians and other scholars as the place where the Lindy effect was first observed. This is the idea that the age of an inanimate object is a good indicator of its future longevity:

> Broadway shows that lasted for, say, one hundred days, had a future life
> expectancy of a hundred more. For those that lasted two hundred days,
> two hundred more. The heuristic became known as the Lindy effect.

Likewise, Judaism, 3,500 years old, will probably last another 3,500; Scientology will be lucky to get another 60. Shakespeare will last longer than Stephen King.

---

[267] Some Jews perform a ritual for the dead upon learning that a fellow Jew, especially a family member, has left the faith, but this "punishment" has not done much to stem the rate of intermarriage or the decline in Jewish religious fervor.

Even living things that do not age on a particular schedule, like trees, tend to follow this rule. It could be because the old ones, having survived, are *anti-fragile*, a concept from Taleb's earlier book by that title; they are not just robust, but gain further robustness from exposure to stresses. Or maybe, like Shakespeare, they're just better.

This principle is very powerful and Taleb applies it to many topics, with the Lindy theme running through the whole book. Academia, for example, sometimes resembles an athletic contest in which the hardest-working or most aggressive participants appear to win. But this is not a good system for discovering truth. "The winner is the one who finishes last," said the philosopher Ludwig Wittgenstein; that is, the academic whose theories are least easily overturned, most enduring, had the best theories.

Investors would do well to understand the application of the Lindy principle to their enterprise. Indexing as a concept is about 70 years old; value investing is even older.[268] These great ideas are unlikely to be overturned any time soon. Instead, improvements around the edges are the best we can expect. The latest idea for earning alpha, whatever it is at the moment, will almost certainly turn out to be a flash in the pan, easily arbitraged away by the time it can be widely implemented.

Why are there so many employees?

To illustrate how the principle of skin in the game applies to labor contracting, Taleb compares the behavior of two private jet pilots. Bob is a freelance contract pilot who is sometimes useful to your little airline but is at other times so busy hauling Saudi princes to fancy resorts that he's not available to fly your airplanes. The result, an occasional stranded planeload of people, is disastrous for your business.

The other, a pilot-employee – I'll call him Bill – does more or less what you want, including working overtime in a pinch. Why the difference? Taleb writes,

> People you find in employment love the regularity of the payroll, with that special envelope on their desk the last day of the month, and without which they would act as a baby deprived of mother's milk... [H]ad Bob been an employee rather than something that appeared to be

---

[268] Index funds, as a concept, started with Jack Bogle's senior thesis at Princeton in 1951. Value investing traces its origins to Graham, Benjamin F., and David L. Dodd. 1934. *Security Analysis* (first edition), New York: Whittlesey House/McGraw Hill.

cheaper, that contractor thing, then you wouldn't be having so much trouble.

Economics dictates that employment is just one of many ways to contract for labor, and a particularly inflexible one that requires you to pay the employee whether you can keep them busy or not. You've probably considered replacing employees with contractors in whatever business you operate or work. Yet there are a lot of employees! Taleb's tale provides a clue to why: "Every organization wants a certain number of people associated with it to be deprived of a certain share of their freedom." Employment is the only legal way to achieve that sort of dependent relationship.

What's the connection to skin in the game? We tend to think of freelancers and entrepreneurs, such as Bob the pilot-contractor, as risk takers, skin-in-the-game players. And they are. But, as Taleb reminds us, "skin in the game is not [about] incentives, but disincentives." You don't want the employee to do what is best for himself in the short run – that's what contractors do – so you set up an alignment of interest between his long-run welfare and yours. As an employee with a family and a mortgage, and considerable costs if he has to get another job and relocate, he has skin in *your* game.

That's why we have so many employees.

Two very different kinds of risk

Because investing is applied philosophy, Taleb's whole book is relevant to investors, but the most directly applicable part is Chapter 19, "The Logic of Risk Taking." He draws the distinction, fundamental but rarely fully understood, between *ensemble probability* and *time probability*. (Like double-entry bookkeeping, this is one of those wonderful ideas that's obvious once you've heard it; less so in advance.) Ensemble probability involves a risk faced by a population at a given point in time, such as that of a hundred people visiting a casino once, where each person can make a one-time, double-or-nothing bet involving his or her entire fortune. In that single visit, about half of them will be ruined. The other half, having doubled their money, will be perfectly fine.

Time probability, in contrast, involves an ongoing risk faced by an individual over time. Consider someone visiting a casino 100 times in succession, also making a double-or-nothing bet involving his entire fortune. In 100 visits, that person *will* be ruined; usually ruin will occur after just a few visits. No one who behaves this way will ever be fine.[269]

With ensemble probability, then, as Taleb explains, "the ruin of one does not affect the ruin of others." With time probability it's the opposite: once you get a sufficiently bad outcome, the game is over and you cannot become un-ruined.[270]

This distinction is relevant to investing because the risks investors face involve time probability, not ensemble probability. In most aspects of life, we are accustomed to thinking about risk in the ensemble sense: a football team has a 2-in-3 chance of winning a game, a disease has a 10% mortality rate. So we are familiar with that kind of risk, and comfortable extending the concept to other aspects of life.

But, in investing, the state of a person's wealth at any point in time is contingent on her wealth at the previous point in time; returns are cumulative; investing exposes us to time risk, that is, cumulative risk. We are not typically able to do the mental approximations needed to think about that – if the risk of getting in a car accident on the way to work is one in 10,000, what is the risk of driving to work 10,000 times? (It's not 100%, nor is it insignificant; it's 64%. You should go to work anyway.[271])

Thus, we need to be very careful when relying on intuition to tell us about investment risk. Investing involves more risk than you think. We also need to be wary of extrapolating from the past (and avoid the temptation that comes from the fact that it's so readily accessible). Paul Samuelson famously said that "we have only one sample of the past," meaning that far more things could have happened than did happen; there's only so much you can learn from studying history. But it's just as important that we will get only one sample of the future! The return pattern that we will experience is just one of the infinitely many possible ones, and it will not be the one that we "expect" statistically; it will be something different, possibly very different.[272]

---

[269] The probability of surviving 100 successive double-or-nothing fair bets with one's fortune intact is about 1 in 10^{30}, the latter representing a number far larger than the number of seconds since the universe began.

[270] I've further simplified Taleb's already simple example by making the bet double-or-nothing and the odds 1:1 (that is, a 50% chance of winning, a fair bet). Taleb's example involves smaller losses.

[271] The right way to think about this is to start with the probability of not getting into an accident, which is .9999. One then takes this number to the 10,000th power, for a result of a (rounding) 36% chance of not getting into an accident in any of 10,000 trials. Thus the probability of getting into an accident is 64%.

[272] This is also the point of my article with Barton Waring, "What Investment Risk Really Is, Illustrated," https://larrysiegel.org/what-investment-risk-really-is-illustrated/.

Are you an IYI? I hope not

Consistent with his famously combative persona, Taleb takes pot shots – frequent and vigorous ones – at intellectuals, or, in his acronym, IYI. An intellectual yet idiot (IYI) is someone who is beloved by the public for his or her knowledgeable airs but who is actually full of baloney, having no practical sense.

Taleb considers Steven Pinker, author of *Enlightenment Now* and a current darling, to be an example, and calls him a "journalistic professor," not the psychologist and linguist that he obviously is. (I reviewed Pinker's book, favorably, in a different *Advisor Perspectives* article.[273])

When one gets past the gratuitous insult, however – Taleb doesn't think much of journalists or professors – he has a point. When a real expert strays from his own field, he is susceptible to making the foolish mistakes of an amateur, except that an amateur is likely to be humbler.

Taleb has not convinced me that Pinker is a wandering amateur. Maybe it's Taleb, not Pinker, who is wandering too far from the core of his knowledge.

Dedicated to the one I love?

Book dedications are rarely interesting; they usually feature one's parent, spouse, or teacher. But, in an odd twist that allows us to see (a little) into Nassim Taleb's mind, he dedicates *Skin in the Game* to two well-known people whom I would have praised less lavishly. First, Ron Paul, "a Roman among Greeks"; second, Ralph Nader, "a Greco-Phoenician saint."

In a self-referential joke, Taleb's comment about Ron Paul reverses the dedication of his earlier book, *The Black Swan*, to the great mathematician Benoit Mandelbrot, "a Greek among Romans." It took me a bit of effort to find out, by searching through Taleb's tweets, that he admires the Romans' practicality as much as the Greeks' gift for abstraction:

> As I came to realize…[,] the Romans were no-B.S. Fat Tonys; they resented grand theories and favored prudent and progressive tinkering.

---

[273] Siegel, Laurence B. 2018. "Is Life Improving? Documenting the Remarkable Progress of Humankind." *Advisor Perspectives* (April 30), https://www.advisorperspectives.com/articles/2018/04/30/is-life-improving-documenting-the-remarkable-progress-of-humankind; also at https://larrysiegel.org/is-life-improving-documenting-the-remarkable-progress-of-humankind/

Much of what they built, from constitution, to Roman law, to bridges, to low income housing, to their literature, to their imperial administration (still around in the structure of the Catholic church), has survived 2000 years.[274]

Paul, a doctor and former congressman from Texas, is an honorable – although occasionally goofy ("audit the Fed") – man who often stands alone in objecting to his colleagues' expedient political follies. I'm not sure (and Taleb doesn't say) why that makes him a Roman, but maybe an encomium is deserved; I would not have singled him out. Did I say Taleb was quirky?

But Ralph Nader a saint? He certainly sacrificed personal income, and subjected himself to harassment, when making the case that U.S. auto companies were making dangerous cars; he had skin in that game. But Nader has a dark side. Despite having taken a poverty vow and very publicly living like a monk, he revealed a personal fortune of $3.8 million in his 2000 presidential election filing – not a large fortune but not monkish either. He has also founded nonprofit organizations that do research of dubious quality, and his latest crusade is a meaningless fight against share buybacks (an important mechanism for enabling investors to get cash flow out of their portfolios). Nader is an odd choice for sainthood.

Skin in the game everywhere

Like many authors who've discovered a principle that they believe applies in many aspects of life, Taleb isn't shy about discussing every aspect he can identify. They include the role of looks in choosing a surgeon: don't choose a dignified, handsome one – one who looks more like a butcher "had to have much to overcome in terms of perception." Military interventionism? He's against it, arguing that policy analysts who make war from comfortable offices don't know what it's really like on the ground and have no personal stake in the consequences. Religions, at least initially, demand extreme sacrifices from their adherents because their leaders know they can only hold the tribe together if its members can see that fellow members have sacrificed too: "The strength of a creed," Taleb writes, "did not rest on 'evidence' of the powers of its gods, but evidence of the skin in the game on the part of its worshippers."

This campfire-style storytelling makes the book seem, in places, more like a

---

[274] Taleb's Facebook post of August 21, 2015, https://www.facebook.com/nntaleb/posts/10153269370143375. I've corrected a number of typos. "Fat Tony," a recurring character in Taleb's books, is an unlettered wise guy who is street-smart and makes money seemingly without trying.

collection of loosely related essays, as I referred to it at the outset, than a coherent book. This approach has an upside and a downside. It's easy to read parts of the book without losing the train of thought, since many of the parts were written as magazine articles and stand well on their own.[275] The downside is that, if you try to read the book as a coherent whole, you'll find it too full of interruptions and asides.

Conclusion

Taleb's writing is nothing if not lively. What other philosopher, let alone investment writer, creates characters like Fat Tony, a worldly-wise trader who cares little for book learning; Yevgenia Nikolayevna Krasnova, a neuroscientist with three philosopher ex-husbands, who writes a runaway best-seller called *A Story of Recursion*; and Nero Tulip, a thinly disguised version of Taleb himself? Taleb entertains, educates, and infuriates all at once, a heady combination for readers who score high on curiosity but frustrating for those who are just in a hurry to gather information and get on with it. This is Sunday afternoon, not Monday morning, reading.

Mercifully, *Skin in the Game* is also relatively short, unlike Taleb's previous book, *Antifragile*. It can be consumed effectively by a casual reader and does not require sustained attention.

Skin in the Game is not Taleb's best book – that's *Fooled by Randomness* – but it's his most accessible. I highly recommend it.

---

[275] Or chapters of the forthcoming book were serialized in magazines – it's hard to tell which.

Chapter 24. The Rules of Growth: Organisms, Cities and Companies

October 2017[276]

What do living organisms, cities, and businesses have in common? They all have organic characteristics: they're born, grow, sometimes shrink, and usually die; they all require energy to maintain and grow; and they all must deal with the sometimes undesirable byproducts of their existence.

Do these wide-ranging behaviors follow simple laws that have explanatory and predictive value? Geoffrey West, a physicist and past president of the multidisciplinary Santa Fe Institute, says "yes...and they are laws of *scale*." Such rules "*quantitatively* describe how almost any measurable characteristic of animals, plants, ecosystems, cities, and companies scales with size."

The biology and physics that underpin these scaling relationships explain why it is unlikely we will ever discover a land mammal much larger than an elephant or much smaller than a mouse, and never the mythical Godzilla of motion picture fame. Weight rises with the cube of length or height, so that, in order to move, hunt, forage, or fight, a creature much larger than an elephant would need muscles bigger than the creature. On the small side, a creature much smaller than a mouse could not exist because its heart could not pump blood through its capillaries. It would need a completely different body plan, such as that of an insect.

Likewise, though the lens of scaling, we can understand why, despite life expectancy increasing by leaps and bounds in the modern era, we should not expect to live beyond age 125. People wear out, not because they are overworked but because their cells are. Metabolism, the internal engine or "fire" of life, damages cells at predictable rates and that process puts a limit on how long we can live, even if all diseases become curable or preventable.

---

[276] Scale has the remarkable subtitle, "The Universal Laws of Growth, Innovation, Sustainability, and the Pace of Life in Organisms, Cities, Economies, and Companies." The author (or his publisher) does not appear burdened by an excess of modesty.

We can also find, in the vocabulary of scale, reasons why cities grow to mammoth size — several metropolitan areas now house 40 million people — even though common sense suggests that smaller units might be more efficient and pleasant. Some of these megacities are evolved versions of settlements that were established millennia ago, by people seeking in cities the same kinds of business and social connections that they do now.

Businesses, which are superficially like cities, in that they are aggregations of people pursuing some activity in common, reach their scale-driven size limits fairly quickly and have surprisingly short lives, although with a long tail: one Japanese business, a builder of Buddhist temples called Kongō Gumi, "lived" for over 1,400 years.

Scale, argues West, explains all of these phenomena.

West makes a valuable contribution to one of the overarching challenges of our times: how to expand the benefits of economic growth experienced by the developed world to billions living in poverty in the developing world while at the same time dealing with twin environmental challenges of pollution and changes to global temperatures. His contribution is the "scaling toolkit," which helps us better understand the resource dynamics of human interaction, people, cities, countries, and the world.

An author who reaches this broadly is bound to overstep. The usual rule applies: Anyone who thinks they have found a single explanation for everything, hasn't. There are limits to what can be explained by scaling factors.

West calls for a "Manhattan-style project or Apollo-style program" in pursuit of a "grand unified theory of sustainability," based on his concern that matters of scale could someday threaten the existence of the human race. I suspect he's talking his book. West's institute and career would benefit immensely from such an effort. Or it could be just what the world needs. We don't know. However, for the non-scientist, West's story of scaling opens a window to the hows and whys of resource dynamics in a growing world economy.

Some Basics

It is well known that there are some basic mathematical relationships between the size and the functional characteristics (say, speed or longevity) of *anything*. Science writers across the generations, from D'Arcy Thompson (*On Growth and Form*, 1917) to Stephen Jay Gould to Matt Ridley, have emphasized this fact.

The relationship usually takes the form of a *power law*. Here is one that is familiar to athletes: The strength of a muscle increases with the area of its cross-section, which is proportional to the *square* of the muscle's thickness; but the weight of the muscle is proportional to the *cube* of its thickness. Thus the strongest athletes, per pound of body weight (not in absolute terms), are the little guys, not the big ones.

This principle applies in shipbuilding, too, and in just about everything else. The grand engineer Isambard Kingdom Brunel, who built Britain's Great Western Railway in 1838, also built a Great Western steamship — the first modern steamship — for travel to North America. This venture succeeded, so he built a second ship, the Great Eastern, much larger so it could power around the Cape of Good Hope to the Far East.

But it was too big!

How can a ship be too big? The energy it uses is proportional not to its length, but to the weight of the water it displaces, which varies as the cube of the ship's length. So the Great Eastern lost boatloads of money and was eventually disassembled for parts. Her top mast still stands at the Liverpool Football Club's stadium, a monument to scaling gone awry.[277]

The Power Law for Organisms

In biology, West argues, a *three-quarters* power law is particularly widespread. (A three-quarters power law takes the form $y \sim x^{3/4}$.) Let's look at the metabolic rate, which is centrally important because it is the internal engine of all living things, the rate at which an organism converts inputs (food) to outputs (work):

> Elephants are roughly 10,000 times (*four* orders of magnitude, 10^4) heavier than rats; consequently they have roughly 10,000 times as many cells. The ¾ power scaling law says that, despite having 10,000 times as many cells to support, the metabolic rate of an elephant (that is, the amount of energy needed to keep it alive) is only 1000 times (*three* orders of magnitude, 10^3) larger than a rat's; note the ratio of 3:4 in the powers of ten. This represents an extraordinary economy of scale [in the use of resources] as size increases.

[277] In a 2002 BBC poll, the British public voted Brunel the second greatest Englishman in history, after Churchill but ahead of Shakespeare, Newton, Darwin, and all of the royals. This result is sometimes said to have been due to a campaign by students at Brunel University. See http://news.bbc.co.uk/2/hi/entertainment/2509465.stm. Brunel is almost completely unknown outside Britain.

Exhibit 24.1 shows this relationship, which also explains the relentless march toward larger size as evolution proceeds: small reptile to dinosaur, eohippus (an early horse about the size of a fox terrier) to modern horse, small sea mammal to whale.[278] Yet, as we saw at the outset, scaling factors also impose limits to size, as the organism encounters tradeoffs between the efficiency of larger size and the handicaps that large size inflicts.

Exhibit 24.1 Relation Between Size (Body Mass) and Metabolic Rate of Animals

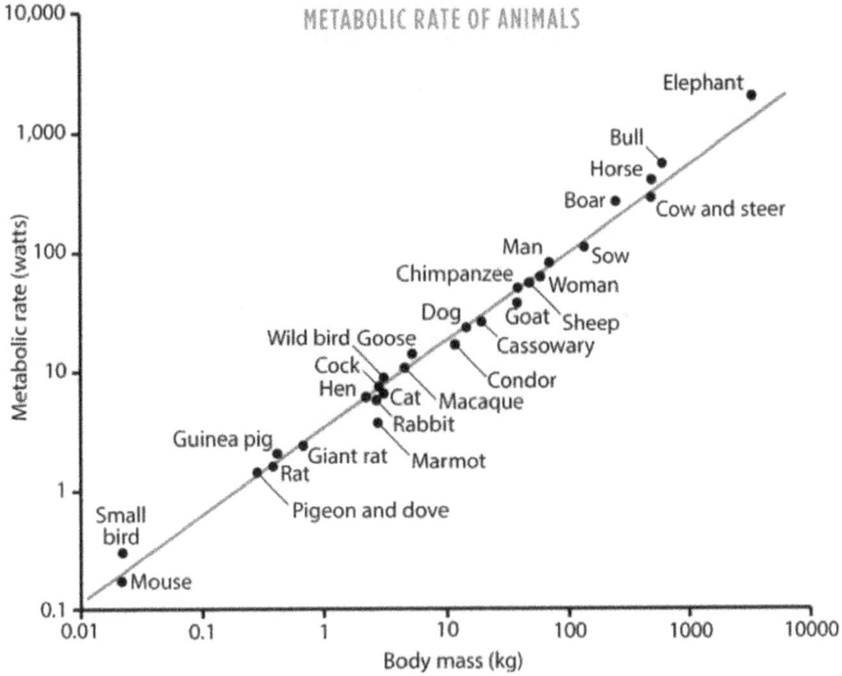

Source: Mann, Charles C. "How Nature Scales Up" (review of Scale by Geoffrey West). *Wall Street Journal*, June 23, 2017. After West [2017], Figure 1 on page 3.

Scale for Schoolchildren

Children learn about scaling early on, not just in the pecking order of the schoolyard but by repeating Jonathan Swift's rhyme from 1733:

[278] We are now supposed to call eohippus ("dawn horse") hyracotherium. Almost no one does, eohippus being much more melodious; and, while the comparison of eohippus to fox terrier is copied from textbook to magazine article to this essay, few people know what a fox terrier is, much less how big they are. Gould [1991] documents the spread of this silly meme, which I used so I could write this footnote. Gould, Stephen Jay. 1991. "The Case of the Creeping Fox Terrier Clone," in *Bully for Brontosaurus*, W. W. Norton & Co.

So, naturalists observe, a flea

Hath smaller fleas that on him prey

And these have smaller still to bite 'em

And so proceed *ad infinitum*.[279]

Packed into those four lines intended for six-year-olds are the concepts of scale, self-similarity, and fractals, the building blocks of West's book and of much of biology, much of urban economics, and — as we will discover — something about the life and death of business corporations too. (Yes, there was a time when six-year-olds could puzzle out "ad infinitum.")

Cities

Cities connect two power laws: (1) The sublinear ¾ power law for the inputs of energy and other services needed as city size increases (metabolism) and (2) the superlinear 1.15 power law as human connections grow 15% faster than city size due to proximity.

The latter power law indicates that each doubling in the size of a city results in a 115% (rather than just 100%) increase in each of the key economic variables such as wages, patents, and industries. Because commerce is transacted more rapidly, *per capita* GDP is higher in larger cities: Los Angeles is richer than Tulsa, which is richer than a typical rural town. The relationship is causal, not coincidental — the connections made possible by the larger city's size created the additional wealth.

If cities consume (relatively) less and produce more as they become larger, no wonder they grow so quickly! And they will continue to do so, adding to the stresses associated with rapid urbanization, especially in developing countries.

Wealth creation has thus proceeded hand-in-hand with the emergence of large cities, always and everywhere: in ancient times, in the last two centuries in what we now call the developed countries, and more recently in the developing ones. While it sometimes seems as though large cities have inordinate numbers of

---

[279] Swift, Jonathan, 1733. "On Poetry: a Rhapsody." Note that the rhyme suggests "flea" was pronounced "flay" in Swift's day, to rhyme with "prey." In 1922, the British mathematician and meteorologist Lewis F. Richardson adapted the poem to self-similarity in fluid dynamics: "Big whorls have little whorls/ Which feed on their velocity/ And little whorls have lesser whorls/ And so on to viscosity." This line of thinking led to Benoit Mandelbrot's (1967) discovery of fractals.

poor people, that is generally because they have migrated there in the hope of ending their poverty quickly — and, more often than not, they do.[280]

Exhibit 24.2 shows the relationship between city size and several attributes of cities: GDP, income, crime, and number of patents created. The slope of all of the relationships is 1.15; that is, the 15% rule applies to each of the attributes. Note that bad attributes (crime) follow the same power law as good ones.

West's investigation of the characteristics of cities is extensive and sophisticated. He is well read on the topic, having consumed not just the works of Jane Jacobs and Lewis Mumford (familiar to beginners in urban geography) but also the more academic contributions of Walter Christaller and Michael Batty. The lengthy section on cities was the most valuable part of *Scale*.[281]

Exhibit 24.2 Predictable Cities: Data from 360 US metropolitan areas show that metrics such as wages and crime scale in the same way with population size.

Source: http://wideurbanworld.blogspot.com/2016/03/settlement-scaling-and-social-science.html. Drawn by Michael E. Smith after Figure 44 on p. 343 of West [2017]. Professor Smith is a colleague of Geoffrey West at Santa Fe Institute.

---

[280] The persistence of relative poverty in minority districts of large U. S. cities can probably be explained by history (the migration of ex-slaves and descendants of slaves in the first century after the Civil War) and poorly conceived social policies. In the U.S., poor urban immigrant communities typically do not stay poor for long, following the pattern seen in other countries. In developing countries, progress from extreme poverty to "ordinary" poverty and, then, sometimes, to non-poverty takes place very quickly in cities, but U. S.-based observers may have difficulty recognizing the fact that ordinary poverty is a huge step up.

[281] This is familiar and friendly territory. Before I studied finance, I studied urban geography at the University of Chicago.

Businesses

West originally set out to extend his research on scale to businesses, but turned to cities because he couldn't, at first, get the business data. It's just as well he turned his attention to cities, because business didn't turn out to be as fruitful a field. Still, in the business world, West found some regularities worth noting.

Companies look superficially a lot like cities: both are voluntary aggregations of people, assembled to pursue a common goal. Both produce and consume resources, compete with other cities or companies, and seek to grow. Both start from essentially nothing and can become very large. However, cities tend to stay in one place, growing amoeba-like into new territory only over decades, while companies can pick up and move quickly and be acquired or dissolved with the stroke of a pen. Moreover, while cities almost never die completely, companies generally do.

West's key findings are: (1) Company sizes follow a Zipf distribution, like cities; and (2) The efficiency of companies — measured, say, by sales or profits per employee — scales sublinearly (that is, at a slower rate than a linear relationship) like organisms.

What an odd beast we have created!

George K. Zipf, a linguist, discovered in the late 1920s that word use in languages follows a power law in which (taking English as the example) the most frequently used word, "the," occurs twice as often as the second most frequent word, "of," and three times as often as the third most frequent word — and so on down to rare words.[282] This power law is observed in many contexts including the populations of cities (New York, 8.5 million; Los Angeles, about half that or 4.2 million; Chicago, about a third that of New York or 2.7 million) and the sizes of companies as measured by profits or sales. The ranking of company sizes is, of course, much more fluid than that of cities — the top-ranked company rarely repeats from one decade to another.

---

[282] Zipf wrote up his "law" with regard to the frequency of words in a language in Selected Studies of the Principle of Relative Frequency in Language, Cambridge, MA: Harvard University Press, 1932, and extended it more broadly in *Human Behavior and the Principle of Least Effort: An Introduction to Human Ecology*, Reading, MA: Addison-Wesley, 1949. Zipf's Law is closely related to the Pareto distribution for incomes, discovered by the Italian economist Vilfredo Pareto in the 1890s (see Hardy [2010]). Hardy, Michael. 2010. "Pareto's Law," *The Mathematical Intelligencer*, Volume 32, Issue 3 (September), pp. 38-43, https://link.springer.com/article/10.1007%2Fs00283-010-9159-2.

West's scaling analysis for the efficiency of companies is summarized in Exhibit 24.3. Each "cloud" represents, respectively, "income, profits, assets, and sales for all 28,853 companies in the United States from 1950 to 2009 plotted logarithmically against their number of employees, showing sublinear scaling with a substantial variance." Data for Chinese companies over a shorter period shows a similar relation, not shown in the exhibit. Thus, in two very different economies, adding more employees does not add to sales or profits at a commensurate rate.

Exhibit 24.3 Income, Profits, Assets, and Sales of U.S. Companies Plotted Against Number of Employees, 28,853 Companies, 1950-2009

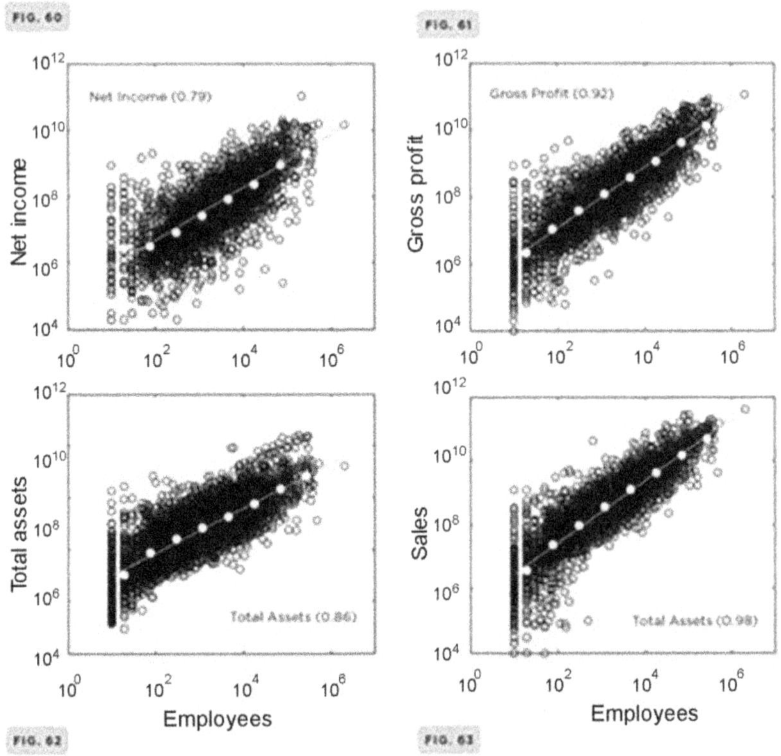

Source: West [2017], p. 388.

"This suggests," West writes,

> that companies are more like organisms than cities and are dominated by a version of economies of scale rather than by increasing returns and innovation. This has profound implications for their...growth and mortality. ...[S]ublinear scaling in biology leads to bounded growth and a finite life span, whereas...the superlinear scaling of cities (and of economies) leads to open-ended growth.

Note that, in Exhibit 24.3, sales do scale almost linearly with number of employees (the slope is 0.98), but net income grows significantly less quickly (the slope is 0.79). This means that costs grow superlinearly with company size, something that almost any corporate employee or manager would have expected.

West also studies company mortality but the results are colored by the fact that companies rarely die completely — they are merged or acquired, or their assets are sold to other companies. Thus the analogy with organisms is incomplete.

Sustainability

In the provocatively named subchapter, "Global Warming, the Exponential Scaling of Temperature, and the Metabolic Theory of Ecology," West issues a call for a new science of ecology or sustainability based on his observations about scale, metabolism, and entropy.

I am a little disappointed that this book, with its valuable contribution to understanding how organisms and organizations grow, starts to slip into just another piece of climate-change advocacy — one calling for a sustainability Manhattan Project involving the extensive and expensive involvement of scientists much like the author himself. While West's basic take on climate change is not very different from that of most scientists, his angle of attack feels a little contrived: If melting ice packs, rising sea levels, steaming hot jungles and deserts, and dangerous weather aren't convincing enough, let's try metabolism. Let's try entropy.

All other things equal, metabolism accelerates exponentially with absolute (Kelvin) temperature, at a rate such that it doubles with each 10°C rise. Fair enough, although I haven't observed tropical human populations metabolizing at double the rate of polar ones so I'm not sure how to apply this principle.

But entropy? West is absolutely correct in saying that, merely by having been alive, an organism leaves the Earth a slightly warmer place, for reasons directly related to the theory of entropy (the second law of thermodynamics). An animal (for example) is a machine for converting fuel to work, but it is not completely efficient at doing that. It gives off some heat as a waste by-product; that is why animals feel warm to the touch. If it were a perfectly efficient machine, its internal fires — its metabolism — could burn at a high temperature but no heat would leak through to the outside, and it would be cold to the touch.

But this process has been going on for much longer than humans have been alive, and the nonhuman biomass on the planet vastly exceeds the human.[283] The resulting heat production has had no measurable effect on anything, with global temperatures affected on a many times larger scale by geological heating and cooling. Between "the Eocene Optimum, 55-45 million years ago, [and]... the [last] Ice Age, which ended just 20,000 years ago....[t]he overall range in temperature was enormous, about 35°F," writes William Menke, a Columbia University geology professor who is as mainstream as you get.[284]

Even if the "social metabolism" of the human race — its energy use from fossil fuels and other technologies — is 100 times its animal metabolism, as West estimates, geological climate change is going to overwhelm metabolic climate change in the long run. Moreover, most scientists believe that the greatest threat to climate stability is the greenhouse effect of CO_2 emissions, not energy use *per se* (which leaks heat into the environment because the conversion of fuel to work is not completely efficient).[285]

Finally, people won't just stay put and watch their environment become unlivable. They will migrate to more comfortable climates.[286] This has happened before, and it has a downside as well as an upside. The downside is the wars, famines, and epidemics that have accompanied climate-motivated mass migrations in the past. The upside is the discovery and settlement of new territories with new resources. We are about out of territories, so mass migration in the future will mostly involve downsides, but, because of technology and civilization, the pain involved will be less than it was in previous episodes.

And there have been previous episodes. We have had warm periods before, recently enough to be documented by those living through it, in the Minoan, Roman, and Medieval warming episodes. The last two were warm enough to convert northern England to a wine-growing region. The rest of recorded history consists of cold periods.

People, then, adapt to their environment, and they adapt their environment to their needs. I am not saying global warming isn't a potentially serious problem — patterns of human settlement are already more or less optimized around the existing climate, so any climate change (warmer or cooler) is disruptive and

---

[283] See https://ourworldindata.org/life-on-earth

[284] http://blogs.ei.columbia.edu/2014/07/11/what-geology-has-to-say-about-global-warming/

[285] From this vantage point, nuclear energy is "clean," even if it is not completely efficient and produces waste heat, because it does not generate CO_2. So are wind, solar, geothermal, and so forth.

[286] Our descendants may also employ mitigation strategies (which were not available in the past) to improve the climate while staying put. See chapter 25 of my book, *Fewer, Richer Greener*.

costly, and can be fatal to populations that are not technologically advanced enough or wealthy enough to adapt or move. Assuming no adaptation, however, is the wrong way to assess the danger.

An Older, Better Grand Unified Theory of Sustainability: Economics

West calls for a grand unified theory of sustainability, based on scale, but we already have one based on incentives, tradeoffs, and opportunity costs: it's called economics. When a resource starts to be scarce, it becomes expensive, so we use less of it. We are also incentivized by its high price to make more of it, or to find substitutes. Thus a "tin" can is made of aluminum and a "silver" photographic plate is made of silicon. We burn natural gas in "wood" stoves and we are about to put robotic "drivers" behind the "wheel" of automobiles.

There is literally no resource that we have run short of without finding either a way to make more of it or an acceptable substitute for it. This process, basic to Adam Smith's vision of a market economy and probably discoverable in the writings of the ancients, is no mystery. It describes how man has adapted to the changing supply of resources and has created a versatile economy that fulfills people's needs even as external circumstances undergo great change.

Having shaped the environment to our advantage in countless ways, we have also depleted or damaged it in others. But, where necessary, we can reverse the process. A generation after adopting meaningful environmental regulation in the United States, many of our polluted waterways are once again sparkling rivers, fit for drinking. We are extracting energy from the wind and sun, at first haltingly but now with increasing efficiency. We are even finding ways to remove carbon dioxide from the atmosphere.

Conclusion

Scale is a mix of wonders and disappointments. Its value is in broadening our intellectual base as we confront the economic and policy decisions we must make, individually and collectively, to adapt as both population and economic output grow. West's work on organisms and especially on cities is compelling. His extension of the concepts of scale to environmental issues is provocative although more speculative.

West's attempt to extend his methods to businesses, however, runs into difficulties caused by the very nature of businesses — unlike organisms, they change ownership, operate under a variety of names and corporate structures, become parts of other businesses, and are nationalized by governments.[287] Are all of the U.S. railroads and airlines that went bankrupt really dead? No, the assets they owned have been redeployed, moving more people and freight more safely using less energy (sublinear scaling!). Even truly dying businesses, like typewriters, leave behind "spare parts" that are often used to build new businesses.[288]

Thus, for investors, the seemingly immutable laws of scale that apply to organisms and cities apply less directly to the understanding of companies' life cycles and prospects. But in this era of superlinear scaling by likes of Google, Facebook, and Amazon, West gives us a framework for thinking about growth and its limits.

So investors will have to look beyond power laws and Zipf distributions to assess the health and longevity of the businesses they are evaluating. They will have to focus on fundamentals — the cost of labor and materials, the demand for the company's service or product, the competitive environment. Active management has not yet been turned into a science, nor do I believe it ever will be.

The author thanks Steve Sexauer (CIO of San Diego County Employees Retirement Association) for extensive comments and assistance.

---

[287] The same ambiguity applies to cities — is Brooklyn a going concern, or did it die when it was merged into New York in 1898? How about Jersey City, which never officially merged but might as well have? Based on what logic can we say that Brooklyn has "expired" but Jersey City is still "alive"?

[288] In a New York Times review of *Scale*, Jonathan Knee, (May 26, 2017, https://www.nytimes.com/2017/05/26/business/dealbook/geoffrey-west-scale-the-universal-laws-of-growth-innovation-sustainability.html), writes,

> Furthermore, the consistent "decay" rates of corporations identified by Mr. West — calculated by the longevity of independent public corporations over time — does not correspond to any consistent change in underlying activity analogous to "death" in living organisms. Even in the context of bankruptcy, which Mr. West looks at separately from corporate "death" from mergers and acquisitions, good businesses with bad capital structures often continue "life" under new corporate form. It is not evident how meaningful mathematical calculations could be that treat such situations the same as failed businesses that are simply liquidated in bankruptcy for scrap value.

Chapter 25. The Unicycling Genius Who Invented Information Theory

A Review of *A Mind at Play*, by Jimmy Soni and Rob Goodman

November 28, 2017

Where do technological innovations come from? We have two mental images. One is of a lone genius working in a laboratory or garage, misunderstood until, at long last, the world appreciates her contribution. The other is of a team of busy bees, experts working at a corporation or government agency, the Manhattan Project being the best-known example.

The life of the inventor, mathematician and engineer Claude Shannon merges the two stereotypes. Temperamentally a loner and very much a genius, Shannon was never misunderstood — at an early age he was a protégé of the MIT School of Engineering dean Vannevar Bush — and he became part of the legendary research team at Bell Laboratories. While no one person invented the computer, Shannon's discovery of the parallelism between the zeroes and ones of binary, or

25-1 Claude Shannon
(photo by Alfred Eisenstaedt)
https://spectrum.ieee.org/tech-history/cyberspace/celebrating-claude-shannon

Boolean, logic and the on-off status of electronic circuits was the concept that made electronic computers possible. And, because Shannon was an engineer as well as a theoretician, he *built* computers, something that the better-known John von Neumann, Norbert Wiener, and Alan Turing never did.

In *A Mind at Play: How Claude Shannon Invented the Information Age*, Jimmy Soni, best known as the former editor of the *Huffington Post*, and Rob Goodman, a graduate student and political speech-writer, chronicle Shannon's life and scientific achievements. Their style blends traditional biographical information with a considerable amount of scientific content. The book is readable and sol-idly written, but falls a little short of captivating.

But Shannon's life and personality are so rich a tale that they shine through the mild blandness of the authors' presentation.

Early Years and Engineering Tomfoolery

A country boy from Michigan who wanted to be an electrical engineer like his distant cousin Thomas Edison, Shannon showed an obvious gift for engineering as a youth: "his creations included a makeshift elevator, a backyard trolley, and a telegraph system that sent coded messages along a barbed-wire fence." He was awkward, looking like he was "always on the verge of being mugged or hit by a bus." Shannon was so self-evidently brilliant that his flight instructor at first de-clined to teach him, fearing he would crash the plane and die, depriving the world of a first-rate mind.

Shannon could also be sublimely silly. He maintained a fleet of unicycles – in-cluding, writes *The New Yorker*'s Siobhan Roberts, "one without pedals, one with a square tire, and a particularly confounding unicycle built for two."[289] He built a robot whose only ability was to turn itself off using a mechanical hand, and invented a flame-throwing trumpet and a rocket-propelled Frisbee. In the au-thors' clever phrase, Shannon "worked with levity and played with gravity" — thus the emphasis, in their title, on a mind that was not at work but at play. Despite some distressing moments, it must have been fun to be Shannon, never feeling as though he had done a day of work in his extraordinarily productive life.

The Magical Parallelism of Bits and Circuits

When Shannon was 22, he wrote a master's thesis that would define his career.[290] "Following a discussion of complex telephone switching circuits with Amos Joel, famed Bell Laboratories expert in the topic," writes *IEEE Spectrum*'s John

---

[289] Roberts, Siobhan. 2016. "Claude Shannon, the Father of the Information Age, Turns 1100100." *The New Yorker* (April 30), https://www.newyorker.com/tech/elements/claude-shannon-the-father-of-the-information-age-turns-1100100.

[290] The thesis, "A Symbolic Analysis of Relay and Switching Circuits," *Transactions*, American Institute of Electrical Engineers, vol. 57 (1938), is at http://www.ccapitalia.net/descarga/docs/1938-shannon-analysis-relay-switching-circuits.pdf.

Horgan,[291]

> Shannon showed how an algebra invented by the British mathematician George Boole in the mid-1800s — which deals with such concepts as "if X or Y happens but not Z, then Q results" — could represent the workings of switches and relays in electronic circuits.
>
> The implications of the paper by the 22-year-old student were profound: Circuit designs could be tested mathematically, before they were built, rather than through tedious trial and error.

Even more important, Shannon demonstrated that the correspondence between Boolean algebraic expressions and electronic circuits is exact, so that if you wanted to construct a machine that could perform operations involving Boolean logic, you could build it out of electronic circuits. That is what a computer is. Consequently, Shannon's paper has been described as the most influential master's thesis ever written.

Almost everyone who uses computers now has some sense of the relationship to Boolean algebra, but Shannon discovered it. Boolean logic and electronic circuits had developed along different paths. The 19th century computing pioneers Charles Babbage, who designed — but did not quite build — a mechanical computer called an analytical engine, and Lady Ada Lovelace (Lord Byron's daughter), who wrote the first algorithmic program for Babbage's proposed machine, followed the Boolean path.

Electronic circuitry emerged from the telephone industry's need to manage a blizzard of intersecting requests for the system to connect phone calls. The two paths collided in Shannon's brain and in his lab, and we now take "logic circuits" for granted.

Genetics as Information Science

Just when Shannon seemed poised to become one of the world's leading electronic engineers and theoreticians, his interests took a 90-degree turn: to population genetics, the topic of his Ph.D. studies at Cold Spring Harbor Laboratory on Long Island, New York. Genetics is, of course, the branch of biology that studies how *information* is transmitted reproductively from one organism to

---

[291] Horgan, John. 2016. "Claude Shannon: Tinkerer, Prankster, and Father of Information Theory." *IEEE Spectrum* (April 27), https://spectrum.ieee.org/tech-history/cyberspace/claude-shannon-tinkerer-prankster-and-father-of-information-theory. Later, John Horgan became a popular writer on science issues and a contributor to Scientific American.

another, and the information is digital (conveyed, we now know, by the locations of the four nitrogenous bases — adenine, thymine, guanine, and cytosine — in a DNA molecule). Thus there is a close connection to Shannon's other work.

This change in direction was spurred by Shannon's mentor and thesis advisor, Vannevar Bush, who remarked, "Just as a special algebra had worked well in his hands on the theory of relays, another special algebra might conceivably handle some of the aspects of Mendelian heredity."[292] Of Shannon's contribution, James F. Crow writes, in *Genetics*,[293]

> The main purpose of [Shannon's] thesis was to develop a genetic algebra. Shannon's formalism was original and quite different from any previous work. The idea was to predict the genetic makeup in future generations of a population starting with arbitrary frequencies.

While this work was original and creative, it remained unpublished and therefore had little influence. Crow concludes,

> Shannon went to work at the Bell Labs immediately after receiving his [Ph.D.] degree. There he found a stimulating environment with outstanding engineers, physicists, and mathematicians interested in communication. This got him started on a new career, and genetics was dropped.

The Theory of Information

Information Is Stochastic

So, what is information theory, Shannon's central achievement? Perhaps the best one-sentence explanation is that it is the science that treats information as *stochastic* rather than *deterministic*.

Whether we know it or not, we usually think of information as deterministic: "five troop ships," an example of a brief message, contains 14 letters and two spaces — that is, three "words" — in a very particular order. There is no mistaking any of the letters or words for anything other than what they are. And when we transmit the message to another person, through the air in a room, through a wire, or wirelessly using satellites, we expect the message to be received

---

[292] http://math.harvard.edu/~ctm/home/text/others/shannon/entropy/entropy.pdf

[293] Crow, James F. 2001. "Shannon's Brief Foray into Genetics." *Genetics*, vol. 159, no. 3 (November 1), pp. 915-917, http://www.genetics.org/content/159/3/915.

exactly as it was sent.

But, it turns out, the message is received exactly as it was sent only because of the intervention of engineers using information theory. These engineers, following principles first established by Shannon, start by recognizing that some information will inevitably be lost in transmission, whether across a room (as in the children's game of "telephone") or in an electronic communications system. There is just no way around information loss. If you push signals, even simple discrete ones like the dots and dashes of Morse code, through a communications system *at or near the capacity* of the system, some of them will come out wrong. That's what "capacity" means.

So the engineers pack extra information into the message to make up for what they expect will be lost. They make the message *redundant*. MIT's Larry Hardesty explains:[294]

> In a noisy channel, the only way to approach zero error is to add some redundancy to a transmission. For instance, if you were trying to transmit a message with only three bits, like 001, you could send it three times: 001001001. If an error crept in, and the receiver received 001011001 instead, she could be reasonably sure that the correct string was 001.

Information theory, then, says that when some of a redundant message is lost, the heart of it is not lost. This is because, as Soni and Goodman tell it, "information is stochastic. It is neither fully unpredictable nor fully determined. It unspools in roughly guessable ways... Whenever we communicate, rules everywhere restrict our freedom to choose the next letter and the next pineapple." The authors, in an excess of cuteness, note that any recipient of the message will figure out that "pineapple" is a transmission error because it makes no sense.

The word that belongs in place of "pineapple" almost has to be "word"; if it's not, we instinctively feel that a rule has been broken. By eliciting the rules of language from large volumes of text, a linguist — or a computer — can take advantage of the partial predictability of language to detect and correct transmission errors.

Capacity, Bandwidth, and Error-Free Message Transmission

Recall that I earlier referred to the capacity of a system. But how do you measure

---

[294] Hardesty, Larry. 2010. "Explained: The Shannon limit." MIT News Office (January 19), http://news.mit.edu/2010/explained-shannon-0115.

the capacity of a message-bearing system? This was one of the central concerns of Shannon's information theory. Hardesty continues:

> Shannon...showed that any communications channel — a telephone line, a radio band, a fiber-optic cable — could be characterized by two factors: bandwidth and noise. Bandwidth is the range of electronic, optical, or electromagnetic frequencies that can be used to transmit a signal; noise is anything that can disturb that signal.
>
> Given a channel with particular bandwidth and noise characteristics, Shannon showed how to calculate the maximum rate at which data can be sent over it with zero error. He called that rate the channel capacity, but today, it's just as often called the Shannon limit.

Recall that Hardesty described adding extra digits to a binary message to help identify and correct mistakes. He explains,

> Any such method of adding extra information to a message so that errors can be corrected is referred to as an error-correcting code. The noisier the channel, the more [of this code] you need.... As codes get longer, however, the transmission rate goes down: you need more bits to send the same fundamental message. So the ideal code would minimize the number of extra bits while maximizing the chance of correcting error.

Shannon wrote the rules for solving this optimization problem in any setting. "He was able to prove," Hardesty writes, "that for any communications channel, there must be an error-correcting code that enables transmissions to approach the Shannon limit." Shannon did not, however, "explain how to construct such a code [that worked with certainty]. Instead, it relied on probabilities" — information being stochastic, or subject to a considerable, but not unlimited, amount of randomness. Hardesty concludes,

> Say you want to send a single four-bit message over a noisy channel. There are 16 possible four-bit messages. Shannon's proof would assign each of them its own randomly selected code — basically, its own serial number.
>
> Consider the case in which the channel is noisy enough that a four-bit message requires an eight-bit code. The receiver, like the sender, would have a codebook that correlates the 16 possible four-bit messages with 16 eight-bit codes. Since there are 256 possible sequences of eight bits, there are at least 240 that don't appear in the codebook. If the receiver receives one of those 240 sequences, she knows that an error has crept into the data. But of the 16 permitted

codes, there's likely to be only one that best fits the received sequence — that differs, say, by only a digit.

Shannon showed that, statistically, if you consider all possible assignments of random codes to messages, there must be at least one that approaches the Shannon limit. The longer the code, the closer you can get: eight-bit codes for four-bit messages wouldn't actually get you very close, but two-thousand-bit codes for thousand-bit messages could.

Thus Shannon outlined the theoretical basis for the methods now used for transmitting information through the phone system, on the Internet, and everywhere else that message senders and recipients rely on getting the message right with very high probability. You pack in extra information, but *not too much* of it — resources are expensive, and you don't get paid for wasting them. The whole design is quite an achievement, economic as well as technological, and it is Shannon's.

Is the Universe a Computer?

While Soni and Goodman explain these principles with some skill, at times their reach exceeds their grasp. At the end of the knowledge-packed chapter 16 of *A Mind at Play*, the authors engage in one of their many expositions that remind us they are not scientists but journalists: "[We] reimagine the universe in the image of our tools. We made clocks, and found the world to be clockwork; steam engines, and found the world to be a machine processing heat." They conclude by saying that, having invented information networks, we found the world to be one of those, too.

But we didn't. We built clocks to imitate the way the Earth rotates beneath the Sun. We built steam engines to do work, but we intuit, correctly, that Earth is not a machine built to do work; it just *is*. And no one seriously believes that the Earth or the universe is a computer. Art imitates nature and not the other way around. The authors would be better off sticking to biography, rather than injecting their homespun philosophy of science in a place where it does not help educate.

World War II: Code Talkers

Like many scientists, Shannon contributed to the war effort on the home front, working on problems of importance to the military. Among the most important problems were encoding messages and breaking the codes used by the enemy, an obvious application of the emerging science of information.

Shannon's approach to codebreaking was closely related to his insight into accurate message transmission, the former constituting a kind of mirror image of the latter. If the letters in a message arrived truly randomly, redundancy would be zero and codebreaking would be impossible. But, Soni and Goodman write, "our messages are less, much less, than fully uncertain." Given part of a message, the next part is somewhat predictable — as we saw with "pineapple." The authors continue, "[Shannon's] work on information and his work on codes grew from a single source: the unexamined statistical nature of messages."

What makes code-cracking possible is redundancy, which "means that more symbols are transmitted in a message than are actually needed to bear the information."[295] We do this in ordinary messages that are not intended to be stuffed into a wire: "When we write English," Shannon said, "half of what we write is determined by the structure of the language and half is chosen freely";[296] he later revised his estimate of the structural part to 80%. If we see the same patterns over and over, and with known frequencies — U after Q, lots of pairs of E's, S's, and T's and almost no pairs of H's and Y's, "of" often followed by "a" or "the" — then we can crack code. And a machine designed to detect subtle statistical properties can help us greatly.

Cracking code, then, resembles the information transmission problem discussed earlier in that both problems involve separating information from noise by understanding their statistical properties. The mirror-image part is that, in one case, the transmitter is trying to maximize the clarity of communication while in the other case he is trying to minimize it — to conceal rather than to reveal.

Cryptography, unlike some other aspects of Shannon's career, is straightforward enough that a skilled popular science writer can teach a great deal about it, and Soni and Goodman do this successfully. Overall, the book is fairly generous in its detailed, elucidating explanations of scientific concepts, and the section on codebreaking is one of the best parts.

Anecdotes and Adventures

That's most of the science in *A Mind at Play*. The rest of the book is a

---

[295] Soni and Goodman (p. 151), quoting David Kahn, a historian of cryptography.

[296] Soni and Goodman, p. 152.

compendium of sometimes brief, sometimes lengthy anecdotes about Shannon's career, personality, colleagues, and adventures. He interacted with many of the other great minds of his time: Norbert Wiener, who thought Shannon's work was following a wrong track (actually both men were pursuing fruitful, but quite different, paths); Marvin Minsky, who suggested the goofy mechanical-hand robot; and even Einstein, who asked him where a cup of tea could be found.

We learn that Shannon built an Erector Set robot that, like Shannon himself, could juggle. He channeled his passion for chess into a design for a chess-playing computer that would influence the builders of Deep Blue a half-century later. He befriended the finance proto-quant Ed Thorp, who introduced him to the joys of gambling and the stock market. Shannon would have made a fine finance quant himself! But the world is probably better off that he chose information technology.

Why Is Claude Shannon Not Better Known?

Claude Shannon is a legend among information scientists, computer engineers, and historians of technology. But, despite his immense contribution to the Information Age, he is not well known to the public, even to those who pay attention to technology and science.

Why not? Rob Goodman, in a *Forbes* article, wrote,[297]

> Because that's how he wanted it. Shannon certainly earned comparisons to the likes of Turing and Einstein during his lifetime...and when Shannon made a surprise appearance at an information theory conference in 1985, the conference chairman reflected, 'It was as if Newton had showed up at a physics conference.'

> But...Shannon consciously stepped away from fame. After the publication of his landmark information theory paper in 1948, he did experience a brief period of notoriety... Yet, at the height of that brief fame, when his information theory had become the buzz-phrase to explain everything from geology to politics to music, Shannon published a four-paragraph article kindly urging the rest of the world to...focus on research...

---

[297] https://www.forbes.com/sites/quora/2017/07/20/claude-shannon-was-a-genius-on-par-with-einstein-and-turing-why-isnt-he-as-famous/amp/

In other words, Shannon was, at heart, a working engineer, and he was uncomfortable making the leap to professional pontificator, public intellectual, or scientific oracle... Those options simply didn't interest him: he preferred to spend his time tinkering in his two-story workshop, inventing new gadgets...and studying the mathematics of juggling.

Goodman also speculates that Shannon wasn't a tragic enough figure to fit our taste in heroes. He did not have a cruel upbringing like Weiner's, nor was he persecuted by his government like Turing. Shannon had a decent life (marred, at its end, by Alzheimer's). On the second try, he had a satisfying marriage. He succeeded at almost everything he tried.

"The 'trouble' with that," Goodman writes, 'is that it doesn't necessarily lend itself to a tidy narrative of 'genius overcoming the odds'...What we take from Shannon's story is a reminder that creatively fruitful lives can also be joyful ones."

Departure

Claude Shannon died in 2001. Rob Goodman writes,

> [T]here's no better memorial to Shannon than the one he planned himself: later in life, but still in a lucid moment, he sketched out a memorial parade for himself featuring a jazz combo, unicycling pallbearers, juggling machines, a "chess float" atop which a human grandmaster squared off against a computer in a live match, a phalanx of joggers, and a 417-instrument marching band.

The procession never took place, of course. But it tells us a great deal about the person who planned it.

Claude Shannon at a Hinge of History

Technology is the driving force of our economy, and investors and their advisors would be wise to learn as much about it and its history as they can. Jimmy Soni and Rob Goodman's *A Mind at Play*, while covering material that is somewhat distant both in time and in topic from today's immediate concerns, opens a window into a crucial period in the creation of the Information Age in which we now live. It is skillfully, although not brilliantly, written, and is a good read.

Thomas Cahill, the historian, likes to refer to "hinges of history," events that, on benefit of reflection, made all the difference in bringing about some important aspect of our world. Located at the end of physics' golden age and the beginning of both the Information Age and the Age of Biology, Claude Shannon's remarkable career is one of those hinges.

And his joyous and quirky life is fun to read about.

Source: https://zhuanlan.zhihu.com/p/83865186

A conversation between Larry and Wayne Wagner

Montage, Laguna Beach, California, October 16, 2018

Wayne Wagner: What path took you to here and now?

Larry Siegel: I'm going to start with Gary Hoover who, during my time as an undergraduate at the University of Chicago from 1971 to 1975, was the only friend of mine who didn't want to get a PhD or save the world or become a backpacker – he wanted to be a *big* business man. Own a department store, as I remember it. As I got to know him I realized he was doing the most interesting work that I was aware of, and I came to think that business was a potential path for me that was both worldly and intellectually stimulating. So Gary arranged for me to get a job with Professor Yale Brozen, who taught at the Graduate School of Business at the university – the school now known as Booth.

Yale Brozen hired me to be a research assistant for his program in industrial organization at Booth. The program was funded by the American Enterprise Institute, so I started circulating among a group of people who were interested in government regulation of business, antitrust, and industrial organization. Yale Brozen helped me get in to the MBA program because I didn't have any work experience.

The first business course that I loved other than Brozen's was Roger Ibbotson's finance course, which came in two parts, Corporate Finance and Investments. I got an A in both, and I was the kind of student who liked to drop by during office hours and talk to the teacher, so he hired me to be his research assistant too. Roger was working on the most peculiar project that I ever heard of: collecting all of the returns on the stock and bond markets back to 1926. He was writing *Stocks, Bonds, Bills and Inflation* with Rex Sinquefield, who was then a vice president and portfolio manager at American National Bank of Chicago.

Wayne: So how did you come to work for Roger Ibbotson for the first 15 years of your career?

Larry: In 1979 I needed a job so I made an appointment to go to Roger's office and talk to him about the job market. He didn't say a word about the job market but instead handed me a pile of paper and said, "Larry, I'm testifying in a utility rate of return case tomorrow." Tomorrow! "And I haven't read this," he said. "Would you please stay up late tonight - read it - write a memo on what it says – and leave it for me in the morning. When you come in tomorrow morning you can prepare me for the hearing."

That was the beginning of Ibbotson Associates. My first office was Roger's floor. He was an early bird and I was a night owl so I was able to take over the desk after he left in the afternoon. I was the first part-time employee, the first full-time employee, and eventually a managing director. After 15 years there I moved on to the Ford Foundation, having watched Ibbotson grow in personnel from zero to a more than a hundred.

Wayne: When was that?

Larry: I left Ibbotson to go to the Ford Foundation in 1994. Linda Strumpf, chief investment officer of the Ford Foundation, hired me to be head of research. What that means at a buy-side institution is: going to manager meetings, trying to pick winning active managers, then doing the performance monitoring and measurement. I also had a role in the asset allocation and risk management of the institution. The most fun part was communicating to trustees: if we were doing well, we could say that we were right, and if we were doing poorly, we could say that we were just early. There is a fine line between being early and being wrong.

Wayne: How did you transition from the Ford Foundation to what you are doing now?

Larry: While at the Ford Foundation, I did a lot of writing for publication and eventually got to where I thought I could go on my own, writing white papers for investment management firms to give to their clients and prospects. I had already been serving as research director of the CFA Institute Research Foundation, part time, while working at the Ford Foundation so I was able to continue in the CFA role, with the income from it providing a base.

I retired from full-time work at age 55, which was in 2009. I had previously sold just about all of my stocks so I avoided the crash. That convinced me I was a genius at timing markets. But I couldn't figure out when to get back in; as stocks rose, the prices all looked too high. But the market doubled and then doubled again, without me in it. So it turned out that I was actually an idiot at timing markets.

Wayne: What part do you look back on as the most satisfactory?

Larry: Three things, one for each phase of my professional life. First, helping to create and interpret the background data for an understanding of the history of capital markets. This has not only grown to be a big business but it's become a fundamental aspect of financial education for the masses. It's on posters in the office of every stockbroker and financial advisor. It's even in high schools – at least, it was in the high school that my son and daughter attended.

Second: my work at the Ford Foundation. I was part of a great institution that does good things for people and I had a role that allowed me to interact with some of the smartest people in the world.

Third, being self-employed since 2009, it's been a lot of fun at having a professional life that's easy, that I'm good at, and that makes a little bit of money. I didn't know if I could do it. I'm not a natural entrepreneur. But, given some good luck and some effort, I am able to spend a lot of time with my wife and sit in my sunroom, or on the beach, writing articles that people say they enjoy reading.

I've also written a non-investment book, called *Fewer, Richer, Greener: Prospects for Humanity in an Age of Abundance.* It is about the future of the human race – I'm a modest guy. The book was published by Wiley in December 2019, and briefly went to #1 in Economics and #1 in History on Amazon before the COVID-19 pandemic quashed the public's desire to read an optimistic book. That is, I presume, only a temporary setback.

Wayne: Who gave direction to your life, and when and how did they do so?

Larry: For now I'm going to skip my wonderful parents and friends, and my wife, and focus on professional people. I think of my mentors as Yale Brozen, Roger Ibbotson, Peter Bernstein, Linda Strumpf, and Barton Waring.

Peter Bernstein, who encouraged me to write and publish, and who published some of my first articles, got me the Ford Foundation job – he introduced me to Linda Strumpf, who as I said was looking for a director of research. Peter and I were friends, and I have tried to model my writing style after his. My conversational approach to writing – trying to draw the reader in as part of an intimate chat in the living room – shows Peter's influence. If you can integrate not just finance, investments, and economics, but philosophy and poetry and a little science, you've provided your readers with a new perspective. That's what Peter did and is what I'm trying to do.

Yale Brozen discovered me as an undergraduate and got me to appreciate the world of business and economics. As I said earlier, he also got me into business school. Roger Ibbotson taught me the whole field of finance as well as how to run an operating business. Linda Strumpf gave me the hands-on opportunity to help manage a large, complex portfolio and introduced me to most of the luminaries of our business.

Finally, Barton Waring is not only a great co-author and a great friend but also put me in the business I'm currently in. When he was at Barclays Global Investors, he hired me to do a lot of the writing I did for them, and that work broadened into the multi-client business that I have now.

Wayne: So you started writing the short pieces early on?

Larry: I began writing them as Ford Foundation internal memos which I called Conference Roundups. I also wrote a lot of articles for publication in journals such as the *Financial Analysts Journal* and the *Journal of Portfolio Management*. Some of these were short essays and some were full-length research pieces. Once I was on my own, the publication Advisor Perspectives invited me to write a series of articles – a mix of book reviews, interviews, research pieces, and think pieces. At about the same time, Ted Aronson thought the writing I was doing would be fun for his readers, who are his firm's clients and prospects, and engaged me to work for him.

Wayne: You're very well-read; how do you pick a topic to write about?

Larry: I follow links on intellectual websites – Tyler Cowen is a good source. He's a professor at George Mason University in Virginia and he has a very popular economics website called Marginal Revolution. People send me things: Jeremy Grantham sends me his letter, Howard Marks sends me his letter, Cliff Asness sends me his Cliff's Perspective, which is sometimes more like a book than a letter. Bill Bernstein is a fine source. Marty Leibowitz is the very definition of an Old Reliable. I get e-mails and tweets from some people who are more retail investor-oriented, like Cullen Roche and Morgan Housel.

Of course, I am not some special person who gets these materials before anyone else – I am just on their distribution lists, although I know them all. Among my personal friends, Steve Sexauer, Barton Waring, and Ted Aronson are very good sources of ideas, as is Bob Huebscher of Advisor Perspectives. I want to thank Ted and Bob for their help with this book.

Reaching beyond economics, there are some people with great web sites. GatesNotes.com is Bill Gates' website. If he mentions a book favorably I will probably read it. I do the same with popular science writers such as Richard Dawkins, Steven Pinker, and Matt Ridley.

Wayne: So that's the top of the funnel. How do ideas get to the bottom?

Larry: I mostly work on things that respond in some way to consumer demand.

Let's say Advisor Perspectives' publisher, Bob Huebscher, is interested in having me write a review of a book – for example, the recent biography of Claude Shannon, the computer genius. The book was called *A Mind at Play* by Jimmy Soni and Rob Goodman. I try to figure out what I know about the topic, which in that case was almost nothing. I am not an electronic engineer. But it turns out I know a little about some related topics, such as the technology industry, and a lot about some more distantly related topics, such as productivity and long-term economic growth. Eventually I am able to write a review that brings together a bunch of different thoughts from different places. I think that's what people enjoy about my writing.

It's ironic. I had never heard of Claude Shannon and, in preparing to write the review, I talked to some computer scientists who told me that they couldn't believe it – it was like an artist who never heard of Pablo Picasso.

Wayne: You've reviewed long and complicated books and academic papers. What comes easily to you? What are the hard parts of reducing and popularizing that material?

Larry: What comes easily to me is writing in a conversational style that approximates what we're doing here now. But I can only do that if I have knowledge of the subject. What does not come easily to me is doing the background work to get up to speed on an unfamiliar topic, because every rock that you turn over has six more rocks under it. I did that for my book, *Fewer, Richer, Greener*. I know some economics but I'm not a demographer or environmental scientist so I had to read three or four books on demography and maybe six or seven on environmental science. It's like a newspaperman's job. You have to be a quick study and be aware of what you don't know as well as what you do know.

When you function that way, you learn only the top layer of a new subject, so you can only teach the top layer. You realize you're going to make some mistakes. You just get to work and start writing. Then, at the revision stage after you've learned more, you take out the mistakes that you can find. Regarding the ones that get left in, you say "all mistakes are solely my responsibility and not those of the many people I've relied on in gathering information."

Wayne: Of the pieces that we've selected here that are going into this book, what's the number one piece that readers should read?

Larry: If they're a professional investor, the first piece they should read is called "Is It Science or Is It Baloney?" The investment business is built on a beautiful edifice of scientific research that the business mines for the pieces of baloney hidden within, so they can sell them for a high fee. This situation is improving and low-fee investment products are on fire, while high fee products are not, but for a very long time the investment business was a way of transferring wealth from the customer to the manager under the cloak of scientific research. (Where are the customers' yachts?) I credit Bill Sharpe, 50-plus years ago, with beginning to fix that.

But when real scientists began to take investing seriously as a field of research, that's when academic work began to be used as a sales tool. In many cases this was done appropriately. As Cliff Asness, a good friend and a valued client, said, you decide what to sell based on your research into what might be good for your customers. So there is no inherent conflict between the manager and the client. Sharing the profits according to some formula, say a performance fee, aligns manager and client interests even more closely. So "Science or Baloney" is not an attack on the business - it's a call for clients to use their head and be aware of what they're getting into when they invest money.

Wayne: Let's take that same idea to the individual investor – the dentist who has put together a million dollars and wants to retire on it at some point.

Larry: "Debunking Nine and a Half Myths of Investing." Professional investors may want to try to pick winning active managers, but I advise individuals to buy index funds and diversify among asset classes. As Cliff Asness said, riffing on Jeremy Siegel, stocks are good for the long run but bonds are also good for the long run. Think about your liabilities; if you're principally trying to fund retirement spending, that liability looks a lot like an inflation-indexed bond, so you might want to hold some of those, along with other inflation hedges.

The long run could be a lot longer than you think. The good news is that, when you retire at 65, you could live for 40 more years. The bad news is that you're going to have to pay for it – so consider blending conventional investing with annuities, especially deferred annuities. Diversifying among annuity issuers will help you reduce the risk of default by the issuer, which is not a trivial concern.

Finally, if you think you're smarter than the market, you're probably not. If you think you're dumber than the market, you're probably not. Professor Meir Statman, another valued colleague and friend, has a sign in his office that says, "You are not so smart and other people are not so stupid."

Wayne: You wrote a book entitled *Fewer, Richer, Greener*. How did that come about?

Larry: It started as a 2012 article in the *Financial Analysts Journal*, and I decided to make a book out of it. I was getting annoyed with my friends who were telling me that the world was going to hell in a hand basket. They generally said this just before they got into their Mercedes and went home.

My long run forecast for the future is for continued economic growth. It will be faster in the developing world than the developed world, which is already rich by any historical standard you'd care to apply.

Looking back, I hear a lot of bellyaching about how tough times are now. The COVID epidemic is a real hardship and a setback for growth, but as Abraham Lincoln said, channeling an ancient Persian proverb, this too shall pass. The reality is that economic conditions have gotten dramatically better in my lifetime. Standards have changed. I went back to the east side of Cleveland and looked at the house I was raised in. It seemed more than adequate at the time. We thought we were lower middle class but now the city can't even give the house away, so it was vacant last time I checked.

In other words, even what it means to be poor has changed: the poor want and can afford better housing than what I had growing up, and I had a hard-working father who never thought he was poor. Standards have also improved in terms of food quality, medical treatments, travel, and a million other things. As Barack Obama said, if you could choose to be born at any time and place in history, it would be right here, right now.

Per capita GDP has been growing in the United States at a rate of about 1.8% per year since the founding of the country. Britain and a few other countries have also grown at about that rate for about that long. Parts of the world that developed later are growing even faster because they don't need to invent the railroad, the telephone, the car, the airplane, and the computer – that has already been done for them. It's easier to play catch-up than to be a pioneer. But there are still a lot of poor people in the world, about half the world population, so we have a lot of work to do.

Wayne: That explains what you mean by "Richer," but what are "Fewer" and "Greener"?

Larry: Fewer? The population explosion is coming to an end. Almost everywhere except in sub-Saharan Africa, fertility rates have dropped to levels that imply a stable or even declining population in the next few decades. Africa will take longer but is moving in the right direction. World population will peak between 10 and 11 billion near the end of this century and then begin to decline. This is unbelievably good news. Only a generation ago, serious thinkers were worried about us starving to death. Now obesity is a bigger problem, even in many developing countries.

Wayne: But you're not forecasting an actual decline in world population in the near future?

Larry: No. But "fewer than expected" does not make a good book title.

Wayne: Greener?

Larry: A clean environment costs a lot of money. Economic growth is good for the environment. A rich society can afford to impose costly environmental regulations, think about the very long term, and try out advanced technologies that help the environment. Stewart Brand has written an excellent book, called *Whole Earth Discipline*, that calls on us to embrace urbanization, nuclear power, genetic engineering of foods, and other forms of environmental engineering as valuable and necessary tools. People who are opposed to them are barking up the wrong tree, and would make us poorer to save the earth when the exact opposite is what is needed.

Wayne: What does all this imply for long-term investors?

Larry: Invest globally, because that is where the growth will be; and equities will be strong performers. The current price of equities worries me in the short to intermediate run, but the going-in price makes less of a difference the longer your time horizon is. And equities are cheaper outside the U.S. than in it.

The U.S. has outperformed the rest of the world for so long now that it's hard to remember that, from 2003 to 2007, the U.S. market roughly doubled but the emerging markets index went up by a factor of five. Something similar happened with the developed non-U.S. markets in the 1980s.

Wayne: I remember it well.

Larry: *You* do, but most people react only to their most recent observation, which is that the S&P 500 has recently been the only asset worth owning. That's ridiculous. So I would diversify internationally. Moreover, diversify among asset classes. Even if equities have the highest expected return and are positioned to take advantage of global growth, nobody over 45 years old should have an all-equity portfolio because we don't live forever and markets sometimes go down and stay down.

Wayne: What about investment professionals - are they adequately filling clients' needs?

Larry: Investment professionals are improving at filling clients' needs. Instead of selling the hot stock of the week, they're selling whole portfolios. These can be portfolios of equities – an equity index fund – or portfolios of asset classes, which can be packaged as a target date fund or asset allocation fund.

But professionals are not communicating the characteristics of these products very well. As a result, an employee participating in a defined contribution retirement plan sometimes signs up for 3 funds on the day that they start a job – the conservative, the moderate, and the aggressive fund. They're all the same fund, of course, just with slightly different betas, slightly different mixes of the underlying products. The employee doesn't know they bought the same underlying product three times and they don't revisit the decision until the day they retire. This may sound like an extreme example but it's really not. The people who are overseeing the client interface are not doing a very good job of it.

However, I think the investment industry has improved its product offering very profoundly from the days of the hot stock of the week and the saying that stocks are not bought, they're sold.

Wayne: Are there any results from your research that you feel you should be incorporating into your personal investing, but haven't?

Larry: I should be looking into a deferred annuity because I write passionately about the need to hedge tail risk. The tail risk, for both you and me, is that we're going to outlive our money. So, according to the work I've done, about 85% of your net worth at age 65 should be in a conventional (albeit conservative) investment portfolio, designed for you to live on until about age 85; and 15% into a deferred annuity that kicks in at age 85. It is designed to pay you until you die – or it can be a "later to die of two spouses" contract – but nothing is left after that, and the annuity is surprisingly affordable because most people either don't live to collect it or don't live very long after they begin collecting. But if you live a very long time, you'll be happy.

The last thing you want to do is what my grandfather did, which is to prepare to live into your 70s or 80s and find out at 103 that he had to ask his kids, who were then in their 70s, for money. If I practice what I preach, that won't happen to me or to the people who follow the strategy in my article with Steve Sexauer, "A Pension Promise to Oneself," and my article with Tom Totten, "Combining Conventional Investing with a Lifetime Income Guarantee." While neither article is in this book, they are on my web site at http://www.larrysiegel.org.

Wayne: Thanks. Anything you ever wanted to do and never took the time to do it?

Larry: I wanted to be a musician but I wasn't disciplined enough to make it a career. My son is a brilliant musician and that's what he is doing. But my great friend and musical collaborator Tom Dundee, who passed away in 2006, made me into a little bit of a rock star – just enough to meet my beautiful wife and a number of other very attractive women. I had to pick just one, and I got the right one. Of course, the reality is that she picked me. Isn't that the way it always works?

Wayne: Who are your favorite musicians?

Larry: Beethoven and Bob Dylan. My favorite musician whom I knew personally was Tom Dundee. I played with him for years.

Tom Dundee's guitar, which he got from Steve Goodman, is now in my family. Steve Goodman owned it when he wrote "City of New Orleans" and "Go Cubs Go." Then Tom Dundee owned it, then me, and my son Josh owns it now.

Wayne: Okay, the last question: what question should I have asked that I didn't ask?

Larry: What has my wife, Connie, done to help me get from there to here? She allowed me to be myself and not think I'm a nut. Not to try to learn my trade because, if she did, we would be competitors. Instead I can decide for myself what to do professionally. Our relationship hinges on many other wonderful and beautiful things but not finance, investing, and economics. She is just there for me.

Wayne: Thank you, Larry.

Index

Montesquieu
Press

About the Author

Laurence B. Siegel is the Gary P. Brinson Director of Research at the CFA Institute Research Foundation and an independent consultant, writer, and speaker. In July 2009 he retired from The Ford Foundation, where he served as director of research in the Investment Division since 1994. From 1979 to 1994 he was a managing director of Ibbotson Associates (now Morningstar).

Larry's book, *Fewer, Richer, Greener: Prospects for Humanity in an Age of Abundance*, was published by Wiley in December 2019 and reached #1 in Economics and #1 in History on Amazon shortly after release. In addition, he has written, co-authored, or edited a large number of journal articles, magazine articles, and CFA Institute Research Foundation monographs. He serves on the board of directors of the Q Group (Institute for Quantitative Research in Finance) and other organizations.

Larry received his BA in urban geography from the University of Chicago in 1975, and his MBA in finance from Chicago Booth in 1977. He lives in Wilmette, Illinois and Del Mar, California. His web site is http://www.larrysiegel.org.

About the Editor

Wayne Wagner's support for Larry Siegel began with Wayne's serving as the Research Committee Chairman of the CFA Institute Research Foundation. Wayne's career has spanned the history of capital market theory since his Wells Fargo days, when he created the operating algorithms for the very first index funds. He was a founding partner at Wilshire Associates, where hie became an investment manager for the state of Minnesota's $1.3 billion Wilshire 5000 Index Fund. As a co-founder of Plexus Group, he specialized in institutional transaction cost consulting.

Wayne is the Editor of *The Complete Guide to Securities Transactions: Enhancing Investment Performance and Controlling Costs* (Wiley, 1969) and co-editor with Ralph Rieves of *Investment Management: Meeting the Noble Challenges of Funding Pensions, Deficits and Growth* (Wiley, 2009.) He was also the co-author of *MILLIONAIRE, The Best Explanation of How an Index Fund Can Turn Your Lunch Money Into a Fortune* (Renaissance Books, 2000.)

Wayne is a graduate of the University of Wisconsin Business School and holds a master's degree from Stanford University's Department of Statistics/Management Science. He taught courses in investment management and securities trading at UCLA and the University of Southern California.

CHANGE YOUR PERSPECTIVE ON LIFE
PROSPECTS FOR HUMANITY IN AN AGE OF ABUNDANCE
FEWER, RICHER, GREENER
LAURENCE B. SIEGEL
JOHN MACKEY
WILEY
"The many young people who seem to share a gloomy view of the future should read the new book by Laurence B. Siegel"
Jason Zweig
The Wall Street Journal
"As the twenty-teens draw to a close, may I wish everybody a Happy New Decade, and recommend a book that convincingly argues in great detail that it will be one.
Matt Ridley
Author of The Rational Optimist
NOW AVAILABLE ON
amazon
BARNES NOBLE
FewerRicherGreener.com

www.ingramcontent.com/pod-product-compliance
Lightning Source LLC
Chambersburg PA
CBHW031503180326
41458CB00044B/6675/J